A VESTERHEIM REPRINT
Vesterheim, The Norwegian-American Museum

The Diary of
Elisabeth Koren

1853-1855

TRANSLATED AND EDITED BY
DAVID T. NELSON

Norwegian-American Historical Association
Northfield, Minnesota
1955

Fifth printing, 1997
Vesterheim, The Norwegian-American Museum

Photographs from the collection of
Vesterheim, The Norwegian-American Museum

Cover Design: Robyn B. Loughran *Design*

ISBN: 1-57216-008-X
Library of Congress Catalog Number: 94-066634

Preface

Six decades after Elisabeth Koren wrote the pioneer diary and letters that make up this volume, she modestly but accurately described them as "simple, unadorned notes." She was then a venerable lady who could look back upon more than four score years, whose life had encompassed virtually the entire sweep of the Norwegian immigrant story, and whose memories were rich and deep. One may regret that she did not write a full-length autobiography recording her experiences and observations and revealing the mature growth of her personality. But the notes from the 1850's are in themselves of genuine value. They mirror the prologue to a larger story. They have the freshness of a contemporary recording of an age long since vanished. They make scenes and events and people of a hundred years ago seem as vivid as those of yesterday and today. Their historical interest is accentuated because they are pictures of beginnings significant in themselves and for their long sequel.

The modern reader journeys vicariously with the diarist across the broad Atlantic in 1853 and on the tortuous and far way to the frontier of the Middle West. The diary describes primitive travel with memorable concreteness: rough and inhospitable taverns, no dome cars on smooth and swift trains but a dugout canoe on the Wisconsin River and a crossing of the Mississippi on ice, an uncomfortable wagon trip through the snow. At journey's end, one views in daily panorama the life of a pastor and his wife in a crowded Iowa log cabin through seasons when bitter winter winds and violent summer storms beat against it, with water seeping in between its ill-plastered walls. Some writers cast a romantic aura over pioneer life, but here are the homely details of log-cabin living. Here are the cooking, the slaughtering, the washing of clothes and interminable scrubbing of floors, the monotonous diet (and smell) of salt pork, the clumsy furniture of domestic manufacture, the hard-working neighbors and friends of the community, the anxieties of communication with the outside world. Mrs. Koren's husband, the young frontier minister, served many congregations, and so there were long days of waiting for his return, lonely introspection for his bride, walks in every kind of weather, and reflections that spanned the space from the frontier to the cherished warmth of her old Norwegian home. One shares the excitement of the Korens as they plan for and achieve a pioneer parsonage of their own, with its privacy and simple charm. One could wish that the indefatigable services of Koren himself, a major figure in Norwegian-American church history, were reported in more detail, yet he is the focus of much of the story. The diary, now made available for the first time in English, is an enrichment of our sources for an understanding of Norwegian-American life on the frontier.

Professor David T. Nelson of Luther College has richly earned the thanks of the Association for the carefully wrought translation and the competent and responsible editing he has supplied the diary and letters. He has contributed a volume that will win a permanent place in the literature not only of the Norwegian immigrants and the Middle West, but also of American history in a wide context.

THEODORE C. BLEGEN

UNIVERSITY OF MINNESOTA

Introduction

The westward tide of migration in the United States that swept from the Appalachians to the Rockies had crossed the Mississippi by 1850, but had not yet filled the vast land areas to the west of the river. As part of this westward movement, Norwegian immigrants, after crossing the Atlantic, had moved into northern Illinois and southern Wisconsin during the 1830's and 1840's. By 1850 the stream of Norwegian settlers had grown larger, had pushed into the central and western areas of Wisconsin, and had made the first crossings of the Mississippi into Iowa and Minnesota. During the 1850's these settlers of Norwegian blood poured across the Mississippi in great numbers. In Iowa, colonies grew up in Clayton, Allamakee, Winneshiek, and Fayette counties in the northeastern corner of the state. The largest of these were on the prairies to the east of the present city of Decorah, a community which received its first settlers in 1849.

The Norwegians who took up land and pioneered this new frontier, whether they came from older settlements in Illinois or Wisconsin or had made the long journey by sea and land direct from Norway, soon felt a need for the church that had been a central point in their life at home. It was the church which in the mother country had cared for their baptism, their instruction and confirmation, their marriage, their holy communion, and their last observances for the dead. Now in a new land, the settlers longed for that which they lacked; they wanted the church, and they wanted men of their own blood and language and faith to conduct the sacred rites to which they had been accustomed. So the arrival of a minister of the gospel was an event eagerly awaited and long planned for.

The time had not yet come when such ministers could be obtained from among Norwegians trained in this country. The pastors who served the early Norwegian settlements in the Midwest were men who had received their training in the old country, had felt the need of ministering to their country-men transplanted afar, and had made the long journey to the New World. They came first to the older Norwegian settle-ments in northern Illinois and southern Wisconsin; later, from these states, the first Norwegian ministers crossed the Mississippi into Iowa.

The Reverend Claus L. Clausen visited the settlements in northeastern Iowa in the summer of 1851, and the Reverend Nils O. Brandt visited them in the autumn of the same year. Pastor Brandt returned to the settlements in 1852 and again in 1853. In 1852 he organized congregations — the first among Norwegian Lutherans in Iowa — at Paint Creek, Turkey River, and Little Iowa (Washington Prairie). That year a letter of call, formulated by Pastor Brandt, was drawn up and signed by 105 members of the three congregations. It was in response to this call that the Reverend Ulrik Vilhelm Koren decided in 1853 to come to America.

He had completed his theological studies for the Lutheran ministry. He received the letter of call from the Iowa settle-ments on June 13, 1853, and was ordained on July 21, 1853, by Bishop J. L. Arup in Christiania.[1] On August 18, 1853, he was married to Else Elisabeth Hysing of Larvik and together they left Norway, September 5, 1853, for America.

Elisabeth Hysing Koren, who had been brought up in a sheltered home in Norway, kept a diary of their voyage across the Atlantic, their journey inland to Iowa, and their life together during most of their first year in the Little Iowa settlement. Not many accounts have been written, or have survived, dealing with the earliest experiences of Norwegian women transplanted to the frontier of the Midwest. Elisabeth Koren's diary is a remarkably full account of her experiences as a pioneer. It gives a vivid picture of the primitive conditions that the twenty-one-year-old wife encountered in Iowa after coming directly from her comfortable and cultured life in Norway. Not least of the hardships was the lack of privacy and the long wait for a home of her own. From December 21, 1853, when she and her husband arrived in the Washington Prairie settlement southeast of Decorah, until October 1, 1854, when they finally moved into the parsonage, the young couple had only temporary lodgings.

After staying three nights in the crowded quarters of the Nils Katterud family, the Korens shared a cabin, 14 by 16 feet, with Erik and Helene Egge and their two young children until March 10, 1854. They then moved in with the Ingebret Sørlands, sharing their cabin until May 2. Next they found shelter in a cabin on the Skaarlia farm. They left August 10 for a trip to Wisconsin, expecting that the promised parsonage would be completed during their absence. They found the parsonage unfinished, however, when they got back September 13. After two nights with the Skaarlias they left September 15 for a visit to some outlying congregations; Mrs. Koren, then an expectant mother, was reassured by the promise that all would be ready when they returned.

On their return September 30, the parsonage was still with-

[1] Jens Laurits Arup, 1793–1874, was at that time a bishop of the Lutheran state church in Christiania.

out doors. They had to go to the Egges and ask for shelter; and that night, says Pastor Koren, "as we sat together on one of the red immigrant chests, I saw, for the first time, tears in my wife's eyes." [2]

But the diary for the most part reveals not emotional crises, but the intelligence, interest, fortitude, and clear vision with which Mrs. Koren met the problems of the frontier and made the transition from her assured station in the old country to the rude conditions of the new.

The late Hanna Astrup Larsen, who knew Elisabeth Koren well, said: "There is a picture of her — taken shortly after her marriage. It shows a round, soft, girlish face, but looking out from it two eyes so clear and steadfast that one is sure she faced the prairie with courage." Miss Larsen continued: "I wish I could make you see Mrs. Koren as she was when, as a little girl, I used to visit in the Washington Prairie parsonage. She seemed to me then the most exquisite creature I had ever seen, and I have seen no one since to make me change my opinion. She was not old even then as we count age now. Her blue eyes were bright, her skin was fresh and clear, her abundant dark hair only lightly touched with silver, but it was always covered with a dainty white lace cap, which she assumed when she was about forty-five and never abandoned. Her dress was sober and simple as that of any well-bred matron in those days. The lace cap was the only touch of luxury, and it seemed to belong to her somehow. It emphasized the purity and serenity of her face." [3]

Else Elisabeth Hysing was born May 24, 1832, in Larvik, Norway, and died June 7, 1918, at Washington Prairie in Winneshiek County, about six miles southeast of Decorah, Iowa. Her parents, who were second cousins, were Ahlert Hysing (1793–1879) and Caroline Mathilde Koren (1801–40). The latter was a daughter of Christiane Birgitte Diderick-

[2] V. Koren, "Nogle erindringer fra min ungdom og fra min første tid i Amerika," in *Symra*, 35 (Decorah, 1905).
[3] Hanna Astrup Larsen, "Address at the Koren Eighty-fifth Anniversary Festival, Decorah, Iowa, September 4, 1938," in *Lutheran Herald*, vol. 23, no. 12, p. 274 (March 21, 1939).

sen Koren, known as "Mother Koren," who had some literary
aspirations and whose diaries have been published in part.[4]
Ahlert Hysing and Caroline Koren were married March 30,
1825, in Ullensaker. The husband was married a second time
September 2, 1842, to Elisabeth Frechland, whose father was
a pastor in Søllerød, Denmark. The children of the first marriage were (in order of birth): Christiane, Elisabeth, Augustinus (Stin), Marie, Thomas, Caroline (Lina), and two boys
who died in infancy.

Elisabeth was eight years old when her mother died. Her
sister Christiane was six years older — a big difference in
age to the younger Elisabeth. Her mother's long illness and
perhaps Elisabeth's tendency to deafness made her a lonely
girl. Moreover, Christiane, in the first year after her mother's
death, spent considerable time at the home of an uncle, and
also with the Winsneses at Vang, east of Hamar. Hanna
Winsnes (of cookbook fame) was a friend of Mrs. Hysing,
and both she and her daughter Maren remained close friends
of the girls.[5]

After her father's second marriage, Elisabeth was twice
sent to Copenhagen in the hope that something could be done
for her hearing, but no good came of it. The school of which
Elisabeth's father was headmaster admitted only boys and
there were no schools for girls, but some of the teachers at
the school gave her private lessons. She attended dancing
school as a child. Her greatest pleasure, however, was working
with her father in their garden. She loved flowers, especially
roses, and continued this interest until she was eighty-three
years old. She was fond of walking, too.

Elisabeth was taught English, but only to read and write it.

[4] Gudrun Johnson, *Slekten Koren*, 1:188; 2:139 (Oslo, 1941).
[5] Hanna Olava Winsnes, nee Strom (1789-1872) was born in Drammen,
Norway, and was married in 1817 to the Reverend Paul Winsnes, who from
1840 to 1875 served the parish of Vang in Hedemark, Norway. She published
poems, short stories, and an excellent book for children; and in 1845
achieved a national reputation with *Lærebog i de forskjellige grene af husholdning* (Textbook in the Various Branches of Housekeeping — Christiania,
1845). The book ran through twelve editions and sold more than fifty
thousand copies.

It may have been thought that because of her deafness she could not learn to speak it. Her teachers were Mary and Jane Archer, members of a Scotch family that had business interests in Larvik. One daughter, Mrs. Jørgensen, was Elisabeth's godmother. Mary Archer was rather emancipated for her time and was the first young woman in Larvik who dared to skate, in the face of the taboo on sports for women.[6]

Elisabeth's father, who had studied theology, became a teacher in the Bergen cathedral school in 1819. Five years later he became the principal of the newly established *real* (modern or science) high school in Larvik on the south coast of Norway. There he had a distinguished career, eventually becoming headmaster. Upon his retirement in 1867 he was made a Knight of the Order of St. Olaf. He was representative from Larvik and Sandefjord to the Storting (parliament) in 1830. For ten consecutive years he was mayor of Larvik. He helped organize the Larvik Savings Bank, was a member of its board of directors from the beginning, and served for twenty years as chairman. The family lived in a large, rambling old manor house (*herregaard*), now a museum. The school occupied the second floor, the Hysings the main part of the first floor, and Dean Münster one wing; the janitor also had rooms there.[7]

Elisabeth's husband, Ulrik Vilhelm Koren, was born December 22, 1826, in Bergen, Norway, and died December 19, 1910, at Washington Prairie, Decorah, Iowa. He and Elisabeth are buried in the cemetery of the Washington Prairie Church. Vilhelm's parents were Paul Schonevig Stub Koren and Henriette Christiane Rulffs (Koren). When Ulrik Vilhelm Koren was only sixteen, his father was killed by an earthquake at Cap Haitien in Haiti, May 7, 1842. The widow and her five children were then left almost destitute and the son had only very meager means while pursuing his

---

[6] A son, Colin, later built the "Fram," the specially constructed steam vessel in which Fridtjof Nansen, the Norwegian arctic explorer, made his famous journey in 1893.

[7] Thomas George Münster (1801–79) was dean in Larvik; Johnson, *Slekten Koren*, 1:68.

studies at the university in Christiania (1844–52) for the Lutheran ministry. During this period he supported himself in part by tutoring and by teaching in the Nissen Latin School. His decision to accept the call from the newly established Lutheran congregations in Winneshiek, Fayette, Clayton, and Allamakee counties in Iowa made him one of the first resident Norwegian Lutheran pastors west of the Mississippi. He continued all his life to serve the congregation that had first called him. He became secretary of the Norwegian Synod in 1855, was its vice-president, 1871–94, was president of the Iowa district, 1876–94, and was president of the Synod, 1894–1910. He played a major part in founding Luther College, in locating it in Decorah, and in selecting the site for its campus. Koren Library at Luther College is named in his honor.

After their marriage in Larvik, the Korens left Norway September 5 on the steamship "Constitution," landed at Kiel, and went by train to Hamburg, whence they were to sail for America.[8] They sailed September 15 and arrived in New York November 20, after a voyage of nine and one half weeks. They left New York December 1 and arrived at the Washington Prairie settlement southeast of Decorah on December 21. Their journey from Larvik had taken fifteen weeks and two days.

Mrs. Koren's diary tells of this journey and, supplemented by letters to her family in Norway, continues the story of life in this frontier Iowa settlement to Sunday, December 3, 1854, just nine days before the birth of her first child, Henriette. The account is then continued by means of extracts from five letters written by Mrs. Koren in 1855.

The first part of the original diary, which deals with the journey from Hamburg to Washington Prairie, appears to have been lost or mislaid. In the transcript of the original (see below) this part is headed "Mammas dagbog fra over-reisen" (Mother's Diary of the Voyage). The remaining por-

[8] Johnson, *Slekten Koren*, 1:67. Ulrik Vilhelm Koren and Elisabeth Hysing were cousins.

tion of the original diary is in the possession of Miss Marie
Koren of Decorah, Iowa, youngest and sole surviving of the
nine children of Vilhelm and Elisabeth Koren. The diary is
written on double-sheet correspondence paper, later neatly
stitched together into six separate parts. Parts 1, 2, 3, and 5,
each containing twenty-four pages, are written on a very good
grade of unruled white paper. Part 4, containing thirty-two
ruled pages, and Part 6, containing twenty pages, are written
on gray-blue paper of considerably poorer quality than that
in the other parts. The diary is written in a very even hand,
but so fine that anyone trying to read it today welcomes the
aid of a magnifying glass.

In 1914 "Extracts from Mrs. Elisabeth Koren's Diary and
Letters from the Fifties" were published by her children, in
the original Norwegian, under the title *Fra pioneertiden:
Uddrag af Fru Elisabeth Korens dagbog og breve fra femtiaarene.* This book, of 210 pages, was published in Decorah.
For it a handwritten transcript had been made from the
original diary. The transcript, which is likewise in Miss
Marie Koren's possession, has been made available to the
translator. A comparison of the transcript with the original
shows that many portions of the original were omitted from
the copy. Likewise, a comparison with the published version
shows that many portions of the transcript were omitted
from the published version.

Except for some minor omissions, usually made to avoid
duplication of material found in the letters, the present
version offers a complete translation of the original diary and
letters, except that the last four letters from 1855 are somewhat abbreviated. Some passages from Dr. Koren's hand as
printed in *Fra pioneertiden* in 1914 are here omitted.

Many of the sentences of the original, the divisions between
which were not always clearly marked, have been broken up
into shorter sentences in the translation. The paragraphing,
beyond that found in the Norwegian printed version, is likewise the work of the translator, who is also responsible for

the division of the diary into chapters and for the chapter headings.

In addition to the acknowledgments that are found in the notes I gratefully acknowledge my indebtedness to Miss Marie Koren, Miss Henriette Naeseth, the late Mrs. Caroline Koren Naeseth, Mr. William Koren, Jr., the late Professor O. A. Tingelstad, Professor W. I. Brandt, Mr. Georg Strandvold, Professor Karl T. Jacobsen, Mrs. Chester H. Cable, Professor S. S. Reque, Mr. William Linnevold, Professor Einar Haugen, Mrs. Elizabeth Seegmiller, the Baker Memorial Library and staff of Dartmouth College, and the Koren Library and staff of Luther College. I am grateful for suggestions and assistance from Dean Theodore C. Blegen. I owe much to Helen T. Katz for her editorial work. To my wife I am indebted in countless ways. I trust all who have helped me will feel some satisfaction in the completed work.

DAVID T. NELSON

LUTHER COLLEGE
DECORAH, IOWA

Contents

Illustrations

The Diary of Elisabeth Koren

1

Leaving Europe

It was a beautiful moonlit evening when, on Thursday, September 15, 1853, accompanied by Consul Lund and his wife, with whom we had spent the previous evening, we boarded the packet "Rhein" to sail for New York.[1] At the wharf we took leave of our friendly hosts and were rowed aboard. It was late — after eleven o'clock — so that I had time only to look about me very hastily and survey our fellow passengers, a number of whom were still up. I caught a glimpse of one woman who vanished into the ladies' saloon. At the table in the gentlemen's saloon sat a woman in a big white cloak with black rosettes; more plain than handsome, she appeared neither young nor old, and was apparently busy

[1] The Korens left Norway on the steamer "Constitution." They arrived in Kiel, Germany, September 8, 1853, and went to Hamburg by rail; there they spent a week as guests of Consul Lund and his wife before sailing for America. Jonas Gabriel Lund (1816–95) was the son of Jonas Smith Lund, a master pilot, and was appointed Norwegian-Swedish vice-consul in Hamburg in 1848, according to information received from the office of foreign affairs in Oslo. The "Rhein," a three-masted bark, carried two hundred steerage passengers, thirty to forty second-class passengers, and a small number of first-class passengers, besides mail and cargo. At that time Elisabeth was twenty-one years old and her husband twenty-six.

1

reading; but to judge from her tear-stained eyes and sorrowful expression, her thoughts were not greatly concentrated on her book. On the sofa sat a woman and a little girl, at their side another woman and a little girl, who appeared to have accompanied them on board.[2] The sorrows of departure did not seem to weigh heavily here. There were also a number of gentlemen, but where they hailed from I do not know. I talked a little with the captain's wife, a pale, melancholy-looking creature dressed in black. I saw no more passengers that evening.

As we had been aboard earlier in the afternoon and had unpacked and arranged our effects, we were able to retire without more ado. I thought how entirely different I should have felt had I gone aboard in Norway to sail directly to America, instead of in this foreign city. And yet I had a very strange feeling; we were, indeed, leaving Europe.

When we awoke next morning, the ship was lying quite on one side, as if we were on a hill, so it was very difficult to walk up and down. We had gone a short distance from Hamburg, had run aground, and, willy-nilly, had to lie there until high tide. I got up too late, of course, for breakfast, but with V.'s help managed just the same to get a cup of coffee and a roll, which tasted very good. Afterwards I was busy inspecting the other passengers and our captain, Mr. Popp, a fine-looking man. He has his wife with him, a pale, agreeable person who speaks very softly and gently and is very fond of her husband. One of my amusements is to watch that large strong man bundle her up so lovingly and fuss over her.

I was busy that morning writing letters home, and sat aft in the ladies' saloon in a most miserable position, wholly aslant, feet highest, and wrote nearly all forenoon. Later we went on deck and gazed at the attractive shore line. Meanwhile we had slipped free and were being towed down the Elbe by a steam tug. The scenery is very beautiful, especially

[2] The woman and the child on the sofa were Madam Zeplin (sometimes called "Smiles" by Elisabeth) and her daughter Franciska.

near Blankenese, a friendly little town lying between two tree-covered heights; each house and cottage has its own garden and lies quite hidden by trees. All day we sat on deck and gazed at the land as long as we could. The tugboat left us that day after having towed us a considerable distance down the river. We had the loveliest moonlight and stayed up as long as possible.

Our fellow passengers appear to be friendly, good-natured people. One of them, Madam Zeplin, is traveling with her little daughter to join her husband in New York. Then there is a Miss Kihn whom I do not care for; a Miss Küsler, a friendly, unpretentious girl, who is to meet her sweetheart and be married in New York; a doctor from Vienna with his wife and son. The doctor is a bearded man, somewhat affected, who is very busy when anyone is ill. His wife is a small, friendly, lively, stout Viennese; but I have trouble understanding her Viennese dialect. Then there is a Danish master carpenter, Juul; and a fat little man with red nose and cheeks who is friendly and attentive to the ladies; and finally Emil, Arthur, and Anna, three small children who are going to their parents in America and have a maid, who is almost square, to look after them. These are the first-cabin passengers.[3] It was rather strange at first to be always on shipboard, and especially to go to our tiny stateroom in the evening and lie in the berths, where, nevertheless, I sleep very well — that is, when I am not thrown about too much.

Friday, September 16. Friday we had the most beautiful weather we could wish for; the passengers were on deck all day. It is very interesting to scan the various physiognomies and observe the different groupings. The women sit or lie about; some read, others knit, some do nothing all day except chat with one another. The men smoke and read. If the weather is fine and the ship steady, the passengers from the

[3] Jean is the name of the doctor's son. The "fat little man" is apparently the one later called the "little Russian"; the children's nurse is sometimes designated as "Fatty." Other persons not included in Mrs. Koren's list appear during the journey who may or may not be first-class passengers.

second cabin usually come with their rugs, which they spread out and sit on, and play chess or cards and infect the air with their vile tobacco.

Early in the morning there is a throng of steerage people on the deck below; the women usually make their toilet there, and eat breakfast. At twelve o'clock one can see them running about with their tin pails to fetch their midday meal, grouping themselves as best they can about the deck to eat it. This day slipped almost imperceptibly away. When there is good weather and calm, one can scarcely distinguish between the days; they are all alike; we walk a little, work, read, and eat; the last affords the greatest variation and the most important occupation, thanks to our capable steward and cook, who prevents it from becoming monotonous. This day we said farewell to Germany and were in the midst of the North Sea.

Saturday, September 17. Saturday and Friday were just alike. The same beautiful weather, the same beautiful moonlight. We took our regular walk morning and evening. The wind was unfavorable and we had to tack, with little success. It is interesting to watch the maneuvers with the sails, and especially to see the captain stand at the helm and give commands; he is in his element there. A man in the steerage died today.

Sunday, September 18. It was strange to spend our first Sunday aboard a vessel; there is almost nothing to differentiate Sunday from the other days of the week. Everything must go its usual way then, as at other times. Moreover, it was not a pleasant day. Vilhelm was not well and stayed in bed most of the time. I sat and read and amused myself by paging through my album. The weather, which had been fine in the forenoon, took a turn for the worse after dinner. The sea became rough; the women were sick and had to retire to their berths; and neither was I entirely well, though only for a moment.

Monday, September 19. Fine weather. The whole day

spent on deck. We passed Helgoland in the forenoon. It is very beautiful, this rock island, and of almost uniform height from the quarter from which we could see it. The red cliffs descend in a sheer perpendicular to the sea on one side, but on the other a plain opens up, where the town lies. The houses seem to go right down to the water. The whole island has a unique appearance, especially when the sun throws its splendor over the red cliffs.[4]

Tuesday and Wednesday, September 20 and 21. Both these days we drifted in the North Sea, because of unfavorable wind and calm, without being able to enter the channel. The weather was fine. Miss Kihn was busy teaching the other three women English. The sun sank in marvelous splendor that evening. It was large and red without rays, and as it went down it formed beautiful landscapes among the golden and many-colored clouds. One of my joys here at sea is to gaze at the sunsets.

Thursday, September 22. A fairly rough sea and an unfavorable wind. The women are sick. The woman from Iowa and I are the only ones who are holding up, but she is somewhat ailing. Two large warships (French) passed us, two smaller ones and two steamships, and many sailing vessels.

Friday, September 23. We saw Dover with its beautiful white chalk cliffs, which on this day, unfortunately, were gray, for there was a heavy, damp fog. The wind was still poor, so we got no farther than Goodwin Sands, I think it is called. There is a pretty lighthouse there. Many ships lay at anchor, large and small. I have never seen anything so beautiful as the sky at sunset.[5]

Saturday, September 24. Early in the morning we passed Beachy Head. Here I saw the chalk cliffs in the full light of day.[6] I stood for a long time and gazed at the waves, which

[4] Helgoland is in the North Sea about eighty miles from Hamburg.

[5] Goodwin Sands are dangerous sandbanks off the coast of Kent, southeast of Ramsgate and northeast of Dover.

[6] Beachy Head is a headland, 575 feet high, in Sussex on the English Channel.

5

broke against the ship and sparkled in different colors. The sea was lovely. The sun's rays brought out rich streaks of green in the water. Toward evening it became so calm that for a long time we were able to sit quietly and gaze at the beautiful starry sky.

Sunday, September 25. It was a stormy day from first to last. It blew hard and the ship rolled in all directions. The chairs came sailing along the floor; dinner landed in our laps. The women were sick; everything was topsy-turvy. The wind grew stronger and stronger; we could hardly keep our seats because of the rolling, and got to our berths with difficulty. The storm raged all night. We could not sleep; it was a disagreeable night, and I was heartily glad when day came. It was a laborious toilet I attempted that morning; it was impossible to stand. A little later in the day the storm subsided; but the strong ground swells are worse. To stand on deck in such a sea, when the ship dips fore and aft and the water is beautifully dark blue with white crests, is thrilling. It is a magnificent sight.

There is much sickness in the steerage; eleven are already dead. One man lost his wife and two or three children; one poor woman, six children. The captain intends to put in to port for the sake of the sick.[7]

Monday, September 26. We tacked all day without being able to make headway. Toward evening, however, we saw land. We tried to take a walk on deck, but I for my part had to give it up. It was quiet on deck, and quiet below; people are sick. That poor man who has had such a loss came up to have a talk with Vilhelm; he was very dejected. There is a Swiss among the steerage passengers who is our favorite. He is an exceptionally handsome, good-natured man. I spoke

---

[7] There was cholera aboard; fourteen people on this ship are said to have died and been buried at sea. *Fra pioneertiden: Uddrag af Fru Elisabeth Korens dagbog og breve fra femtiaarene,* 17 (Decorah, Iowa, 1914); V. Koren, "Nogle erindringer fra min ungdom og fra min første tid i Amerika" (Reminiscences from My Youth and from My First Years in America), in *Symra,* 20 (1905).

with him this morning for a time. He would not talk about
Switzerland; he must be homesick.

Wednesday, September 28. The first thing we heard this
morning was the Swiss, yodeling. When we arrived on deck,
we saw the Isle of Wight. It was blowing hard; we were
rapidly approaching land. It was a joy to see green meadows
and trees once more. The nearer we came, the prettier Wight
was. First we saw fertile fields; the land was rolling, not high,
no trees, few houses. As we passed the lighthouse, the lovely
gardens and parks came into view, and farther in the distance
the pretty town of Ryde; to the left, farther inland, the
queen's summer residence, surrounded by parks. Below and
to the left lie one charming villa and cottage after another,
extending from the sea far inland. On the other side we have
Portsmouth with its fortifications and ships.[8]

There was a strong wind as we sailed in. It was very interesting to see the pilot, in his little boat, working his way
through the waves to come aboard, now up on the crest, now
almost hidden by the waves, and then the young boy rowing
back alone — on the boat was written "Mary Cowes." There
then, at this pretty spot, we entered. A doctor came aboard
to look after the sick. He and a second man — a ship broker
or whatever he was — were very civil. One wanted us to go to
Wight, the other to Portsmouth. It was a relief to have the
ship at rest and to eat in peace once more. There is a hub-
bub overhead; the whole steerage is on deck.

Thursday, September 29. Today I have been in England —
walked about in lovely Ryde. It is interesting to have been
in old England. This was a busy place this forenoon — so
many men. The pilot had dinner aboard yesterday; it made
a good impression to see him say grace with bowed head and
hand before his eyes. After breakfast today the captain, his
wife, the doctor, and we rowed ashore. The march up the

---

[8] Ryde is a watering place on the Isle of Wight in the English Channel
off the south coast of England, opposite Portsmouth on the English main-
land; Portsmouth is a seaport and naval base.

pier was a long one; at the far end there is a sort of pavilion where ladies sit and read and take the sea air.

Ryde is undoubtedly a very handsome place. All the houses are small and pretty — for individual families. The shops are remarkably fine; all, even to the butchers' stalls with their carved turrets, display unusual taste. There were many inviting fruit shops. We walked through a bazaar that was closed; the prettiest thing there was a collection of various sorts of marble, alabaster, and conch shells. But most attractive of all are the cottages. I cannot imagine anything more inviting, comfortable, and genuinely pretty than these small houses with their gardens and charming entrances, with ivy completely covering the walls. Even the roof of one thatched cottage was completely covered by vines, and its entrance was inlaid with conch shells. There are many pretty churches.

We wandered about in several quarters, stopped at a confectioner's, and returned just in time to meet the others at the dinner table. Our little Russian, who is unusually gay these days, presented each of the women with a jug and each of the men with a clay pipe, the latter to be tried over coffee. We sat a long time about the coffee table and chatted, enveloped in a cloud of smoke; afterwards the gentlemen played whist and the ladies amused themselves as usual by solving riddles, the regular occupations here in the evening.

Friday, September 30. Breakfast tasted unusually good today. We had fresh English bread, fresh milk for our coffee; and we all have splendid appetites. The Russian treated us to English cake.

The weather was beautiful; all the women went ashore, walked about the city and its environs, looked up and down the streets to find a good confectioner, and finally succeeded. Preus distinguished himself by speaking German and running here and there for us.[9] We went past an exceptionally pretty bathing place with the most attractive little bath-

[9] This was Jacob Preus, a brother of the Reverend Adolph C. Preus; he entered business in Madison, Wisconsin, and in the late fifties moved to California; Reverend J. C. K. Preus of Minneapolis to the editor, February 2, 1955.

houses. I sat far out on the pier and gazed at all the various lords (?), ladies (?), and children who came and went on the steamboats which, every half hour, put in from every quarter. I expected to get a chance to see the much-talked-of English nobility, but found only new and very pretty attire.

About five o'clock we returned and had an excellent dinner, except that there were too many currants in the pudding. When I had eaten, I read until Juul came and asked us to look at the great steamer that was to go to America. I stayed on deck for a time and spoke to the mate and to some children whose parents are ill.

We women sat and chatted and wondered what had become of our husbands. Toward evening they at last returned, except for the doctor and the Russian. When, later, these two also returned, the latter was in an altogether splendid humor and hit upon a thousand things to pass the evening, which was indeed a success. We played a game of oracles, solved puzzles, etc. Miss Kihn was in her glory. The captain and the Russian chaff a great deal with her. She is quick enough in answering them. But her smile was tiring beyond all reason this evening. The crew members were gay; they had a fiddler aboard, and shouted, sang, and roistered quite dreadfully.

Saturday, October 1. It is raining with all its might today; we shall certainly not get ashore. Altogether, we have now been aboard fourteen days. I have written industriously in these pages, and have at last made up a part of what I had neglected; but many incidents and impressions unfortunately were lost before they could be recorded here. Vilhelm has written to Johan, and I to Marie.[10]

The other women are gathered in their own saloon. Miss Kihn is reading an English phrase book, and has "Smiles" as her most industrious pupil. The doctor's wife apparently is

[10] Boycke Johan Rulffs Koren (1828–1909), then lieutenant and later rear admiral in the Royal Norwegian Navy, was one of Ulrik Vilhelm Koren's two younger brothers. In October, 1853, he married Marie Louise Münster, who had been a bridesmaid at Elisabeth's wedding; Gudrun Johnson, *Slekten Koren*, 1:68 (Oslo, 1941). Marie Louise Munster was daughter of Dean Münster, pastor at Larvik.

9

not well these days. She was not herself yesterday, either. Mr. Juul is invisible save in the morning and at mealtimes. Kihn's English does not amount to much, since she does not know how anything is spelled. How tiresome the women were yesterday when they had to stop and look in the windows of all the shops! In the bazaar it was beyond all reason. The men played whist last night. Vilhelm was in a heated dispute, being the only one to defend Denmark against the Germans. It was no easy matter — one against three — and in the German language to boot. The dispute continued nearly all evening; we others kept quiet and listened.[11]

Sunday, October 2. We did not go ashore today as we had intended. The weather was glorious but the sea was too rough for the women; so we had to be content with walking the deck and gazing at the lovely scene and all the gulls that fly about us. There is much activity where we are anchored; many steamers come and go, and pretty yachts with their masters and families sail about, to and fro, outside our windows.

It is quiet today. I miss the gay little Russian; he could put life into the party. We have now had dinner, and it was a poor one. The meat was not done and the plum pudding was not good, either. The Russian has returned, but it is still as quiet as ever here. I think most of our group are overcome by sleepiness; they do nothing but yawn, with the exception of Kihn and me, who are reading. Now they are going to have another round of cards, so I will finish *Chuzzlewit*.[12]

I have now finished *Chuzzlewit*, and become more and more attached to Dickens the more I read. The air is raw this evening; the captain has fortified us with a glass of raspberry cordial, and I am going to bed.

Monday, October 3. All forenoon we sat in the men's saloon working busily, Mrs. Popp, Kihn, and I. The other

[11] This dispute probably dealt with the Schleswig-Holstein question, which had been under discussion for some time. Eventually a crisis led to the Austro-Prussian attack upon Denmark in 1864 and the loss to Denmark of the two duchies.

[12] Charles Dickens, *The Life and Adventures of Martin Chuzzlewit* (London, 1844).

two women are inseparable; they always sit by themselves and read their letters to each other. Mr. Juul came down and called me on deck to look at some large fish that were swimming about our ship. He is always so thoughtful about calling me whenever there is anything to see. Otherwise I am on deck as little as possible these days. It is not pleasant when the whole steerage is up there. If the dinner was poor yesterday, the meal today made up for it, with a dish of fried flounder as a bonus.

As soon as we had eaten, Vilhelm, the doctor and his wife, the Russian, Kihn, Küsler and I went ashore in Ryde. We strolled all the way through the town and beyond it, as we had agreed to do, and had a lovely walk, ascending all the time through pretty parks, past "Uncle Tom's Cabin," past two attractive gated dwellings, low, thatched houses covered with ivy, and on the outskirts past a beautiful wood which led to a pretty red building with a style all its own — many small towers, octagonal rooms. On the other side of the road we found the prettiest hedge I have yet seen, with small arched entrances covered and almost hidden by vines. We went a long way, to a turn of the road where we had an unobstructed view, and then turned back. The Russian had a girl on each arm — a neat trio.

After we had returned to town and were wandering among the shops, we were surprised by the captain and his wife, who had followed us in the boat. We went in, bought gloves, and afterwards stopped to eat cakes and buy bonbons, and thereafter, well content with our visit to Ryde, rowed back to the ship. We had an excellent supper consisting of oysters, broiled chops, and potatoes. It lasted a long time, for nothing is so tiresome as oysters, particularly when one does not eat them. Later the Russian was in a merry mood and kept everyone's laughing muscles busy; but alas, it did me no good, I have such a hard time understanding him, and moreover, I have to play peekaboo with him if I am to see him, since we always sit with the large mast between us.[13]

[13] Mrs. Koren was somewhat hard of hearing and resorted to lip reading.

Tuesday, October 4. The doctor's wife entertained us this forenoon by telling us of Vienna and the Hungarians. She is a vivacious woman; she has enjoyed life, heart and soul, I dare say, and has done her share of work, too, when necessary. When it rains and blows all day long, as it does today, so that we cannot go on deck, we become quite alarmed at our good appetites and capacity for food. It seems as if we do nothing but eat. We had a good laugh during our evening meal when the doctor's wife, creeping on all fours, sewed Mr. Giering fast to his chair; Mr. Juul discovered it and laughed so hard I thought he would have hysterics, and he set us all to laughing. I knitted, and read Irving's "Sketches." [14] Kihn is making small shoes for the captain's children, and sits whispering to his wife. Küsler works steadily, mending her cloak. The men do nothing but smoke from morning to evening.

Wednesday, October 5. Today is apparently going to be just like yesterday. The weather is not particularly good, the wind dead against us.

I sit here waiting for coffee and laugh at the steward who, as he went to get a clean tablecloth and noticed that Vilhelm was not yet up, said very hesitatingly: "Herr Pastor! Kaffee! Wollen Sie so gut sein?" [15] We shall soon see if it has the desired result. There he comes with English — or whatever they are — hard biscuits.. They will taste good. Juul must be writing to half of Copenhagen, for he now starts in anew. He is a strange fellow. We had the pleasant diversion this forenoon of having Vilhelm read aloud to us from *Frithjofs saga*.[16] My work went busily on.[17] We are having the same weather — sun and rain alternately, and contrary winds.

We took a little turn after coffee this morning, and tried to appease Mr. Giering's resentment at the prank last evening,

[14] Giering, who is mentioned frequently in Mrs. Koren's account of the voyage, is apparently a writer. He is one of several persons in the diary who have not been successfully identified. By the "Sketches" she means Washington Irving's *Sketch Book of Geoffrey Crayon, Gent.* (New York, 1820).

[15] "Coffee, reverend sir, if you please?"

[16] Esaias Tegner, *Frithjofs saga*, translated from the Swedish by C. Momsen (Christiania, 1843).

[17] Probably her tatting or crocheting.

but were not quite successful. The rain drove us below and held us there until we had eaten a good dinner with a new kind of rice pudding for dessert; then Vilhelm and some of the group went ashore; I stayed on deck a long time and enjoyed the beautiful evening. Many ships lie here and, like us, wait for the wind. The doctor entertained us, until the others came home, by reading aloud a tiresome novel which has been read once before.

Thursday, October 6. We have now lain here more than eight days; still no wind.. The same gray, foggy weather. I must be about unusually early, for not even Mr. Juul is up. One day cannot be distinguished from another. Vilhelm and the doctor played chess; Giering read aloud to us. We stayed up fairly late on this beautiful evening. Kihn makes herself more and more conspicuous, but not to her advantage.

Friday, October 7. Today, like yesterday, no change. We do the same things, eat about the same, the doctor reads aloud the same — in short, all is identical, save that Kihn has hit upon the idea of giving the dog a little of everything choice, to the vexation of the rest of us.[18] We stayed up tonight until we were tired, watched the crew try their strength against one another and saw the mate come off winner over all.[19] In the morning Vilhelm and the captain played chess; Kihn and Mrs. Popp racked their brains writing verses about the captain; he then of course was full of praise for the authoresses.

Saturday, October 8. The weather is beautiful today; we were on deck all forenoon, and watched while the anchor was weighed and the sails maneuvered. However, we got nowhere before the anchor had to be dropped again; so we are lying here once more. After dinner we took a beautiful trip to Ryde with the captain; and now I hope that I have seen lovely Ryde with its charming cottages for the last time. A captain from Hamburg accompanied us; he stayed for the evening and played whist.

[18] The captain's poodle was called Kiddy.
[19] Apparently some kind of wrestling game was being attempted.

13

2

Wind, Weather, and Sea

Sunday, October 9. Today we weighed anchor in good wind and fair weather. God be praised, we are under way again! Everything takes on an entirely different aspect when we are sailing and the ship is moving a little. The women begin to droop, lie as long as possible on deck, and, for the most part, sleep. Kihn is in bed; I wish she would try to stay up. Vilhelm read a sermon for Mr. Juul and me. We are sailing out the same way we came in, unfortunately, so we shall not see Cowes.[1] On the other hand, we discovered a second pretty spot on Wight — a couple of inland towns which we had sailed past so early in the morning that we did not see them.

It is now afternoon. The personnel at dinner is again reduced to the same number as during the last heavy sea. The women sat down to dinner with the best intentions, but to fulfill them was beyond their strength. One after the other vanished, until only Küsler and I remained. Juul regales us

[1] Cowes is a small seaport on the north coast of the Isle of Wight, now famous as a yachting port.

with stories of the Danish king and his frugality at meals. He tells a story in quite an amusing way.

Monday, October 10. Today it looks a little better than yesterday. The women are all on deck and lie about in groups. Even the woman from Hamburg has come up, and sits close to me, weeping. Perhaps she is homesick, poor creature; she is not easy to make out. The weather is beautiful — fairly warm; but I wish we had a little more wind. At the moment Vilhelm is below, reading. Now I am to help "Fräulein Braut" solve some of Schiller's riddles.[2] A wagtail is flying about the ship — a friendly greeting from land.

It is now afternoon. The cook has given us a new dish, some of his dumplings — large flour dumplings which have no taste at all and which he serves with boiled meat. I have been on deck all day and am now sitting here waiting for Vilhelm to come up and walk with me. I hope he will not be too late for this beautiful sunset. Such a summer evening is indeed beautiful; the sun, about to set, gilds the heavens on one side, and on the other the moon is already throwing its beams across the water — nothing else to see but an unending stretch of sea and the heaven above it.

Wednesday, October 12. We have a fair wind today and are making good progress; the sea is very rough, and all, even Küsler, are seasick, so that I was the only woman at the dinner table. Now we begin with our old diversion of watching the dishes and plates move about of their own accord.

One is hardly himself at sea, however, even if one is quite well. I have no desire to do anything, and cannot fix my thoughts upon anything. All day I am up in the clouds and when I go below in the evening and the men begin to play, I am usually overcome by an unconquerable drowsiness that lasts until we are ready to eat. Then, happily, I wake up, especially when we have lobscouse.[3] Such is my condition

[2] "Fräulein Braut" was "Miss Bride"; that is, Miss Küsler, who was to be married in New York. By Schiller's riddles Elisabeth no doubt meant the problems of reading Schiller in the original.

[3] Lobscouse is a nautical term for a stew of meat, vegetables, ship biscuit, and so forth, baked or stewed.

when we have really heavy seas; not otherwise, fortunately. Here on board I forget everything, too — even everything I read.

Thursday, October 13. We have, praise God, the same good wind today; we sail rapidly, nine miles to the watch; and the weather is beautiful — warm for the month of October. We sat on deck all morning, Vilhelm reading a paper dealing with emigration, and I amusing myself with *Pickwick*; it makes good reading on deck, where people talk noisily on all sides and are teasing Kiddy, the captain's dog. I simply cannot bring myself to like the barking; it reminds me too much of land.[4]

There come all the passengers from the second class with their rugs and cushions, and encamp, one resting on the other in a lovely group. It is amusing to see all the different positions. There lie the doctor and his wife; they look miserable, both of them. The captain and his wife are near by. The American is sleeping, stretched out full length, using his wife, who is also sleeping, as a pillow. The pharmacist lies directly in front of me in his beautiful red-checked riding habit with the American's foot to support his head. The elderly woman, the stout girl and the slender one, and all the children are in a snug little group; and we sit nearest the wheel, a little removed from them all. Juul is in high spirits today. The heavier the seas, the more he laughs.

Yesterday the sea was so rough and the pitching so strong that I dreaded the night a little. We did not go on deck after noon, but were very comfortable below. By the time we had lit a light I was so sleepy that I had no desire to attempt anything, and went to bed early after first making ready a glass of fruit juice and water to refresh myself with if I should wake during the night. But I never wakened. It was bright day when I opened my eyes, greatly amazed that I had slept so well and the ship was rolling so little. When I got up I

[4] Charles Dickens, *The Posthumous Papers of the Pickwick Club* (London, 1837).

was surprised to see all the women busy with their toilet. We drank our coffee, which tasted good, for we had milk, and ate some of Mrs. Garrigues' good biscuits.[5]

After that I read Schiller's *Jungfrau von Orleans* until Vilhelm came in, and now am sitting in my usual place with my cloak wrapped about me, listening to a few second-class passengers behind me playing dominoes and counting, now in English, now in French.[6] The rest of the company are making a fearful racket, for they tie rope around one another's feet and try to pull one another down. Kihn is well today and is crocheting with all her might, but the rest look rather pale. In contrast to yesterday, I have been wide-awake and cheerful today, have eaten fried ham and potatoes, and have had more than one good laugh out of Juul.

Saturday, October 15. We had a very stormy night. The ship rolled much more than last time; everything was topsy-turvy in our cabin. I woke up in the middle of the night, and when one is once wide-awake it is not easy to get to sleep again. It is hard to lie awake and be thrown about and listen to the creaking and whistling and uproar. It is fine to have day dawn at last and be finished with the laborious task of dressing. The wind shifted suddenly late last night and is fairly good; but we make little headway, the sea is so high. We sat on deck all morning, well bundled up, a large heap of sails at our backs, and chatted and were very comfortable, except that Vilhelm was not entirely well.

I have never seen the sea so rough as today; there were really mountains and valleys. It was interesting to watch. It is beautiful when the sun shines on the high wave crests until they become clear and transparent and take on a greenish color. A little dark bird flew astern the ship all morning. In the afternoon I slept a while, chatted with Kihn; after supper I was on deck in the glorious moonlight, and have been very comfortable despite the stormy weather.

[5] Mrs. Garrigues entertained the Korens at her home while they were in Hamburg; *Fra pioneertiden*, 10.

[6] Friedrich Schiller, *Die Jungfrau von Orleans* (Berlin, 1802).

Diary of Elisabeth Koren

Sunday, October 16. Nothing, indeed, is so changeable as wind, weather, and sea. Last evening it was calmer than one who had seen it in the forenoon could have believed possible; last night we lay quite on one side and rolled heavily. I was awakened by one of the armchairs in the saloon crashing against our wall; it was gloomy and black outside; the rain poured down.

I was glad it was not long until daybreak. Chairs, tables, and everything movable lay in confusion inside. Madam Zeplin sat completely disconsolate on her bed, which had been thoroughly soaked. The cabins to windward were a pitiful sight. No one can stay on his feet. We had been served coffee without mishap with a little of the precious milk in it, and were quietly eating; but then all at once there was a lurch; the milk pitcher came sailing over Madam Zeplin and me, and biscuits, knives, and plates were all helter-skelter. The most amusing thing was to watch the steward, who is otherwise so nimble and dexterous, slip and fall every time he tried to help wipe up. A storm is raging today, so we shall have to stay below. Yesterday a sail blew to pieces.

We have been below nearly all forenoon, each in his armchair, talking away the time, but we went up to watch the enormous waves for a while before noon. It is dreadful how rough the sea is. The waves break over the forecastle every moment, and now and then one comes over the fore part of the deck and washes down through the skylight.

Dinner today was a comical affair. We managed to get to our places without losing our balance, and waited for the soup, which the steward managed to bring with considerable trouble, now by crouching down, now by making use of a tranquil moment to dash forward a little. One of us had to hold the tureen; and each one, balancing his bowl in his hand, hurried to eat his soup before it landed in his lap. Then came the roast chicken; but the poor creatures doubtless fancied that they were alive, so restless were they on the platter. The captain fortunately got hold of one, Vilhelm

18

looked after two, and Mr. Giering, not to be outdone, impaled the fourth upon his fork and held it in the air. We found ourselves busy, each one holding on to something as it came in, one the peas, another the gravy. The steward had been careful enough to pour the juice off the beets, but the chicken gravy did not seem to like that and gave them a portion of its own fat; and just as I was thinking of getting some gravy for my meat, it came over very gallantly and gave me a little. The dessert was managed peacefully, Vilhelm sitting in an armchair, his chin on his hand and all the dessert plates in his lap. The large bread pudding reached the table safe and sound and tasted very good.

The rough stormy weather lasted all evening; one gets so weary of the perpetual motion. The captain and Giering got Juul to play whist with them, to their great pleasure.

Monday, October 17. I become quite frightened with each new date I set down; the seventeenth already, and still contrary winds and a frightfully rough sea. We must be driven backward. The weather is clear. Last night it was bad indeed; but I slept better than previously. I usually get up as soon as day dawns. It looks dismal and cheerless here today. None of the servants has come in. Mr. Juul is the only one who is up; he stands at his usual post in the passageway. Just now he had to spring aside; a wave swept almost full upon him. A little later another came, of much greater strength and duration, and washed over half the deck. There comes the maid almost crying, completely soaked. Many who came up from the steerage with their tin cups were drenched.

Tuesday, October 18. This was not a pleasant day, especially because it was so disagreeable in the saloon—foul air. Stormy weather continued yesterday, though it was a little better after noon. For a few minutes the ship would be quite still, then it would lurch. The noon meal was fairly peaceful; I think only the gravy boat overturned. We sat on deck for a while yesterday, nevertheless, and saw a ship pass us; it is cheerful to see a sailing vessel once more. But we were driven below by a sea which struck us head on, and as there are not many places that are comfortable in so strong a wind, we remained below the rest of the day. I was so sleepy that I turned in before nine o'clock, and yet slept all night in spite of the rolling, and so did not have to use the lemon cookies I had placed near at hand.

The weather is fine today, the wind a little better, but not particularly good. The ship is steadier, the sick are getting up. Here comes the doctor's wife; she looks ill. The elderly woman and all the children are up too. Everything has a bright appearance—quite different from yesterday. Ah! that we might have such beautiful weather and a good wind for a time! But it is still so cold that we cannot go on deck. Vilhelm has become quite gay over a copy of Christiania *Posten* he has found.

Wednesday, October 19. Yesterday's respite did not last long. It was very cold, but we sat on deck for a time nevertheless; it is much pleasanter than below. Toward evening the wind picked up more and more, and ended with a violent storm—the worst we have yet experienced—which lasted all night. Now the sea is perhaps a trifle calmer and the weather clear, but last night it was horrid. Still, I slept now and then. A ship passed us last evening. It was a lovely sight to see it draw away under full sail. Now a large ship sails past again. The wind is the same as yesterday.

Thursday, October 20. One day is like the other, calm during the day and stormy at night, and a contrary wind. Yesterday evening it was so calm that Kihn and Mrs. Popp came in and played dominoes. I knitted and read *Wallenstein,* and slept very well last night in spite of the noise and uproar.[7] Everything fell down, glass was broken, armchairs crashed against our wall every moment; it was frightful, too, the way the ship heeled over. We came close to falling out of our berths, and everything that was not fastened moved toward those who slept leeward.

[7] Friedrich Schiller, *Wallenstein, ein dramatisches Gedicht* (Tübingen, Germany, 1800).

I am now through with my sick visits—the customary round I make every morning — and sit here waiting for coffee. Juul is quite in despair over the wind. He thinks, I dare say, that it is lasting too long to be merely laughed at. It rained hard last night and is still raining a little, so we will probably not be lucky enough to get on deck.

Friday, October 21. We have had fearful weather. Last night it was very stormy and rainy. It was still blowing hard when I got up, and the sea was very rough; but the sun was shining brightly and I thought we would have a calm day. It turned out to be far otherwise. We were sitting peacefully at the coffee table, and the ship was almost motionless, when all at once there came a lurch that tipped over everything standing on the table and spilled all the milk on me. The wind increased more and more, a pair of sails went to pieces, and all the sails had to be made fast except a small one (the standing jib or whatever it was), which was to help keep the ship a little steadier on the waves.

So long as we had that one, the ship was, indeed, much steadier; and if I had not heard the dreadful howling and din of the wind I could have fancied the weather was beautiful and calm. But the sail went to pieces; and then, quite helpless, we were thrown about and rolled frightfully. The doors to the ladies' saloon flew open and shut constantly; shutters were put in place on the windows, and the poor women, who were all in bed, were left in the dark. The topmasts gave way. The captain and the crew had more than enough to do to get down everything that had gone to pieces. Two men stood at the wheel all day. The sea was frightfully rough, all spume and spindrift; rain came down violently a couple of times. It was an anxious day.

It was almost impossible to sit in the saloon. For a part of the forenoon we sat in our stateroom and read. Later I lay down with Mrs. Popp on her army bed; it was a relief to get that repose. It is so tiring to be thrown about continually without a rest for one's head. The dog, too, was uneasy; he is as good

21

as a barometer in a storm. The barometer, which had stood near storm, began to rise toward noon, and the wind subsided a little, but the rolling naturally became worse. At dinner the steward had to carry the soup to us one plate at a time; it is a wonder he was able to get food cooked at all.

Yesterday afternoon I spent some time with the women in their cabins until the lamp was lit. Then I took up my tatting. It helps a good deal to be working. Unfortunately the filter machine broke down, so we shall have poor drinking water hereafter. We have sea water to wash in. I was on deck a little while before we had our evening meal. It is still blowing fairly hard and the ship is pitching violently.

It was a strange sensation to stand there on deck, where everything had been in such uproar. The sky was so fair; it seems to me I have never seen the stars so large and beautiful before. It was lovely to watch the phosphorescence in the sea. The ship lay and rocked without a single sail and with broken mastheads. Strange it was to stand there on the lonely ship in the middle of the Atlantic Ocean, and then to think how easily a misfortune could have occurred earlier in the day, an event which God graciously averted.

I should not have believed that we would be able to sit down so peacefully to our herring salad that evening. Below the companionway there was a picturesque scene. There sat the captain, with a flaming red muffler about his neck, the mate, and a couple of others, busily mending and patching sails by the light of a large lantern held by a sailor sitting in the middle. Around them all was dark, the lone light from the lantern throwing a strange glimmer on the nearest objects.

Saturday, October 22. God be praised for the peaceful night and the good sleep I have had! Would that the other passengers might also soon be similarly refreshed! But the movements of the ship disturb them too much. It has been raining very hard. Now the sun is shining, and the wind is favorable, but weak. The women are beginning to come in. There is the doctor's wife; she looks exhausted, poor thing, and yet she generally looks so bright. The mate is looking at the barometer; his expression is quite cheerful, so apparently it is rising a little. I do not need to ask him; his face is barometer enough. He has a splendid face, that mate.

The wind became worse later in the day, though we could still sail by it. I went on deck and staggered back and forth a little. It is too cold to remain seated, and the deck, moreover, is full of torn sails and other reminders of yesterday. I spent nearly all day reading and sewing. Today, for the first time in many days, the table was fully occupied at noon.

Sunday, October 23. The wind is bad and Juul says we are not holding our course; but he is not much to rely on. The night was calm and gave the sick a good rest. It is fourteen days since we left beautiful Ryde. I have been on deck with Vilhelm to breathe a little fresh air. Walking was out of the question; so we stood and watched the captain mending sails and enjoyed the beautiful sky. I went in and visited with Miss Kihn until mealtime. She is a strange person; she told me yesterday all sorts of things about her affairs, her engagement, etc. The men played whist and were invited by the second cabin to have punch; but the invitation was not accepted save by the captain, who was called there. I sat and tatted until I was sleepy. The other women go to bed so early. The doctor's wife is still sick, poor thing.

Monday, October 24. Well, today everything has received legs on which to walk or wings with which to fly. We roll intolerably. It is dark without and dark within. The wind is still bad, though it could be worse. I stayed in and conversed on topics one and two, the custómary themes: wind and weather, and how long we shall be en route. I sit here now waiting for coffee, and reflect how odd it is that you are now having your morning coffee at home.

Yesterday it was very cold; today, mild and rainy. It is raining heavily without a letup; it is as disagreeable as possible. The steward and the two tiresome maids go in and out and let the doors stand open and slam; Juul is now working to repair the lock and lets us get a clear view of the deck, which is inundated, with dripping men going by, wet to the skin.

In here it does not look very gay either. Vilhelm sits in a corner and reads with an earnestness and calm which are interrupted only when his chair, without warning, takes him for a little ride. "Smiles" is sewing and is chewing on her biscuits; she does not look merry, that is certain; she deserves praise, however, for she does what she can to get well and does not give up. Miss Küsler sits just opposite me with her stocking, looking very melancholy. Mr. Giering is quiet. All are dispirited because of the wind. How tiresome it is that they are German! I have such difficulty in talking to them and following a conversation. If only we could sit on deck awhile! Here, indeed, it is hardly possible for us to converse with each other. We sit where we sit, it is so difficult to move from the sofas. This is a sad picture of the day, and one might believe I am out of sorts to see everything in so dark a light; but on the contrary I am not. I am in high spirits.

Wednesday, October 26. I forgot to write yesterday, and now I do not remember in what way yesterday was remarkable. It is not easy to distinguish one day from another. I know that I was entirely alone. The women were inside all day. Madam Zeplin was sick and remained abed; I sat with her until breakfast time, and sewed and read afterwards, as I usually do when I am not with the women. The doctor's wife is very sick; it must be dreadful to be seasick so long.

One can stay on deck only long enough to get fresh air; it is too cold to sit down and one cannot walk. I stand and hold on firmly, and for amusement I watch the water foam about the ship. There is great activity on deck; they are busy repairing all the damage. The weather is alternately foggy and clear, the wind not particularly good. We have a peculiar schedule on board now; the steward lets hardly half the usual time go by between meals. An English ship sailed by us yesterday at close quarters. It is a pleasure to meet a vessel; everyone comes on deck to watch it.

I am sitting on deck writing this, well bundled up and surrounded by sails. All the women are up, Miss Kihn included. It is a long time since we have gathered in our usual fashion. The weather is very fine, too. Reclining at ease, I crocheted, with Preus, sitting on a heap of sails, to talk to. The other men played whist; they are carrying it quite far now, playing in the middle of the forenoon. The scene before me is a varied one. Women are lying and sitting all around me; some are reading, others are working or sleeping.

Where no one is sitting, the deck is full of rope and sail and seamen, smoking. Our last sheep has been slaughtered and hangs from the mast. The pigs below are grunting; their fate is approaching. The shrouds are hung full of sailors' trousers and shirts, creating an illusion of people whole or cut in half as they hang there ballooning in the wind. The lowest deck is full of steerage passengers, who look weak and exhausted. Such is the appearance of the world in which we are living; and beyond, in all directions, the immense ocean, so peaceful today, without a single sail, and the clear sky above.

One gets very dull during the day; everyone complains of it. It comes no doubt from our idle, monotonous, sedentary life. The evening was lovely yesterday; we were up late. I like so much to see the transition from light to darkness and to watch the stars as they come out.

Thursday, October 27. Sleep refreshes in quite a different way when the ship is steady. I found that out last night. Everything looks brighter as the women now come in for coffee; and since the weather is fine, the day will no doubt be spent on deck.

Nothing came of that, for we had rain instead of sunshine. The rain let up in the afternoon and the ship was then so steady that for the first time in many days we were able to walk a little. In the evening we saw a star larger and brighter than I had ever seen. The evening passed quietly with whist for the gentlemen, reading for the ladies. I always sit up longer than the others. The wind turned suddenly to the east this forenoon and there was rejoicing and gladness. But just as quickly as it had turned east, it turned north; still, that is better than it was.

Friday, October 28. The sea is quite calm and peaceful today; a studding sail is up, indicating that the breath of wind we have is after all, good.[8] Now if it will only blow up a little more, later in the day! I think the women can thank Vilhelm that they are more patient and contented with our headway than before; it helped considerably to show them, from newspaper accounts of emigration, that many have been more unfortunate with wind and weather than we.

Now the day begins again with me sitting inside alone as usual, waiting for coffee and for company to help me drink it. Here is Miss Kihn; she distinguishes herself more and more each day by performing experiments with her food, presumably to amuse us.

After breakfast we went on deck; I was busy with my lace, and was vexed at hearing the prattle of others about nothing at all and at their familiarity with "Fatty," until Vilhelm came up. The sea and wind were still calm. Then came "Wollen Sie so gut sein," inviting us to a meal of sago soup and that pickled meat which Vilhelm and I cannot endure.[9] It was better today, however; and then those dumplings, too, that the Germans are so fond of, which have no taste at all; possibly they could be eaten with prunes. "Die wunderschönen Klöse, ach, wie freue ich mich!" was what I heard over and over, all forenoon.[10]

Mr. Jäger took a bath today; I hope it agrees with him. Afterward he was busy helping the sailors with their work and was everywhere at once. He is a queer person, that Jäger; no matter how cold it is, he goes about in the same thin gray coat, without a cap; he is always in good humor. There are a German and his wife who have spent some time in America—disagreeable persons, so exceedingly self-satisfied and tiresome to look at.

[8] The studding sail is a light sail set at the side of a principal square sail of a vessel in free winds to increase its speed.
[9] Mrs. Koren designates the steward by the phrase he constantly used.
[10] "Those marvelous dumplings — oh, how I enjoy them!"

Mr. Giering has given us a puzzle to solve, consisting of a ring which is artfully entangled in cords. The puzzle is to free the ring from all these cords. It looks impossible. We use all our ingenuity. A little gold crucifix has been put up as a prize. I shall not forget Miss Kihn when she saw it. I was very much afraid V. would become really angry. She has something to say about everything and therefore often says something tactless. Besides, she must be very silly, though she passes here for a genius.

Now we are to eat; I had better lay this aside. What will it be tonight—stewed codfish or lobscouse, or perhaps neither? The meal is over; we had ham and potatoes. Kihn, the doctor's wife, and Mrs. Popp took their meal on the floor, kept in continual laughter by Kihn's witticisms, which unfortunately I could not catch.

It is evening again and everything takes its usual course. The whist game is at the end of the table, the children on one side, talking. Juul, with his bandaged eye, sits with his hands on the table and stares. "Smiles" sews and nods. Kihn lies on the floor as usual with her head against the medicine chest, on which the doctor's wife, who is now much better, is sitting.

I went on deck and watched the phosphorescence, which is extremely bright this evening. It is very pretty to see the sparkling white foam of the waves as they sweep along. We are making good headway this evening—eight miles, they reckon. The ship lies quite over on one side, so we shall be lucky if we do not fall out of our berths.

3

Slow Headway in the Atlantic

Saturday, October 29. It looks bad for the women today; the sea is rather rough and the ship is rolling violently. The poor doctor's wife is sick again, and she so sorely needed more days of rest. Mrs. Popp is ill today too; she is very dispirited because of the wind and weather and everything. It is now afternoon; the lamps have just been lit. We have had, and still are having, a stormy day. It has blown almost as violently as during the last storm, but I think that nothing more than a pair of sails has gone to pieces.

Vilhelm took me on deck for a time to watch the stormy sea. It is interesting when it is so angry; how it broods and breaks and what a pretty color the wave crests have as they rush on! It is fascinating to be up forward and see the ship plunge its prow into the water, and watch the waves boil and foam about while the ship momentarily lies upon its side, so that it seems to touch the surface of the water. It seems impossible that the mountainous waves will not crash upon and flood the whole deck. Seldom indeed, is the sea higher than today. I think I have never been out in such a wind before. I could scarcely draw my breath, and my face became quite salty from the sea spray.

When we came down again we found the company at breakfast; we, too, sat down to eat and to help hold the unruly dishes and plates. Vilhelm was going to stop the butter plate from fleeing, and stuck all five fingers very deftly into the butter, whereupon Juul remarked very dryly, "You need not be afraid of breaking your fingers there." The doctor's wife lay on the floor for a time; but the doors began to bang open and shut so violently that she took to her cabin. Madam Zeplin also took to her berth. Miss Küsler and I then sat alone once more and worked with all our might. One gets so dreadfully tired of the endless movement without a support for one's head. We lay down and rested a while and then sat by ourselves and chatted till noon. No doubt wholly out of concern for our comfort, the steward gave us pease porridge today instead of soup.

Vilhelm is stretched out asleep; he is so sluggish today. I have suddenly become wide awake, although I may be lulled to sleep again listening to Franciska and Jean's monotonous song.[1] Giering already begins to nod. The wind is so contrary that we are steering just opposite to where we should. It would be splendid to get a somewhat calm night now after such a day. My handwriting shows clearly enough how we are still rolling; it is certainly not very easy to write.

Sunday, October 30. This is the seventh Sunday we have spent on board. I am not fond of Sundays here; they pass about the same as other days of the week. Most of the time the crew has even more to do, for there is generally bad weather on Sundays. Yesterday's strong wind is still with us, though fortunately it is not so warm as yesterday. It was then 18 degrees in the saloon—so oppressive and disagreeable.[2]

Now, with great inconvenience, we have drunk our coffee, which today "tasted strong as water," as Giering said. I have

[1] Franciska is Madam Zeplin's daughter; Jean is the Viennese doctor's son.
[2] Eighteen degrees centigrade would correspond to 64.4 degrees Fahrenheit.

been reading Spitta's hymns and am about to teach Miss Küsler some paradigms.[3] V. is reading, the doctor, too. Giering is conversing with the doctor's wife, who has progressed so far that she is lying on the floor in the little entry to her cabin. Juul is trying to solve Giering's puzzle. Madam Zeplin is in her berth, Mrs. Popp and Kihn in theirs, but I think the latter will grace us with her presence later on.

The tiresome children — how many times we have had to tell them, in vain, to be quiet this evening! Before I lie down, however, I shall see if it is possible to write a couple of words despite this fearful rolling; the wind has increased rather than fallen off today; it is still storming. Such weather is unpleasant, aside from the annoyance of not being able to sit anywhere without that howling, whistling, and cracking. We—that is V. and I—have nevertheless passed the day gaily in animated conversation.

The noonday meal was the most impossible one we have had so far, it seems to me, for it is out of the question to describe how it looked with rice, peas, and potatoes everywhere. My admiration for the steward's dexterity increases with each meal in rough weather; I do not understand how he can shuffle the pudding safely the length of the slippery deck. We lay down and rested a couple of hours after dinner. When I came in, half the saloon was full of sail that the captain is busily occupied in repairing. So many sails are going to pieces that they must hurry. The others sat about, wholly or half asleep, and consequently little interested, until it was time to eat; then they are forced to stay awake, since there are so many lively dishes to take care of.

It is now late, but I have no desire to go to my berth while it is so rough; but I shall nevertheless be compelled to do so, for there is no indication that the wind will subside. May God let the night pass quietly and give the sick a chance to sleep! It is already late at home. It is odd to think of this difference in

[3] Karl Johann Philipp Spitta (1801-59) was a German clergyman and hymn writer.

time; when I got up this morning, people were already going to church at home, or were returning, if there was an early service.

Monday, October 31. It was a frightfully stormy night. God be praised that all has gone so well! I do not mind lying awake now as much as I did in the beginning. The storm is still with us; no sail can be set. The wind blows from many directions during the day. The weather is fair.

Evening. The day has passed fairly quietly, nevertheless. It blew hard, but not so hard as yesterday. It is still blowing, but today the men could play their whist in peace, unlike the last time, when the captain had the tricks which belonged to him, and also those which did not, constantly in his lap.

The noon table looked so neat and clean that it was a delight. We are acquiring more and more dexterity; yesterday, however, the coffeepot came dancing into Küsler's lap, the hot coffee naturally all over her, and I, who sat at her side, had my share too. Our meals are important business for us; therefore I relate so faithfully what occurs at them. I have actually been comfortable during these stormy days, when indeed there is little that is agreeable, and have passed the time working, chatting, reading, and paying visits to the poor women. Now I am off to bed. I cannot understand how I slept so well last night during that terrible storm.

Tuesday evening, November 1. This has been a gloomy, rainy day. Such days are scarcely agreeable on board. All the women stayed inside and lay about on the floor, and looked just as melancholy as the weather. I sat, very industrious, and finished crocheting my piece of lace this forenoon. V. read and played dominoes, and now is busy with whist. In the forenoon the weather was very calm, the sea naturally still rough after yesterday; but toward evening it began to blow increasingly hard, and the dog went about uneasily with his tongue hanging from his mouth — a sure sign of storm. It was almost storming when I went to bed, prepared to pass an uneasy, wakeful night; but this, God be thanked, did not happen.

Wednesday, November 2. The wind is such that we are making progress today, and the barometer is rising. For the most part I have ceased to inquire concerning wind and navigation now, for I never get anything but an unfavorable answer. It looks as if we shall have fine weather today. I shall spend the time sewing and reading *Don Carlos*.[4]

Now it is evening; we have eaten our boiled potatoes and herring, to which Miss Kihn has looked forward since she awakened this morning. In the forenoon I helped Mrs. Popp and Miss Kihn eat a plate of potatoes and butter. During breakfast Kihn entertained us with a lecture on cooking and what pertains thereto. She is tireless. The men played whist in the forenoon. When they do not play whist, they play dominoes, that is, Giering and the captain do; Vilhelm reads. We have had a calm day; it blows very little. The women have their mattresses and blankets on the floor, where they spend the day when they are not eating.

Thursday, November 3. For the first time in a long while I am seated on deck, writing. The weather is beautiful; the sky is clear with a few white, transparent clouds here and there; the great ocean is as calm and smooth as a lake. Mr. Jäger is sitting in one of the boats, amusing himself by fishing up seaweed that drifts by; I got some of it as a souvenir of the Atlantic Ocean. Twice I have been lured from my seat to see a shark that never would show itself after I got there. The deck is littered with sails, and the passengers are camped about, enjoying this day of rest; indeed, they needed it after all the stormy weather, though I should prefer a little wind to this calm. Vilhelm is standing in the shrouds, gazing down into the sea.

I recognize a delicious odor from the kitchen; we shall no doubt soon be going down to eat. I know the bill of fare already from Miss Kihn. Today she even had to bring out her cookbook at breakfast.

I am enjoying *Pickwick*, which is well suited for reading here. We have seen many fish today — they were thought to be

[4] Friedrich Schiller, *Don Carlos, Infant von Spanien* (Leipzig, 1787).

porpoises. After dinner I felt I must go on deck again immediately to make the most of the beautiful day, and arrived just in time to gaze at the sunset. I had to go down for V., who was sitting over his coffee cup, and we rejoiced together at the beautiful sight. More gorgeous brilliancy of color I have never seen, but the sunset we saw at Dover with the soft, fine shadings appealed to me more. Long, long after the sun had set, the sky continued to change colors — most beautiful and remarkable tints — and to throw reflections on the sea. It spread farther and farther until at last we lay wholly surrounded by its splendor. And then the transition to darkness, when the stars began to appear and the new moon showed itself — yes, it was beautiful, all of it. Sunsets are indeed loveliest at sea.

We walked up and down until I was very tired and went below, and I sit here writing, with Vilhelm by my side jotting down his observations from Hamburg, all the children boisterous just in front of us, Giering humming on the opposite side of the mast, and noise from the steward's mortar out in the pantry. He must be going to surprise us with something special this evening. If he does he will surpass himself today, for the noon meal was excellent. We were able to eat it in peace instead of having to sit and watch our plates and then, despite all our trouble, getting something spilled on ourselves. It is really fine to have such a calm day now and then and see everyone once more about the table.

Friday, November 4. I hurried out of my berth this morning upon seeing a bright red streak in our little window recess, and hoped to see the sunrise, but I did not succeed, arriving on deck too late. So I went to bed again, fell asleep, and slept so long, of course, that I was almost too late for coffee instead of being one of the first there, as I usually am. I do wish, however, that I might once be up early enough to see a sunrise.

I have been on deck for a time. The morning was beautiful, but now the sky is quite overcast. I saw several small black stormy petrels. The barometer is falling, and soon the surface of the ocean, which is now so calm, will take on a different

33

aspect. All are sitting very quietly at their work, waiting for the second act of eating, which Kihn never ceases to spice up. The doctor's wife is sitting in her corner with "Fatty" beside her. V. and Giering are playing dominoes as usual; the latter is the champion here, however. The captain sat up and read pirate tales until two o'clock last night, so he is not yet visible. One could easily become melancholy looking at his wife, she seems so completely disconsolate.

Now the sun has come out and the fine weather has lured us on deck. V. is sitting in the top; I wish he were down — I cannot reconcile myself to seeing him aloft. We have a splendid west wind, but since, unfortunately, we must go west, we cannot rejoice greatly over it. The captain is so disheartened because of the wind that he will not leave his berth. "Smiles" sits and talks busily with that old woman; everyone appears to be much taken with her.[5] I am tired of listening to their prattle. The wind is becoming stronger and stronger; our rest will soon end, I fear.

We are sitting in a long row with our backs toward the ship's staircase. On the floor to my left I have Madam Zeplin in busy conversation with "the old one"; by her side sits the doctor's wife, "Fatty" at her feet. Anna lies spread out in all directions. On my other side I have Kihn and Küsler. There comes the doctor. What a relief! He has had his long locks cut! I hope V. will not make use of the same barber, but rather keep his wavy hair until we get ashore.

The doctor, who is certainly the most affectionate, if not the most cheerful, husband in the world, seats himself by the side of his wife, lets her lean her head against his shoulder and in a whispering voice begins to read aloud for her one of Giering's interesting tales. Since she looks at the book with him all the time, she could easily dispense with his voice. That is their customary occupation when they are not munching figs or talking to Jean. They certainly look anything but merry.

[5] The top on which Vilhelm was sitting was a platform surrounding the head of the lower mast. It is not known which of the passengers "that old woman" or "the old one" is.

Look! There we really have the captain, his wife, and his pirate tale. He has realized at last that the wind took no notice of his wrath but blew merrily to the east, and has left his berth. He has now made up a couch of rugs for his wife, and starts in on his story, lying by her side. Kihn, who follows Mrs. Popp like a faithful hound, no sooner noticed that there was a little place left on the latter's blanket than she crawled over there with the remark to me that now I could make myself so much more comfortable. She left just at the right time for V. to come and take her place.

V., as usual, was busy hushing the children and calling his favorite, Emil, over to him; Emil is now lying by his side and learning to distinguish between colors. The Swiss has been yodeling very prettily today; he is lying on the roof of the second cabin entertaining the steerage passengers, who are very merry. We sat on deck until we were agreeably interrupted by "Wollen Sie so gut sein," who must have suspected how hungry we were, to judge by the substantial dinner he gave us.

The lamps are now lit and one by one the passengers come below, while the captain throws a bundle of cloaks and blankets down through the skylight. I have not been on deck since noon, but have been sitting below with V., who smoked his pipe and drank coffee with Giering. We have eaten supper — the women except Küsler, who sews and nods as usual, and the captain's wife, who, for what reason I do not know, always sleeps on the floor at the door of her cabin instead of in her berth. The steward is very busy pounding; it must be on account of the doctor's birthday. Now I shall put this away and finish my stocking before I go to bed.

Saturday, November 5. Breakfast is over. The weather is raw and wet; we had the porthole open for a moment, but had to close it because of rain. Madam Zeplin is sitting on the floor in a corner of the ladies' saloon, the door of which is closed. She looks very miserable. Her mouth is closed; I do not know whether she is nearer to sleeping or crying; now

35

and then she makes a pitiful attempt to sew or read. "The old one" has kept a little life in her by conversation, but now has moved over to the companionway or corridor, as Kihn calls it, to bless the doctor's wife with her presence. The doctor sits in the other corner studying an English grammar; he looks like a gray rainy day. Küsler, as usual, is sitting by my side sewing; I see now, however, she has laid aside her stocking and started in on *Maria Stuart,* which she finds "sehr hübsch"; but I have a vague misgiving she does not find it particularly interesting.[6]

Vilhelm and Giering have concluded their customary morning session of dominoes, which lasts from coffee to breakfast, and now are seated on opposite sides of the table, reading two very different books. The captain is sitting on the medicine chest in great sea boots, buried in his interesting book. Mrs. Popp is lying as usual in the doorway, with the most melancholy expression in the world. She is reading Schiller, I believe; but no, it is one of the interesting pirate tales; no wonder, then, that her face has an expression of terror. Kihn came with her rug just as her mistress appeared in the doorway, and now lies at her feet, sharing her interest in those terrifying stories. I see that she too has got herself one of the tales and laid her *Meister* on the shelf. Oh, well, it is no doubt likely that her "Meisterwerke" became too heavy for her, "hubsch" as they were.[7] The merriest of the whole party are the children, who in their usual fashion are busy at one end of the table with their houses and their inhabitants, and shout, talk, and sing all at once.[8]

I hope that it will be a little gayer here tomorrow, that the sea will be as calm as today, and that we can eat the steward's cakes in peace. The wind is probably a trifle better than yesterday and the ship is fairly steady. Now I shall start

[6] Friedrich Schiller, *Maria Stuart, ein Trauerspiel* (Tübingen, 1801). "Sehr hübsch" means "very nice."

[7] Johann Wolfgang von Goethe, *Wilhelm Meisters Lehrjahre* (Berlin, 1795-96). "Meisterwerke" are masterpieces.

[8] The houses and inhabitants were probably cut from paper. Mrs. Koren was skillful at making them.

on my stocking again and see what best suits my taste today, *Pickwick* or *The Alhambra*.[9] There comes that affected steward, puffing, and pushing the children aside; he is after a bottle of milk, I see, which he very carefully puts in his pocket, presumably so that we shall not begin to wonder why he has quit giving us milk for our coffee in the morning. It must be going into the puddings.

Now the lamps are lit and everything is almost as usual except that V., Giering, and the doctor are playing whist, something they have not done these last days. Through the open door I catch a glimpse of the captain, who is sleeping. His wife, like a faithful dog, lies on guard at the entrance to the holy of holies with the poodle sleeping at her feet. Madam Zeplin is sleeping in her corner with her nose in the air. "The old one" is stretched out on the floor, with her feet near the doctor's wife and her head near Zeplin, in order not to treat either of them in stepmotherly fashion. Everyone is certainly sleeping soundly, for no one has been wakened, even by little Anna's talk and shouting. When she no longer has Giering to fuss with her she is a nuisance to the other children, and at this moment is being carried out, shrieking, by her dear uncle steward. Juul as usual stands back of one of the players, looking on.

I went on deck for a while; it is good to get up there and breathe a little fresh air when one has been below in one spot all day — even if it is not very agreeable on deck, as was the case this afternoon. It was cold and the wind blew hard. The ship was making headway, but it was listing considerably. The sea looked cold and gray, just as on a winter's day at home. The wind is still unfavorable. A flock of gulls flew about the ship, quite near. I stood for a time and watched them as they flew straight into the wind slowly and with difficulty, then like an arrow back again and down into the water to rock a little on the waves, and then again into the air.

[9] Washington Irving. *The Alhambra: A Series of Tales and Sketches of the Moors and Spaniards* (Philadelphia, 1832).

Sunday, November 6. Today is our doctor's birthday; I just now congratulated him as he came from his cabin, all spick-and-span. The weather, too, is celebrating the day with beautiful sunshine. The changeable barometer again stands at fair; this time nothing came of the storm that I expected. The wind is the same as yesterday. Now we shall begin the first act, which opens with the drinking of coffee. I see that the steward treats us to biscuits today; that is no doubt on account of the birthday.

The day will soon be over; the third act of eating has just ended. It has been so cold today that we had to sit with heavy shawls on. We did a double-time march on deck this morning to warm up a little. It was just like a winter's day — cold and sharp. After breakfast, at which we received a kümmel to break the chill, we went to our cabin. V. read a sermon and the rest of the morning we remained there, where it is always best to be, until we were called in to dinner and the old scenes again.

In honor of the doctor there was a really festive touch to the dinner. We had chicken broth, roast chicken with peas and potatoes, and a compote of pears, or whatever it was. The captain served Rhine wine and champagne. As nearly all the steward's wineglasses had been broken, the doctor's health was drunk in a beautiful medley of coffee cups, big German beer glasses, and wineglasses. Well, it tasted just as good. The health was drunk; the doctor drank first with the captain and his wife and thereafter passed around and drank and spoke a word or two with each one individually. Whether that is the usual custom on board ship, or whether it was from the impulse of his own kind heart, I do not know. For dessert our steward had baked macaroons and other cakes, all very excellent, and a welcome change from the pudding.

After the meal the men had cigars with their coffee and played a round of whist. I have been sitting between Zeplin and Kihn, reading Dickens and listening to Küsler, who has just finished *Jungfrau von Orleans* and now has started on

Maria Stuart, wondering whether there ever was such a person as Jeanne d'Arc, or whether it was not simply a figment of the imagination on Schiller's part; and every moment she bursts out with, "It is frightful, indeed, the intrigues that were carried on at such courts, and that Elizabeth must really have been a dreadful queen." She has not read very widely in history.

The doctor's wife is lying in her corridor, where her husband also has passed the greater part of the day, sitting behind her and reading pirate tales aloud; he does not look like a happy-birthday child. Mrs. Popp is lying in her doorway, with Kihn, near at hand as usual, giving extracts from the cookbook. The captain reclines near them and is teasing his wife in his usual way by snapping his fingers in her face and throwing paper on her, which Kihn carefully picks off, protecting her against his attack. It is their daily sport, of which I am very tired. The card game is in full swing again. The day has gone quickly and quite agreeably despite the cold. Küsler is beginning to nod over her *Maria*; I think I too shall soon go to bed, for it is cold.

Monday, November 7. The wind is favorable, and that causes everything to have a noticeably brighter appearance. The weather is beautiful but cold. The coffee tray has been removed. V. and Giering are playing dominoes; the children have not yet begun their usual sport. The doctor's wife has actually been on deck but came down again pale and frozen. Küsler is knitting; the other women have not come in; Miss Küsler and Mrs. Popp were still lying here on the floor when V. turned in last night, Mrs. Popp sleeping, as she does nearly all the time, the other with her Leibrock, which she told me was very interesting — "es sind wunderhübsche" and "wundervolle Geschichten." I do not doubt at all that they are "wundervolle." [10]

We have kept company with a sailing vessel today — the

---

[10] The reference is probably to J. L. August Leibrock (1782–1853), an extremely prolific writer of German popular novels. The expressions in German mean, "They are exceedingly beautiful," and "wonderful stories."

first since we left the channel. Most of the time we have been sailing away from it, and it is already far astern.

It is evening and just time for bed as I am writing this. All the women have gone to their cabins with the exception of Mrs. Popp, who is sleeping in her doorway, to the great inconvenience of the steward, who has difficulty enough maneuvering past her without bumping her face. So I sit alone among the four men, who are reading; Juul always leaves as soon as he has eaten.

This has been an exceptionally pleasant day. Everyone was heartened by the fair wind and calm sea. All have been on deck, something they have not done for quite a while. I, too, was on deck for a short time this forenoon. I enjoyed watching the gulls and other birds that fly so near our ship. The rest of the day was passed in knitting the last stitches on my stockings and reading the *Cricket*.[11] In short, the day has passed very well.

Now the wind is increasing in strength; the ship begins to heave and the tiresome doors of the ladies' saloon to slam. It must be raining, I think, since the captain has put on his sou'wester. He has just had to lay aside his prized book and go on deck in the rain and wind; that is quite another thing. We are sailing rapidly this evening — a strong wind and a smooth sea. The phosphorescence of the sea is very bright. I have been gazing at the luminous foam through our little porthole; it looks very pretty against the black sea. We are careening sharply. It is well that I do not have the upper berth and am in no danger of falling out. Now I must turn my nose to the wall; I hope then I may sleep well despite the heel of the ship.

Tuesday, November 8. Yesterday and today — what a contrast! Yesterday a favorable wind and calm sea. The barometer stood at fair, higher than it has been before. Everyone was well; even the doctor's wife was able to sit up all day. Today it is storming. The ship rolls dreadfully. The barometer

[11] Charles Dickens, *The Cricket on the Hearth* (London, 1846).

stands almost on "fair." I could hear that the women were sick long before I went in to see them. They were naturally quite depressed. Still the sun shines beautifully. Our joy in the favorable wind was short-lived; yet who knows, it may soon come again.

We must retire in darkness now, for there is no more oil. After I had lain down I heard a sharp crack; it was a boom that had broken off; fortunately no one was hurt.[12] I slept well, and as usual dreamed myself in this or that place in Norway. This time I was home. I awoke at five-thirty. V. woke up, too, lit a match, and looked at his watch. Afterwards I fell sound asleep and was awakened again by a loud noise. A wave had struck violently against our porthole, had washed over the deck and down again. I am seated now waiting for coffee and the coffee drinkers, settled very carefully to wind-ward so that I shall not have coffee spilled on me.

Coffee is over, and tasted excellent, especially since Madam Zeplin served her prepared milk and the biscuits, which are very good. Everything went well; not a drop was spilled. I hope dinner will go just as well. I think the steward is trying to make a mush of our soup so that we shall not spill. Just now Vilhelm came down from the deck to say that it is very cold — it is snowing and hailing and the wind is bad; but he trusts that this weather will not last long. We must live in hopes.

Wednesday, November 9. It was stormy and cold yesterday. We spent the morning in our little cabin — it is always best there — until it was time to go in and enjoy our "Kirschen mit Klöse," which tasted very good and warmed us up well, and was followed by fricasseed chicken with raisins and almonds.[13] I read the rest of the day, for it was too cold to work, and when the weather is so bad I never desire to do anything. Today, too, it is cold and gray; the barometer, it is true, stands at fair, but otherwise I see no signs of good weather.

---

[12] The spanker boom had snapped off because of a sudden shift of the wind, according to an account of the day by Pastor Koren: *Fra pioneertiden,* 44.

[13] "Kirschen mit Klöse" are cherries with dumplings.

41

The sea is calm; still the ship rolls considerably because of the ground swells. The wind is bad, but we are, nevertheless, now off the Newfoundland banks.

Juul came down this morning and brought me a button which had come up with the lead; I have put it away as a souvenir of Newfoundland. One wonders whom it may have belonged to, possibly someone unhappily drowned. V., half-frozen, came down from the deck just now and said there was a flock of birds to be seen, and the first sign that we were approaching land — a fishing buoy. He is now playing dominoes with Giering, who sits wrapped in his fur coat with the collar up over his ears. He is more susceptible to cold than the women, who do not even use wool stockings. Of course they usually lie wrapped in their rugs.

Well, things look about as usual. Breakfast, which went exceptionally smoothly today, is over. The captain has gone to his cabin (the curtain of which is not drawn aside, as his wife has not yet made her appearance), where he is smoking his shag, I imagine, and presumably reading his Leibrock. The doctor's wife lies in her doorway with "Fatty" at her feet; just now she left and was replaced by "the old one." Madam Zeplin is not well and keeps to her bed, as Miss Kihn too is doing, though not for that reason. The fact is she finds the day very long and stays abed almost all forenoon in order to shorten it. Miss Küsler is just as smiling as ever, possibly a bit more so since the sea is so calm; she has bundled herself up in all the traveling things she has and now trips up and down the deck with "Brother-in-law," who is certainly the most good-natured person one can imagine.[14] The rest of the day has passed as usual. The lighting is rather poor in the evening, for we have only one lamp, and when a card game is in progress, it is difficult to get a place where one can see. It is fortunate that half the group lies on the floor.

Thursday, November 10. Today it is blowing very hard,

[14] Shag is a strong coarse tobacco cut into fine shreds. Mrs. Koren uses the expression *Schwager*. As Miss Küsler was going to America to be married, the man was probably a prospective brother-in-law.

and the wind, as usual, is bad. There were such brilliant northern lights that the captain woke V., who got up and went on deck. Küsler is here, too, the only one of the women. It has been storming all day; but now the wind has subsided, and as a result we roll from side to side. Now came a lurch worse than all the others; both doors slammed shut; the trunk, bandbox, and all things movable in the ladies' saloon were hurled back and forth and came to rest at last to leeward. The lid of Kihn's trunk flew open and the contents were strewn all about.

V. sat and chatted a little with Juul this afternoon and discovered he was acquainted with the *konferentsraad*, and is a half brother of Sarzs the wholesaler.[15] I sat knitting and was very sleepy until mealtime; then, after a very excellent lobscouse, I became wide awake and bore myself bravely until I went to bed, which indeed I was forced to do, so as not to be thrown off the sofa by the rolling.

Friday, November 11. Today is the captain's birthday. I had hoped he might get a favorable wind to cheer him, but the prospect is depressing. It looks as if it will blow just as hard as yesterday. The barometer stands at "fair," but I long ago ceased to place any reliance in that. It cannot be right. Today even lazy Kihn must be getting up, since it is her dear captain's birthday.

Evening. Well, this day too is at an end, and a pleasant day it has certainly been. The weather turned fair and the wind better. There is beautiful moonlight now, but it is very cold. Mr. Giering composed a song in honor of the day. When we had drunk our coffee, the steward was ceremoniously ushered in to present a letter of congratulations to the captain. V., Giering, and the doctor placed themselves before the curtain to the sleeping room and sang the afore-mentioned song. The captain came in to breakfast and served a bottle of kümmel to warm us up a little, and V. was of course very zealous in seeing that Kihn got a full glass.

[15] *Konferentsraad* means "councilor."

Today, too, Mrs. Popp did not get farther than her door. I was not at all satisfied with the steward; he had not made the slightest effort to provide a more festive meal; on the contrary, it was worse than usual. The bread pudding had gone to pieces and tasted just like the rusks broken up in milk that little children get; but later we had champagne, drank healths, and were merry.

The men started their whist when the lamp was lit. Up to that time the captain, his wife, Kihn, Kiddy, and Anna had made a charming picture on the floor. As we sat at the evening table, we were interrupted by music; four of the steerage passengers had come to bring their felicitations, too. They remained a long time entertaining us with all sorts of dance music. The captain and Kihn took a turn at a dance in the ladies' saloon, then he and I; but it is not an easy matter to dance while a ship is rolling. Later we grownups sat in a group on the floor. Küsler is sitting, just as sweet and blue-fingered as ever, by my side. Mrs. Popp lies asleep on the floor and Kihn too. How long will they keep the captain from getting to bed?

4

The Land Was, after All, America

Saturday, November 12. Not until the day was so well advanced as to light up our stateroom — and it must have been well advanced to do that with such a little hole for a window — did I awake with that pleasant refreshed feeling which a restful couch gives, when one is not thrown about in every direction and not awakened by creaking and the noise of sailors. I would gladly have slept even longer and continued my pleasant dreams (for when the ship is steady, I am lazy). But I had a suspicion I would have to hurry to be in time for my coffee and to give my lord husband, who, be it said, showed no sign of being ready to wake up, time for his, too; consequently I got up and went to the porthole as usual, first to look at the watch, which confirmed my suspicions, and next to look at the sea, which was calm. Sky and sea gave promise of a beautiful, quiet day, with which we should be well content were it not that we wish so much to make faster progress.

I was soon dressed, for I did not need at any moment to

drop everything and hold on. Usually, just as I am doing my best to wash, there comes a lurch; then I must drop the sponge and put both wet hands against the wall; then up with them into the basin again in the hope that I may get through before the next lurch comes; and that procedure I generally repeat many times. I managed to get a glass of water with which to rinse my mouth; ordinarily that is a rare accomplishment; and we were fortunate enough to get in on time and enjoy our coffee with the women, which is also a rarity.

V. went on deck and came down with the news that it was still too cold up there. Accordingly we sat and worked very industriously, without speaking save for a word now and then, and watching what the steward brought up from the storeroom so as to guess what we should have for dinner. Vilhelm was jotting down his notes, and since he smiled now and then it must have been something good he was writing. Giering read and I read, too, and thus the time passed. We began to wonder why breakfast never came. At last the plates were passed and then white bread and biscuits. "Kein schwarzes Brot!" went the exclamation from one to the other, and Miss Kihn made faces at the sausage.[1] Giering put on his fur coat and went on deck, as he always does while the table is being set. Now — breakfast has been eaten, accompanied by talk about sausage, mites in biscuits, and worms (very appetizing). Then there was a general breaking up to go on deck.

After having been below so long, it was pleasant to breathe the beautiful fresh air. Nor was it so cold any more. The sun was shining, beautiful and warm; it looked like a midsummer, not a November day. But that, indeed, is something I do not like about the sea — one cannot tell whether it is winter or summer. For a long time we walked back and forth talking. Madam Zeplin, smiling enough to show her teeth, which is a sign that she is well satisfied, and fastening a pair of languishing eyes on us as she goes by, holds Küsler by the

[1] "Kein schwarzes Brot!" means "No dark bread!"

arm, the latter with her usual smile. She ought to be painted in the traveling dress she has on, with the great fleecy shoes on her feet. Later we stood and amused ourselves by watching how gracefully the gulls rested on the water and by noting how long a bottle thrown overboard would float before sinking. Then I talked a little with the doctor's wife; she predicted bad weather because she had rheumatism toward evening.

All had the most excellent appetites. Kihn, especially, distinguished herself by the quantity of food she consumed and the speed with which that quantity disappeared. At last we were through and the table was cleared. Giering was so eager to start the card game that he dealt before the forks were removed. We took up our work, at the same time playing a very interesting game that consisted of imitating something which Mrs. Popp said first. If one failed, there was a forfeit.

At last there was talk of a dance and dancing. The ship rode as easily as in a harbor. I do not know what the captain was thinking of, but he sent the steward to the second cabin to ask the men if they wished to dance; if so, the ladies were here. I do not know what the ladies would have done if the men had taken the invitation seriously, but they had sense enough not to do so. I was glad. It is later than usual this evening; all have gone to bed except the captain, his wife, and Kihn, who are on deck and revel in the lovely moonlight. I thought I ought to be sensible and so I did not go on deck, but went below instead.

Sunday, November 13. I awakened today greatly surprised to find V. almost dressed. It was not yet seven-thirty. When he actually does get up first, it is really early. The ship is just as steady as yesterday, but the weather is rather cloudy. I found everyone busy with coffee when I came in. The steward surprised us with rusks, two for each of us. When the two that were left over vanished, the steward suddenly noticed that Juul, who was on deck, had not had any and asked quite angrily who had taken the rusks. After breakfast we went up for a walk and listened to Juul pour out his anger on the steward; the latter had offended him by failing to call him for coffee today. Juul was really angry; he just wished that he knew German so that he might tell the steward off properly. I thought they were the best friends in the world.

When I went below, I was kept busy cutting out horses and other marvels for the children until breakfast was served — fried pork liver and rice with butter, cinnamon, and sugar (a remarkable combination). Afterward we retired to read a sermon, and remained until we were called for the noon meal. There is no end to chickens here, I believe; today soup and roast again, and rusk pudding for dessert.

We were happy to get coffee right after dinner, and cakes, too. They were almond tarts, a birthday present from the steward to the captain, although because of wind and weather they were a couple of days late. Some of the company went on deck after dinner but soon came down, chased inside by the gray, wet weather. The wind increased, the ship's movements also, and Mrs. Popp and Miss Kihn retired to their seats on the floor. We had had the impression that the wind was not especially favorable until V. opened the skylight and called down that the studding sail was set.[2] "What is the studding sail?" asked the women. It was explained, and there was rejoicing. Madam Zeplin came down with her face all smiles and her teeth protruding as far as she could get them and said, nodding in all directions, "Der Leesegel ist auf, der Leesegel ist auf."[3]

The captain came below and lay on the floor beside his wife to sleep. His faithful poodle lay beside them, and they had enough to do, trying to quiet the restless children. The doctor and his wife clung to each other in a corner and looked very miserable, she on the floor, holding her husband's hand; he, with a languishing look, leaned against her.

Meanwhile we have had a pleasant twilight hour. V. came

[2] See chapter 2, footnote 8.
[3] "The studding sail is set."

below and sat beside me and sang, a diversion I found very agreeable, and I wished the steward far away when he came to light the lamp. Now the pleasant twilight has been replaced by the prosy moonlight of the lamp saying its dismal farewell: it burns for the last time tonight. The captain and his family are still lying on the floor. Juul is sitting behind the mast reading, and listens while I hear V.'s lesson in English. Zeplin knits, Küsler reads, the children clamor; that is the picture here this evening. There is no end to the talk about food today.

Sunday, November 13.[4] Southwest of the Newfoundland banks. We had a fine breeze from the south and, with all sails set, were making a speed of eight or nine knots until eleven o'clock at night. After the evening meal we sat chatting of this and that. The captain was obviously in good humor and related stories of "my Gung," his former captain, Wilkens, now harbor master in Hamburg. (Tales of hurricanes: it had blown so hard the pigs had lost all their bristles — all the paint was gone from the ship's side — the whole rigging had blown away without anyone's having noticed it. And pirate tales of how he frightened the pirates in the West Indies with his guns.) At last only the captain, Giering, and I were left, as usual. We lit our cigars, talked of the voyage, and the chart of the Atlantic was brought out.

"Tomorrow we shall be in a new chart," said the captain, and pointed out to us where we now were, about sixteen to eighteen miles east of Sable Island.[5] "We are holding our course straight toward it," said he, "but all the time we have been farther south than our reckoning shows, and we will pass it about here," he added, pointing with his finger on the chart.

---

[4] This account of the events of November 13 was written by Vilhelm Koren; see *Fra pioneertiden,* 49.

[5] Sable Island is a low sandy island eighty-five miles east of Nova Scotia about twenty miles long and one mile wide, with dangerous sandbars running out seventeen miles into the ocean. It is often referred to as the "graveyard of the Atlantic," more than two hundred recorded wrecks having taken place there. There was no lighthouse until 1873.

"Too bad there is no light there," was said lightheartedly; then we reckoned how long it would take us to pass the banks.

"Tell the lookout that this time he must keep a sharp watch," I said in jest.

After that we went up into the moonlight awhile and then below to bed. Toward morning I awoke in a state of strange anxiety, very close to fright. Nonsense, said I to myself, turned over, and after a while fell asleep again.

I am sure I had not slept long when I was roused all at once by a violent wrench. I wondered whether I had been dreaming; at the same moment there was the sound of footsteps on the deck, and then again a jar. The captain's voice with three or four orders, one after the other; once more a shock and increased tumult — all in the course of a few moments. In a flash it was clear to me that there was danger and that it was time to dress quickly. I had scarcely got my trousers and boots on when crying and wailing and howling from the cabin and the staterooms aft were mingled with the other uproar. I stuck my head out; there they were, all in the greatest excitement, but only women.

"We have had a collision," said the captain's wife to my question. "There is great danger."

It was a tense moment: I was at the same time uneasy and very calm. I awakened Leis, who had felt the shocks in her sleep but had not thereafter heard much more of the noise than she usually did. I told her to dress herself in all haste and to be prepared, for it was possible there was danger ahead. I picked up my watch and put it in my pocket, opened all the drawers and took a coat and my pea jacket together with my traveling bag with the papers, asked Leis if there was anything she wished to have. No. She was fairly calm too.[6]

After all that, which did not take a quarter of the time it takes to write it, I hurried out to the confusion on deck. The pumps were going steadily and the ship bore away under topsail. There was no other ship to be seen. There were many

[6] "Leis" or "Eleis" is a shortened form of the name Elisabeth.

distracted faces, and the brave Swede stood and cried. At last I got the news — I think from Preus — that we had struck upon the banks near Sable Island; I could see the land to the southeast.[7] It was impossible to get any information as to our whereabouts, whether we were clear of the banks, whether we might expect new blows, or whether we had received damage. So I went down to the others — tried to reassure them — and then went with Leis into our stateroom, where I tried to bring us both to a calm and Christian composure.

In a little while I went out again — it was beginning to grow light — and not long afterward heard with joy the captain's words that we were safely over. After staying a while longer in our stateroom, I heard the steward give the call for coffee, an invitation which I cannot remember ever before having accepted with so much pleasure. The captain explained that our course had been badly steered last night, else we should have passed north of the banks. Later in the day the wind increased, and in the evening we lay again with a close-reefed topsail — that is our usual spread of canvas on this voyage. A fairly heavy sea.[8]

Tuesday, November 15. It is not blowing hard today and the ship is fairly steady, but now and then it lurches so that those seated to windward fall over backward, and I, seated to leeward, am brought to a standing position. What a pity we cannot keep a good wind more than a day! Thus it has been throughout the voyage, the few times we have had a fair wind. Today, I dare say we are not making much progress. Now I shall visit my patients and see how they are. It is evening now, we have eaten, I am tired and sleepy, and will only remark that the day has passed as usual. The weather turned fair, but cold.

Wednesday, November 16. The sun was already shining through the little porthole and down through the glass in the deck above, when I awakened after sleeping all night without

[7] The Preus mentioned was Jacob Preus. See chapter 1. footnote 9.
[8] Pastor Koren's account ends here.

interruption. Yes, Vilhelm was still sleeping, and since his watch had stopped and I had no idea of the time, I let him sleep and hurried through my toilet. When I went in for a glass of water as usual, I found almost everyone at the coffee table. I hurried in again and roused my lord consort, who asked me, a little peevishly, why I had not awakened him earlier. My excuse had to be that the watch had stopped; I felt that he could still get there in time. I went in, drank my coffee, buttered some bread for V., and had just poured a cup of coffee to take to him when he appeared. That was fast work.

We were pleased with the good wind and fine weather, but were annoyed by the dirty fat girl who, unabashed, came and sat down by the doctor's wife as she was winding yarn near the ladies' saloon, and also by the doctor's wife for always tolerating the girl near her.[9] "The old one," too, has advanced from below to windward. V. wrote and I took out my knitting and *Alhambra*.

I have just been on deck to breathe the fresh air, and found there the same intimate group that had vexed us below. Mrs. Popp has progressed as far as her doorway and lies on the floor with Kihn; but it does not look as though the fair wind will be able to brighten her pitiful face. Now the usual entertainment begins as Jean is placed in a corner to learn a verse by heart. But he proves to be lazy. The doctor scolds, and the whole scene ends, as usual, in tears.

The day is now so far advanced that a lamp is lit; we have a lamp again, fortunately; we are burning sweet oil. V., who has just finished a fine speech for Arthur, is reading. Kihn crochets and has a headache. Z. smiles and knits. Franciska and Jean quarrel and fight. Küsler sits puzzling her brain over a crocheting design. The captain and his wife lie on the floor, sleeping, I think. The doctor and his wife sit in the darkened part of the room; he has his arm about her neck, she strokes him caressingly under the chin. I cannot see Mr. G., but I can hear him behind the mast, entertaining himself with Anna and asking

---

[9] The "dirty fat girl" is apparently the children's nurse.

her whether her name is Anna Boll or Anna Weber, which has been the moot question since we came aboard. Juul comes in, puts his cap on the stove, stands a moment by one of the sofas, goes into his cabin for a moment, then takes his cap and goes out again.

Verily the cookbook has appeared again; it passes all bounds. It is Kihn and Zeplin. The former's headache apparently goes away when she becomes stimulated — as she always does when the talk is about food. The day has passed as usual. We ate a good dinner in peace — sat so long at the table that it was too late to start the whist game. The dominoes began to move again. I took a chair in a corner and let my thoughts wander off to Alhambra. Then there was coffee, and then it became dark. V. went on deck, but came back, sat down, and began to sing; and so the time passed until the lamp was lit.

Thursday, November 17. I was so late today that V. had to bring me my coffee and rusks. The wind, thank God, is fair today, too, and that has a cheering influence upon all save Mrs. Popp, who sits with just as many wrinkles in her brow as ever and, after the captain has gone out, asks Mr. Giering, with her usual anxiety, when we may expect to reach port and how the barometer is. She is sitting in her corner with Miss Kihn by her side; the latter has borrowed Dickens' *Christmas Carol*, with which she is now occupied.[10] I really believe she finds it more interesting to braid Anna's hair in little pigtails all over her head than to pore over a book of which she does not understand a word, according to V.'s opinion. Mr. Giering, who is always willing to make himself useful, is writing something for the captain. The rest of the company is on deck, although the prospect is not very inviting, for the day is gray and wet.

Friday, November 18. Yesterday was really a festive day. At the noon meal the captain ordered the steward to prepare a punch for the evening. But we had codfish, anyway. Most of us are satisfied with potatoes and butter when we have that. We went into our cabin. V. was reading some of his notes to

[10] Charles Dickens, *A Christmas Carol* (London, 1843).

me when we heard the conversation become very animated in the saloon and went in to see what it was about. We found Juul surrounded by all the passengers, holding a pretty little waterfowl in his hand; it had fallen upon the deck and he had clapped his cap over it. Since it was wounded in the breast, it was sentenced to die and thereafter to be stuffed and mounted. Amidst the excitement, meanwhile, coffee had been brought in, and we seated ourselves at the table. I can hardly remember when everything has had such a cozy, homelike appearance. All were in a cheerful mood. We sat about for a time, each one at his task, and afterward went on deck until the light was lit.

The evening passed as usual until supper, consisting of stewed codfish, was brought in. Later we had punch. It was very good and was soon gone. The captain ordered more, together with small biscuits, raisins, and almonds, whereat the steward looked anything but pleased. Healths were drunk, the captain's, "Miss Bride's," etc. First, songs were sung by those who knew any. Then it was decided that all were to sing, whether they knew any or not, under penalty of forfeit. Juul, assisted by V., sang "King Christian." Then "the old one" came trembling forth and bleated something, I know not what. The doctor, too, offered his best in a song and the company found it very entertaining. Franciska, accompanied by her mother, sang "Freut euch des Lebens." [11] Each one offered his mite save three stiff-necked persons, of whom I was one. Forfeits were required, but we were graciously exempted from redeeming them. Then they sang with great earnestness and with tears in their eyes "Du, du liegst mir im Herzen," or whatever it is.[12] V. sang with them, the most pitiful expression on his face.

Juul took his cup (on board ship one uses what one has), went over to the captain and said a few words, half German and half Danish, of which the sense was that he wished to

[11] "Kong Christian stod ved højen mast" (King Christian Stood by the Lofty Mast), first line of the Danish national anthem, by Johannes Ewald; and "Rejoice Ye in Living," a song by Martin Usteri dating from 1793.
[12] "You Live in My Heart," German folk song.

drink the captain's health, whereupon he came over and asked
V. to join him in a song for the *skaal*. Together they sang "Og
dette skal være." [13] Juul shouted "Hurrah!" so that the rafters
rang and afterwards drank with us all. He was in high spirits,
and laughed in chorus with "the old one," who became so gay
that she sang incessantly and began to propose what game we
should play, when the talk turned to that problem. Fortunately, her proposal was rejected, but it was certainly just as good
as the one that was accepted. This consisted of saying some
nonsense which each one was to repeat, with a forfeit if he
failed. This is a great favorite here, and each outdoes the other
in coining words which do not belong to any language and are
almost impossible to pronounce.

We were in full swing when the mate stuck his head in the
door and said, "Herr Kapitän! Regen und Brise." [14] The captain went out and the women became uneasy. "What is
'Brise'?" asked the doctor's wife, who has no more idea than the
man in the moon about such things. They recovered quickly,
however, when they understood what it was, and became just as
merry as ever. The captain returned and the sport went on
anew. "Es war ein grüner Jäger," etc.[15] Juul was witty. The
banal forfeits were redeemed and the captain kissed Kihr
despite much opposition on her part, all to the great merriment
of that agreeable audience who remained at the doorways of
their cabins. Thus the evening passed, and a part of the night,
too, for it must have been almost one o'clock before we got
to bed.

[13] *Skaal* is Norwegian for a toast. The song goes as follows:

> Og dette skal være Kapteinens Skaal,
> Og dette skal være Kapteinens Skaal,
> Og Skam faa dem som ikke
> Kapteinens Skaal vil drikke,
> Hurra, hurra, den Skaalen er bra, hurra!

> And this shall be the captain's *skaal*,
> And this shall be the captain's *skaal*,
> And shame on those who shrink
> The captain's *skaal* to drink,
> Hurrah, hurrah, the *skaal* is braw, hurrah!

[14] "Rain and wind, sir."
[15] "There was a verdant hunter."

Today the sea is smooth and there is a calm. What little wind there is, is not of the best. We are only a score of miles from New York. If we could just get a little breeze soon! It is gray and damp again today; but I have been on deck awhile this forenoon, nevertheless, and watched two sailing vessels.

We had sat down, the captain and his wife, Giering, V., and I, around the table near the stove and were struggling with Giering's knot when there was a knock at the door.[16] "Come in!" But no one came. V. went over and opened the door and there stood the ship's painter. He came in, went up to the captain, and began to mumble something to the effect that the pharmacist had threatened to throw a wine bottle in his face and in several ways had insulted him. I thought he was drunk, but this was not true; he stammers badly and has a disagreeable voice. The captain went out. Then the door opened again and that disgusting pharmacist, after a couple of vain attempts, came in so drunk that he could scarcely stand on his feet, and began to abuse the painter and the other men. The captain came back at last and took him out. The painter remained and ate dinner and is now playing whist.

The past two days have been more pleasant; it is cleaner and neater in the saloon. All are up and well. The doctor's wife, wisely enough, keeps on deck for the most part. Zeplin and Küsler walk in turn with the patient brother-in-law.[17] Küsler has been in and out, smiling constantly, wrapped up in her pretty traveling costume, and now has found refuge on one of the sofas with her blue stockings and *Don Carlos*, which is brought along for appearance's sake, for it is certainly not there to be read. The lamp has just been lit. We are lucky to have it.

Across the table from me (I am sitting in my usual place close to the mast) sits the doctor's wife playing with Anna. "Fatty" leans against the chair behind her, and waits to put Anna to bed. Madam Zeplin sits there, too, with her everlast-

[16] For a description of Giering's puzzle, see p. 27.
[17] See chapter 3, footnote 14.

ing embroidery, which she thinks troubles her eyes less than reading. That is a puzzle to me. Franciska sits by her, quiet for a change, and is ruining a pair of scissors by cutting holes in wood. Jean stands beside her, without quarreling, and amuses himself by trying on a three-cornered paper hat from all angles. Kihn and Mrs. Popp have vanished into the darkness of the captain's cabin, and no doubt find it interesting to lie on the bed there, for they do not come back. The doctor is lying down because of a headache. The other men have a light at the other end of the table and are playing whist. Juul stands watching them, as usual. Arthur is chased to bed crying, while Emil stands very serious and attentive and observes the players. That is the picture here this evening. The ship is steady, of course, since the scene has this appearance, and God grant that we may have a good wind tonight.

Saturday, November 19. I was not quite through with my toilet this morning when V., who at last was awake, said, "We must be getting the pilot; I thought the mate told the captain that just now." I hurried in and found the captain there. The pilot had come and American newspapers lay on the table. I went back with that news and eagerly seized the newspapers in hope of finding something from Europe, but in vain; every thing except that. I was very curious to see this first Yankee, but was much disappointed, when he came in to drink a cup of coffee, to find, instead of a seaman, a man in a light gray coat and immense collar who looked more like a country squire. Our quiet English pilot, with his knowing smile, was something quite different. We went on deck; there was nothing but thick fog and it was wet and unpleasant, and so I soon went below.

The women are in a radiant mood. Madam Zeplin's face is one big smile with her teeth the center of it. "Miss Bride" is somewhat quiet and languishing, naturally enough, I think. It is not an easy matter to make a voyage to New York to be married. Presumably the steward is very glad at the prospect of being rid of us soon, but he expresses his joy very generously

by serving us delicacies; thus we had excellent butter and biscuits for coffee this morning and pork chops for breakfast.

After we had finished the chops, the pilot went on deck. The
captain, who remained seated awhile, suddenly became uneasy
and sprang to his feet. Something seemed to be wrong. V.
dashed into our room and looked out, and called to let me
know that we were very near land. We had been aground for a
moment, but fortunately had slipped free again. Whether it
was only the fog that was responsible for this, I do not
know.

We have now had our first glimpse of America — Long
Island. It reminded me a little of England — the same grayish-
white rock; but it was too cold and raw outside to enjoy the
view. It is fairly calm again today. I wish the fog would blow
away, so that we might catch a glimpse of the beauty of the
famous harbor.

Sunday, November 20. Today at last we arrived at Staten
Island, but, to our great disgust, had to drop anchor and await
further orders. The reason was that all the steerage passengers
had to appear before the doctor to show that they were well,
and all did so, in fact, save two tiresome persons who would not
stir from their beds. One was faint from seasickness and had a
swollen cheek, the other was sick from having eaten too much,
with the result, it was said, that when the doctor saw them
lying abed in broad daylight he thought they were very sick,
and we had to stay in quarantine. Now there was grief and
confusion; and most annoyed of all was our good friend Mr.
Giering, who had believed so firmly that he would be able to
sleep in New York tonight. The captain went ashore and we
passed the evening as well as we could, but we were no wiser
when he returned. Nothing had been decided. All that time
we had waited in vain.

Since we had the most beautiful sunshine and a clear dark-
blue sky, we could really enjoy the beautiful view as we entered the harbor. We were up early, V. even before the sun.
When I came in, I found the whole steerage on the quarter-
deck and heard cries of "Land!" We hurried on deck and

caught our first glimpse of America. It was beautiful — some bluffs with white buildings. After breakfast we went on deck again and remained there.

It grew more beautiful as we sailed along. We had Long Island to our right, Staten Island to our left. Long Island is less attractive; the country is more level and monotonous — woods and fields with buildings here and there. On the opposite side, however, there were several elevations; the lower area is mainly cultivated land; in the background are woods of evergreen and leafy trees; villas are scattered here and there. Some, with towers, loomed up in the midst of the woods on the upper heights; others were surrounded by gardens and level meadows. They looked very new — as if the landscaping was unfinished. The most charming ones lay close to the water, thickly surrounded by trees, all with verandas. There were likewise many buildings in poor taste. Several things reminded me of home — two large poplars outside a house made me think of our poplars at home on Storgaden.[18]

Yes, it was a joy once more to see land, and we shouted when we saw a carriage driving along or people walking on shore. But there was melancholy in knowing that this land was, after all, America; and the anticipation or joy that, especially during the first part of our voyage, I thought I would feel so strongly on reaching land, was not present in the degree I had expected, for here everything was foreign. There was no one waiting for us; it was not like traveling in Europe; still I was heartily glad and thankful that the voyage was safely over.

We very soon began to notice something of the rush and bustle of New York. There was a mass of shipping; steamships passed to and fro. Tugs were towing one big ship after another. One towed us away. There were at least four emigrant ships lying there; one of them, a German ship, with a great many passengers, cried out "Hurrah!" as we passed by. The captain brought us letters from home and from Johan. Good news, praise God!

[18] Storgaden was the principal street in Larvik, Mrs. Koren's native town in Norway.

5

New York and the Journey to Koshkonong

Monday, November 21. This has been the most disagreeable day of the voyage. It rained all day. The captain went ashore, leaving orders for us to remain aboard until further notice; but the steerage folk were taken ashore on a tug. The customs officers came aboard and looked through our luggage; they were very civil. V. went out in his rain cape. Wohlenberg, Kihn's brother, came to the ship to talk to her. Madam Zeplin walked about, wondering why her husband did not come. We stood in the captain's cabin and passed the time gazing down on the deck, where there was a throng of people so clean and well dressed that we did not recognize them.

We had gotten our trunk up from the hold and had begun to pack our things, when we were interrupted by an order from an official who was aboard to hurry ashore right away, every last one of us, as the ship was to be fumigated. Everyone was sure there must be a misunderstanding and began to make objections. Kihn cried; Küsler thought it best to go just the same. I let them prattle and simply hurried with my packing. The steward set the table and kept saying, "Wollen Sie nicht so gut

sein und Platz nehmen, sonst kriegen Sie nichts." [1] We followed his good advice and had finished our broth when an
order came from the mate, who of course was in command,
that we had to leave. Then there was confusion. V. comforted
Kihn and Zeplin and promised to look after them.

While the confusion was at its height, a counterorder came
to the effect that we could remain; the tugs would wait no
longer. We were very happy to be able to turn to the fresh beef,
which we had looked forward to for so long; it tasted delicious,
even though the potatoes were cold. Miss Kihn dried her tears
and joined the other women in praise of V.'s goodness; I was
quite proud of my husband. We spent a pleasant evening after
that, for the captain came aboard with the information that the
ship was first to be fumigated, then would dock in New York
the following day. I shall not forget poor Madam Zeplin's disappointment when she heard that the captain had spoken with
her husband and that he was well, but still had not come
aboard.

Tuesday, November 22. The father of the children has come
aboard. It was a pleasure and joy to see his meeting with them
and his happiness at being with them. Little Anna gave many
a questioning look before she dared to remain with him, but
now she walks very contentedly up and down the deck in her
cloth coat. The fumigators have been aboard and refreshed
our organs of smell; now we are under way to the great city,
New York. The fog is disgusting; it keeps us from seeing
things. It is too bad for Zeplin that her husband never comes;
he must be a strange creature. I have been on deck to see what
I could see, and have marveled at the forest of masts in all
directions, and all the steamships with one deck above another. V. is in raptures over all these beautiful ships.

We are now lying at the wharf. Miss Kihn's brother is here.
That is kind of him. While we were sitting at the table Mr.
Zeplin came at last; but what an unpleasant impression his
cold greeting and his whole being made upon me! "Have you

[1] "Please take your places; otherwise you will get nothing."

brought the collars and clothes for me?" was his first question. She trembles when she speaks to him. The first man to come aboard was a Norwegian, Arnesen, a sailmaker, who is a good friend of the captain.[2] It was fun to hear him; he speaks genuine Christiania Norwegian, even though he has been away from home so long.

We have been ashore with the captain. First we went up Broadway and into Taylor's Restaurant.[3] How splendid it is! It is extremely large, with a balcony over half of it. The other half is an open floor. Above are two hundred gaslights, some chandeliers, some glass candelabra; below, sixty or eighty lights. The floor is set with tables, and along the walls at each table are lovely semicircular sofas covered with crimson velvet. In the center is a large fountain, partly of marble, partly of glass, in which goldfish are swimming. We had a hot meal and ices, marveling at the more than ample American servings. We then proceeded to the celebrated Barnum's Museum.[4] The most remarkable things we saw there were two giraffes, fifteen feet high, and a woman with a great beard on her face. She sat on a platform, decked out for exhibition like a strange animal, with bare neck and arms and a diadem on her head. Her little husband sat with both feet in a window recess, reading a paper. There was much to see, good and bad, all mixed together.

We also went to a theater and saw "Uncle Tom's Cabin," which was frightfully distorted of course; but it was quite amusing to see something of that sort and to observe the Americans' taste.[5] When Eva, an affected little girl, fell into the water, or someone was killed, they laughed and clapped as loud as they could. Naturally they had taken care to make Topsy as preposterous as possible, without allowing her to im-

[2] The *New York City Directory* for 1853-54 lists a Frederick E. Arnesen, sailmaker, at 80 West Street.
[3] There was a Taylor Hotel at 28 Cortlandt Street, according to the *New York City Directory*.
[4] The Phineas T. Barnum Museum was located at the corner of Broadway and Ann Street, about four blocks from the Taylor Hotel.
[5] Harriet Beecher Stowe's *Uncle Tom's Cabin, or Life among the Lowly* was published in Boston in 1852.

prove later. One pretty thing, however, was the scenery. One saw the varied landscape along the Mississippi. Some of that, like the sunset and dawn, was really beautiful. The theater itself was attractive, too.

Wednesday, November 23. Today Schlytter was on board and brought us a letter from Sellø. It was naturally very pleasant to talk with a person from Larvik again. Hvoslef, the merchant, came, too, and invited us for tomorrow. Schlytter came on board after we had eaten, and he went ashore with V. All day the ship was full of people, businessmen and friends. All the passengers left except the doctor and his wife.[6]

There was an unpleasant episode this evening. Just after V. had left, the doctor's wife came aboard anxious and distressed. She had taken a little walk near the ship with her husband, who is greatly disheartened at his prospects since his arrival here and was strangely upset this forenoon. While they were thus walking together, he suddenly tore himself away from her and vanished. Oh, how worried we were as to what he might do in that condition! The steward went ashore to see what he could do. When V. came, he and the mate took a lantern and looked for him on the wharf, but in vain. Time passed; the steward returned intoxicated and came to blows with the mate and the maids. The doctor's wife, poor creature, was very composed and quiet; at last she went to bed. The captain, too, returned. The mate arranged to sleep in the saloon, and we also went to bed.

Thursday, November 24. God be praised, the doctor has come back. He came this morning and told a story of having traveled for fourteen hours, back and forth, between Brooklyn and New York. Now, in spite of all our precautions, he has gone ashore again. The mate was supposed to look after him, but lost him. The captain intended to go ashore; we were to go

[6] Schlytter and Hvoslef were friends of the Korens who lived in New York. Sellø (Selje) is a parsonage in Nordfiord about thirty-five miles north of Bergen, Norway. The Reverend Wilhelm Frimann Koren (1801-91), an uncle of Vilhelm Koren, was pastor there; Johnson, *Slekten Koren*, 1:64. Pastor Koren's mother stayed at Sellø with Wilhelm Koren for a time.

to Hvoslef's. He and Schlytter came and called for us. But that poor wife could not be left alone. After some discussion we decided the men would go aboard again after we had eaten.

It was pleasant to get away from the cold ship to a comfortable, nicely furnished room with a fine big fireplace full of glowing coals, and to be received cordially by a sweet little matron with a young child on her arm and another holding on to her dress. It was a very pleasant day. The men left and were gone a long time, but we entertained ourselves as best we could. They accompanied us to the ship, where we are still staying.

Friday, November 25. The day was really to have been used for writing home; but there have been many interruptions. The doctor is fairly well. He has been bled and his wife has gone ashore with him. V. is ashore with Schlytter, who this evening takes us to Captain Mølbach, and tomorrow we move ashore.

Saturday, November 26. We had a cozy evening yesterday; it was so good to be able to speak Norwegian once more. Today we were up early to get our chests sent off, and have now moved ashore to lodge with that Danish family, where we are living in a fairly large room — not handsome, however — taking our meals with the family.[7] While V. was aboard getting our things, Schlytter, that splendid person, who is a great help and comfort to us, talked to me about everything, old or new. V. called for me later, when we went with the Hvoslefs to see the Crystal Palace.[8] We drove there in an omnibus, were delayed incessantly on crowded Broadway, and as a consequence found time to observe a number of elegant carriages with their lordly occupants.

It is really interesting to have been there. The building is pleasing from outside and magnificent within. I had expected

[7] Mrs. Koren mentions, *post*, p. 68, that the name of their hostess was Madam Scot; apparently she was Mrs. Frederick Schott. The *New York City Directory* for 1852 lists a "Frederick Schott, hotel," at 90 Greenwich Street.

[8] The Crystal Palace was so named because of the large amount of glass used in its construction. It was erected in 1853 on Sixth Avenue between Fortieth and Forty-second streets, and was destroyed by fire in 1858.

to find more glass in the roof. Among the things that made the deepest impression on me was a group by Thorwaldsen, a figure of Christ and a baptismal font, very charmingly arranged in a semicircle, with draperies of purple velvet in the background, and a wreath of evergreen above each figure.[9] That spot had something solemn and awe-inspiring about it. There were many other marble figures, too, but I did not care for most of them. Among the loveliest and most gorgeous exhibits was the silverwork from England. The watches from Geneva were remarkably fine, one pair not larger than a Norwegian two-shilling piece. A large number of pretty pieces of wood carving from Switzerland. The French porcelain and the Beauvais tapestries, which looked just like beautiful paintings, were lovely. Gorgeous Brussels rugs, silhouettes from fine daguerreotypes, pieces of furniture, carriages, some matchless fireplaces of marble and carved wood — well, I do not know what could have been missing. One could spend many days instead of our five hours. With all the countless gaslights burning, it looked splendid, especially when one had a clear view from above.

I was quite depressed at seeing the Norwegian and Swedish section, it was so poor. A few carved bowls and spoons, a few hideous crocheted pieces, and insignificant trifles made up the greater part of it. Then there were a Wergeland poster and some iron articles. From Sweden several beautifully bound books — Tegner, Charles XII, and others. A colossal Amazon in bronze, a magnificent piece of work (German), was undoubtedly one of the best things. It was happily placed. In the center of the building stands a huge bronzed plaster of Paris statue of Washington on horseback. Near by are two beautiful marble candelabra, very large. Everywhere were many knickknacks. A whole street, Greenwich Street (where we are living for the present), with emigrants who have just landed, was very well worked out in sugar. Perfumes in abundance. There

---

[9] The sculptor was Albert Bartholomew (Bertel) Thorwaldsen (1770-1844). A replica of Thorwaldsen's Christ was placed above the altar of the Washington Prairie Church and adorns it to this day.

is a large collection of paintings, among them a couple by Gude.[10]

We grew very tired looking at all this and went into one of the many restaurants, where we refreshed ourselves with tea and bread. Thereupon we continued our wanderings until eight o'clock. Then we entered one of those very large cars which are drawn on rails and are very comfortable; they run smoothly and are said not to jump the track. We went into Taylor's, had a hot dinner and ices, and then took leave of each other, well content with that afternoon. The Crystal Palace was impressive from the outside when it was lit up. It was interesting as we drove along to see all the different large, well-lighted shops of every kind. When we reached home, we found a letter from Consul Bech inviting us to visit him.[11]

Sunday, November 27. We have good weather again today, fairly cold. This morning I went down to breakfast. We eat in the basement. That seemed quite odd and was new to me. There is a large square room with a vault of brickwork in one wall, in which there is a cookstove. The rest of the wall is taken up by a large table for washing; there is also an ordinary stove, a rocking chair, and a nice sofa. In one corner was the breakfast table, very neatly and nicely set, and from the ceiling hung a pipe with two gas jets, which were lit, since it does not get light very early in this nether world. In this cross between a kitchen and a living room the family is usually found; they live in cramped quarters, as do most people here. On the wall hang great bundles of onions and of dried lemon peel. The lady of the house is a friendly woman, typically Danish, although she has been here so long. The room where we live is the assembly room for the Scandinavian Society; there is a

[10] Henrik Arnold Wergeland (1808-45) was a Norwegian lyric poet and dramatist, and Esaias Tegner (1782-1846), a Swedish poet. Charles XII (1682-1718), hero-king of Sweden, reigned 1697-1718. Hans Fredrik Gude (1825-1903) was a Norwegian landscape painter.

[11] Edward Bech, Danish consul in Poughkeepsie, New York, was the owner of iron works that were located on the river front there; information supplied by Mrs. Amy Ver Nooy, of the Adriance Memorial Library in Poughkeepsie, from the local city directories of the 1850's. Consul Bech entertained the Korens at his home the weekend of December 2, 1853.

piano, some music, and a large bookcase with good books on several subjects.[12]

Monday, November 28. We ate dinner downstairs by gaslight yesterday, but did not find it particularly pleasant, since the other lodgers also eat there on Sunday. However, they appear to be quiet, unassuming persons (Danish). Preus was here for coffee. We sat and chatted until Schlytter and Hvoslef came to take us home with them. We had another pleasant evening and find both husband and wife more and more attractive. The time passed quickly in lively conversation. The men drank toddy, we ate cakes and drank lemonade, and before we realized it, it was eleven o'clock. Schlytter saw us home; and now I hear him coming for V.

Tuesday, November 29. V. and Schlytter took me to Mølbach's yesterday, where I was to stay while they ran their errands. We sat quite cozily working and talking, but were interrupted for a time by two tailors who were arguing loudly about fashions. At last, to our relief, they left. Some time later V. came to ask in Schlytter's behalf how I was getting on. We sent him on his way with the message that I did not intend to come home for dinner; thereupon Mrs. M. and I sat down to our noonday meal. We sat some time over coffee and afterwards were planning to go up Broadway to see the crowds in the city, when word came that a German captain's wife was coming to call. That was a disappointment, but there was nothing to do about it; and we had to do our best to keep a conversation going in German until Mølbach and V. came and helped us. Mrs. M. played, and the evening passed very agreeably, even though I was tired.

Wednesday, November 30. We have just finished our breakfast, and have had a visit from a *bergenser*, Mr. Rein.[13] Preus

---

[12] Det Skandinaviske Selskab was organized July 9, 1844, at the home of Christian Hansen, 117 Washington Street, New York, and was composed of Norwegians, Swedes, and Danes. It went out of existence about 1910. See A. N. Rygg, *Norwegians in New York 1825-1925* (Brooklyn, n.d.); Theodore C. Blegen, *Norwegian Migration to America: The American Transition,* 287 (Northfield, 1940).

[13] A *bergenser* is a native of Bergen, Norway.

is brushing his shoes with all his might, and we are waiting for Schlytter. The weather is mild and fine. Mrs. M. told me a great deal about American women. Many, even though their husbands earn much more than Mølbach, still have no servants, but do their own scrubbing and other work, and afterward clothe themselves in velvet and silk and promenade up and down Broadway. They do not see their husbands save for brief visits, as the latter seldom eat at home. She knew some, she said, who spend a thousand dollars just for clothes, and yet these ladies oftentimes scarcely have decent bedding or table linen. V. and Schlytter, as usual, had business affairs that took them out; I stayed home and reread letters. We had dinner and listened to Madam Scot's [*Schott's*] Danish chatter about food and American fashions. Immediately afterward Schlytter came with Westergaard to accompany us to the well-known Greenwood Cemetery.[14]

We took an omnibus and got off at the entrance, in order to see everything better. Whoever first conceived the idea of laying out a cemetery there had good taste indeed. It covers a very large area. The piece of land which was chosen for it is very pleasant — rolling, with lovely lakes and beautiful trees. It seems strange to walk among the dead all that distance; yet one could easily forget them, since, because of the cemetery's great extent, the graves are scattered. One is aware only of walking in a pretty park, until suddenly one is aroused to consciousness by a group of white memorial markers or a monument that gleams from the top of a grass-covered knoll.[15]

Mortuary vaults are very numerous. Interment is in a knoll with an entrance like a chapel's; some, in Gothic style, were very pretty, while others looked more like fireplaces than

[14] Rein and Westergaard, apparently acquaintances of the Korens in New York City, are not listed in the city directory for that year and have not been identified elsewhere.

[15] Greenwood Cemetery, which is about a square mile in area, has its main entrance at Fifth Avenue and Twenty-sixth Street in Brooklyn. It was opened in 1850 and is considered one of the outstanding cemeteries of the New York City area.

anything else. A few monuments had a beautiful location down by a lake. We examined a number of monuments in detail; one for a woman was especially fine. There was one which was quite comical — a captain, life-size, who stood looking through an octant. The man is still living and now and then goes to gaze at his epitaph. The prettiest one we saw was for a French woman who died by falling from a horse. There were many charming monuments for children. Here there is a strange custom of placing the child's playthings on the grave. There were some glass cases with whole exhibits inside. We walked about until dark and went home satisfied that we had done justice to that beautiful cemetery.

By mistake we almost took separate omnibuses home. V., that coffee man, is not himself when he does not get his coffee in the afternoon, as was the case today. He decided that since he could not get coffee, he would nevertheless have something, and took Schlytter with him. Westergaard and I hurried into an omnibus with no one in it; it soon filled up, and when the men came there was just one place for Schlytter, who took V. upon his lap, and after much trouble and after having sung and talked nicely to him, got the unruly child to sit still.

The driver cracked the whip, but we had gone only a few steps when the omnibus stopped; something had gone wrong, and we waited patiently until we heard the welcome "Go ahead!" The same thing happened once more before we reached Brooklyn and went aboard the handsome ferry, as they call the steamboats between New York and Brooklyn, which soon brought us to the other side. There we boarded a streetcar, and found the same women who had followed us all the way. They burst into gales of laughter over our meeting again. We were at Hvoslef's again in the evening, where as usual our hostess was gracious, regaling us with eggnog and other good things.

Thursday, December 1. We had just finished our breakfast when Mrs. Mølbach paid us a visit, then Schlytter, who went out with V. and bought a trunk. Mrs. Mølbach left a little later and we took a tour up Broadway. It is amusing to go there at least once and look at the traffic and activity, the splendid shops, and all the different faces. When we got home we found Consul Bech, who had come to the city again to find us. He urgently invited us to visit him Friday; we could then leave Saturday. As we had decided definitely to depart Friday morning, we said no. But there was no gainsaying him. He wished us welcome to his home when he left, and we finally decided to go by way of Poughkeepsie.

Mrs. M. came again in the afternoon to take us to see an exceptionally fine steamship. It is very large, and arranged comfortably and elegantly. From there we went on board the "Rhein" to say good-by. It grieved me to say farewell to our genial captain and his wife. Schlytter had dinner with us in the evening. The Mølbachs came up to say good-by; we had not run across them earlier. We packed, and went to bed late; and at nine o'clock next morning we sat in the railway coach on the way to Poughkeepsie, accompanied by Schlytter, who went a little way with us.

It is a beautiful route; we have the Hudson River on one side with its lovely shore, which consists alternately of gray-white, wooded bluffs of even height, cultivated fields, and small, neat villages. The roadbed follows the water's edge. In some places the river cuts into the bank, and the track is laid over the water.

At twelve-thirty we arrived at Poughkeepsie, and found a carriage waiting to take us to Bech's. We were cordially received by Mrs. Bech; the consul arrived a little later. We drank hot chocolate and admired the pretty rooms, especially the conservatory. We had dinner; the evening passed in a very lively discussion of religious affairs on the part of V., Mrs. B., and the consul. On Saturday the consul and V. were at the factory while his wife, the children, and I went for a drive in and around the town. The surroundings are very charming. A Danish gentleman came and remained until

Sunday evening. Sunday we attended the Episcopal church. I like their service very much except for their custom of half mumbling their prayers, which are otherwise very beautiful. The sermon is the least part of the service. Sunday passed quietly and peacefully. I went to bed early, as I did not feel well.

Thursday, December 8. I am now sitting aboard a large elegant steamer on the way from Chicago to Milwaukee. The weather is beautiful and calm, so that I can continue quite at ease my description of the journey from Poughkeepsie. Monday morning, the fifth, we took leave of our friendly hostess and, accompanied by the consul, went to the station. The consul wanted to go with us to Utica, but was unable to, and sent his servant with us part of the way to see us safely to another train. We left at ten-thirty. A short time afterward a gentleman approached and began to talk to us about Mr. Bech and "help." We did not fully understand him, and V. dismissed him rather shortly. We asked the servant who it was, and learned that he was a friend of Bech's. The servant went over and spoke to him, and so did V. When we came to Albany, where we changed trains, he obtained seats for us. He himself sat behind us. We conversed as best we could; he treated us to apples and nuts. He was a friendly, amiable man. He left us in Utica, where we arrived at three o'clock.

The day was gloomy and a little snow fell. The landscape was most charming during the first part of the journey through the Mohawk Valley and over the Mohawk Canal; later the land became more level and monotonous. At nine o'clock we arrived at Buffalo, having traveled about four hundred English miles. We were rather tired and wanted to stay overnight there; we escaped safely at last from the importunate cabmen and arrived at a hotel; got a room with a brisk fire in the fireplace. A little bustling person came bowing and scraping and said, "Supper is ready"; so we went down and found, as usual in these hotels, many small dishes, meat, good bread, but poor tea and coffee. At seven o'clock next morning we walked in rain and mud to the station. It was not easy to find a place in the crowded coaches.[16]

We traveled this day through Ohio; stopped longest in Cleveland. The weather was beautiful later in the day. The land is rather uniformly level, with many groves of leafy trees, some firs scattered here and there, many orchards, small lakes, long stretches of woods and uncultivated land where occasionally one spies a wretched little log cabin, and sometimes a man in the woods with an ax on his shoulder. The train stops are frequent. We passed through several places, among others South Bend, where one could see the beginnings of buildings of considerable size. At one station an excellent horse-drawn machine for sawing wood caught our attention. In the afternoon we crossed into northern Indiana, but there was no difference in the nature of the land. At one of the changes of cars we got a disagreeable old woman behind us who entertained and amused the rest of the company by relating her travels and rattling on as if they were all ignoramuses.

At Cleveland we had considerable trouble finding the right train; when we did, the coaches were so crowded we were lucky to get a seat, and could hold it only by remaining in it; but we stopped so long that it was vexing not to be able to go out to get a little food. We met Mr. Pauli there; he told us that when we reached Toledo we would have to cross the bay before we could get the other train. It was between nine and ten when we arrived in Toledo. We followed the crowd and arrived, just as we had expected, on board a steamboat, where we waited a long time without going anywhere. When at last we reached the far shore, no train was to be seen; we made inquiries and heard that it had gone. The next train was at three o'clock in the morning. There was nothing we could do about it. We met a gentleman who showed us to an omnibus which took us to a hotel where we could wait. We went down

[16] The first railroad between Buffalo and Chicago had been completed in the fall of 1953, according to Pastor Koren; *Symra,* 21 (1905). In the paragraph that follows, Mrs. Koren gets a little ahead of her story by discussing South Bend and Indiana before she has left Ohio.

to supper, and then spent the time in a room with two women and some children who were to leave with us. I wrapped my shaw about me and lay down with my coat over me and slept quite splendidly until the omnibus came to take us to the station.

The coaches were filled with an unpleasant mixed company, which one must put up with here where there is only one class. Near the large cities it is all right, but as we get farther west, the passengers are mainly farm folk. The seats are so comfortable that I did not feel much fatigue. I slept part of the time, as there was the same monotonous, fairly level land. We stopped very often and waited several times for locomotives to pass us. The coaches are always full of newsboys who offer apples and cookies for sale; at intervals they are kind enough to go about with water; they also sell books and magazines.

It became more level as we neared Chicago. Michigan looked yellow and unattractive. Great deserted prairies with woods on the horizon — in which at times one caught a glimpse of a little cabin — swampy or covered with a growth of marsh grass. The prairie nearest Chicago was more cultivated and settled; large orchards were planted there. Finally, at four o'clock, we arrived in Chicago; that much of our journey was safely past. We have seen almost no snow or ice on the whole trip, and for the most part only leafy trees.

We took the omnibus to the Matteson Hotel and got a room.[17] V. went down for our luggage; after many vain attempts I was at last lucky enough to get a servant to make a fire. V. looked up Unonius, the pastor, who came back with him and sat here awhile.[18] He was very friendly, expressed

[17] The Matteson House, a neat and plain red brick structure, four stories high, was at the corner of Dearborn and Randolph streets. It opened in the early fifties and was considered a first-class hotel. It was destroyed in the great fire of 1871. See *Guide to the City of Chicago* (Chicago, 1868); and J. S. Currey, *Chicago: Its History and Its Builders* (Chicago, 1918).

[18] Gustaf Elias Marius Unonius (1810-1902) was a Swedish Lutheran pastor who founded a Scandinavian settlement at Pine Lake, Wisconsin, in 1841. Subsequently he was ordained an Episcopal minister; he went to Chicago in 1849 to work among Norwegians and Swedes there. He first met the Korens in Hamburg in 1853; he gave them advice about Iowa, which he had visited. See Blegen, *American Transition*, 123, 126, 128, 129; *Fra pioneertiden*, 12.

his regrets that we had not come directly to him; but as we were to leave early in the morning, we were unwilling to make any change. He had been on the point of leaving for a party when V. came. When he had gone, we went down to supper in a very large dining room. Everything in this hotel looks very grand and costly. Who would believe that when Pastor Unonius came here twelve years ago there was no trace of a city, and he had to live in a wretched log cabin? Now it is a flourishing city with shops just as fine as New York's, if not finer. Naturally one gets the same impression here, as everywhere on our journey, that everything is still in its beginnings. At eight o'clock this morning we boarded a boat for Milwaukee, where we will arrive soon, I suppose, since it is now half past three.

This is a remarkably fine steamer. The upper saloon, where we are — there are two decks — is extremely large, lacquered white with richly gilded borders and carvings, four large, handsome chandeliers, several gilded mirrors. The floor is covered with expensive carpets, and there are mahogany tables with marble tops, velvet-upholstered sofas and chairs. Doors along the walls open into the cabins. The passengers, however, are not at all suited to this elegance — a mixed company here as everywhere. A young woman sitting opposite is clothed in silk from top to toe, with white kid gloves, and looks as though she were much taken with herself and her finery. Her husband, on the other hand, does not look very elegant. Beside her sits a woman with a number of children, who is quite boldly taking down her hair. One sees all kinds of shoes, too, some small, narrow, and polished as if made to tread upon silk and velvet; others large, heavy, dirty, whose owners should be forbidden to walk upon these lovely carpets.

About five o'clock we landed in Milwaukee. Since our train had already left, we had to wait until eight o'clock the next morning. We hurried from breakfast into a bus, and were taken first to the steamer, much to our alarm; then by good fortune we got into the bus again and to the train — only one

car. Beautiful weather. We arrived in Milton about twelve
o'clock. I went into the Milton House, sat down in a rocking
chair, and gazed at all the gimcracks in the room.[19] V. made
an effort to get a horse, but in vain. We discovered that the
little white-haired boy near the stove was Norwegian. We ate
dinner in company with a very mixed group. Preus left with
the baggage.[20] Later we got a lumber wagon and a most
learned driver; expecting every moment to tip over, we came
at last safely to Koshkonong.[21] We surprised the [Adolph C.]
Preuses in the midst of butchering, but were welcomed very
warmly. We found it rather strange in that little house to
begin with. Sunday was pleasant; we took a drive. The parsonage is a fairly large log cabin with whitewashed walls and
unbelievably simple furniture; but it is cozy, and the Preuses
are unusually kind and friendly.[22]

Monday, the twelfth, I wrote home. Preus and V. were
gone all day. In the evening H. Preus came to take us to his
home the following day.[23] We left Koshkonong on the thirteenth at eleven o'clock.

[19] Milton is fifty-five miles southwest of Milwaukee. The Milton House still
stands and is today maintained as the museum and headquarters of the Milton
Historical Society. This building, reported to be the first concrete structure
in the United States, was built in 1844 by Joseph Goodrich, who continued to
operate it as a public inn until his death in 1867; Margaret Gleason, reference
librarian, State Historial Society of Wisconsin, to the editor, February 8, 1955.
[20] This is no doubt the Jacob Preus whom the Korens had met on the ship.
[21] Pastor Koren states that the driver was an American about twenty years
old, who apparently was a college student during the winter; *Symra*, 21 (1905).
Koshkonong parsonage was fifteen miles north of Milton.
[22] The Reverend Adolph C. Preus (1814-78) migrated to America in 1850 and
was pastor at Koshkonong until 1860; he was president of the Norwegian Synod,
1853-62; in 1872 he returned to Norway.
[23] The Reverend Herman A. Preus (1825-94) migrated to America in 1851;
he was pastor at Spring Prairie, Wisconsin, about fifteen miles northeast of
Madison, 1851-94; and he was president of the Norwegian Synod, 1862-94.

6

From Koshkonong to Iowa

It was a gray but not very cold morning, the fourteenth of December, when we set out for Spring Prairie, driven by Pastor Herman Preus in his buggy.[1] It is not more than twenty-five miles between Koshkonong and Spring Prairie, but to us it seemed twice as long, we went so very slowly. We had a good deal of baggage with us. Preus and I sat in the front seat, he upon a high pile of horse blankets and sheepskins so as not to be inconvenienced by the large trunk which he had between his legs, I well packed in with buffalo robes both over and

[1] This account was written beginning January 20, 1854, after the Korens had reached their destination in Iowa. Mrs. Koren mistakenly wrote "fourteenth" in place of "thirteenth." The chronology of the trip from New York to Washington Prairie is as follows: Friday, December 2, New York to Poughkeepsie; Monday, December 5, Poughkeepsie to Buffalo; Tuesday, December 6, Buffalo to Toledo; Wednesday, December 7, Toledo to Chicago; Thursday, December 8, Chicago to Milwaukee; Friday, December 9, Milwaukee to Koshkonong; Tuesday, December 13, Koshkonong to Spring Prairie; Thursday, December 15, Spring Prairie to a tavern beyond Madison; Friday, December 16, from the tavern to Dodgeville; Sunday, December 18, from Dodgeville to a tavern; Monday, December 19, from the tavern to Prairie du Chien; Tuesday, December 20, from Prairie du Chien to McGregor, Iowa; Wednesday, December 21, from McGregor to Washington Prairie.

under me and Mrs. Linka's great sheepskin shoes on my feet.[2]
The rear seat had been removed to make room for the chests
and bags. On one of these chests sat Vilhelm, with my brown
cloak over him, not very warm to be sure, so he jumped off
from time to time to walk. In addition he had a bad cold and
became hoarser and hoarser as we progressed further, so that
I was quite alarmed. In this manner we went along carefully
and slowly.

The landscape was not especially beautiful — or possibly the
gray light failed to make it attractive. The roads were bad — no
snow, but deep ruts and mud. We stopped a couple of times to
water the horses. Preus then had to get down in the mud and
soil his buffalo shoes; so each time he got up again, he would
throw the shoe that would have been next to me into the back
of the wagon.[3] Vilhelm kept wanting to walk to get rid of his
cold, but we still had too far to go. Preus said he could walk
the last mile; but it seemed never to come. I have never driven
so slowly.

It now became dark; Vilhelm got down, Preus and I sat and
chatted quite comfortably and soon were some distance ahead.
We were driving over the prairie; it was so dark that we could
not see the road. Preus lost it, and drove back and forth and in
a circle to find it again. I imagine Vilhelm, who was far behind,
could scarcely have had any idea of what we were up to. He
mounted again when he caught up to us, and after some searching we hit upon the right road; but it was no easy matter, for
the whole prairie was burned black and there was not a star to
be seen. We were lucky enough to escape being hemmed in by
fences, and at last saw light in a house. It was the parsonage.

[2] Mrs. Linka, the former Caroline Dorthea Margrethe Keyser, was the wife
of Herman A. Preus. For her own account of life in a pioneer parsonage, see
Linka's Diary on Land and Sea, 1845–1864 (Minneapolis, 1952).

[3] Buffalo shoes were made of buffalo hide and served much the same purpose as overshoes. They were made with the fur outside and were "big and
walloping," according to Mr. William Linnevold, a resident of Decorah, who
remembers them well. Mr. Linnevold, now (in 1955) seventy-seven years old,
is a grandson of Magnus Arneson Linnevold, who took land on Washington
Prairie in 1853. William Linnevold had a wide acquaintance among the early
families and has written several articles on pioneer days. See "Minder fra
nybyggertiden," in *Decorah-posten*, appearing weekly May 24–July 5, 1929.

Preus lifted me over the mud and into the kitchen. From there we came into a large room with a stove in the center, a table with a light between the two windows, and on one side two doors, one leading to the study and the other to a little bedroom. Between these two doors a stairway with a loose trap door led up to the loft; below this was the entrance to the cellar, and on the wall hung coats and wraps. Despite all this there was something very cozy in the large whitewashed or, more accurately, gray-washed room.

A small, plump young woman in a blue dress and a little white cap, with a bright, lively countenance greeted us graciously. This, then, was Mrs. Linka, of whom I had formed quite another conception. I was immediately much taken with her — such an active, cheerful person. She had expected us for dinner and had just started coffee when we came, and now she went back and forth, with her businesslike little cap on her head, preparing supper for us. It consisted of excellent fricasseed chicken that put to shame her husband's remarks about her poor skill as a cook. Afterward Master Christian came in; he was afraid of the strangers. Linka asked about the news from Christiania; she was so hoarse, however, she could scarcely talk, and as we others were tired from our journey we soon went to bed.[4]

The next morning I was the first one up. I stood underneath the stairs and paged through a book. A couple of people came to speak to the pastor; after a bit they got tired of waiting and went over and tried the door to the study, whereupon little Christian came running out half dressed, with the pastor himself following, in his shirt sleeves with a towel in his hand, to bring him back. At last they were all ready and we sat down at the breakfast table. Vilhelm felt a little better later in the day and went out with Preus.

It was so muddy that we ventured out only to look at a pig and a cow that were to be slaughtered, preferring to sit inside

[4] For Mrs. Preus's account of her preparations for the Korens' visit, see *Linka's Diary*, 241. "Master Christian," later the Reverend C. K. Preus, was president of Luther College in Decorah, Iowa, 1902–21.

and talk. I asked for and received various bits of good advice.
Meanwhile the men returned, we ate our dinner, and had a
cozy hour over coffee, after which they again left us. When
it got dark we stirred up the fire, drew our chairs nearer, and
continued our chat. When V. and P. came back, there was
much discussion as to whether we should leave one of our
trunks behind; this was finally decided, and so I had to get
everything into the room and undertake a thorough repacking. Linka was busy in the kitchen baking pancakes for our
lunch on the journey. The evening passed very agreeably after
the repacking was finished.

We were to start early next morning, but Lars kept us waiting so long that we finally concluded he had changed his
mind.[5] At last he came. It was eleven o'clock before we started.
Linka drove with us to Lars's house; here he was to get something, and we had to taste his beer. We said farewell to the
Preuses, promised to write soon, and began our journey.
There was cloudy weather and a tiresome road over black,
ugly prairies all the way until we were near Madison. Since V.
was hardly in condition to talk, we sat with scarcely a word all
forenoon. Near Madison we met two wagons with Indians;
farthest back in the wagons sat the chiefs, their faces painted
red, their heads uncovered and adorned with feathers. They
made a brave show as they sat there wrapped up in their white
and colored blankets.

Madison is situated very charmingly on the banks of a lake
— it was good to see water again — and looks as if it might
become a good-sized city. Here we were to eat dinner, but the
question was, in which tavern.[6] There were enough of them to
choose from, and Lars seemed to have a great inclination toward one of the small, low ones just at the entrance to the

[5] Lars J. Møen, a blacksmith from Voss who had settled at Spring Prairie,
was to drive the Korens to a point on the Wisconsin River near where it
empties into the Mississippi. When Herman Preus and his wife first arrived
in Spring Prairie in September, 1851, they were housed with Lars Møen,
whose cabin was the one nearest to the site for the parsonage; *Linka's
Diary,* 193.
[6] "Tavern" was the usual designation for the kind of inn found on the
frontier.

town. However, we drove farther. Vilhelm went into several shops, from which expeditions he returned with a large, atrocious-looking umbrella and a scarf for me; then we alighted outside the Madison House, a large building that promised well. We did, indeed, come into a handsome room, from which we had a view of the city hall, which stands on a fenced-in enclosure with trees planted about. Here we ate dinner, consisting of the usual pie and roast turkey, not to forget all the side dishes which are found on an American table — beets, cold meats, cucumbers, conserves, and I know not what.

Vilhelm went out again, and I was engaged in conversation by a Norwegian who was working there and who every now and again found some pretext for coming into the room to speak to me. Lars came back with the wagon, Vilhelm a little later; so we took to the road again in the hope of reaching the nearest tavern before dark.[7] Since Lars knew the road to Madison, but not a bit farther, we now had to inquire our way as best we could, nor did we meet many people without halting them with our questions. I became so tired of driving that day, especially when it grew dark, that I fell asleep with my head on Vilhelm's shoulder, while he held the buffalo robe firmly about me. I did not awaken until we stopped outside a tavern, and when I got inside, I was so frozen I vowed never again to sleep in the wagon. Vilhelm went with me into the room. When Lars noticed that he had settled down there, he came over to the door very cautiously and beckoned to make him understand that that was the "Ladies Parlor," and that no males might remain. What, then, must he not have thought of Vilhelm, who, notwithstanding this, very calmly settled down in the "Ladies Parlor"!

At length the evening meal was ready, and it tasted good after the long drive. Just opposite us sat Lars and next to him a lively, very talkative man whose bright eyes were often fastened upon us while he was asking Lars about us, and who was very

[7] The vehicle was probably a lumber wagon, but the terms used by Mrs. Koren make it difficult to identify it.

busy serving us everything on the table. We got a bedroom
that had a warm stovepipe passing through it; the furnishings,
aside from the bed, were limited to a chair and a little table;
I had a good laugh when I came in and found Vilhelm standing in front of the mirror with a candle in his hand, gazing at
his fat face very carefully and seriously, and saying, "Really, I
am becoming a pope!" After that discovery he sat down in a
rocking chair, which went to pieces with a loud crash, whatever the cause might be — the pope's weight, or my clothes,
which were hanging on it.

I awoke and looked at the watch; it was half past five, so I
hurried out of bed. The moon was shining into our room. I
managed to light a candle and looked again at the watch,
which now, it was apparent, stood at two o'clock. I was not
troubled by my mistake and lay down again to sleep, not without waking several times and looking at the watch, which at
last really did indicate five-thirty. I dressed and groped my way
in the darkness down the stairs to get some water to wash in.
The maid was to bring it immediately, so I went up and waited
a while; but no one came. Then the bell rang for breakfast, so
that at last I had to go down again.

One has to be his own servant in these taverns. Two things
are considered luxuries here; namely, a bellpull in the bedroom and candle snuffers. When I came down I discovered
that the maid had brought water and a towel to the washstand
which stood in the "parlor." It is the custom here, it seems,
to dress — and thereupon go down to the parlor and wash — a
custom which is not so absurd, indeed, since the bedrooms are
cold to wash in and are not warmed up so early as the parlor.
Meanwhile, since we had no love for that custom, I brought
the water pitcher and its appurtenances, at great risk to their
existence, safely upstairs and to my joy found Vilhelm, the
sluggard, almost dressed. Right after this there was a knocking
at each door to announce, "Breakfast is ready." We found the
same company there as in the evening and Vilhelm had a conversation with the old landlord, in which the latter told a long

history of a Norwegian maid who had worked for them and had been most remarkable in every way.

It was at least seven o'clock, though it was not yet quite light, when we set out again; we were to reach Dodgeville by evening.[8] We soon discovered that our driver, Lars Møen, was both a kind and worthy man. He is a smith from Voss, and Pastor Preus's right hand. We enjoyed talking with him, and this morning we talked about America and asked him about the country here.

"I suppose there are many birds here, Lars?" I asked.

"Oh yes, there are plenty of birds, but they do not sing as they do at home; it used to be so beautiful to hear their warbling in the evening," he answered quite sadly.

His answer caused our eyes to flash the same thought to each other. It always makes me sad when I hear that in America the birds do not sing, and the flowers have no fragrance. I feel as if something of the finest were lacking, as if no real joy could be felt in nature; and so my thoughts turn with added melancholy to the beautiful summer evenings at home.

We had the same cloudy weather and monotonous scenery as on the preceding day. After eating several pancakes and having with great pains persuaded Lars to take one, I found it not too cold to amuse myself by cracking nuts, left over from the railway journey — though Vilhelm disdained them. At dinner-time we discovered an inn in the town of Moundville, where we rested the horses and warmed ourselves with a cup of coffee, which we obtained after a long wait — just as bad here as everywhere. Lars had a substantial dinner. Finally the horses had rested long enough, and we departed.[9]

We were now approaching the Blue Mounds. The country became more hilly and woody. The roads were generally very bad. Vilhelm and Lars often walked a stretch to get their blood in circulation. We saw the Blue Mounds becoming blue in the distance and discovered to our joy several hilly knolls

[8] Dodgeville, Wisconsin, is forty-three miles west of Madison.
[9] Moundville (spelled Mountville in the original) was twenty-five miles west of Madison. In 1881 the name was changed to Blue Mounds.

where a fir had found lodging and fastened its roots.[10] There were not many settlers along this road. Lars was so careful with his horses, keeping them at a walk, that it seemed doubtful we would reach Dodgeville before some time at night. When we had passed through the Blue Mounds, Lars began to inquire even more eagerly concerning the road. "How far is it to the next tavern? Right way to Dodgeville, sir?" These questions were directed to every human being we met, or saw within hearing. It did not bother Lars that he asked the same person twice, which was the case with a man who drove past us several times and whom we at last met outside a house. He very likely thought we had a screw loose.

Toward Dodgeville the country was level again. We drove across a very extensive prairie just as the sun went down. Here for the first time we had an opportunity to get a full view of an American sunset. We found ourselves, as mentioned, in the midst of a great, black, desolate prairie. The sky had been covered with gray clouds all day, but by one of those frequent and sudden changes of weather it became clear, and let us see the sun go down in great splendor, gilding a great sweep of the heavens; at the same time darkness rapidly overspread the opposite part of the sky and looked as if it would throw itself upon the daylight and destroy it, as indeed it did within a few moments, while isolated stars twinkled here and there. Directly in front of us, where the prairie rose a little, we saw a man on horseback silhouetted for a moment sharply against the sunlight, completing the scene, and thereupon coming toward us at full gallop. Aside from ourselves, the man and horse were the only living creatures to be seen.

When we had driven a bit farther, we saw a glare far away upon the prairie. "There goes a prairie fire," said Lars. While we were talking of this, Vilhelm said, "Turn around." I did so, and saw the full moon rising over the horizon. Its light had a marvelous effect upon the black prairie, heightened even more

[10] The mounds are a little to the west and north of the village of Blue Mounds and reach an elevation of 1300 feet.

by the prairie fire on the other side. There was an air of un-reality in driving here, especially as the moon soon hid itself behind the clouds and we could no longer see the road.

We did not know exactly where we were driving, and were glad to discover a light gleaming in a valley. Lars gave V. the reins, and after some trouble with an ill-tempered dog, got safely to a house, and brought back the information that we were on the right road and not far from Dodgeville. It was farther than we had been told, but at last we saw some houses, and glad I was, for towards evening I always become weary and tired of driving, and even peevish too, I fear. It appeared that Dodgeville consisted of three parts; at any rate, we drove through two small places before we came to Dodgeville proper. Here, then, we began to ask for Preus among all the Norwe-gians we met; but no one had any information.[11]

We were thinking of going to a tavern when a Norwegian blacksmith asked if we would not go with him to his home. We did, and came into a warm, crowded room, where there were several small children. Marit, the lady of the house, ap-peared immediately and was much surprised to find guests. They appeared to be good people but were, without doubt, much "Yankeefied." It was so crowded and stuffy that I had no great desire to stay, but we could hardly decline their friendly invitation. At that time I was not yet accustomed to native rural hospitality. We had not been there long before Pastor Preus came; he had asked for us in all the taverns, and was happy to find us at last. Marit, meanwhile, had prepared a meal. V. and P. took a walk after we had eaten; I remained behind and was annoyed by the children, who now had supper with their parents, got what they demanded, and were untidy beyond all description. P. returned with V. and stayed until almost nine o'clock.

We were not up early the next morning, so Marit felt justi-fied in knocking repeatedly on our door and asking us to hurry

[11] They were inquiring for either A. C. Preus or H. A. Preus; the context does not indicate which.

to the breakfast table, which was set out with many kinds of bread. Because one of his horses had not eaten either in the evening or in the morning, Lars was much troubled and was reluctant to go farther. Inquiries for a conveyance were therefore made in several places, but in vain. It was exasperating, but there was nothing else to do; we had to wait until the following day and see how the horse was. Lars, poor fellow, was very much embarrassed. He was reluctant to break his word, would gladly see us safely on our way, but his dear horse was not well.

We took a walk with Preus and called on a fine young couple, Arne and Birgitte, with whom we were to stay that night, to my great satisfaction, for I liked them and their accommodations much better. We had dinner at the smith's and spent the evening at Arne's, where Preus was, too. Lars brought an Iowa man, John, to talk with Vilhelm; he was to leave the next morning. There was another discussion about our journey, one plan after another was proposed, so that I was thoroughly weary both of that and of the journey, and came very near falling asleep. We now had a good bedroom, to which I retired early.

Sunday morning Preus came over again, Lars a little later. There was the same talk back and forth; an American was brought in who would drive us, but he was so unreasonable in his demands that even Lars considered that arrangement out of the question. "You will have to drive them yourself," said Preus once more to Lars, and with that it was settled, to my great relief; I was so reluctant to give him up. His dear horse had eaten a little in the morning. This gave him more courage, and people who understood such matters believed there was no danger. Meanwhile, with all this talk the forenoon was far advanced, so we had to hurry away. We then took leave of Preus, who had been so friendly and helpful to us. He packed me in well, we nodded to the friendly Birgitte, who stood with her little child at the window, and drove away across the prairies, where there was scarcely a house to be seen.

It was cold and raw; V. jumped down often, Lars, too. I sat in the wagon and laughed to see them running, each on his side of the wagon, V. in his raincoat, sou'wester, and great sea boots, Lars hobbling along with his cap down over his face. Not until we reached Wingville did we see any trees.[12] That little place lies beautifully in a narrow, heavily overgrown valley. It was past noon when we arrived there. Lars went in to find out how far it was to a tavern. Ten miles to one in a wood, fifteen to a second one, was the answer. We asked several whom we met the same question and always got different answers, so we were just as wise as before and simply had to hurry as much as we could to reach a destination while it was light. The horse was doing very well; he was as frisky as ever.

We had no sooner left the valley of Wingville when we again saw endless prairies before us, and not a house nor a tree. On one of these prairies we had our midday meal. There was a roast quail for each of us, on which we gnawed; the meat was delicious, but our fingers froze and we could not eat the bread and butter which went with it. Lars took his quail at last, too, not without much coaxing; he was always reluctant to deprive us of any of our provisions. Afterwards, we ate candy. Vilhelm was almost over his cold.

The ten miles to the house in the wood seemed never to end. V. was quite convinced that what he saw on the horizon was a house. Yes, we thought so, too, but then discovered a gleam of light some distance from the road on the left side. Lars went in and came back and said it was a tavern, and he thought it would be sensible to stop overnight there. Therefore we drove in; but it turned out to consist of only one room; so, after some deliberation, we decided we would rather drive five miles farther and get a decent room.

Miles become twice as long in the evening and so they seemed now. We had no idea about the road, and drove with the stars as our guides until we reached a house where Lars

[12] Wingville, now known as Montfort, is a small settlement in Wingville Township, sixteen miles west of Dodgeville.

again went in and came back, quite aghast at how filthy and horrid it was. We were on the right road and would soon reach the tavern, he had been told. So it turned out, and we were glad to get into a warm, orderly room and take off our many wraps. We found a long table set in a large side room, which was likewise the kitchen, where an elderly widow, proprietress of the house, was supervising two young girls preparing food. The other persons in the room were a young couple with two handsome children, with whom Vilhelm amused himself and to whom he gave candy. They, too, were going to Iowa, but to a different part than we.

Then Lars and we had something to eat and enjoyed it heartily. As I was tired and wished to see our bedchamber, the landlady took her candle and accompanied us upstairs to a little room. There stood a bed with its right foot against the window, taking up all the space except a passageway just large enough for a little chest and two persons (that is to say, when they did not move about). On the wall hung the girls' starched muslin dresses; there was no chair, no washstand, and what was worse, no stove, so that it was icy cold — and we had been looking forward with joy to a good, warm room after the cold day! That cubbyhole and a similar one about a foot wider were the only ones we had to choose from. The large warm one below, the farmer's family was to have, for they had come first, and having small children, no doubt needed it, too.

My desire to get to bed subsided as I looked at that cold room; so I went down and sat near the stove and talked with the landlady, who brought out her clay pipe and began to smoke. Remarkably enough, neither she nor the girls were especially inquisitive, garrulous as they otherwise were. Never have I experienced anything so cold as that night; it was as if we were lying out under the open sky; and then, too, it was one of the coldest nights that winter. I was not tempted to sleep late in the morning, and was glad to get on some clothes and complete my toilet downstairs, where it was comfortable and warm, and pleasant to see the preparations for a good breakfast. No one had come in yet; the hour was only five-thirty. It was past seven, however, before I got all my numerous shawls tied up in front of my nose and mouth and Lars was ready to drive.

It was a cold day. The sun was shining brightly, however, and warmed us a little as we drove through the valley which leads away from the house. We had driven a good mile along the way when I discovered I had forgotten my umbrella. Lars went back, and we prepared ourselves for a good long wait, for we knew his slowness. Vilhelm was not able to go in his place, for he had put on his raincoat and it had now frozen quite stiff, and crackled and cracked with every movement. He was annoyed because of this, and because I had been so idiotic as to persuade him to put it on. Who, indeed, could have imagined that the miserable raincoat would have caused so much bother? After much trouble, and some damage to the coat, he finally succeeded in getting down and walking back and forth a little until Lars at last came puffing along with the umbrella.

And it was well we got it. Our road lay over prairies all the way, with a frosty wind so fierce and biting that I do not know how we would have fared if we had not had the large umbrella to protect us; but under it we sat fairly warm and cozy until we came to a narrow, thickly overgrown valley, and were able to tell, because the prairie had disappeared, that we were approaching the Wisconsin River. Lars explained to me what kind of trees we were passing, and I exerted myself to look at them from under the umbrella and the scarf on my forehead. Vilhelm got down, leaving the umbrella to me, and was far behind most of the time.

The road, which of course was bad after we left the prairie, now became quite impossible. The wagon tilted far to one side, with two wheels almost in the air. I had to lie crosswise in it and had plenty of trouble holding myself in and seeing that the umbrella did not become enmeshed in the wheel or entangled in the stuff that lay in the back. Thus it went, now up, now down, in fairly deep snow over a hill. On one side the ground sloped precipitously upward, on the other abruptly down into the valley. To make things even worse, the scarf on my forehead slipped down so I could not see, and I dared not speak to Lars for fear of distracting him from minding the horses. I sat there, half laughing and half crying, as patiently as I could, and prepared for an upset at any moment. Lars, however, brought his horses safely over the difficult place, V. came up soon afterward and freed me from my clothes and from the umbrella, which was not needed in the valley, and restored me to balance, for I had been so stiffened with coats and shawls that I lay where I lay.

We were now able to laugh at my tragicomical account of my misfortune (I wish that someone could have sketched it), of which Vilhelm naturally had had no conception because he was walking far behind, deep in contemplation of the marvelous valley, which now held all my attention, too. It was wild and primitive. It did not look as if the sound of an ax had ever echoed among the old oaks, which stood in picturesque groups interspersed with saplings — some bowed down, others thrown upon each other by the wind, still others half dead, embraced by fresh vines which at times had quite overrun and covered old dead trunks that long since had lost their crowns. There were some wild fruit trees and thickets round about; it must be beautiful when the leaves are light green and the fruit trees in bloom.

The valley broadened, the trees thinned out, and now we were surrounded by grassy heights with a tree here and there; and alongside these heights from time to time cliffs jutted out in wonderful, fairyland formations — at times, indeed, whole barricades and fortifications. These strange bluffs, which V. with great difficulty enabled me to see by turning my wrapped-up head around, continued all the way until we were quite near the river. Then the valley opened up and sloped very gently down to the water. Here we were again surrounded by woods on both sides, with the remarkable bluffs at the back.

We drove down to the ferry and found the river, as we feared, full of drift ice, and saw no possibility of getting across with horses. We then had to drive back to another road, said to lead to the upper ferry; here the horses were unhitched and tied to the front of the wagon, in which oats were placed for them. V. and Lars went to look for the ferryman, and I remained behind, passing the time in the back of the wagon as best I could, gazing at the beautiful landscape about me and eating the rest of Mrs. P.'s cakes, while in front the horses devoured their oats and frightened me with their friskiness. While I was sitting there, two Yankees came up who also wanted to cross the river; they talked with me for a time before they continued on the same road as the others. I waited a long time and froze my feet thoroughly, until at last I heard them coming with the ferryman and his boy, who were to help with the baggage. Lars and the horses were to remain behind and we were to be taken across in a canoe.[13]

Each was well loaded with his portion of the baggage, and I set out ahead, accompanied by the ferry boy, who had to take my hand and help me cross a pool of water on some timbers; my feet were so stiff I could hardly walk. We went through a wilderness of bushes and undergrowth until we came to a little stream over which there was a bridge. I became much frightened to hear that V. had crossed it, for it lay more under water than above. It had been broken down by a Norwegian driving over it, they said. I was unable to get across; so we went farther up along the bank. Here the ferryman went ahead and tried the ice, which held, and led us safely over to the other side. Then we halted to see how Lars was faring; he had taken the way across the dilapidated bridge, dragging one of our chests after him; thank goodness, everything went well, but it looked dangerous. Not long afterward, we stood by the river.

The ice was solid for some distance; so the luggage had to be pulled out upon it before it could be moved into the canoe

[13] The Wisconsin River flows into the Mississippi below Prairie du Chien. The ferry was near the site of present-day Bridgeport, Wisconsin.

which was to take us across later. We went into the woods for shelter for the time being, I with my buffalo shoes on my hands to warm them. The canoe came back, we said our farewells to Lars, asked him to greet the P.'s, and, wishing each other a joyous Christmas festival, went our ways. I was quite grieved to lose him; he had been so kind to us, and he now stood and waited on the shore until he saw us safely across. I was very much frightened at going right out to the edge of the ice, which we had to do in order to get into the canoe. Here we seated ourselves in the bottom, holding on firmly, with one hand on each side and our hearts in our mouths. We really had to sit still in that little, light canoe, if we did not wish to see ourselves overturned. The ferrymen stood, one in each end, and made their way between the ice cakes with their paddles. They were Frenchmen, and showed their lively dispositions by shouting and yelling like wild creatures, encouraging us not to be frightened. That was not necessary. Nevertheless, I was glad to reach the shore.[14]

We went to the top of a steep hill to the ferryman's home, which has a charming view over the river and its beautiful banks. Here we arranged for horses to Prairie du Chien. They could not come before seven o'clock, however; so we ate supper with this black-eyed French family. The horses we got were fast and the coachman talkative. He spoke a great deal about a Norwegian minister who always stayed with him when he was in that neighborhood and called his house his home. There was bright starlight, but it was dark, so we could not see how things looked; no doubt there was only black prairie. The five miles were soon left behind us; we alighted at the Hotel Phoenix and go a room so scantily furnished that we had to ask a Norwegian boy who was carrying wood to get us another chair.[15]

[14] Vilhelm Koren has given a graphic account of this crossing in *Symra*, 23 (1905).
[15] The minister was probably Nils O. Brandt (1824–1921), pioneer pastor in Wisconsin, Iowa, and Minnesota, and eventually a teacher at Luther College in Decorah. Brandt organized the first Norwegian congregations in Iowa. See

The next morning Vilhelm went out to find someone to take us across the Mississippi, which was frozen over but could not be crossed by horses. I passed the time, meanwhile, as best I could. First I tried to converse with the Yankee maid who was tidying the room, but received no other answer than a stupid look and "Ma'am?" so I soon tired of that. I sat down and ate some of the nuts which Preus had given me in Dodge-ville, and wrote a little until V. returned and said we could not get away until after dinner. V. left again and came back a number of times with various purchases. At twelve o'clock we had a fair dinner — and presently the buggy came, driven by a little man who was called "Doctor," with an immense woolly hat, and a pair of gold spectacles on his nose. We drove off, the doctor on V.'s lap. I tried to get some idea of the appearance of the town. It lies in a large flat valley, surrounded by bare hills, has a thousand inhabitants, but will not increase in size until the railroad comes.[16]

After we reached the river, the horses were unhitched. The doctor went ahead, trying the ice with a long stake, and helped Vilhelm draw the buggy, in which I sat; a Norwegian boy pushed from behind; and so we proceeded — as much as pos-sible across islets, then alternately over ice and trees, a mile or so across in all. When we reached the other shore the boy stayed with the equipment and we followed the doctor down a remarkable road through the sloughs along the river. I had to take off my shawl.

We stopped at the American House, and V. went to look for a conveyance. I passed the time watching servants decorate a room with garlands for a ball, and conversing with the two

ante, editor's introduction, p. viii. The Phoenix Hotel was a brick and frame structure on Main Street, one block south of Main and Blackhawk, in Prairie du Chien; Mrs. Florence Bittner, curator of Villa Louis in Prairie du Chien, to the editor, June 14, 1955.

[16] Prairie du Chien, oldest town in Wisconsin, is on the Mississippi three miles above the mouth of the Wisconsin River. It was a meeting place for traders and Indians even before 1700. The French gave it the name "Prairie of the Dog" because it had been the home of an Indian chief called "The Dog." The French and the British successively maintained military posts there, and the United States built Fort Crawford there in 1816.

Norwegian maids until V. returned.[17] We could not get horses until morning, and had to be ready for an early start. We asked to be shown a room, and had our choice between a large one with a stovepipe to warm it and a little one without a stove. The large one had this "but" attached to it, however, that adjoining it were the quarters of a Yankee and his wife who were spoken of very mysteriously and were not expected home until late. We settled down in the room which was supposed to be warm, but had not been there long before we discovered at least three broken windowpanes. V. took all the pillows he could find and stopped up the holes; it was still cold. A warm room is always difficult to find in an American tavern. We drew the table close to the stovepipe, trimmed our candle with a hairpin, and spent the time as best we could until the bell rang for supper. Later we decided on the inner sleeping chamber, cold as it was; we stuffed shawls around the window and went to bed early, for I was tired of sitting around freezing.

When we came down next morning, we found both maids busy baking biscuits. We asked for breakfast, but were told that until the landlord came we could not be served; he himself had to be present at the table. This was a strange custom, that the guests had to wait for the landlord in order to get food. But there was nothing to be done. They did not dare go in at our request and disturb that stupid landlord; it was annoying, for it was late and we wanted to get away. In the meantime it appeared that our horse was just as unreliable as the landlord. The latter came sauntering in at last, seized a large bell, slammed open the street door, and stood there ringing with all his might. Now at last the time had come.

While we were eating, the wagon came, and we hurried to

[17] The Korens had now reached the west bank of the Mississippi and were spending the night in a hotel in McGregor, Iowa. Mrs. Koren mentions later (January 12) that the two girls were the daughters of Thorbjørn Omager of the Turkey River settlement. In 1852 the American House was a frame structure 16 x 20, situated close to the river; this information, from the *North Iowa Times* (McGregor), August 26, 1875, was furnished by Mrs. Lena D. Myer of McGregor, Iowa.

get away from that tiresome place. It was dark and snow was falling. Our driver was a young Scotchman with an attractive face. We stopped outside his home while he went in for his shawl, which he wanted me to put on. Then he seated himself again and started to drive. At once we recognized a strong smell of spirits and discovered that the Scotchman was literally swimming in whisky. In sitting down he had broken his whisky flask, poor fellow. But he was not slow, he ran into the house again, emptied his pocket, folded his shawl up in the pool of whisky, and drove merrily on.

We had a sheltered road during the first part of the way through the McGregor Valley, before we reached the dusty, cold prairies. One mile, two, four, six miles, the Scotchman announced very accurately, pointing down at the side of the road, where we, too, discovered the markings on some small flat stones, which would not need many inches of snow to cover them. These, then, were the mileposts in this country; they are perhaps better than none at all. "I am going to see if he knows any of the Scottish melodies," said V. and began to sing. It was not long before the Scot joined in, and he continued through most of the trip to sing his Scottish ballads in a very appealing way. He told us he was twenty-three years old, and his wife not yet twenty. They had been married four years and had had three children, of whom only one was living. When we asked him if his wife was Scotch, he answered, "Oh yes, certainly. I would not have a Yankee; they only eat candy all day long."

When we came to Monona (a couple of houses and two shops), we stopped a long time while he went in and got himself a dram.[18] He also provided himself with a new flask of whisky, to which he applied himself diligently.

"You should beware of drinking so much whisky," said Vilhelm.

"What does your wife say about it?" I asked.

"Oh, she says I'm a naughty boy," he answered, but assured

[18] Monona is fifteen miles west of McGregor.

us at the same time that it was never found in his house; it was only on trips that he indulged.

Naturally we were curious to see the nature of the land in Iowa, but we discovered no marked change, except that the prairies were more hilly and the road even more natural (that is, as nature had formed it) than in Wisconsin. Late in the day we came to a very large stretch of woods where the road forked, and the Scot insisted that our road was the narrower one (which, as it turned out, led up to a little house). Vilhelm thought not, but naturally, the driver ought to know best. So we drove the narrow road, which was wrong, of course, and then back between deep snow and thickets until we came to the right road again. It did not look as if we would reach our destination early; the horses were sluggish; nor did it help matters that the driver continually called to them, "Show that you are worth your thousand dollars!" We made slow progress at best.

Vilhelm, as usual, walked now and then. Meanwhile the Scot was as merry as ever: he ran, sang, took a pull at his bottle from time to time, and froze thoroughly nevertheless; he marveled that I kept up my spirits. "It would have been different if she had been a Yankee!" he said, and was just as eager as we to arrive soon at the first Norwegian house. He inquired faithfully, too, whenever he could, how much farther it was to the first Norwegian. The sun had long since gone down; we all began to feel cold. I pulled and tugged at my buffalo robe, as usual, to get it close about me. At last we discovered, on our left, the first house. Here, then, it was; happy were we and happy was the Scot. He was hoping, in fact, that he might get home soon enough to attend the ball at the American House.

"Does Mr. Johnson live here?" he cried when we came to the vicinity of the aforementioned house and spied a man standing outside.

"Yes!" shouted the man, and Mr. Johnson, tall and erect, came forward. He was good enough to come over to us at once, and, extending his hand to Vilhelm, wished him welcome when he heard who he was. He told us Nils Katterud lived about two miles farther on, and that it was easier to get to him, as the road to Knud Aarthun's was full of twists and turns; and to one of these men we intended to go.[19] He mounted his horse at once and rode ahead to show us the way.[20].

[19] This first Norwegian farmer whom the Korens met when they neared Washington Prairie was Gullik Johnson Rønningen, whose family now goes by the name of Running. He lived on the northeast quarter of Section 13, Springfield Township, Winneshiek County. Nils Hanson Katterud (1798–1895) and his wife Liv lived on the southeast quarter of Section 1, Springfield Township. The Washington Prairie Church was later erected about half a mile south and a little west of their place. Knud Aarthun, his wife Anne, their eight children, and a paternal uncle and his family lived together in one cabin during the winter of 1853–54 on the northwest quarter of Section 6, Frankville Township. Aarthun eventually moved to Minnesota, and it is said that Ortonville, Minnesota, is named for him or for one of his sons. Valuable information on families and farms in the Washington Prairie area has been supplied to the editor by Mr. William Linnevold of Decorah.

[20] This ends the account of the journey from New York. The diary now begins again, with some duplication of what has been related.

7

A Log Cabin Far Inland

Wednesday, December 21, 1853. It was probably close to
six in the evening when we reached the first Norwegian house
in Iowa. With Mr. Johnson in the lead, we set out as on
parade, over stump and stubble. I have never seen such a
road. All went well for a time; Mr. Johnson was sometimes
ahead, sometimes alongside, talking to us. I was freezing and
the others were, too, I suspect. Vilhelm raised himself to
get my buffalo robe better about me, but thereby lost his
sou'wester and got off to look for it. We continued up and
down the slippery hills until I asked the driver to stop and
wait for Vilhelm; it took a while, but at last he came, quite
breathless from running after his sou'wester, which he had
lost several times.

We went on again until we came to a house where our
guide went in to get the man of the house to accompany us
farther; his name was Erik Egge.[1] Our Scot made a place for

---

[1] Erik P. Egge (1826-1905) came to the United States from Hadeland, Norway,
in 1848, and to Winneshiek County in 1851, where he took land in the southwest quarter of Section 6, Frankville Township. He, his wife Helene (1824-

97

him on a chest by his side, and the expedition again got under way. I thought to myself that these were two long miles indeed; but they ended, without other misfortune than Vilhelm's loss of one mitten. We were not shaken out of the wagon, Erik did not fall from his unsteady seat, and we all came safe and sound to Katterud's house. Vilhelm went in to find out whether they could put us up and came back immediately with the man of the house and a chair to help me down from my high seat.

We came into a room that did not look very attractive. It was a fairly good-sized room with a large stove in the center. The floor was wet; a girl with a mop was busy swabbing one end of the room, which was partitioned off partly by a thin wall and partly by a curtain, behind which one caught a glimpse of a bed — all very simple and plain. Log walls cemented with clay, as usual. We were very kindly received by an elderly man, an even older wife, and the daughter, who helped me off with my things, made excuses because it was so untidy — they had washed clothes — and drew a rocking chair up to the fire for me.

Nils and his family appeared very happy at having this pastor, for whom they had long waited in vain, so suddenly saddled on them. They brought forth the best the house offered, and on the whole were so friendly that we soon felt at home and chatted away a couple of hours very pleasantly, until at last, tired and sleepy, we went to our bedroom, that is to say, up to the loft, where in addition to us, were a sister-in-law of Nils and three children who had also recently come to this country.[2] It was a good warm bed and we slept well, but it was cold getting up in the morning. [*December 22.*] We

1902), and Helene's two children by a former marriage shared their cabin with the Korens from December 24, 1853 until March 10, 1854. The original cabin has been preserved and is a part of the outdoor museum on the campus of Luther College in Decorah, Iowa. The Egge farm was about five miles southeast of Decorah and three quarters of a mile south of Iowa highway 9. See E. C. Bailey, *Past and Present of Winneshiek County, Iowa*, 2:307 (Chicago, 1913).

[2] The sister-in-law was Kari, wife of Ola Katterud. She and her three children were staying temporarily with Nils Katterud; V. Koren, in *Symra*, 25 (1905).

had recognized the smell of fried pork, the usual meat for all meals, and hurried down, where we found everything looking better than on the evening before. A neat breakfast table was set, to which V., Nils, and I sat down first, thereafter the wife and daughter.

Nils is a small man with an odd face set off by fairly long, light hair and a pair of twinkling and smiling bright eyes; he talks slowly with a very broad East Norwegian accent and no doubt passes for a wit in his family, who laugh at anything he says. He is a kind, friendly man. His wife looks old, trembles considerably, is kind and good, and always manages to get in her say. The daughter does not talk much, but accomplishes so much the more; she has a pleasing manner.[3] There is a wholesome relation between the family and the sister-in law who is there, and I like the whole group very well.

Nils had to go up to Thrond Lommen's, he said, to announce the arrival of the pastor.[4] Vilhelm wished to go along; so in the forenoon they set off afoot and I was left alone with the women. We spent the time as best we could. I asked for and received information about all sorts of things. We had pork sausage, bread and butter, and coffee, which takes the place of soup here, and fired the stove steadily. Outside it was snowing and blowing; our walkers were having bad weather.

In the afternoon the wife of Suckow, the shoemaker, came for a visit, and later Knud Aarthun, who stayed until the

[3] The daughter, Mari Katterud, was, at the age of fifteen, the first public-school teacher in Winneshiek County. This school, located on Ole Gjermund Johnson Hedalen's farm, the southwest quarter of Section 31, Glenwood Township, was built in 1852. The first confirmation in the settlement was held there in 1855. Mari later married Lt. Ole A. Anderson, a veteran of the Civil War who was a nephew of the Reverend Nils O. Brandt. See A. Jacobsen, "Reminiscences of Pioneer Norwegians," in G. W. Anderson and I. B. Goodwin, *Atlas of Winneshiek County, Iowa*, sec. 2, p. 11 (Davenport, Iowa, 1905); Linnevold, in *Decorah-posten*, June 14, 1929.

[4] Thrond Lommen (1792-1856) of Valdres, Norway, and his son, Gudbrand T. Lommen settled on Section 33, Decorah Township, Winneshiek County, in 1851. Gudbrand T. Lommen later married Elizabeth Lomen, sister of the Reverend Nils O. Brandt and widow of Jørgen Lomen; W. E. Alexander, *Hostory of Winneshiek and Allamakee Counties, Iowa*, 132 (Sioux City, Iowa, 1882); and a personal interview with Professor S. S. Reque of Decorah, Iowa, a grandson of Pastor Brandt.

others came back.[5] They returned just after we had lit the lamp. Knud, who must be a very fine man, stayed and helped eat the *flødegrød* which Nil's wife served, and afterwards remained until late in the evening talking with Vilhelm.[6] I went to bed early in the loft, where I sleep just as well as in the most splendid chamber, except that it is so cold mornings and evenings; it happens to be unusually cold these days. This was the twenty-second, Vilhelm's birthday. Last year on this day he came to Larvik to visit me, and today we are sitting in a log cabin far inland in America!

Friday, December 23. I was awakened today, too, by the smell of fried pork and coffee, hurried to dress, got a basin of water, went outside the house to brush my teeth, and then sat down to the pork, which, curiously enough, tastes just as good to me every time I eat it; that is, morning, noon, and night. The weather has been delightful today, but fairly cold. Nils and Knud are trying to find us another lodging, for it is too crowded to remain here. They would like to place us with the Ingebret Sørlands, who have the most room, but do not seem eager to take us in. I hope that something will be decided soon, so that Vilhelm may have some quiet for study.[7]

He studied this forenoon; I took my knitting and visited with the family until dinnertime. When we had eaten, Vilhelm and I took a walk. First we went to Ingebret, who was very friendly and seemed to be quite willing to receive us in his home; but his wife said very frankly that she was afraid there would be too much for her to do. It is very nice there;

---

[5] Lars Johan Suckow and his wife Sigrid (Siri) lived about three quarters of a mile east of the present Washington Prairie Church. A son, Christopher Suckow, attended Luther College, 1863-64, and died in the Civil War; information from William Linnevold; see also Gisle Bothne, *Det norske Luther College, 1861-1897*, 360 (Decorah, 1897).

[6] *Flødegrød* is a dish made by slowly cooking thick sour cream, to which flour and milk are added. It may be served with sugar and cinnamon or with raspberry juice.

[7] Ingebret (Embret) Gulbrandson Sørland (1824-1901) settled on Section 1, Springfield Township, Winneshiek County, in 1851. He was married to Eli Clement Skaarlia (1826-1879). The family now goes under the name of Soland; Alexander, *Winneshiek and Allamakee Counties*, 629; markers in the Washington Prairie cemetery.

in that respect we certainly could not get a better arrangement. But it is better, I think, to have crowded quarters than to be received with reluctance. From there we made our way across the fields and thought of going over to Knud Aarthun's, but we sensibly gave that up, for we did not know the way and wandered into a wood which we soon had to get out of. It was not passable for me with my long skirts — any more than the hazel brush through which we did force our way later; Vilhelm always plunges into the very midst of the hazel brush. When we got out of that, we found the tracks of a deer; eventually we reached home without encountering anything more unusual.

In the evening Knud came and said it had been decided that we were to live with the Erik Egges, and could move when we pleased. He stayed for the evening; a couple of other farmers were here for a time, too. Vilhelm would have liked to sit up part of the night to study, but the cold became so biting that it was impossible. Ugh! how cold it was to go to bed that night in the breezy loft where, besides us, Nils's sister-in-law, Kari, and her three children are sleeping! The space that is not taken by the beds is filled with the family's clothes, chests of drawers, meal sacks, etc. Such was the appearance of our first bedroom in our new home.

Christmas Eve, 1853. This was a strange Christmas Eve, indeed; so different from any I have ever known before. Here we sat, Vilhelm and I, separated for the first time from relatives and friends, in a little log cabin far inland in America. For supper we had spareribs and coffee. As we sit here now, we get a little light from a lead dish in which there are tallow scraps and a little rag for a wick, placed on an overturned salt container.[8] Vilhelm is studying his sermon for tomorrow. We are expecting Erik back from Decorah any moment; he is bringing the bed in which we are to sleep, as well as some candles.

[8] The container was possibly a small wooden keg or box in which salt was usually kept.

After dinner today, Nils hitched up his oxen. We said farewell to our friendly hosts, promised to visit them often, and seated ourselves in the sleigh, Vilhelm on the chest in back, I on the one in front, holding on as best we could, for the road was not what you would call smooth. Nils walked at the side with a long stick, thrust at the oxen, spoke his "Ha!" and "Gee!" and talked with us. At last, right side up, we halted the oxen outside Erik's house, and entered a room which, though clean, did not have the most pleasing odor, because it had just been scrubbed by Helene, mistress of the house.

The house is fourteen by sixteen feet, divided by curtains of calico into two rooms, one of which affords space for two beds, which extend along one wall of the house and are separated from each other by a second curtain. Nils put our things in the loft, said "Go 'long!" to the oxen, and drove home again. Helene, who appears to be a kind, friendly woman, brought out beer and *fattigmandsbakkels* for us; after that, accompanied by Per and Kari, three and four years old, we went up to the loft to put our things somewhat in order.[9] I cannot imagine how Vilhelm will get any quiet for study here, it will be so crowded.

What a contrast between this evening and a year ago! I am happy and content that we are here in time for the Christmas festival — there is such joy over the pastor's coming — but it grieves me to think of Father and the others whom I miss, for the first time, on this Christmas Eve. Vilhelm took a walk with me. The evening is lovely; it was good to get outside a little. Oh, how beautiful the sky is! The stars are much brighter and seem larger than at home.

Now Erik and Knud have come back loaded with all sorts of things. There has been a great to-do to get the bed up. Knud has just left and Erik and Helene have gone to bed, so

---

[9] *Fattigmandsbakkels,* literally "poor man's cakes," are a favorite Norwegian pastry. Kari and Per were Helene's children by her first husband, Anders Egge. Kari later married Embret Clement Skaarlia; information received from William Linnevold.

that it is quiet and peaceful for Vilhelm, who no doubt will sit up a long time. I am weary and am going to bed.

First Christmas Day Evening. Today, before a large group of listeners, Vilhelm preached his first sermon. The service was held in the largest room they could find, at the home of Thorgrim Busness.[10] When the service was over, I talked with several people — as many as I could, for it was so crowded that one could not move. It pleases and interests me to see and talk to all these different people, our Norwegian farm folk, with whom I have had so little acquaintance up to this time. I find many of them attractive; I like those best who have no city flourish about them, but come up, take me by the hand and say, "Well, we wish you welcome to America!" Then, generally, a number of questions follow. "Where do you come from? Have you parents and relatives? There was great sorrow when you were to leave, I imagine?" Also at times, "My, that is a lovely brooch you have there!" followed by careful examination and admiration of what I am wearing.

When we came home we found guests, several of Helene's relatives. Dinner was waiting for us. It snowed and the weather was bad, so we remained quietly inside. The two young girls stayed here over night. Suckow, the shoemaker, came over for a couple of hours. The conversation turned upon sectarians and hymn melodies until after supper; then Suckow left.[11] Vilhelm studied for the following day and I read *Elisa*.[12] Tomorrow I expect to go with him five miles

[10] Thorgrim Busness settled on the northeast quarter of Section 7 in Frankville Township, Winneshiek County, in 1851; his farm was about a mile and a quarter east of the site of the Washington Prairie Church, and is now occupied by Howard Viste. The original cabin still stands, but has been used as a chicken coop; Linnevold in *Decorah-posten*, June 14, 1929, and in a personal interview with the editor.

[11] "In all parts of the frontier, Norwegian immigrants were influenced to a greater or less degree by the powerful, friendly, and aggressively zealous American churches." The story "involves, among others, the Quakers, the Baptists, the Mormons, the Methodists, and the Episcopalians"; Blegen, *American Transition*, 103, 105. The term "sectarians" was rather loosely applied to any non-Lutheran group and at times even to those within the Lutheran fold.

[12] Friedrich Wilhelm Krummacher, *Elisa* (Elberfeld, Germany, 1837-41).

into the country, where services are to be held. Nils K. is to drive us.

Second Christmas Day. We came back a little while ago from Ingebret Haugen's.[13] I am very glad I went; otherwise I should have missed an enjoyable day. At eight-thirty Nils stopped outside the door with his two daughters, who were to go with us. There was a cold wind. Helene had lent me a good heavy coat, so I was warm enough to enjoy the beautiful drive. The road went up and down hill, through a long, narrow, unusual valley, where there were rocks like those near the high ridges along the Wisconsin River. When we had passed through the valley, we saw the Little Iowa River, along the banks of which, as everywhere along the rivers here, it was very beautiful, though only sparsely settled. Not far from there lies Decorah, which looks at least more imposing than Milton and has a pretty location.[14] A couple of miles beyond Decorah is Ingebret's house, where the service was to be held that day; it is on the edge of a large wood where there is said to be an abundance of wild grapes and other fruit.

We came into a good-sized room with two beds, one above the other, along the wall; in the lower of these lay the husband, who had been sickly for a long time. The remaining furniture of the room consisted of a large motley-painted cupboard and a second one of black walnut, a wood which is beautiful for furniture (though the farmers much prefer fir painted in gaudy colors), a table, chairs, the usual stove — in the center of one wall — and a hole in the ceiling, through which a stairway leads up to the loft; the rest of the room was

---

[13] Ingebret Peterson Haugen is said to have bought the Henry M. Rice trading post situated on the northwest quarter of Section 31, Decorah Township, Winneshiek County, in 1849. Rice was later United States senator from Minnesota. In Haugen's home was formulated and signed, in October, 1852, the letter of call that eventually resulted in Pastor Koren's coming to America; Alexander, *Winneshiek and Allamakee Counties*, 185, 187.

[14] The Little Iowa is the Upper Iowa River, which flows through Howard, Winneshiek, and Allamakee counties, to empty into the Mississippi. Decorah, by 1854, had expanded from the three cabins that were there in 1851 to "a little village of fifteen to twenty buildings, counting hotels, stores, stables, shops, and buildings of all kinds." Bailey, *Winneshiek County*, 2:190.

filled with rough planks laid upon blocks cut from trees, upon which some members of the congregation had already taken seats.

The lady of the house, Ingrid, a neat, active farm woman who still wears part of her national costume, helped me off with my wraps, got me a seat, offered me something to drink, and showed her friendliness in many ways. We had planned, as soon as the service was over, to drive back with Nils; but this was not to be thought of. Mother Ingrid wanted us to eat dinner, and even to remain for the night; this we could not do, so she had to content herself with having us for dinner this time.

I enjoyed being there and talking with people; there were many openhearted, fine folk. A young, handsome woman from Valdres (Ola Bergan was her husband's name, I think) won my heart especially. I also met both the sisters of Pastor Brandt and their husbands, friendly people who have retained their Valdres dialect; they pressed us to visit them when services are to be held in their neighborhood. I also enjoyed talking with an old woman from Valdres who knew Christie when he was pastor there and who was very eager to get news of all his children.[15]

At length they gradually left, each for his home, with the exception of Anne Aarthun and Mari Sørland, with whom it was now my lot to converse and to hear Anne chide Mari because she had not given us lodging.[16] At the front of the room Vilhelm was talking with the men; at the back Ingrid kept on with her affairs and was busy beyond all measure. She is

[15] Ola Bergan and his wife Kari lived in Section 2, Springfield Township, Winneshiek County. One of Pastor Brandt's sisters was Elizabeth (Mrs. Jørgen) Lomen, who, after Lomen's death, married Gudbrand T. Lommen. The other was Mrs. Ivar J. Ringestad, who with her husband settled on the south half of Section 29, Madison Township, Winneshiek County; interview with Professor S. S. Reque of Decorah, Iowa; A. Bredesen, "Pastor Nils Brandts erindringer," in *Symra*, 99 (1907); Charles H. Sparks, *History of Winneshiek County with Biographical Sketches of Its Eminent Men*, 28 (Decorah, 1877). The Reverend Edvard Christie (1770-1847) was a cousin of Pastor Koren's grandfather; Johnson, *Slekten Koren*, 1:41.
[16] "Mari Sørland" is no doubt an error for "Eli Sørland." Eli Skaarlia married Ingebret Sørland in 1850.

an active, capable woman, and how nicely she manages everything! It was a pleasure to watch her.

First she brought out homemade wild grape wine and *fattigmandsbakkels,* leading one person after another to the table and urging him to eat and drink. "Why, come now, you must not be bashful; drink all of it, this will not harm you." At last she had her table loaded with fried pork, spareribs, sausage, bread, butter, cakes, and excellent coffee. Mother [*Anne*] Aarthun took it upon herself to look after me, and gave orders right and left. "Knud, give me the potatoes for the pastor's wife. Ingrid, will you pour some coffee for the missus?" At last, well fortified, we had to think of going home. Knud invited us to drive with him, as his sleigh was supposed to be warmer than the wagon, and so indeed it proved to be.

It was a pleasant drive home, for it was no longer blowing. Anne and Knud entertained us with horrid stories of snakes, and we made fast progress until we came to Thrond Lommen's. There we simply had to turn in, for he is Knud's best friend, he said, and it would not do to pass him by. The entrance to Thrond's house is not very nice; one has to cross an area something like a dunghill, where horses, oxen, cattle, swine, hens, and all kinds of four-legged and two-legged creatures wander about amiably together. Thrond lives in a very large room which houses, besides him and his family, also half a score of newcomers for the winter. His elderly wife met me with many heartfelt and pious wishes that our coming hither might be a blessing both for us and others.

After we had tasted her Christmas beer, we hurried away to reach home before darkness fell; but it overtook us just the same. Anne invited us to have dinner with her tomorrow, and we promised to come. We found the supper table set and Helene waiting for us with her pork. Suckow was there, too, and ate with us. It is quite comical to hear him; he speaks such absolutely pure *bergensk,* and has a slight burr.[17]

[17] *Bergensk* is a dialect spoken by the natives of Bergen, Norway.

Tuesday, December 27. We have just come back from Aarthun's. Because Vilhelm was busy with his affairs and I was helping Helene sew curtains for the beds before we set out, it got so late that Anne met us on the road, fearing we might not keep our word. It would have been better if she had not — we can hardly ever be alone. It is a poor house that Knud has, and too small for his large family; he has eight children, and this winter his paternal uncle and family are living with him. He is a handsome old man, the uncle, though he did not seem very happy at having emigrated; he felt that they were in straitened circumstances — the house and other things — in which opinion, indeed, he may be right.

I soon wished myself home again, I cannot deny it; it was hot, there were so many children, and it is not always pleasant to watch Anne's naïve, free and easy manners. At the same time, they are so friendly, these people, and in every way make it so comfortable for us that I am ashamed of being critical. I took a walk with Anne across their fields after dinner, went in and looked at her favorite horse, etc.; Vilhelm and the uncle roamed about by themselves. Knud was not home, and had not yet come when we left, which was four o'clock, I think.

Helene had just finished her curtain when we came home; I helped her get it up, and have spent the rest of the evening writing. Vilhelm is writing too; Erik is studying the same *Emigranten* for the third evening in a row. Helene is in bed, whither I, too, now consider betaking myself.[18]

Wednesday, December 28. It was so lovely out this morning that I remained wholly lost in contemplation when I went outdoors as usual to brush my teeth. The sun had just risen; its beams made the frosted hazel brush gleam as if covered with diamonds and gave the woods the golden appearance of a beautiful autumn day. After working industri-

[18] *Emigranten* was one of the earliest of the Norwegian-language newspapers. It was published at Inmansville, Wisconsin, 1852-57, and at Madison, Wisconsin, 1857-68.

ously for a time, we agreed to take a walk in the beautiful weather. I went up to the loft to put on my things and Vilhelm, as usual, began to ponder what he should put on his feet — traveling boots, buffalo shoes, or overshoes. It turned out to be the last, and we began our ramble. We had to trot through a thick hazel brush, of course, to avoid a little detour before we came down to the main road. The snow lay deep there and the result was that Vilhelm got his overshoes full of snow and decided to go back and change. I continued on my way and turned around just at the right moment to see my lord husband, arrayed in his great boots, making most graceful leaps over the hazel bushes.

We went on in the best of spirits, glad to be alone for a while, until we met Nils Katterud outside his door, with his brother.[19] We went in and found them already busy with dinner. So varied are the hours here — one has dinner when it is not long since the other has finished his breakfast. Mother Katterud insisted we should take off our wraps and eat; but as we had come to get Nils to show us the land for the parsonage, we chose to wait until he had eaten; and that took a long time, for Nils eats slowly and talks slowly, and both things always have to be done at the same time.[20]

We finally got him away, however, and then waded right through all the snow across Nils's fields, which adjoin that [parsonage] land. I have no fault to find with the property; it is pleasant and could certainly be made a cozy place to live. It is fairly hilly, with small woods here and there. The house would be situated in the shelter of one of these, but of course it has not yet been decided whether we shall live there. It took a long time to go over it all and for Nils to explain in detail everything about it. At last we turned back and made our way through some high hazel brush mixed with wild

[19] The brother was probably Ola Katterud, whose family was sharing the Nils Katterud cabin. For a note on the Ola Katterud family, see footnote 2 to this chapter.

[20] Liv Katterud (1795-1861) was Nils's wife. The original tract for the parsonage was eighty acres, the east half of the northwest quarter of Section 12, Springfield Township, Winneshiek County, Iowa.

VILHELM AND ELISABETH KOREN IN 1853
[From photographs in the possesion of Mrs. David T. Nelson]

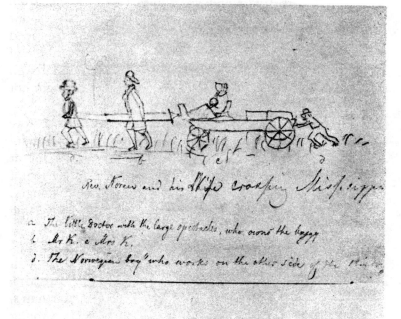

Rev. Koren and his Wife crossing Mississippi

a. The little Doctor with the large spectacles, who owns the buggy
b. Mr K. c Mrs K.
d. The Norwegian boy who works on the other side of the river

Mr K and his Wife crossing Wisconsin River
a. Icecakes. b. The two howling half breed Frenchmen
c. Mr K. d Mrs K.

THE KORENS CROSSING THE WISCONSIN AND MISSISSIPPI RIVERS
[From sketches by Pastor Koren in the possession of Miss Marie Koren]

plum trees, which in summer is almost impenetrable; from there through virgin woods, where the branches struck our ears and caught in my clothes, though fortunately I escaped without a tear or mishap. After having crossed the stubble of a cornfield, we came upon a regular road again, said farewell to our guide, and walked briskly on so that Helene might not have to wait dinner too long.

We did not get farther than Ingebret's, however, before we stopped, this time to have a little talk with him and another man, who, unfortunately, was on horseback; for at sight of that horse, Vilhelm stood and talked so long that I became quite impatient. I was tired and hot and hungry. Well, at last he was through, and we went on, conversing with the man on horseback, who left at the same time.

When we came home, we found a neighbor's wife, whom I had not seen before, visiting Helene; she stayed and ate with us, but left immediately afterwards. I sat down to write Mrs. [Linka] Preus, and Vilhelm started out for Knud Aarthun's, but came back at once with Anne, who drove in with a young couple — a Norwegian from Drammen, Ole Hegge by name, I think, who is married to a Danish woman. Probably they came to pay us a visit; they were profuse in their invitations that we visit them. I do not recall where they live. I tried to converse with the Danish woman, but it was not easy. They left soon after Helene had crept down into the cellar for beer and up to the loft for *bakkels* for them. Vilhelm rode with them and I busied myself with letters again until dark, when Vilhelm came back without having found Knud.

The light was lit, the pork set on the fire. In an effort to get tea somewhat as it should be I took it upon myself to make it; but it is no easy task with such poor tea, and I had no great luck with it, either, especially since Helene, without my knowing a thing about it, filled the kettle with water. We had to drink it, thin as it was, and talked about what poor groceries one gets in this country. We passed the rest of the evening writing and incessantly trimming the candle with big shears, for snuffers are a luxury in America.

Thursday, December 29. The weather is dreadful today. Snow, and on top of it a biting, piercing wind. God be praised, we did not go to Paint Creek today, but can sit in a warm room.[21] Two people have been here from Minnesota this forenoon — handsome, attractive men — to speak with Vilhelm. The Norwegians must be a handsome people; I am now meeting a great many from all districts of Norway, and there are so many fine folk among them. I have written diligently all day and I got some clothes ready for Vilhelm for his journey tomorrow. Knud came over while we were eating supper and brought Vilhelm a letter from Minnesota with a request for him to come up there as soon as possible. We decided to leave [for Paint Creek] tomorrow at ten o'clock. I hope we have better weather than today so that I may go, too.

Paint Creek, New Year's Eve, 1853. Today I am writing my diary in the home of Sivert Vold.[22] This is a very large room, running the length of the house, with an ordinary little stove in the center which falls far short of heating so large a room to the proper temperature. The house, though new, is a poor sort of place. The floor consists of unfinished planks, which bob up and down when walked on. At one end is a passage to the cellar, covered with a couple of loose boards laid an inch apart. The ceiling, likewise, consists of rough boards, through which one can see into the loft and even catch a glimpse of the sky through the roof. There is a bed near the cellar trap door, and beneath that a chest which is drawn out in the evening to provide a couch for the family's youngest members. On the other side of the window there are shelves full of tools.

At the farther end of the room Ingeborg has her milk

[21] Paint Creek is in Allamakee County, east of Waukon, Iowa. It runs through present-day Waterville. The Norwegians arrived there in 1850 and settled to the north of the creek. In all their early records and in Mrs. Koren's diary it is referred to as Painted Creek.

[22] Sivert (Sjur) Vold, a native of Voss, Norway, his wife Ingeborg, and his family arrived in the Paint Creek settlement in 1850; I. Rudolph Gronlid, "The Beginnings of Norwegian Settlements in Iowa," 41. This is a manuscript thesis submitted for the degree of master of arts at the State University of Iowa in 1928. A copy is in the library of Luther College.

shelves and other kitchen articles. The table at which I am sitting is close to the stove; and about it, as usual, there is a circle of chairs, distinguished by the variety of their shapes and materials; and on these chairs Sivert and his sons, as many as can find places, are sitting. Ingeborg, the lady of the house, a handsome, attractive woman who always goes about with a nice white cap on her head, is busy preparing dinner, with her two small daughters as helpers, and at this moment is in the act of baking biscuits for us. Here, then, I am spending my first New Year's Eve in America.

We came here late yesterday evening. It had been agreed that we should leave home at ten o'clock. Early in the morning Erik went over to help Knud with his sleigh. We were ready at the right time, but eleven, twelve, one came, and still no sleigh. Now we became really impatient and Vilhelm went over to Knud's. Helene hurried to get some dinner ready and I set the table. Just as it was ready, they came at last; something had gone wrong with the sleigh and it had to be repaired. We did not get away until two.

The weather was changeable, now snow, now sunshine. The first part of the journey lay across a long prairie where, as always, the wind was cold. The land soon took on quite a different appearance; it formed great hollows, somewhat like basins, with steeply sloping sides. The woods were fairly open here and the road followed a ridge with these hollows on both sides, up hill and down. It continued thus quite a distance before we came to the prairie again. Here we lost our way and drove back and forth a little until we met a Yankee who rode some distance with us and put us on the right road.

We made the trip in a long sleigh, its bottom covered with hay and a board, on which we sat, laid crosswise in the back part of the sleigh. Knud sat in front. We had not driven far before his seat plumped down; a little later we met a like fate. After a couple of vain attempts to make the board stay, we chose to sit in the bottom of the sleigh, a change which made us far more comfortable, too.

Some time after we had driven past a couple of houses (the beginning of the county seat of Allamakee County), we met a Norwegian from Paint Creek; he assured us that it was too late for us to reach the *vossing* with whom we had thought to spend the night, and invited us to go home with him.[23] Not long afterward we met a group of men who looked like Yankees in their blue coats and low-crowned hats, but turned out to be the very ones we had intended to visit — Sivert Vold and his sons. They now went back with us and we continued our journey to their home. It is not pleasant to drive so late at night; it gets very cold, and the road seems twice as long.

My feet were freezing, though they were packed in hay, and I had only one wish — to get into a house soon; it seemed as if that time would never come. At last, however, we saw a light and soon were sitting in Sivert's home. It had a cheerless look with a tallow lamp set high up on a shelf, throwing a dim light over a room very much in disorder — a pile of shavings in one corner and everything scattered over the floor. The family was probably preparing for bed and not in the least expecting such a visit.

Ingeborg received us cordially, brought out a mug of excellent milk to refresh us, and hurried to prepare our supper. I was a little crestfallen as I sat there by the stove and looked about me in the dark room with the open floor and ceiling, and began to wonder where we would sleep. I wished I had remained at home instead of coming along, and at the same time was ashamed for letting myself be so easily disheartened; but it was really a bit venturesome to set forth in this manner without knowing either how far we had to travel or where we were going to stay.

That mood, however, did not last long. The people were very friendly. They gave us their own bed and they themselves went to sleep in the loft; and when they had all gone up and we were alone I am sure I did not regret having come

[23] The county seat of Allamakee County is now Waukon. A *vossing* is a native of Voss, Norway.

along. Vilhelm took the tallow lamp and made a careful examination of the bed and sheets, and even spilled tallow on them in his zeal. We slept very well on our straw and were wakened early the next morning by the man of the house putting wood in the stove. Ingeborg came down soon afterward and began her morning preparations; I hurried to dress myself before the men came down —one must watch his chance.

We have had beautiful sunshine today. In the forenoon, accompanied by Baard, we first went to the nearest neighbor, whom we found in the midst of housecleaning.[24] From there we went to another cabin and came into a little, low room, where there was a stench of snuff and tobacco that was almost unbearable. Here we found, besides several childen, two old women in their mountain dress; the older of them was pounding snuff in a wooden mortar with a trembling hand.

"I use snuff, I do, Father," she said and offered some in her hand.

Then she whispered to Baard to ask if this was indeed the pastor whom they were waiting for. She was very happy when she heard that it was. She is the oldest woman we have seen here, almost eighty, and came three or four years ago. She is very active for her age and has two sons here; one of them was the man we met on the road yesterday. Her daughter-in-law came in, too, and wanted us to stay and have coffee, but we did not do so. It was wonderful to get outside and away from that smell of snuff.

From here we walked down one steep hill and up another to a cabin on the other side of the valley. Here we encountered a woman and a number of children in a little log house with no partition between the loft and the lower room; everything, however, had a clean and neat appearance. All the children, from the largest to the smallest, were so clean it was a delight to see them; it is really very seldom that they are not smeared with that everlasting molasses that they eat.

[24] Baard was Sivert Vold's son.

We had come a long way, and it was heavy walking in the deep snow with the smooth buffalo shoes; I slipped continually, fell down a couple of times, and had to listen to Vilhelm laugh, and poke fun at me too, because, as he said, I got so cross.

It is beautiful here, very hilly, with woods in abundance; on the horizon one sees the bluffs along the Mississippi. Along the river it is not so pleasant as here, although more picturesque. I was glad to reach home and get a little of the good milk that Ingeborg always has on hand.

The service is to be held here tomorrow; so they have been busy arranging everything and getting the seats ready. It is now late evening; Vilhelm is occupied with his sermon for tomorrow. This year will soon be at an end — this year which has been so rich in experience and of so much significance for us both. God grant that the new year, which we shall now begin in this foreign country, may be a blessing both to ourselves and to others!

My pen has been resting a little, while I sat thinking of Father and all the dear ones in our distant native land; and I am sure we have been constantly in their thoughts this evening. On such occasions they are doubly missed. May God bless this year for them too! Last year I began the new year clad in bobbinet, dancing away with roses in my hair. This year I am sitting here with Vilhelm in this bare room, where tomorrow he is to conduct divine services for all these people who so long have lacked a pastor. Still, this is best.

8

This Must Be the Pastor's Wife

New Year's Day, 1854. It starts out cold, this new year. It is
no small matter that so many people — and so many little
children among them — dared venture out as were gathered
this morning. Services here always seem peculiarly affecting
and impressive to me. It is so wonderful to see our people
in this foreign land streaming together from every direction,
and to feel the devotion and attention with which they sing
their hymns and listen to the pastor. It all has quite a different
aspect from what I have been accustomed to.[1]

As usual I visited with people after the service was over. I
especially enjoyed a naïve little woman from Valdres. First
she came over and took me by the hand and wished me welcome to this country and said, "You have had a tiring journey,
I am sure, but you look so nice in spite of it; and the pastor,
he looks so nice, too." Afterwards she said, "You must really
be awfully young, aren't you?"

[1] See chapter 7, footnote 21. The Paint Creek congregation was organized
some time before January, 1851. The first religious services in the area were
held July 2-4, 1851, by the Reverend C. L. Clausen; he was paid a fee of
twenty dollars. See Gronlid, "Norwegian Settlements in Iowa," 47, 48, 49, 51.

"How old do you think I am?" I asked her.

"Well, you must be sixteen, I suppose," she said.

Then I told her my age, whereupon she turned to Ingeborg [Vold], saying: "Why, would you ever have believed that, Ingeborg, so fair and young as she looks? And she puts up so patiently with being here, though she has lived in the city and is accustomed to fine houses and such; and she is not a bit haughty or proud or unwilling even to look at us, as many are."

The woman and her whole manner were a great delight to me; our conversation ended with repeated invitations to visit her. I also spoke with several newcomers, of whom there are many; in general they are not very well satisfied, though that is nearly always the case with newcomers. One of the neighbor women stayed to help Ingeborg with the meals. Møller from Bergen was here too and had dinner.[2] Now they have all gone home and the day will soon be over, so I will lay this away for the evening.

Tuesday, January 3. We are back again in our own quarters. Vilhelm is drawing a map, Helene is baking bread, and Per and Kari romp noisily about with great mustaches of molasses as usual.

We set out from Sivert's at eleven o'clock yesterday. For the last time Ingeborg gave us delicious milk to warm us. It was not nearly so cold as the day before, but just the same, though I sat in the bottom of the sleigh packed in hay, my feet froze more than they ever had, so I was very glad to get into a warm room and have a cup of hot tea. Vilhelm has such a bad cold, too, and such a pain in his back this morning that he could scarcely get up; he is now somewhat better, praise God. I have been writing without interruption all day. Vilhelm was just here and asked if I did not wish to take a walk — not a bad idea, perhaps, after sitting still so long; so, for the time being, the writing will have to wait.

[2] This was probably J. S. Møller, who settled in the Paint Creek area in 1850. Gronlid, "Norwegian Settlements in Iowa," 41.

Just a few words before I go to bed. As I mentioned, we took a walk over toward Knud's — I was much afraid Vilhelm might fall on the slippery road and thus make his back worse. There was a fresh, mild wind. We talked of how we hoped to have things here, and what a joy it will be when we are in our own home and I am expecting Vilhelm from one of his trips and have arranged the room cozily and have the tea table set.

I took out my knitting this evening; Vilhelm read aloud his descriptions of our journey, which gave great pleasure not only to us but also to Erik and Helene.[3] So the time passed until we were to eat, after which I began a letter home and Vilhelm turned to his work.

Wednesday, January 4. This morning I ruled books for Vilhelm until I had all ten fingers smeared with ink; but I had the job done, too. The wife of Suckow, the shoemaker, has been here, and later a man who wished to be enrolled in the congregation — a lively, talkative man, who interrupted my writing considerably. Vilhelm's back is better today, praise God. He has a good many things to get ready for Friday, but has no peace because of the two children; as usual, he will have to make use of the night. All day long, one person after the other takes up the refrain, "Be quiet, Kari!" and "Can you not hold your tongue, Per?" But the youngsters are lively and it is not easy to make them sit like statues all the time, poor dears.

As usual I have been writing all day — as long as I was able to see. Then I again received an invitation to take a walk, but had no great desire to go out in the bitter wind. Vilhelm said, "You are really tiresome," and went up to the loft, from which he came down with his buffalo shoes on; he said that he would go out and chop wood, since I did not wish to walk, and anyway the wood chopping would help his ailing back. A remarkable cure, indeed! I heard the sound of his ax, but it was not long before he came in and we sat down on a bench

[3] These notes, in Pastor Koren's hand, are in the possession of Miss Marie Koren of Decorah, Iowa.

by the stove, in which the fire was burning merrily; outside, the storm was howling and caused us doubly to appreciate how pleasant it was in a warm room lit by the fire. Vilhelm whistled songs, making our thoughts wander back to our dear native land. Now it is very quiet here. Helene and the children are in bed; only Erik is still sitting up, smoking his evening pipe by the stove. I am laying my letter aside for the night; I am very tired of so much writing and am going to bed.

Thursday, January 5. While I was home this forenoon writing, there was a knock at the door, and in came a big tall farmer to speak with Vilhelm. They were soon on religious topics, and then it turned out that the man belonged to the so-called Franckeans.[4] He is one of their lay preachers and is supposed to be among the most uncompromising. He had a great many Bible passages at the tip of his tongue but never replied directly to what Vilhelm said. No matter what Vilhelm advanced, his answer was quite beside the point. There was no way of dealing with him. One might just as well have remained silent, a procedure Vilhelm at last followed, so that now the layman, when he holds his meeting this evening, can say that he "so far prevailed upon him that he had to keep silent and could not answer a word," a boast he had already made about [Pastor] Brandt after a similar conversation with him. I marveled that Vilhelm was so patient and answered him so quietly; I expected several times that they would come to blows. This was the first we saw of these so-much-talked-of sectarians.

[4] The Franckean Synod of New York was organized in 1837 and eventually became part of the United Lutheran Church in America. It has been designated as the most liberal Lutheran synod in this country. Most of the Norwegian adherents of the Franckean Synod joined the Synod of Northern Illinois in 1851. The Norwegian settlers near what is now the Springfield Church in Section 17, Springfield Township, Winneshiek County, were early attracted to liberal groups in which lay activity was prominent. Peter Asbjørnsen Mehus was active among these settlers in 1851–52. Johns. Johannessen (J. J. Johnson — 1826–1902) belonged to the Northern Illinois Synod; he served the Springfield congregation, 1853–56. See Blegen, *American Transition*, 150, 152; Bredesen, in *Symra*, 101 (1907); Rasmus Malmin, O. M. Norlie, and O. A. Tingelstad, *Who's Who among Pastors in All the Norwegian Lutheran Synods of America, 1843–1927*, 286 (Minneapolis, 1928).

I make slow progress with my letter.[5] There have been so many interruptions by visitors today. Vilhelm was lying down, resting a little, but had been there only a few minutes when first one and then another came. The last was Knud, who had supper with us and has just left. Now Vilhelm and I are sitting here alone. He has to make use of the night hours again today; it is a shame. Just so he does not become really ill! Tonight, moreover, it is frightfully cold. I hope it turns milder before he has to set out. Now I shall try to sneak to bed, and silence my squeaking shoes as far as possible so that Vilhelm will not be disturbed, nor Helene and Erik hear them.

Epiphany.[6] Beautiful sunshine, but nipping frost today. I was quite short of breath from the crisp air when we went to Thorgrim's this forenoon, expecting, with my slippery buffalo shoes, to fall any moment on the even more slippery roads.

A crowd gathered today, and there was communion for the first time. It is really remarkable that the service can be conducted with as much order and dignity as it is. I did not have my customary visit with the people today, they left so quickly. I drove home, sitting in Anne Aarthun's lap, with a little man from Valdres. At the door I met two rather unpleasant-looking women. Helene had found them outside her door when she got home. The one was a Franckean, the other a Methodist.[7] They had been at the meeting. I do not understand what they wanted, either there or here.

It was so intolerably hot at Thorgrim's and so cold and unpleasant here when we came home that Vilhelm caught a bad cold in his throat. I have a touch of it, too, in my nose. It was not long, however, before we had the room warm and were sitting down to our pork and coffee, after which Vilhelm lit

[5] In the early days, letters were usually long, composed with great pains, and written in a fine hand on both sides of the paper. Often they were written over a period of several days or weeks. Postage was high. Pastor Koren said that in 1853 it cost him 54 cents to mail a single letter to Norway; Koren, *Samlede skrifter*, 4:112 (Decorah, Iowa, 1912).

[6] The feast of Epiphany, or Twelfth-night, falls on January 6.

[7] In 1852 Norwegian Methodists organized a congregation in Winneshiek County under the leadership of O.P. Petersen, a missionary; Blegen, *American Transition*, 120.

his pipe and we moved over to the stove and talked about Ryde and foreign lands. Erik did not fail to have his say, too, repeating literally whatever Vilhelm said. He is a fine fellow but very boring when he simply repeats what others say. We sat pleasantly thus for a time until Vilhelm lay down on the bed to rest a little. Then we sat in the darkness by the light of the stove, each one lost in his own thoughts. This is the most pleasant hour of the day — twilight; then one can sit so peacefully and let one's thoughts wander where they most like to dwell. I have been writing since we got a light. The room is filled with the smell of fried onions, I see Helene taking her toasted bread from the pan; so it is time to wake Vilhelm.

A couple of hours later: It was hard to get Vilhelm awake; he answered yes, but continued to doze, so at last I had to pull him out of bed. Now he is sitting directly in front of me, writing, and since he maintains that I disturb him, I shall betake myself to bed. It's all nonsense that I disturb him; I sit absolutely quiet and write; as a matter of fact he does not need to look at me. However, I had better be an obedient wife and conform to my husband's desire, much as I should like to complete my letter this evening.

Saturday, January 7. There is no end to the changes of weather here. Today it is most beautiful again, far from cold; and yesterday — especially last night — it was so biting cold that Vilhelm had to go to bed early, for it was impossible to keep the room at all warm. Today he is to visit the western settlements; his good friend, "the dapper bachelor" Halvor, is to drive him. I have just packed his things, while he is busy preparing a supply of pens for me. And now Helene has lunch ready.[8]

It is evening. Halvor came at four o'clock instead of twelve;

[8] Pastor Koren preached at Hans O. Aakre's home in the northeast quarter of Section 1, Sumner Township, Winneshiek County, on Sunday, January 8; *Symra*, 27 (1905). William Linnevold says that Halvor, the dapper bachelor, was Halvor Tollefsjord, who often drove for Pastor Koren and whose cabin was south of the Egges' farm. The pens were cut from goose quills. On the western settlements, see chapter 12, footnote 17.

that is too bad, for now they must drive very late in the evening. I think that "woman's trumpery," as he called my red cloak, will come in very handy. This is the first time I have been left alone; let me now see to it that I keep up my courage and do not become moody or any such nonsense!

After Vilhelm's departure, which did not take place until he had delivered a moving exhortation to Per which I hope will bear fruit, Helene set about scrubbing the floor, and I put on my things and went out, glad to be able to escape the raw vapors. Without paying particular attention to direction, I started out, preoccupied with thoughts of this last half year and all its remarkable events, until I stood outside Ingebret Sørland's house, and was thereby made conscious of the strange certainty that here I was, roaming about quite alone far inland in America on the far side of the Mississippi. I went in to Ingebret's, since I had come so far, and found his wife busy baking bread. Her husband also came in. I sat there for a while, chatted about the Franckeans and this and that, drank beer and ate cakes, and thereupon turned my nose homeward. Like a ninny, I lost the way, got well into a field and saw fences on every side before I noticed it, and was thoroughly vexed that I had to go back so far in the deep snow.

When I came home, I had the satisfaction of finding a dry, warm room with the teakettle humming merrily on the stove. Erik is not home, so Helene and I have been sitting here together. While knitting, I have listened to her tell of her experiences since she came to America; she has been through a great deal. At last she turned to her preparations for supper and I to this work of writing. There, I hear Erik coming; I must put things away so the table can be set.[9]

They are really nature's children, these farmers. There is

---

[9] Helene had been married in Norway to Anders Egge. The family left for America in 1852; Anders died of cholera either aboard ship or in Wisconsin. In the same year Helene, with her two children Per and Kari and her two stepchildren Anders and Anne, went to live with her sister, Mrs. Hans Eggebraaten, in Glenwood Township, Winneshiek County. In 1853 Helene met and married Erik Egge; Linnevold in *Decorah-posten*, May 31, 1929; interview with Mrs. Paul Egge of Frankville Township, Winneshiek County.

nothing wrong with that; but it can irk one considerably, as, for example, a moment ago while we were eating. Erik, who had had supper at Suckow's, did not eat with us, but drew off his shoes and socks, put both his feet on a stool, and began quite unabashed to rub them with turpentine; my appetite was not particularly sharpened by either his manners or the awful smell. On the whole we have to shut our eyes and ears as much as possible to preserve our appetite and good humor when our finer sensibilities are offended by these rustic manners; fortunately, they usually have the opposite effect, however; one glance at each other, and we have a hard time to keep from bursting into laughter.

Sunday evening, January 8. This day too will soon be over. I am sitting here half expecting Vilhelm, if Halvor by chance drives him home this evening as he said he would; but it is hardly likely. I was up early this morning, was glad to see the beautiful weather that Vilhelm is having, and thought of going over to Katterud's, when just at that moment Helene asked if I would like to go to the Aarthuns, whom she had promised to visit today. I made no objections, and so after breakfast, when I had read a sermon and Helene was through with her affairs, we set out, Helene with Kari on her back.

The Aarthun family had evidently not been stirring as early as we. Anne was sitting half-dressed in the middle of the floor with her youngest child on her lap and the others about her. Knud was busy with a saddle. On the table lay potato peelings, meat bones, and other remains of their breakfast. In the corner sat the aunt, with hair uncombed like all the others. It wasn't a very attractive scene and it made me wish Helene had not hurried so to get started. They gave the impression, however, of being glad to see us.

Anne soon brought about some sort of order and refreshed us with a glass of good beer and not-so-good cake. I moved my chair as far from the stove as possible and talked with Knud while the others were busy with dinner. As usual the conversation soon turned to the Methodists and Franckeans, after

which Anne started her customary theme of how glad she was
the pastor had come. She just wished we would continue to
live here; we could not find a more pleasant spot in the settlement, she was sure of that. Then we talked about flowers
(which Anne knows rather well) and about which ones do
best here. I noticed a piece of birchbark on the stove and
heard, to my joy, that Knud has birch trees in his woods. Later
Anne admired the "awfully pretty sleeves and collar" which
I had on, and wished very much her daughters could sew so that
they might have something pretty for confirmation. I offered
to teach them the art, at which they were greatly pleased.
Anne is always talking about getting one of her daughters to
work for us.

We went home early, accompanied by Anne, who talked
with Helene of how they would have "pleasure jaunts," indeed, if we came to live in the neighborhood; and thereupon
she asked if I cared to take a drive with them to visit Helene's
sister and several others on Sunday, when Vilhelm is away.
"It would really be fun to show them our pastor's wife," she
said. Here at home we found Suckow, who sat and chatted
with us for a couple of hours in his Bergen dialect.

I am now sitting up alone listening for the sound of a wagon,
but in vain. I'm afraid he will not come this evening. So I had
better go to bed and not disturb the others longer.

Monday, January 9. I had to wait until it was all of four this
afternoon before Vilhelm came and, to tell the truth, I was
glad of the wait, for we have been in a mess here all day.
Helene had a large washing, and I did not care to have Vilhelm come in and turn up his nose at the wet floor and the
nasty lye smell.[10]

I was awakened this morning by hearing Per scream, "Kari,
Kari!" at the top of his voice. "Hold your tongue, young fellow!" I called, very sharply, from behind my curtain. My
words had their effect, for he did not know just where the

[10] It was customary to make lye from wood ashes, wood being the usual
stove fuel. Lye mixed with drippings made good soap; but the lye odor was
probably unusually strong in the homemade product.

voice came from. There was no one in the house except the children and me. I put my head out between the curtains and discovered the wash boiler standing on the stove full of snow and Helene outside the window with a bucket getting more. That made me recall this miserable washing and got me up in a hurry.

I wanted to be through with it soon as possible, but my patience was to be tried a little first. Helene went to Suckow's for a kettle while I sat and plied my needle on some of Vilhelm's things, waiting for the snow to melt. That took an eternity, however, and it was late in the forenoon before the washing began. Helene, with her copper kettle on the floor in the middle of the room, rubbed away on her washboard with a fury that made her face glisten with countless beads of perspiration. Now and then she gave Per or Kari a good smack on the cheek with one of the wet pieces when they got too much in her way. I stood at the table with my fine linens and sorrowfully watched the great pond which spread farther and farther around Helene's kettle, thinking to myself, "Now we shall see Vilhelm return right in the midst of all this."

It was then somewhere near noon, according to our reckoning at least; such a luxury as a timepiece we do not have. So the pork was fried, the coffee made, and Erik and I sat down to eat. Finally we reached the point where the clothes were to be hung up. I wrapped my apron about my head and went out to the hazel bushes, where the wash is now hanging — and in here a beautiful row of stockings too. Now, I thought, we are through at last and can put things in order. But no, first the whole floor had to be washed. "I must make use of my good lye water while I have it; there is nothing like it to wash off the fat stains," said Helene, and began to scrub with all her might. There was nothing to be done. I put wood in the stove, opened the door, moved the table over to the driest spot in the room, and took up my letter to Christiane.[11]

[11] Christiane Koren Hysing (1826–80) was Elisabeth's sister in Norway; Johnson, *Slekten Koren*, 1:188.

At last Vilhelm came. I believe I shall reconcile myself somewhat to his frequent journeys, for I look forward with so much joy to his return. He had fared well, met friendly people, and brought me a large supply of nuts, which Erik has been busy cracking, and we eating, this evening. They are very hard to crack, have the same shape as chestnuts, and taste like walnuts.[12] They grow wild in the woods. Well, tonight I shall escape going to bed at half-past eight — unless Vilhelm takes it into his head that I disturb him and chases me to bed.

Tuesday, January 10. It is almost evening; I expect Vilhelm any moment. He went six miles "southward" this morning to make arrangements about hiring a horse. I walked with him a long way on the road; it was beautiful to be out in the lovely morning hour. It was like a spring day. When the sun shines and it does not blow, the weather is beautiful here; the sky is so pure and clear and the atmosphere so extraordinarily transparent. We went some distance over a prairie. There was nothing to see but the friendly groves of trees on the farms adjoining the parsonage land. We separated on the top of a hill and I wandered back well content with the walk; I came home with wet feet and little desire to iron my blue dress.

While I was busy with that task (Helene had gone out), I had a visit from a dalesman, who appeared to be about seventy years old. "This must be the pastor's wife, I suppose," said he to me, " a hearty welcome to you!" It was strange to hear that old man call me "Mother." He wished to get work at the pastor's.[13]

I struggled with my dress until Helene came home. It was a tiresome job, for the dress is so awful that I can hardly wear it; all the spots, which are a reminder of our days aboard ship, have turned white, and since there are many of them, one can readily imagine how it looks.

My noon meal, consisting of coffee and bread and butter, I

[12] They were probably hickory nuts.
[13] A dalesman was one who came originally from one of the valleys in Norway. The old man was the father of John Dysja, whom the Korens visited later, on January 25.

ate alone today, and then read a little before I took out my writing case. I had not written many lines, when Knud Aarthun and a man from Minnesota who wished to talk to Vilhelm came in and sat down and interrupted me. I had to talk to them, of course, and at last brought out my knitting, for I saw no indications that they would leave. At last it dawned on them that it was really time to end their visit, and they left, saying they would come back later. This they did, too, coming before we were to eat, and leaving only now, near nine o'clock. There was so much chatter that I had to put my writing aside.

Vilhelm came back before it was dark; he had gone various roundabout ways before he reached his destination, and had found things disagreeable and squalid at the home that he visited. Early tomorrow he goes to Decorah with Knud and will doubtless be gone all day, and day after tomorrow there is to be a meeting of the congregation; so he is never home even when he is supposed to be. Now I had better get to bed and try to be up early tomorrow for my ironing.

Wednesday, January 11. I have had a busy day. Vilhelm left for Decorah after breakfast, at which we were surprised with roast prairie chicken, which one of Knud's boys had brought over and which tasted delicious. When Vilhelm had gone, I began to starch my clothes. I did not finish my ironing until it was almost dark. (It is not easy to iron shirts for the first time.) I went outside the house a little to breathe the fresh air, and I enjoyed the beautiful evening star, the lovely sky, the moon, and everything. I walked about for a time and looked every now and then to see if Vilhelm might not be coming, but in vain; so I went in and took up my knitting until the light was lit, for then, naturally, my dear writing case had to come out again. It was not opened, however, for Ingebret Sørland came in, and Vilhelm a little later. Then Nils came; both had supper here. I tried to write, but was continually disturbed by talk about certificates, counties, stations, and Nils's comical answers when he was asked about the date of his birth and when he was married.[14] In general men are not very good at remembering these dates.

I had to go out once more and admire the radiant evening star, and at the same time I inspected a marvelous contrivance in which Vilhelm is to ride when he takes trips.[15] Afterwards we talked of all sorts of things, and Vilhelm made the most wonderful drawings of an overcoat which I am to make for him and for which he had brought home the material. It is very late tonight; I had better begin to clear away the countless things with which the bed is always covered.

Thursday, January 12. Vilhelm and Erik just drove off to Thrond Lommen's, where the meeting is to be held. They rode in that remarkable sleigh Erik has manufactured; it looked as if they might fall out of it, each from his own side, but I hope not. I went out and tried it first by driving around the field; it went quite famously. We are expecting Anne Aarthun over today; she is hardly likely to keep us waiting long, I imagine. Helene is baking biscuits for the occasion. Now she has gone out to "water the cattle," and I have my attention divided between this task of writing, Kari and Per, and a milk pot which I am to keep from boiling over. The congregation will certainly not gather early today; it is almost eleven o'clock and still people keep going by.

The day is gray, but not cold. I must go out and take a walk; if I were not expecting Anne, I would walk to Katterud's. Now I am going to work on my letters to Norway so that they finally may be finished and sent.

Our guest just left; it is well past five, I imagine. She kept

[14] Mrs. Koren uses the word "stations," but she probably should have written "sections." Pastor Koren wrote, "It was only after I had learned how the country, in surveys, was divided into townships and sections that I found something by which to guide myself"; *Symra,* 27 (1905).

[15] The pastor described his vehicle as follows: "You would have been amused to see my primitive means of travel: my first sleigh, consisting of runners and thills in one, constructed from two long hickory limbs, on top of which there was a little box with a board over it to be used as a seat, all put together with wooden pins without the help of a single nail. Or my first carriage, a single wagon with wooden axles and linchpins, and no springs under the seat. Or my first harness, in which all the running parts, including the reins, were made of clothesline"; *Symra,* 29 (1905).

us waiting a long time, so long that we ate dinner and I sat down again to write, thinking she would not come today. It was not long, however, before Kari cried that she saw Aarthun; a moment later she knocked at the door. Helene put the coffeepot back on the fire and I had to join the party and taste her biscuits, which were much to her credit. Anne asked me to show her some of my fine linens and I did so, to her enjoyment and Helene's. They inspected and admired every piece and were not through until it was time to fetch a light.

Soon afterward a man from Turkey River came; he wanted to give the pastor the necessary directions, for he believed he was unacquainted down there, he said; I think Vilhelm will be pleased to have a guide. He was a comical, laughing little man; he questioned me about a great many things, marveled greatly that I, who am so young, can be satisfied to stay here, and invited me repeatedly to accompany Vilhelm when he goes down there.[16]

"What is it you are knitting there?" said he to me, "that isn't a garter, is it?" (I had just begun to crochet a waist.)

"No, I should say not!" answered Anne. "Here, I'll just show you something," and she held up a finished bodice.

I looked down so as not to laugh too much at the interest and wonder with which he gazed on that piece of work and puzzled over the manner in which it was made; thereupon he expatiated very elaborately on how clever they were at handwork in the eastern part of Norway.

"But you will have to make your clothes over now, won't you?" said he.

They cannot conceive that people use the same styles in Norway as here. He accompanied Anne home; so now Helene

[16] The man from Turkey River was John Andreas Anderson Axdal. Axdal and his wife Martha Malene Larsdatter were members of the Stavanger settlement south and east of Calmar. It seems probable that they took land in Military Township, Winneshick County, in 1850 or early 1851; A. Bredesen, in *Symra*, 101 (1907); "Ministerialbog for Little Iowa norsk-evangelist lutherske menighed." The latter is a manuscript volume now on file at the Koren Library, Luther College. The Turkey River settlement was in Read, Wagner, and Marion townships in Clayton County, and extended westward into Fayette County; Gronlid, "Norwegian Settlements in Iowa," 21.

and I sit alone and wait for Vilhelm and Erik to return. Helene watches her potato kettle and her pork, goes outside every moment or two to listen for their coming, and keeps thinking she hears someone talking along the road; but just the same, I do not see them. But I am very hungry, and am going to set the table; then, surely, they will come.

True enough, it was just as I thought: we had scarcely made the table ready before Erik arrived — but without the pastor. He had remained behind and did not get here until an hour later, and then had his first chance at a bite to eat. The meeting had gone well, it seems. Tomorrow a couple are to be married; they are coming here. What fearful weather we have all of a sudden! It is blowing violently.

Friday, January 13. The weather was disagreeable last night; the wind woke me several times. Thank God Vilhelm was not out on a journey! Now if he will only wait until tomorrow, for we have the same wind today and it is exceedingly cold. I do not believe the bridal couple will come today. Ingebret Sørland brought over some certificates while we were eating breakfast. When that was finished, Helene wanted to scrub the floor, since there was to be a wedding, she said, and she had the water all ready; but Vilhelm protested, and now I shall have that pleasure tomorrow after he has left.

The man from Turkey River is here and is giving an account of where he lives and where the other settlements are. I think Vilhelm is discovering that there are more waiting and asking for him than he had dreamed of. He is really a comical little man, this John Andreas [Axdal]. He just came over to me and said: "You write beautifully, you do! My, how beautifully you write!" Doubtless it did not enter his mind that I was writing of him.

It was really a good thing Helene did not scrub her floor. Just now two men, Thorgrim and another, came stamping in with their dirty wet boots.[17] I don't know what they want; they have seated themselves on the kitchen bench, where one

[17] "Thorgrim and another" were Thorgrim Busness and Thorbjørn Omager.

of them is talking to John and Thorgrim is smoking some abominable tobacco and spitting on the floor with abandon. I cannot understand why there is not a spittoon, and a mat for wiping the feet. Apparently that is not done here.

Evening has come at last. I do not know why this day has seemed so long — perhaps because there have been so many people here; the more variety there is, the longer seems the time. John and the men ended their talk at last. We discovered that the stranger was Thorbjørn Omager, whose daughters we had met in McGregor; we now gave him the greetings from them, and he was much pleased at receiving them.[18] He very eagerly offered Vilhelm his services to describe the road he should follow on his journey. Thereupon arose a laughable dispute between him and John, for the latter thought that since he lived down there and had just made the journey up here, he ought to have better information than the former. I wish I could repeat John's dry, quiet answers, which called forth much laughter from all those present. At last he won the victory, too, and it was decided Vilhelm should follow his instructions. Now there remained the question whether they should venture out in that wind.

John stayed and took dinner with us, as Vilhelm wanted to wait a little to see if the bridal couple would not make their appearance, as had been agreed. The clock was near two and no one had come. They had just decided to postpone their trip until early tomorrow morning when there was a knock at the door and two men came in. It was the bridegroom and one of his friends, the former quite drunk; the other I thought was sober, but still he was not very steady. The bridegroom wanted to have the marriage ceremony performed; the bride was waiting in a house in the neighborhood, he said. Of course, this could not be done. Vilhelm took him outside to talk to him seriously. While they were outside, John began making observations on the fact that the bridegroom came to be married without having his bride along.

---

[18] See *ante*, page 93.

"Yes," answered Ola's friend, "she should have been with us, it is true; but this is a strange affair. He is so contrary, this fellow. The arrangements are not the same here as they were in Larvik or Skien," he added, turning to me.[19]

I asked, "Are you possibly from one of those places?"

"Yes, sir," he answered, "I crossed over in one of Treschow's vessels, the brig 'Lolland.' " [20]

Meanwhile Vilhelm and Ola came in again; Ola persisted in wanting the marriage this evening. Vilhelm said no, he would stop there on his way tomorrow; otherwise they would have to wait until he came back. They did not like to agree to that and asked if they could come early in the morning; this request was then granted and now we are expecting the bridal couple tomorrow at eight o'clock. Then, I hope, he will at least be sober. Poor bride! To get a man who drinks!

John went over to Nils Katterud's and it has been quiet here since. Vilhelm set to work again; I crocheted; Erik contemplated my work very attentively and tended the fire in the stove efficiently; Helene was frying pancakes for us for supper and now and then hushing the children. It turned dark early; we sat for a time by the light of the stove and talked of our friends at home before we lit the lamp and ate supper. After we had finished and had been busy with our work for a time, and Helene had gone to bed, Vilhelm looked at his watch — and who would have believed it? It was only seven o'clock. Helene ought to get enough sleep tonight. But then we are to be up early in the morning and have everything ready. God be praised, Vilhelm did not leave early today! It has been very cold. I hope the weather will be better in the morning so that he will not freeze too much in his open sleigh! Now he is going to sit up and work half the night again.

Saturday, January 14. It is evening; I have just finished supper — roast quail, which Helene had brought from Aar-

---

[19] Skien is a town in Norway about sixty miles from Oslo.

[20] The Treschow family, friends of the Hysings, were the owners of Fritsøhus, manor house at Larvik (Mrs. Koren's original home), and also of Fritsøverk, an important industrial establishment of southern Norway. They owned a number of merchant vessels.

thun's, and fresh biscuits. I ate alone, for Erik is at Suckow's. Although the children have been put to bed, there is not much peace, for they are making a great racket. This switch Helene just brought in is surely the third today, but it is used probably just to scare them. Her usual method of punishing them is first to say, "If you do not keep quiet, I shall pull your hair, you rascal." And if that does not help, she watches for the moment when they come near her and plucks them by their thin hair. That happened this noon to Per. He paused a moment, then said, "That hurts, it does," and then stormed away just as merrily as before.

Well, the bridal party came on time today. We had just finished breakfast (while we were eating, John [Andreas Axdal] and Eli Sørland came in), cleared the table, and spread a cloth over it, when they came. Today, they were sober. Ugh! that must be an unpleasant way to be married! The bride's sister and brother were with her. I had to hurry and pack Vilhelm's things while the bridal party was still here. He did not get away, however, until ten o'clock.[21] Eli left soon afterward, and Helene began to dust and have a grand cleaning, so I thought it best to take a walk while that was in progress. I walked almost to Aarthun's, rejoiced at the good weather Vilhelm is having, and came home with a good appetite.

I read a little in Welhaven's "Travel Sketches," but noticed that I was not in a mood to read such descriptions from Norway, and broke off and sat down to write Marie.[22] I was busy with this until dark; then I poked the fire in the stove, drew my bench nearer to it, and fell into musings, from which I was roused now and then to hush Kari and Per. Thus I sat, quite alone, until Helene came back and gave my thoughts a different turn. The light was lit, supper prepared and eaten. Erik has come home and the whole family is already in bed. I am going to read a little before I follow their example.

[21] Pastor Koren preached in the Turkey River settlement near Clermont on January 15 and succeeding days, and in Paint Creek on January 22.

[22] J. S. C. Welhaven, *Reisebilleder og digte* (Travel Sketches and Poems — Christiania, 1851). Christine Marie Cappelen Hysing (1836–67) was a younger sister of Elisabeth Koren; Johnson, *Slekten Koren*, 1:188.

9

Clumsy, Bundled-up Women

Sunday, January 15. I dreamed last night I was home in Larvik in the *herregaard*.[1] Petra Castberg had come over to go with us to a ball; we had completed our toilet and were just driving over to where the ball was to be held when I woke up. I shall not forget my amazement when I looked about me in this little room with curtains on all sides, and the peculiar feeling when I realized at last that I was so far from the scenes with which I had just been occupied that I lay here in Erik's little cabin, far inland in America, that I was married, that Vilhelm was a pastor and was today to conduct a service in one of the settlements. It was strange to think of it all, and I stayed awake until it was light and there was movement in the house. Then I, too, got up.

When we had eaten, I read a sermon, which Erik later read

[1] The *herregaard* was a large wooden building built in Larvik as a manor house a century or more before the time of this narrative. During the 1850's it housed an advanced school for boys. Elisabeth Koren's father was headmaster of the school and lived in one part of the building, while Dean Münster, the pastor of the city, resided in another part. The *herregaard* also contained the classrooms and a theater.

133

aloud to Helene. While he was reading, Suckow came. He sat here for a while before he went on to Katterud's, where the meeting is to be held today. I had thought of going over in the forenoon, but now I shall wait until another time. I shall spend the day writing to Sellø; then I can send my letter home.[2]

Now it is time for dinner and we have both potatoes and onions, as well as pork. I wonder how many of the congregation were able to come to services where Vilhelm is today. Here the weather is so disagreeable that I have not been outside.

It is now bedtime; true, it is not yet nine o'clock, but when Vilhelm is away, I generally shorten the evening somewhat. I have been reading aloud to Erik and Helene from Welhaven's "Travel Sketches" this evening. (Today I am able to read them.) It was a great pleasure, especially for Erik, who is acquainted with many of the places described and knows several of the people.

Monday, January 16. Today I was up early — before it was light. Helene asked if I wanted any clothes washed, as she was going to wash. I answered yes, and struggled for a time with my things. It has been very quiet here this forenoon; I have scarcely heard a sound save Helene's splashing in the water. This is because Kari was given a piece of cloth and a needle to play with and so let Per play alone with his blocks. I wish it might be this way when Vilhelm is home. Erik was in the woods. I ate biscuits and drank coffee for dinner, but declined the pork. Later in the afternoon Helene was through with her washing and wanted to scrub the floor. I protested that it was really too much to scrub both Saturday and Monday — but in vain. So I resorted to my usual expedient under such circumstances — took my hat and coat and went out.

I thought of going on a tour of discovery to see if I could not find new paths, but gave that up as soon as I stuck my nose out the door. My face tingled so that I was afraid of

[2] On Sellø, see chapter 5, footnote 6.

paying too dearly if I should go astray, and therefore I prudently took the path across Erik's field to Sørland's and the path beyond to Katterud's. I turned off before I reached there, circled around, and came back by the way we had taken home from the parsonage land. Since that time I had forgotten how it looked there; I found it extraordinarily pretty, an effect to which the evening sun contributed, throwing its splendor over the landscape and through the trees. When I got home I found Helene waiting with some anxiety for Erik, who had not yet returned, though he had left early that morning and had not taken lunch with him. It became dark. I walked back and forth knitting. Helene made pancakes, the children were noisy, but still no Erik. At last he came and all was well; he had only been delayed.

Tuesday, January 17. I was up very early today, too; but no wonder, for I had gone to bed at eight o'clock. Long after the others had gone to bed last night, I was writing and thinking of continuing my letter. But then it seemed so disagreeable to sit alone — I heard so many sounds — in short, I was like a child who is afraid to be alone. Therefore I hurried to bed and stuck my face under the feather quilt. I lay awake for a long time, thinking of my earliest childhood and recalling several scenes very vividly.

Now it is evening again. The household has gone to bed, but I am still sitting here with a little writing, which I did not get done earlier because Erik asked me if I would not be so kind as to read a little to him from that *boka* ("Travel Sketches").[3] He listens very attentively, even to the descriptions of nature. Helene, busy crushing something in a mortar, takes care to stop her work every time the talk is of people and fairies, but when Welhaven shows enthusiasm for the evening sun's splendor, the dark woods and deep waters, she pounds away merrily.

We were at Sørland's for dinner today. We walked over at ten o'clock this morning, taking the road across the fields.

[3] *Boka* is dialect for book.

Helene had Per on her arm, wrapped in shawls, and a switch in her hand to drive the cows before her to be watered. I walked behind holding Kari by the hand; then came the heifer, bringing up the rear. Kari and I did not manage well. First we both fell down on a slippery hill. Then, as we approached the house, the dogs came barking and jumping toward us, and Kari screamed at the top of her voice and clung to me so that I could neither get loose nor chase the dogs away. At last Eli heard us and came out and rescued us from our distress. She was home alone. Ingebret did not come until three o'clock, when we were ready to go. We had a very pleasant time there; I was busy with my work and Eli set out a plentiful supply of good food. She is a very tidy housekeeper; it is less primitive, too — both saltcellars and pepperboxes.

I wish I knew how Vilhelm is faring and whether he found a good place. Just so he does not come to half-open houses where he will freeze at night!

Wednesday, January 18. I was awakened this morning by light in the room; I peeped out between the curtains and discovered that Erik was already having breakfast. Contrary to custom, I was very sleepy today, and so I rested a little longer until it became lighter and I heard Erik and his oxen leave for the woods. It had snowed during the night, and the morning was dark and gray to begin with; but soon there came one of those sudden changes of weather which sent all the grayness flying and brought us the most beautiful sunshine instead. I hurried to finish my letter to Sellø, then sealed the one to Larvik, and went over to see if Suckow might be going to town. I found only his wife, who said he would not be going before Monday.

I sat there for a while, but was really afraid to look about me in that wretched room. Ugh, it was a trial to go in there after the bright, cheerful sunshine outside. It was stuffy and untidy, though that was not surprising in such a little room with so many children, and then that poor crippled girl who hops about on the dirty floor. Sigrid invited me to have dinner, but I just could not do it. I was eager to get outside, and it was not until I had walked some distance that the fresh winter morning began to blot out the pitiful picture I had just seen.

I was already inside the gate when it occurred to me to go to Aarthun's and ask about sending my letter. It was very lucky that I did, for now Ola is going to Trout River with my letter and one for his father.[4] I sat there for a little while and had a glass of beer. Anne walked part of the way home with me. Some distance from our cabin, I caught the smell of fresh bread and found that Helene had baked biscuits, whose excellence I have just sampled for dinner.

It is now evening, nearly nine o'clock. I read the conclusion of the "Travel Sketches" to Erik and Helene this evening, and thereafter talked with them about Norway. Erik thought it would be very nice to visit all the places he had just heard described, for it was mighty fine there, and to hear someone read about them gives one such a longing.

"And you, Helene," said I, "would you not like to see the places where you lived as a child?"

"Oh, it would really be fun to talk with the people there, but otherwise, well . . . ." answered she.

Nature, it seems, holds no allure for her; but she wishes she might now and then hear the birds sing.

"The songs of the birds are not beautiful here," she said when we talked about that, "and it was really gay at home, wasn't it? When we went out early in the morning, there was such a warbling — yes, it was so lively. And the song thrush — he was a fellow with a merry note, indeed! Here one hears only that ugly frog, who croaks so that people cannot sleep."

---

[4] Trout River is a small stream running north through Frankville and Glenwood townships to the Upper Iowa River. A post office and store were located near the stream on John McKay's land, about three miles east of Erik Egge's (now the Clarence Haugen farm in Winneshiek County). The post office was later moved to Frankville; Sparks, *History of Winneshiek County*, 117; and information furnished by William Linnevold. Ola may have been Ola Katterud, either the elder or the younger.

Diary of Elisabeth Koren

Thursday, January 19. Today I starched and ironed until it was time for dinner; after eating, I took a book and had a long siesta. I was reading some of Ingemann's tales, but they did not especially please me.[5] I had thought of taking a walk in the afternoon but the weather became so bitter and horrid, with snow and wind, that my walk was confined to going back and forth outside the house to get a breath of fresh air. I wonder whether Vilhelm went to Paint Creek today? I hope he does not go until tomorrow, and then gets better weather. It is dreadful how dark the evenings are now.

I sat and crocheted this morning; I felt I ought to write a little, but had no desire to. I talked a bit with Helene, but that did not interest me; what I could talk about with her did not suit my mood, and so I abandoned myself to my own musings. These soon took a brighter turn than they had earlier, and made the hours, which had begun to hang heavy on my hands, pass quickly. I was really not unhappy earlier in the day. No, it was just trifles, such as the unpleasant smell of fried pork, the roasting of coffee, Helene's coughing, the noise of the children, and then finally Erik's bad tobacco — all of which made the room disagreeable to me and made me wish I had someone to talk to. I will not deny that I wished Vilhelm were home. That mood lasted a while but ended with my poking fun at myself because I let these trifles put me out of humor and, as I said, I was soon in good spirits again.

During the twilight Erik cracked nuts and we ate. For supper Helene surprised me with a soup made from meat, beets, and potatoes. It tasted good, for it was long since I had had soup, but it would have tasted even better if we had had it at noon instead of evening, which I told her, too, for the second time. I read aloud again this evening — I enjoy doing it because I see the others get such pleasure from it. Today I read from *The English Reader* and translated from the newspaper

[5] Bernhard S. Ingemann (1789–1862) was a Danish poet, dramatist, and writer of historical novels.

— very fluently.[6] For a change, Helene went to bed at six o'clock this evening and fell asleep immediately without, as usual, making known her approval of what I read from behind the curtain. Therefore Erik and I sat alone this evening. Now he has gone to bed. I shall read a little first before I do likewise.

Friday, January 20. It is only seven-thirty, and I have already had breakfast and am writing. There was such noise and commotion here this morning that I had to wake up whether I wished to or not. Unluckily Erik went to the woods today, instead of to Decorah as I had hoped; by now there really must be at least an *Emigranten* with European news at the post office.

Today, no doubt, Vilhelm will go to Paint Creek. He will have bad weather, it is true; but it is not cold, God be praised, so I need not be afraid he will freeze his nose and ears (provided the weather is the same there as here). I had planned to go to Katterud's today, but now I shall wait until Sunday; then Helene can go along, and she will probably be glad to do so. This morning I shall begin the description of our journey from Koshkonong to Iowa.

It is now noon. While I was busy with the account of our journey and Helene had gone out to water the cattle, three men came stamping into the room and, remarking it was "mighty cold," seated themselves by the stove, shook the snow out of their boots, lighted their pipes, and made themselves comfortable. "You must be the pastor's wife," said one of them, a friendly little man. I asked them if they wished to speak to the pastor. No, they did not wish that. They did belong to the congregation, I was able to gather, but had not been at the meeting of the congregation. They were also very eager to have the parsonage located here. They were from Telemark, where Dean Bech has been pastor; they made some inquiries about him when they heard where I was from, and

[6] Lindley Murray, *The English Reader, or Pieces in Prose and Poetry Selected from the Best Writers* (London, 1799).

also about Castberg, whom they knew through Bech.[7] I enjoyed talking with them, since they knew these pastors. After
sitting here a while, they left. I do not know what they
wanted. They had not known that the pastor was away and
probably they wished to see him.

Evening. The weather is dreadful, with a stronger wind
than I have ever known here. Erik came home from the
woods early, but did not dare go to Decorah, where he should
have gone. The wind takes hold as if it would blow the whole
house down, and tugs at the door. Would to God I knew
where Vilhelm is! If he is at Sivert Vold's, it will be grim and
cold. It is so disagreeable that I am going to bed at eight
o'clock.

Saturday, January 21. I read a sermon aloud and spent all
morning reading. It has been so cold today, I was glad to stay
inside instead of going to Katterud's; it does not look as if I
shall get there. My thoughts wander early and late to Paint
Creek. Ugh! how cold it must be at Sivert Vold's! Vilhelm
will certainly catch a bad cold.

Erik went to Aarthun's this afternoon. Just after he left
we had a visit from Suckow, with whom I had an entertaining conversation on paintings, landscape painters, nature,
and flowers. He is really not so bad to talk to; he has a little
notion of everything and does not pretend to understand and
know things he does not; he likes to learn about them. At
least he does not say "Yes, yes," and repeat exactly what I
say; that is fearfully tiresome.

I hope there may be better weather tomorrow (this evening there is such lovely, bright starlight), so Erik can get
away to Decorah and learn whether or not there are letters.
How I long to receive them! It does not look as if I shall be

[7] Dean Thomas Bech (1798–1862) was pastor in Laurdal in central Telemark, Norway, 1822–34, and at Tjødling, just east of Larvik, 1834–62; J.B.
Halvorsen, ed., *Norsk forfatter-lexikon, 1814–1880,* 1:185 (Christiania, 1885).
The Reverend P.H. Castberg (1794-1858) served as pastor in Larvik and in
Sandeherred, 1833–58; he was also for many years a member of the Storting,
or Norwegian parliament; Edv. Bull and others, ed., *Norsk biografisk leksikon,*
2:514 (Christiania, 1923).

THE EGGE CABIN

INTERIOR OF THE EGGE CABIN

able to surprise Vilhelm, when he comes home, with the good news that our baggage has arrived; yet, who knows?

It is really ridiculous to go to bed when it is barely eight o'clock — one will certainly get fat from such laziness — but what am I to do? It is so cold and unpleasant to sit here alone; moreover, I disturb the others when I am up longer. I shall have to console myself with the thought that I am up early in the morning.

Monday, January 23. This morning I was awakened by the pleasant news that the weather was good enough for Erik to go to Decorah; now we may soon expect his return, for it is four o'clock. I was at Katterud's today. I returned a couple of hours ago — unfortunately, just as the floor scrubbing was about to begin. Monday is one of Helene's busy days. First she bakes bread; then she washes clothes; then the floor simply must be scrubbed with "that good lye water," which I wish were in Blocksberg; and now I hear her down in the cellar, cutting and sawing with all her might to repair something on the cellar steps.[8] Every moment or two I must look up from my work to see that Per does not fall through the opening.

I probably would not have gone to Katterud's today except to borrow an eyestone, as they call it, to see if it can make little Kari's eye well again.[9] Apparently she has something in it. It was a little past eight this morning when I set out. The sun shone brightly enough, but had no warmth in its rays. It was so cold that I glanced neither right nor left but hurried on as fast as I could. When I reached Sørland's I thought at first of going in to warm my feet but did not do so; instead, I took a short cut, thinking to make better time. I might have spared myself the trouble; the road had not been used and

---

[8] Blockberg refers to the Brocken, summit of the Harz Mountains in Germany. In legend the Brocken is the haunt of witches. To wish someone or something in Blocksberg was a common expression.

[9] An eyestone is a small, smooth, lens-shaped object, such as a crab's-eye or the operculum of a small marine shell, formerly used to remove a foreign substance from the eye. It was placed under the eyelid at the inner corner and worked its way out at the outer corner, often bringing the substance with it.

was so drifted over that I found it hard to make my way through the deep snow and keep off the irrepressible Sørland dogs. It was pleasant and warm in the Sørland woods, but the road got no better. A man had gone there before me, and I made the most desperate efforts to step in his tracks, but with my best exertion could not escape plumping down between each footprint. He must have been a giant!

At last I got through and paused on the hill, taken completely by surprise by the charming view. The land behind Nils's house and the ridges on the horizon were lighted up beautifully by the morning sun. When I reached the fence, the road became really bad; I have never seen such bad roads. But I found it a very interesting experience, and stopped at last, good and warm, with my big shoes full of snow, outside Nils's door. Here, as usual, I found the family sitting about the stove freezing and was received with much wonderment that I was out in such cold. I did not get away from there until after dinner; I was treated to *melkevælling,* which I had not tasted in five months. While that was being made, I had a good visit with Mother Katterud, in which Nils also took part while he was reviving his old crafts and sewing a vest.[10]

Evening. Erik has returned — there are no letters! I must be patient! He brought along *Emigranten,* however, with a little in it about Europe. The Turk, God be praised, is still winning against that odious Russian, but all the dispatches are so vague, and from the second of November. How does it look now? [11]

Well, Vilhelm will have no letter to cheer him when he gets home; I hope the cold weather does not prevent him from returning as he planned. We really have reading matter in the house for a long time now in *Emigranten.* Helene, using her index finger, is reading half-aloud a fearful story which makes her forget it is long past her customary bedtime,

---

[10] *Melkevælling* is a milk soup made by boiling milk and thickening it with flour, rice, or barley.

[11] She is anxious about the progress of the Crimean War.

while Erik is lost in amazement at the price at which some bulls were sold in England.

Tuesday, January 24. Today I had a surprise. In the morning I had been busy teaching the A B C's to Kari and trying to give her some idea of knitting. Then there was a visit from a very reticent man who wished to talk with Erik. Then for a while after dinner I was busy with the account of our journey and was just thinking of laying it aside to take a walk while the sun was still up. At that moment I chanced to look out the window and whom should I see but Vilhelm driving in at full speed and stopping just outside the door. I ran out at once — walking would hardly be the term for it. I had not expected him for a day or two. It was delightful to be surprised in this way. He was hale and hearty and had not even caught a chill; but it had been wretchedly cold. He had traveled thirty miles alone in that biting wind Friday without knowing the road; and at Sivert Vold's it had been so cold that the sheet had frozen between him and his bedfellow, and the pillow was covered with frost.

He will not be home long this time. He is to be away Thursday and Friday and leaves again Saturday to be gone several days; but I shall rejoice that he is home now and that he returned so early. I am so glad when he comes. He has so much to tell me, and reads my diary to learn how I have fared while he was away. And once we get our own home, it will be even better; then I shall really be able to take care of him and then we shall have everything cozy. How I look forward to that time — and Vilhelm not less than I!

Wednesday, January 25. It is already evening, but I really do not know where the day has gone. This morning I was writing, but did not accomplish much. This afternoon I helped Helene make communion wafers.

Vilhelm and I took a walk over to John Dysja, or some such name, where we had not been before. The road (if it can be called a road) went uphill all the way and I became very tired; I am unaccustomed to hills now. Outside the house we met John's father, the same friendly old man who asked for work and calls me "Mother." We went there to learn how John was; he had had trouble with his eye. His wife came over to us yesterday to learn whether Vilhelm or I might know a remedy for it. When we asked whether there were not some other people, older, more experienced, whom he might consult, she answered it would hardly be of any use to go to others if we did not know what to do; she thought she could not find anyone better than we. Yet she could hardly have turned to anyone more inexperienced in such matters.[12]

John was better, as it turned out. Conditions were fairly good there, and, best of all, the people were cheerful. They wanted us to stay for supper, but we did not do so, fearing it would become so dark that we would lose the only existing trace of the road, namely, the track left by Erik's sleigh. This morning a cold wind was blowing; while we were out, it was very mild, with fog and a drizzle of rain. The weather is extraordinary! Well, there comes Helene with the cloth to cover the table and I must vacate my place.

Thursday, January 26. Today I am alone. Vilhelm set out this morning to go seven miles, I do not know where, to hold services.[13] I ironed a little and kept busy with my work as usual in the morning and had dinner just at noon. After dinner I took my knitting and buried myself completely in Alhambra's ruins, with its mysterious secret chambers, enchanted treasures guarded by petrified Moors, and the marvelous legends about most beautiful princesses. This so occupied my mind that I did not notice the time, and it became so late I had to hurry to get in my walk before sundown.

So I went out to the road, turned my nose to all four corners of the earth to find where the wind was from, and

[12] John Dysja, formerly of Telemark, Norway, lived on the east half of Section 6 in Frankville Township, Winneshiek County. The Bauder farm is now in approximately the same spot; information received from William Linnevold.
[13] The pastor probably went to Glenwood Township; later in the account of January 26 it is mentioned that he went where Helene's two sisters lived. Mrs. Eggebraaten was one of them; she lived in Glenwood Township.

144

then took my bearings. The result was that I steered my course directly east, where there was a kind of road across a field (that is, a sleigh had been through there), barely passable in the snow. I followed that road until I discovered the traces of a sleigh headed directly north; I had not been there before, so I had to investigate, and followed the tracks until I saw John Dysja's house straight ahead of me on the hill. I did not attempt to go farther, but returned home well pleased with my new road. It will be a pretty walk in summer. The weather was fresh and delightful. I reached home hungry as a wolf and had to go straight to the cupboard and get a biscuit.

A little after dark Vilhelm returned. He was rather offended that I had not worried over his not getting home until dark. Now he is in the midst of his writing and talks to himself about sections and such tiresome matters, and I keep thinking he is speaking to me and become confused in my work. Helene, whose talkativeness knows no bounds when the conversation concerns the place where her two sisters live (where Vilhelm was today), chatters and asks questions in her shrill voice, but it can scarcely be said that she gets much of an answer. Now she stands with a cloth on her arm and for the third time asks if she may set the table. But Vilhelm is stubborn and will not give in.

I hope we shall have good weather tomorrow, for I am to go with him to Thrond Lommen's. I cannot imagine how I shall be able to ride in that absurd sleigh; I suppose what it will come to is that I shall be sitting in the bottom toward the front, half buried in hay. Tonight I shall no doubt be chased to bed at nine o'clock, since Vilhelm is to sit up and work. He is really mean.

Friday, January 27. I went along to Lommen's just the same, and without sitting in the bottom of the sleigh, either. Yet I almost stayed home, scared out by the rather strong wind this morning. But I wanted to make the trip and already had my things on before I really noticed how cold the wind was. "Never mind," thought I, "you can ride as far as Kat-terud's at least, and see how it goes." So, tucking myself in as well as I could, I took my seat in the sleigh, which is so nar-row that Vilhelm had scarcely any room. That made little difference, however, for he had to walk the greater part of the way to keep the sleigh from overturning. By the time we came to Nils's place, I had decided to continue; it did not seem to blow so hard as at Erik's. Here the horse was watered and we had a chance to ask Nils about the road. He wanted to go with us, but did not dare because he was not feeling well. But he accompanied us some distance until we reached the right road. From there we had to fend for ourselves.

As a great deal of snow had fallen, Vilhelm had his hands full with the sleigh, though it is light as a feather. Then, too, he made many complaints about what a nuisance it was to trans-port clumsy, bundled-up women, who just sit wherever they plump down. I comforted myself with the thought that it was his own fault I was with him. Moreover, it seems to me I managed all right; I kept a good firm hold and balanced myself as well as I could. When the road sloped a little to the side Vilhelm was on, I sat quite comfortably; but if the slope was in the opposite direction, it often looked dangerous. "You need not worry, we'll come out all right; when the sleigh leans like that, it is no trick to stay on unless, of course, you fall out of your own accord," said my lord husband very wisely. Well, that was just the question — whether I should fall out or not. Fortunately I escaped and we came safely through the snow to the traveled road.

This one had been driven on quite a little and for a time all went well, until we reached a place where it followed the side of a sharply sloping, slippery hill. Here Vilhelm had to get out, go round to the other side, and support me and the sleigh, just as farmers do when they get to a slippery hill with a big load of wood which they fear their horses cannot man-age alone. We got past that difficult spot safely and on to the main road, as people here call a kind of lane with hedges on both sides. We followed that until we came to the "white house," which was our mark of identification for Ola Lommen's house, where we were to get more detailed directions.[14]

Here we met a little boy who was not afraid to use his vocal organs, and in a high-pitched voice he explained to us "that we should go neither to right nor left of the fence, but just straight ahead." With that information we set off for the fence and drove straight into a valley full of snow. Then we came to the top of a hill. At the foot of this there was a cabin situated very conveniently to help us choose aright among the many roads we now discovered. While I stayed on the crest, Vilhelm went down to the cabin. He went in and came out at once with a woman with whom he began violent gesticulations, the meaning of which I was attempting to grasp when they suddenly ceased, and Vilhelm, turning, beckoned to me. "Go along, Peter," I said and drove very nicely down the hill until Vilhelm met me.

We had not gone much farther before the horse plunged into snow up to his belly; it was dreadful how the snow had accumulated in that valley. We, that is, Vilhelm and his stiff-legged traveling companion, worked their way through as best they could; I sat like a bundle of traveling clothes, and balanced from side to side. It was not long before we stopped again, in doubt as to which of three roads to choose. We decided on the middle one, which brought us along a ridge and into a valley where, according to Vilhelm's reckoning, Thrond ought to be living. We soon realized that it was not so, for we saw a brook with trees on either side; besides, the hills near Thrond's are not so rocky. But we decided to follow the road, in the hope it would lead to a house. We drove and drove until we ran squarely into a big haystack, which stood there as if to make fun of us; the road went no farther.

There was now nothing else to do but turn around and try

[14] A. O. Lommen and his wife Seigie settled on the northwest quarter of Section 2, Springfield Township, Winneshiek County, in June, 1850; Sparks, *History of Winneshiek County*, 26. For many years the family has spelled the name "Lomen."

to get over the hill. We succeeded. "What sort of creature has passed here?" said Vilhelm, and indeed the tracks in the road did look unusual. We followed another road some distance until we saw a cabin; there an American woman informed us that she understood Lommen lived two miles back in the direction from which we had come. Now, then, back over our tracks we went as fast as we could; Peter was not spared. I wonder how long a detour we made. The weather had become so lovely that the delay would have made no difference, only Vilhelm was expected at a definite hour. It was twelve o'clock by the time that we reached Thrond's house.

After the services and a chat with the people (so much was a little pretentious, which I do not like) we had to eat dinner, and we got Ola Bergan and his family to wait for us and show us the road home. I sat on a sheepskin in the bottom of Ola's sleigh until we reached his house; in this way Vilhelm was sure of not overturning me on that part of the road. I sat and talked with Kari (she was that pretty Valdres woman) while Ola was getting his oxen ready. Vilhelm drove round and paid us a visit now and then, and at last whipped up Peter and vanished. We were not far behind, either; I have never seen oxen trot and actually gallop as these did. Consequently we were not on the road long before we got to Ola's house, where we found Vilhelm busy watering his horse.[15] From there we proceeded in Vilhelm's sleigh again; it was so dark we could scarcely follow our tracks. At last we reached Katterud's gate, where Ola let us in, and we arrived at home without an upset or other misfortune. We found Knud here; he ate supper with us and finally left at a late hour; he is always so slow in leaving.[16]

Saturday, January 28. Vilhelm should have gone to Whisky Grove today, but the weather was so horrid, with wind and

[15] On Ola Bergan, see chapter 7, footnote 15.
[16] The gate was opened by Ola Katterud, brother of Nils Katterud. Knud was probably Knud Aarthun.

drifting snow, that it was impossible to see the road.[17] As it became worse later in the day, he postponed his journey until tomorrow, and I am glad. In such drifting snow what might not happen to one who has never gone that road before? Now he has gone for Suckow, who perhaps will accompany him and show him the way. He is to leave tomorrow morning at seven and will not come back until Thursday; then he is to go to Minnesota and will be away a long time, I imagine. It is just one trip after another.

I do not know what has come over me to make me so industrious this evening; I have neither read nor written as usual, but have crocheted and crocheted without even looking up, save when Vilhelm disturbed me by speaking English.

[17] Whisky Grove was an early name for Calmar, Iowa, twelve miles southwest of Decorah.

10

Our Appetites Seldom Fail

Sunday, January 29. Today the whole household was on its feet early because of Vilhelm's departure. He got away at seven-thirty, but Suckow did not go with him, and I wonder how he will manage to find his way. It is not cold today — cloudy and mild.

It is already evening. The forenoon passed quietly in reading. Helene expressed a strong desire to visit some *hadelæn-dinger* when she had tidied up after dinner, and I thought of going along.[1] But Erik saved us the trip because he himself went out after dinner. Helene could not be persuaded to go alone. She went to Sørland's for water, and it looked as if she might have changed her mind on the way and decided to pay some visits, for it seemed that she would never return. I had just opened my writing case to write when there was a knock at the door. It was Sigrid Suckow. She stayed (though I cannot say I enjoyed it) until dark, when both Erik and Helene came back.

---

[1] *Hadelændinger* are people from the Hadeland district north of Oslo, Norway.

Then there was a lively conversation and some surprise over an English Sunday school conducted by a Methodist today at Katterud's. He lets the children recite some verses of the Testament from memory, whereupon they, or rather, he, explains them. Now the explanation can scarcely be correct, because the explainer is a Methodist; therefore Sigrid dared not let her boys go there until Suckow himself had been there. And she thought it strange that Katterud should have the school at his place, for Mari surely must be sufficiently enlightened to know it was wrong.[2] After airing her views on sectarians at some length, Mother Suckow left at last and we lit the light and ate our evening meal. Since then I have been writing. It is not yet eight o'clock, but the whole family is fast asleep. I, too, shall bring the day to a close; it has seemed unusually long.

Monday, January 30. Just as I was about to drink my coffee this morning, Embret came very opportunely and gave Helene some milk, so that I got an excellent cup of coffee. They are very good about furnishing us milk.

I have had a visit from an old man, who brought his certificate to the pastor. He handed me both that and a passport and said, "You will have to look at them yourself; I am not sure which is the certificate." He sat and smoked his pipe, chatting busily with Helene about horse trading, land, and I know not what.

There is an air almost of summer here today. Helene, at the washtub, has beads of perspiration on her face. The door is wide open, to the great joy of Kari and Per, who are very busy carrying chips from the stove and throwing them in the face of a cow that apparently intends soon to pay us a visit in the house. But they are suddenly frightened from their play by hearing Helene stamp the floor and cry: "Stop carrying out my chips! Have you ever seen such youngsters? I'll just teach you a good lesson." Thereupon they look at each other, somewhat bewildered, Per with the most smiling expression,

[2] On Mari Katterud, see chapter 7, footnote 3.

and then begin to shout, "Sørli, Sørland!" to Sørland, whom they see driving back and forth in his field.

Today I must try to take a turn outside while the floor is being washed. Vilhelm, fortunately, has very fine weather; there is a little wind, it is true, but it is very mild. I wish the sun would shine for a moment so that we might set this tiresome clock, which is never wound at the right time and is always stopping. We live in constant ignorance of the time while Vilhelm is away.

I had just begun to eat my pork at noon when I heard someone driving in, and who should it be but Vilhelm. I rushed out, calling, "Are you crazy, coming home so soon?" And the answer was, "Well, well, that was really a beautiful welcome!" No doubt he was right about that, too; but I was really just as much frightened as pleased for the moment. Fortunately, it was only that he had found time to come home for a little visit; tomorrow, of course, he leaves again. Still, there had been something wrong; he turned his ankle yesterday and had to stay in bed after the services were over. Today, God be praised, it was much better and he was able to take a walk with me.

Tuesday, January 31. What lovely weather Vilhelm has for his trip! It has been just like a spring day. I sat by the open door all day. This morning I wrote to Mrs. Bech and began a letter to Mrs. Lund.[3] Suckow paid me a little visit; tomorrow, at last, he is going to Decorah. If he does not get anything else, I hope he will at least bring Vilhelm's table back with him.

A few moments ago I came back from a walk. I had almost given up the idea, for Helene did not return from Suckow's, where she had gone, and I dared not leave the children. Just as the sun was going down I left, strolling along the cattle path toward Sørland's. I was thinking that it was a long time since I had seen a really beautiful sunset — nor did I see one today; but if the sunset was not beautiful, the evening sky

[3] Mrs. Bech entertained the Korens in Poughkeepsie; Mrs. Lund was the Korens' hostess in Hamburg.

was so much the lovelier. It was beautiful in the woods; I sauntered about quite slowly, as is my habit on summer evenings, and instead of flowers I examined the withered stalks and tried to make out what species they were. It was so quiet; I did not see or hear a solitary person all the way. On my return I dropped in at Eli's to quench my thirst, but found neither human being nor water. How I wish Vilhelm had been with me, and there had been a mountain from which we could have surveyed the whole lovely scene! And how I also hope he will go there with me some moonlit evening, for then everything must be very beautiful! If only he could stay home and find time!

Now I shall have supper. Erik is at Suckow's, as usual. Helene is baking potatoes and has just threatened Per with a whipping; he therefore has retired under the table and begun to call, "I am sitting under the table, ma, I am!" [4] Now he has ventured out, after having pulled off one of his stockings; he has wrapped it very carefully around a warm potato on which he is gnawing with much satisfaction. Kari is howling. It is very warm inside, and so every few moments I open the door and gaze at the beautiful stars, which tonight are unusually brilliant. Such is our life here this evening. Now I shall sit down to my knitting and a book.

Wednesday, February 1. After a nap and a rest after iron ing this morning, I put on my shawl and my high boots and went over to Katterud's. It was well I had on high boots; galoshes would soon have drowned in such plish-plash. There were great puddles that I had to cross; but that was not the worst. In order to avoid the deep ox tracks, which were full of water, I had to follow the runners of a sleigh, and as it is not easy to walk a crack, I had a very difficult time until I got into the woods, where the sun had left a little piece of passable road.

[4] The exclamation "ma" was a favorite with Helene Egge, and as used by Per does not mean "mother"; it is the dialect equivalent of *maa du vite,* or, in English, "you must know," or "you know." This information was supplied by Mrs. C. A. Naeseth, daughter of the Korens. Mrs. Naeseth (Caroline Mathilda Koren) was born January 21, 1857 and died in 1945.

The Katterud family was well. Nils sat yawning over *Maanedstidende,* and complaining that he felt lazy.[5] Liv wished very much I would stay there overnight. I declined with thanks, but could not escape taking off my things. Fortunately I had my crocheting in my pocket, so I did not sit altogether idle. Mother Katterud and her daughter were soon busy at the stove, and set the table with cakes and *flødegrød.* She loves to entertain, does Mother Liv. The food tasted very good, too, and would have tasted even better if it had been a little later than five o'clock. But Liv was considerate; she decided, since I was not to be there overnight, that they ought not to keep me too late.

I have been disappointed, sad to say, in my hopes for the letters and the table. Suckow was unable to ford the river because the water was too high, and therefore did not bring the table with him; but as for the letters — I can't understand that — not a word from anyone.

Everything looks as usual here this evening. Erik fills the room with his awful tobacco; Helene, yawning over her stockings, blows her nose, and sighs a bit. Per at last has talked himself to sleep, having experienced many kinds of misfortune throughout the course of the day — he overturned a mug of beer on the floor, and fell down in the mud outside the door; he was picked up out of this and, amid many an angry exclamation, was wiped off with the dirty straw which serves in place of a doormat, and then was chased into the house with a whack which sped him swiftly to the other end of the room and gave me a good laugh. I sit here writing and rejoice in the thought that Vilhelm will be home tomorrow. I wish I knew how his foot is.

Thursday, February 2. It is already six o'clock and no Vilhelm. He is not likely to come this evening; it was not certain he could come today, and moreover he has told me he will

[5] *Maanedstidende* was a Norwegian-language church paper published by the Norwegian Synod, 1851-53. Under the name *Kirkelig maanedstidende* it resumed publication in 1856 and continued until 1874. From 1874 to 1917 it was published under the name *Evangelisk luthersk kirketidende.*

always start early enough to reach his destination while it is light; so I will not be alarmed. I wish I knew whether his foot is all right. But it is annoying that he does not come; now he will hardly be home at all before going to Minnesota.

I have just returned from an unexpected drive. It happened that I walked up the road toward Decorah, to meet Vilhelm if possible, and I went in at Aarthun's to make sure of the road. The horses stood there harnessed for a quick trip to Rognald Belle's, and they invited me to go with them.[6] I did so, thinking we would follow the road to Decorah. I was mistaken in this, but I did not regret the drive, for Vilhelm had not yet arrived when I returned. I should hardly like to have him do that. The weather was beautiful and the road to Rognald's interesting; it goes through a long, narrow valley with those remarkable, exposed bluffs which one generally finds only along the rivers. We drove as if our lives were at stake. Knud's horses were so wild that it was just good fortune that we missed bouncing out of the sleigh, each on his own side. Knud was not far from it once.

At Rognald's I was much surprised to find the same little person who always sings her hymns so fervently on Sundays. Since they were in full swing with their floor scrubbing after having washed clothes, it was not altogether pleasant, though the house is a large new one. We stayed there only a few moments, during which I talked to an old man lying on a bed, and made an effort to get down a bowl of boiling hot milk which the old mother gave me. Full gallop we went on the way home, first to Aarthun's with Anne, then Knud drove me here. The weather was fine and it was a brisk drive.

Now, I see, Helene is setting the table. She apparently decided that Vilhelm is not likely to come this evening, and I am forced to believe the same.

Friday, February 3. I had no more than sat down to the

[6] Rognald Belle (Vesle Rognald) was from Sogn, Norway. He lived on the northeast quarter of Section 5, Frankville Township, Winneshiek County; information from William Linnevold and from Mrs. Henriette Vikesland Roberts of Decorah, a great-granddaughter of Rognald Belle.

table yesterday when there was a knock at the door; in came Vilhelm and happy was I. He was cold and stiff after a twelve-mile ride, all of it on my account. He had not wanted me to become alarmed when he did not return as agreed, for he had stated so definitely that he would come while there was still daylight. This arrangement must now be changed, for difficulties can arise so easily that it is impossible to decide beforehand when he will return. I believe our arrangement will have to be this; I must try to be as brave as possible and not be too anxious if he is not home on schedule. He had broken his sleigh in a thousand pieces on an open prairie, had managed with great difficulty to carry his things to Jørgen Lomen's, and he had ridden home from there with my brown shawl (which is useful for everything) as a saddle.[7] God be praised, he has come. It was certainly considerate of him to ride that long way in the cold. His foot is well again, and out there to the west he lives high as far as food is concerned. He wounds Helene's heart by telling about the *flødegrød*, apple charlotte, roast chicken, and I know not how many other glorious things he has had.

We cannot say that we live so exceptionally well here. The dishes vary from boiled pork to fried pork, rare to well done, with coffee in addition (milk when we can get it), good bread and butter. To this are added now and then potatoes, which are now all gone; fried onions, once in a while; and, above all, the glass jar of pickles. That is our meal, morning, noon, and evening. But our appetites seldom fail. And even though we might find food twice as good at many places, I have not found any other place where I would rather live.

This afternoon we took a walk to Katterud's in the lovely weather. Vilhelm has to borrow a saddle, since he now no longer has an equipage. Well, so long as he does not have to ride horseback to Minnesota, it may be all right to ride on

[7] Jørgen Lomen had a farm north of Conover in the southwest quarter of Section 10, Calmar Township, Winneshiek County, which is now the Puffer farm; Bredesen in *Symra*, 99 (1907); and information from Professor S. S. Reque. See chapter 7, footnote 4.

short trips. We set out across the field — Vilhelm, in order
not to be altogether too unsociable, pulling Peter, who had
no special desire for the expedition, behind him; and thus
we came to a creek where Peter was to have refreshed himself with a drop of water; but he found, unfortunately, only
ice, at which he became so offended he turned his nose homeward and would hardly obey his master and follow.[8] At this
point we discovered that the garment that had served earlier
as a saddle was gone; but with confidence in Iowa's safe
roads (safe because no one ever travels them) we let it lie
wherever it might be and continued our way, with Peter,
who now was meek enough, limping along ahead down to
Nils's spring, where he found the water he wanted so much.

As Nils was not home, Liv and Vilhelm ransacked the loft
and found the wished-for saddle. We did not stay many minutes and had not gone far on the way home when we met a
man with a sleigh. He turned out to be Peter's old master;
he desired to have his treasure home again, and had brought
along a pretty, frisky little pony in exchange. I rode back
with Mr. Norsving, much afraid that I should fall out of his
precarious sleigh and very busy in conversation. "Had it ever
occurred to you it would be cold in America?" he asked. I
have heard that question often. I wonder what sort of ideas
these newcomers have of the country. I believe that even
after they hear of something disagreeable, they must first see
it with their own eyes before they can believe that all is not
roses in their dear America.[9]

Anne, Helene's stepdaughter, was here when we returned.[10] Vilhelm walked over to see Halvor (the dapper bache-

[8] Peter was a horse obtained by the pastor from Knut T. Norsving.

[9] Knut Tollef Norsving, from Valdres, Norway, settled in Section 30,
Frankville Township, in 1850, about five miles south of Erik Egge's property;
Linnevold in *Decorah-posten*, June 14, 1929. Norsving's grandson, of the
same name, was the operator of oil and other properties in California.

[10] Anne Egge, daughter of Helene's first husband, Anders Egge, by his first
wife, later married Mons Grinager, an immigrant from Hadeland, Norway.
Grinager worked for a time for Erik Egge. In 1861 he enlisted in the Fif-
teenth Wisconsin Volunteer Infantry, and was chosen captain of Company
K. See Linnevold in *Decorah-posten*, June 7, 1929.

lor), from where he returned this moment and said Halvor would take him to Minnesota with his horses and buggy; so now he will have a good conveyance.

Saturday, February 4. While we were eating last night, Knud came over with Vilhelm's friend Erik Sleen, the schoolteacher from Minnesota who is to go with Vilhelm. He is said to be well informed and intelligent. They sat and talked until it was very late and I was very sleepy, as were the others, too, I think. Helene shows no embarrassment, but goes to bed no matter how many guests are here.

I wrote industriously all day in the belief that Vilhelm would be going to the post office; but the worthy pastor decided differently and went only for a short ride on his new horse. The latter did not seem to meet with his approval, but what the trouble was, I do not know. At any rate he soon had enough of riding and asked me if I cared to take a little walk; nor did I need to be asked a second time. Vilhelm was going over to his special friend Halvor, who is to be his driver tomorrow. I had not been there before and was pleased to find a clean, orderly cabin, although a veritable crowd of people live there. His place is well situated, and he is the neighbor nearest to the parsonage land. The evening was beautiful; it is really a joy to have Vilhelm with me for a walk; most of the time I have to go and philosophize alone.

Sunday, February 5. Well, I am alone again and will no doubt be alone all week. How I long for the time when there will be a little less traveling, a little more reasonable arrangement, for this one is really all wrong, and, what is worse, is not likely to get better soon.[11]

Vilhelm did not get away until late, because he had to wait for his things to be brought from Aarthun's. At last Erik had to go after them; he came back with the news that the boy who was sick there had died the night before. So it was to end that way!

[11] On this trip Pastor Koren went to Minnesota, where he conducted his first service at Spring Grove on February 9.

While I was writing this afternoon, I was astonished to see Anne [Aarthun] and her old aunt in the doorway. It seemed strange to me that she would care to visit strangers just after such a sorrow; but they must feel or bear their sorrow in a different way from what I could. As I listened to their way of talking of it, I was not able to say a word. "It is a good thing there are no small children," said Anne, "after all, it will not be so difficult for them to manage." It seemed as if the main thing they were thinking of was that the father would not now have his son to help with the work. The mother, too, sat calmly and took part in the talk. They stayed a long time, ate and drank, and left only when it became dark.

It will really be good to have one's own home — how trying such visits can be sometimes, especially on Sunday! Here I sit; I cannot read or busy myself with anything if I am not to offend the guests. I can indeed talk to them, and do so, too, and it is probably my own fault that I find these conversations of so little interest. This is not always true, to be sure; but at times the wish to have a cultured person to talk to becomes very strong. My thoughts prefer to linger elsewhere, and find it intolerable to have to turn back to cattle and swine. Perhaps it will be no different when I have my own home and have similar visits. Oh, yes, it will surely be different. Then I shall be mistress in my own home! Yes, that will be glorious! And then when the pastor returns from his journeys, there certainly will be rejoicing!

Vilhelm has really fine weather for his journey today. I wonder if he has arrived yet; I am glad there is moonlight. It is very quiet here this evening, for Per and Kari have behaved better than yesterday and are now resting with their mother on the bed. Her cough is better, too, and causes less disturbance. Erik is away and Anne [Egge] is studying *Missionsbladet,* and reads half aloud of course, as most of them do. It is a curious custom.[12]

[12] *Missionsbladet* was a semimonthly missionary magazine published in Norway, 1827-60.

Monday, February 6. Today I dispatched my big batch of mail. I hope it will not be too long en route. I was really glad when I had sealed all the letters. When that was done I put on my things to get a little fresh air after the soap and lye odors I have been breathing all day. I took the road to Sør-land's, my favorite walk, but came close to turning back when I came down the hill and met all Erik's cattle pursued by Ingebret's dogs. The dogs barked, the cows bellowed and tried to gore. I plucked up courage and got safely past the whole herd and into the woods. It was not so pleasant there today, for the air was heavy and gray, but it was very quiet — I heard the sound of Ingebret's ax for a moment but saw not a person on the whole walk.

When I was out of the woods, I took the road to the parsonage land. Here to my joy I found tracks made by Vilhelm and Peter. I amused myself by following them until they suddenly turned off I know not where, and I then found myself on the knoll on the parsonage land with that fine view before me. There is a marvelous blue color which at times settles down on the hills at the horizon. Today it varied from a deep sea blue to the loveliest light sky blue. Then I wanted to see how the spot looked where the house was to be placed; I found the spot, too, but not the little valley with the spring. I went on across the hard crust of the snow, which at times carried me and at times let me plump down up to the tops of my high shoes. I walked about amidst the withered foliage and examined the trees to see if I could find some grape-vines, but found not a one, unfortunately. On the other hand I discovered that all the high flower stalks and raspberry stalks were full of delicate vines.

I made a wide circle through the woods and found the tracks of a man, but they stopped suddenly; and so I left the woods and crossed the hard snow, looking for a road, for I did not care to return the way I had come. At last I found a sort of lane I thought would probably lead me to the dapper bachelor's. I was not wrong, and soon came to a regular

road and at last to a human habitation. I wonder if Vilhelm
has taken this road over the bridge under the high trees
which leads to Halvor's; there is a rather wide brook and it is
quite romantic. This is another pretty summer walk for me.

Now I hurried home. I had been walking so long it was
beginning to get dark, and the moon could not penetrate the
dense air. Helene thought I had gone in somewhere for the
evening. As I came in, I met the foster-daughter; she looked
distressed and worn with weeping, poor thing, and had come
to ask Erik to make a coffin for her brother. Think of sending the sister over to get the carpenter to make the coffin for
her dead brother!

It is late (according to the time schedule of this house). A
bed has been made for Anne [Egge] and Kari on the floor;
they are all sound asleep save Erik, whom the missionary
paper keeps awake.

Tuesday, February 7. Knud has gone to Decorah in Erik's
stead and has just driven away with my letters and Erik's wheat.
The wheat today brought the whole household into activity.
There was the machine, of course, to clean it. The cattle
made use of the opportunity whenever no one was watching
and ate heartily. This caused the children to cry out, "The
cows are stealing, ma, they are," which brought Helene from
her washtubs in a hurry and out the door scolding and swing-
ing about her with the wet clothes. This was repeated time
and time again and brought first one, then another, outside,
so that it was exceptionally lively here yesterday morning.
While I sit here writing, I am constantly interrupted by Helene, who is quite in despair over Per's increasing fatness,
does not know how she is ever going to get his pantaloons
large enough, and asks my advice about it.

It is now past eight o'clock. I am waiting for Erik and
Helene to come back from Aarthun's, where they went for
the funeral. Helene had been invited, and Erik had brought
a message that if "the pastor's wife" should care to come with
her, she would be very welcome. I did not care to do this,

much to the astonishment of Helene, who was unable to understand why I did not grasp the opportunity with open arms. They seem to go to a funeral as to a feast. Instead of that I took a very melancholy walk in the Sørland wood; it was not I, but the woods and air which were melancholy. I dropped in on Eli [Sørland], had cake, and talked with her and also with Kari at Katterud's.

When I got home, I was surprised by Halvor, who brought me a greeting from Vilhelm. That was very pleasant. I had no idea he had returned so soon and would gladly have talked longer with him if he had not had to hurry so because of his restless horses. It was good of Vilhelm to send him.

It is taking a long time for them to return from the funeral. I sit here with sleeping beings on all sides of me. Kari and Per rolled about on the mattress on the floor until they fell asleep; they are still lying there, Per with his nose in the air. Anders, Helene's stepson, who came here this forenoon, laid both his arms on the kitchen bench, buried his face in them, and sits snoring full blast.[13] Anne sits with a book in her hands, nodding until her head touches the book and rouses her for a moment. Such is the scene this evening.

Knud got only halfway to Decorah; he met a man on the road who told him the mill had had a breakdown; so he turned back again, and brought us neither table nor chairs, nor *Emigranten,* nor letters. How tiresome!

Wednesday, February 8. We have just finished supper. Helene made soup, which might have been good enough if she had not put in some lumps of meal which were supposed to be dumplings. I thought of "die schönen Klöse," which we despised aboard ship; they were matchless indeed, compared with these.[14] However, I ate a little of the soup and almost laughed aloud when, after I had refused the meat, Erik said, "Perhaps you liked the soup so well you filled up on that." Rognald's brother is here helping Erik. They both very

[13] Anders Anderson Egge was Helene's stepson, the son of her first husband by an earlier marriage; information received from William Linnevold.
[14] See chapter 2, footnote 10.

eagerly scan *Emigranten,* which Erik brought from Decorah; he was there this morning, but afoot, so we have not yet obtained our things, which it seems will never get here. No letters. I wish I could stop expecting them; then I should not be so disappointed every time Erik comes home empty-handed.

There have been many people here today. Eli, with her milk pail, was first, then Sigrid Suckow; both of them spent all forenoon here. Several men also came to talk to Erik. Helene had no more than cleared the table before she had to set it again, and so all day long we have had a constant smell of pork. Anne, from her place by the window, spied out who was coming, one after the other, whether walking or driving. Of course this is not something that happens every day, so it is not strange that both large and small have felt impelled to run from window to window to figure out who the next ones might be. We have also had a visit from two peddlers, or whatever one calls such itinerant people. They had a great deal of trumpery for sale, which Helene and Anne went outside to examine, while I stood at the window with the children and looked at the pretty horses, which ought to be used for something better than this.

Erik brought candle snuffers with him from Decorah, to the great joy of Per and Kari, who do not tire of looking at them, and of me no less; I am thereby relieved of the necessity, every time I have snuffed the light, of going over to the stove to throw the wick into the fire. Per is giving our laughing muscles no rest; he was told to be quiet and go to sleep; but instead, like a little brownie in his red cap, he is lying in the middle of the large bed, acting like a clown, as he often does, and mimicking everything that is said.

Thursday, February 9. This time Vilhelm has beautiful weather for his travels. It is a lovely evening. Just as the sun was setting, I took a walk to where Halvor lives and came home by moonlight. Vilhelm really must go over there with me at sunset; it was lovely this afternoon. There are many charming walks hereabouts. I thought of crawling under a fence to a road at the left of Halvor's which probably led to Ingebret's; but as I did not know how far it might be, I took the same road home, gazed at the moon, and watched the stars come out.

I have been very industrious today — ironed, cut out a basque and apron for Kari, finished my waist, read for a long time after dinner — and I marvel that tomorrow is already Friday. This week has gone remarkably fast, and that is unusual, for Vilhelm is away; when he is gone the days are long, as a rule. Yes, Sunday was long enough this time, too, but now Saturday will be here day after tomorrow.

I ate some time ago, fortunately; otherwise I should have quite lost my appetite watching Erik and Tollef. They are eating soup with pork and dumplings swimming in fat and are conscientiously licking the backs of their spoons after each mouthful.[15]

That poor clock dangling on the wall can never, it seems, be left in peace. Yesterday Helene could not get the clock to go fast enough, so she moved it ahead one half hour after another, and this evening she has fussed and tinkered with it until it stands completely still. Well, now we shall have to use the sun for a clock, if it will only be kind enough to show itself! That clock causes Helene endless trouble. At a moment when we are sitting quite peacefully, she is likely to cry out, "Can't you be quiet, children, so I can hear if the clock is running?" If, as is usually the case, it is not running, she takes it down, gets on her knees before the table, and begins to shake and wind it endlessly until she has it running again after a fashion — as long as that lasts.

Friday, February 10. I just returned from my usual walk and brought back a splendid appetite, which fortunately will soon be satisfied, for Helene is already setting the table. My walk took me to Aarthun's; I went in for a while to assure

[15] Tollef has not been identified. He may have been a carpenter working for Erik Egge, who put up a number of buildings in the settlement.

myself that the old aunt was not offended because I had
not come the other day. She had not been; and I was glad I
had not gone when Helene finally came home that evening
(which was not until after ten — Anne had fallen fast asleep)
and told me there had been a great many strangers. "It was
well that madam was not there," she added, "for she would
not have felt at home, the floor was so dirty, and the room
was so warm and filled with children." That might not have
been so bad, but to see a lively party on such an occasion
would not have been pleasant. From Helene's account it seems
that they had visited and enjoyed themselves as best they
could.

I had company home in the person of my little friend
Karen, who was going to Erik's to get an auger, and talked
and prattled the whole way. There has been a great rummag-
ing about in the loft today to move the clothes and set up a
quilt frame for Helene, who is going to tie a quilt; in this
work I am to have my share.[16]

It is really a pity Erik did not go for the table and chairs
as he said he would; now we shall not have even them when
Vilhelm returns. Tomorrow by this time he will be here, I
hope. Today he was to be at Erik [Sleen], the schoolmaster's.[17]
This week I have done hardly any writing save in my diary; I
had no special desire to do so, and since there was no hurry,
I preferred to put it off.

[16] Karen was possibly one of the Aarthun children.
[17] Erik Ellefson Sleen was the first treasurer of the Spring Grove-Big Canoe
(Minnesota) congregation, 1855; O. M. Norlie, *Norsk lutherske menigheder i
Amerika, 1843-1916*, 1:454 (Minneapolis, 1918). Norlie erroneously spells the
name Steen. According to Professor S. S. Reque of Decorah, who met a
descendant of Erik Sleen at the hundredth anniversary of the Big Canoe congregation, Sleen lived in the Big Canoe neighborhood. He later moved to
Lansing, Iowa, and then to South Dakota, where he became somewhat prominent in politics.

11

The Land for the Parsonage

Sunday, February 19. It is now more than a week since I
have had my diary out; my eyes have pained me — a cold from
a draft, perhaps — so that I have been unable to work, much
less write. Now, God be praised, I am well again; I was really
tired of sitting so long with nothing to occupy me but some
knitting. But I have had Vilhelm home all the past week,
God be praised. It is a long time since he has been left in
peace for so many days. Now he is on the move again; he left
at eight this morning for Whisky Grove, where he will stay a
couple of days. He went by sleigh (a half-finished sleigh
without a seat, sitting on my cloak, with his bag tied on behind), and probably has not made fast progress, for it has been
so mild these last days that most of the snow has melted.

We had much company today. They have just gone, and
have left me a quiet hour before sundown to do a little writing; I dare not yet use my eyes by candlelight. I had just laid
my book away, after having read a sermon, when Anne Aarthun came over with at least five children, the oldest not yet

nine, the youngest not a year old. All these youngsters, together with Kari and Per, made the house lively indeed today; they stormed the stairs to the loft until they were tired enough to accept the more peaceful diversion of driving the sleighs and horses and looking after the chickens which I cut out for them; it kept my fingers busy.[1] Suckow, with his wife and little Ludvig, came over before Anne and her flock started home; they talked of pastors and sectarians, as he always does when Sigrid is with him. They have gone now, too, and everything is back to normal. Helene swept the room for the seventh time this afternoon; now she is waiting for the water to boil so she can cook porridge, and is scolding Per, who every now and then peeks under the lid and cries, "Now it's boiling, ma."

I am sitting by the window at Vilhelm's table, glad I can begin this work again. I have been so much at a loss without it that I have quite forgotten how the days passed this last week.

Last Saturday afternoon, while I was in the loft with Anne (we were just putting the finishing touches on a quilt, and had been busy all day), the pastor appeared, driving up in state with a team and everything, and a boy for driver. This time he had been in Minnesota. From now on his journeys will be a little more sensible, I hope. He had work enough that week — preached every other day and had twelve baptisms in one day, besides all the other duties.

On Sunday, services were held at Rognald Belle's, or Vesle Rognald, as he is called.[2] I drove there with Erik Skaarlia, Eli's father, in a wagon drawn by oxen, which I thought would never get us there, so slowly did they drag themselves along. It was quite a procession! Guri Skaarlia sat in front, enthroned upon a little footstool; Helene, Anne, and I on a board in the middle; behind us sat Eli on a heap of hay, and then we had three of Ingebret's pigs galloping after us like a

---

[1] The sleighs and animals were of course cut from paper.
[2] *Vesle* might be translated as "younger," "little," or "junior."

pack of hounds.[3] It was a perfect spring day. A large crowd had gathered at Rognald's, where a few boards in the ceiling had been taken up so that many could take places in the loft. We stayed as usual and had dinner, the Aarthun family, too. Furniture is scarce at Vesle Rognald's — no chairs, and only a large chest to serve as a table. We drove home with Knud. All the low places were under water, it was so mild that day.

On Monday one of my eyes began to pain me. But it was not so bad that I could not put a bandage over it and go for a walk with Vilhelm in the beautiful weather. We followed a road across Erik's field, which I had not crossed before, and saw two deer. They stood still quite near at hand and looked at us, then took flight, leaping out of sight with the most graceful movements. It is strange that they live so close to human habitations.

We called on the Skaarlias, whom we had not visited before. Here the walls were whitewashed and everything was so clean and shining that it was a delight. As we declined to stay for supper, we were given delicious milk to refresh us, and cakes. We went home by way of the Kvale land, and, in looking about for a nice building site, sank to our knees in the snow through the deceptive top crust, and had to cut the most pitiful capers to get on top again. Then we got into the woods, where the branches, which reach almost to the ground, caught my coat and veil so that I could scarcely get through. Since Vilhelm led the way, we went right through high hazel brush, of course; in short, we had a most laborious march until we got out of the Kvale land and into Sørland's territory. Tomorrow the decision will be made as to whether it shall continue to be called the Kvale land or shall become our dwelling place.[4]

[3] Erik Clementson Skaarlia was the father of Eli Sørland and of Embret, who worked for a time at the parsonage. The family later took the name of Clement. They now live in Section 1, Springfield Township, Winneshiek County. The Korens moved to the Skaarlia home May 2, 1854. In the original text Mrs. Koren here calls Mrs. Skaarlia *Skaarlikjærringa;* that is "the Skaarlia woman."

[4] According to William Linnevold, Iver Peterson Kvale lived to the west of the parsonage land. He also owned the eighty-acre tract to the east that was bought for the parsonage in Section 12, Springfield Township.

Knud-on-the-Hill and Ingeborg came over to talk to Vilhelm and stayed until late in the evening. I had not pictured Knud-on-the-Hill, of whom people speak so often, as such a small, quiet, sensible man.[5] We got to bed late that evening. Erik had gone to Decorah with Suckow and Knud [Aarthun]. When it got to be nine and then ten o'clock and he had not returned, Helene began to cry and carry on because he was not home; she just would not listen to reason, and at last took Anne and went to Aarthun's to see what she could learn. Vilhelm and I were alone with the two children; he would have gone with her, had I not been reluctant to stay alone. No doubt the men ended up at Katterud's for dinner, unless they went farther to look for land.

Today an American was here and took Anne into his service, so now I cannot get her even if I wished to. Paulsen in Decorah outdoes himself in sending us gifts. Recently we received four fowls, and yesterday Erik brought eggs from him. So today I had a splendid dinner consisting of soft-boiled eggs and fried partridge. It is a welcome change from that everlasting salt pork.[6]

Wednesday, February 22. It was almost three o'clock before Vilhelm returned yesterday, and then all he did was pack his gown in my old brown cloak, which has to be used in so many ways, fasten it as best he could on the back of his horse, and ride away. Now and then he gave the dangling bundle a shove to keep it in some sort of equilibrium. He did not expect to get back that evening and I was just as well pleased, for it became very dark, and the road passes over a black prairie.

The Kvale land has been purchased for the parsonage; that is the result of the committee's meeting this time, an outcome with which we are well satisfied. I like the land very much, provided water is not too hard to get. Now, at last, it is time

[5] William Linnevold believes that Knud and Ingeborg were Knud and Ingeborg Hauge, who settled on the northwest quarter of Section 2, Springfield Township, Winneshiek County.

[6] Anne is presumably Anne Egge, Helene Egge's stepdaughter. Paulsen is thought by Mr. Linnevold to have been a real-estate operator.

to think of the parsonage. We must go up there, if Vilhelm can only find time, and pick out an appropriate building site. It is decided, then, that we shall be living here where we first found shelter, in the most densely populated part of the settlement; it is very pleasant, too, to live so near people.

I waited a long time for Vilhelm this morning. We had promised to visit Ingebret, and I had just thought of going on ahead when Vilhelm came riding at full gallop with a red-checkered cotton handkerchief tied about his ears as a protection against the strong wind. He had spent the night at the bride's home, where there had been a big party. But I went on ahead to Sørland's just the same, hurrying as fast as I could to get down into the valley away from the biting wind. But it seems I was not to make much speed, for when I reached the brook, I found it had left its banks and filled the valley where we usually cross it. I walked back and forth, looking for a place to get across, and at last came to a place where a narrow plank had been laid. It was so slippery and icy that I was fairly sure that I would fall if I went out on it. But I was going to attempt it and, was just waiting for an opportune moment before a new gust of wind came, when I saw Ingebret run down from the house and take a course in another direction. I turned that way, too, and found a passable crossing.

The brook looked so different; where it was deepest, it had swelled into a veritable lake and the large trees stood far out in the water. Ingebret cuts down so much of his timber. I do wish he would not chop down those pretty trees that are standing on both sides of the brook. We say enough to him about it, both Vilhelm and I, but we do not seem to make any great impression. "Eli, she wants to see the fields," he says; but really it is just on account of those wretched cattle, which always must come first.

Old Thrond Lommen had dinner there and talked about the parsonage land; Ingebret is not at all satisfied with the purchase of it. Ingebret, by the way, sat and talked a great deal about this and that and said, "It is very queer — every-thing about this affair — one would hardly believe it." Eli set forth great quantities of food at noon and again at four. We ate what we could and went home.

When we got home, there was still a little hour of twilight; then Vilhelm turned to his work and kept busy until the family had gone to bed. When they have done so, we have a gay time to ourselves, communicate by means of notes, prac-tice pantomime, at which we have become fairly adept, and are just like two children, happy to be free from all restraint for a little while.

Thursday, February 23. Vilhelm is away today, too; there is a meeting at Sørland's about building the church. Perhaps he will soon be back; he went there early this forenoon, after first having seen Erik off to fetch Torger Luraas' wagon so that he will have something to travel in when he goes to Paint Creek Saturday.[7]

The snow has melted now. The wind is so cold that I do not feel like taking a walk. I sat and read and knitted, and was tired of having to stop so often because first Suckow, then Aarthun dropped in; it is hardly proper for me to con-tinue to read then — in any event I dare not do it, for I do not want these good men to have any cause for criticism.

It is now evening. I am expecting Vilhelm any moment; the meeting must soon be over. The evening has gone much more rapidly than it usually does when Vilhelm is away. Helene is sewing a new hat for herself; she has a veritable passion for such bonnets, as she calls them. This is the fourth since we came here. And when this task is in process, her in-dustry surpasses all bounds; she scarcely even has time to watch the pork. Per sits at the table with two bonnets on and jabbers so that we can scarcely hear our own voices. I cro-cheted and thought of how we may best arrange our future

[7] Torger Luraas took land in Section 31, Highland Township, Winneshiek County; the property was situated about eleven miles northeast of Decorah. This information was received from his granddaughter, Mrs. John Thingvold of Decorah.

home. And now we must eat, for it does not look as if Vilhelm will honor us with his presence.

Friday, February 24. Vilhelm came back yesterday just as
I had eaten. He was well satisfied with the outcome of the
meeting about building the church. There was general agreement, and a great many things were decided. In the future,
services are to be held in three places in the settlement — in
our neighborhood they will be at Vesle Rognald's, so we shall
not have very far to go. When the candidates for confirmation also meet in one place I hope there will be fewer trips
for Vilhelm — at any rate not such long ones. Subscription
lists for the parsonage land have also been started; so it looks
now as though there is daylight ahead.

Erik surprised us by getting home with the wagon last night,
and now Vilhelm has something in which to ride to Paint
Creek tomorrow. Knud Aarthun brought his two daughters
to register.[8] Vilhelm examined them at such length that they
stayed and helped us eat our last partridge, which was excellent. I should not mind if Paulsen sent us more. We have
lived like lords lately, with soft-boiled eggs for breakfast and
wild fowl for dinner. Now that glory is past and pork will
have to do for a day.

We have had most beautiful spring weather; the sun is
actually getting higher; it is just as high now as in April or
May at home. We have the door open and go in and out without wraps. I knit and watch Kari and Per so that they do not
stray into all the ponds. Vilhelm, with Knud, inspects his
wagon from time to time and chases the Sørland pigs, which
are very fond of our society and roam about rooting up the
ground; there are six of them, each one fatter and uglier than
the next, and they sniff and grunt, to our disgust, but to Per's
great delight, for he is never happier than when he sees them
all around him and can cry, "Here come the piggies; come
piggy, piggy!" When we get our own house, one of the first
things will be to get a fence about it so that I may escape

[8] That is, to register for confirmation.

this business of having the cows wash the windows for me with their muzzles.

Today Vilhelm took a holiday, as he says, and we have used that holiday for a long walk on our land. We left while the sun was still high and went around Tollefsjord's farm to the parsonage land. It was so warm I could hardly bear to keep my shawl on, and Vilhelm did not even wear a scarf. We walked all over the land looking for a suitable location for the house. It is not hard to find pretty sites. There is one elevation from which one has as lovely a view as I have seen here — across field and meadow, woods and ridges. The house is not to be there, however, but on a slope nearby, closer to the woods. I shall be happy if it is placed there; it will be some distance from the spring, but that always happens if the building site is to be at all attractive. We also went down to the spring and walked about in the water and mud.

We rejoiced over the natural beauty of the location and are happy indeed that it was chosen. We went home by way of Sørland's and stopped to gaze at my rugged old oak, which, Vilhelm tried to maintain, is no finer than many of its neighbors. If it is not, it is at least more imposing; it is immense in extent and circumference. It is the largest oak I have seen.[9]

We spent the greater part of the evening near the open door, behind us a stove that was red-hot because of some peas which had been given to Helene that had to be cooked for a long time before they became tender. Erik drew a sketch of our house, but it was rejected. Vilhelm was more successful, but concluded that if they do not build the house larger than they are now planning, we shall scarcely be able to move about in it.

Saturday, February 25. It is so dark both outside and inside

[9] Mrs. Caroline K. Naeseth says that in the woods to the north of the parsonage "there was an old oak, called the Big Oak, which had, I believe, seven large trunks with one crown. It stood on a green slope, and the branches spread far out and hung down low so that they formed the most delightful arbor. Everyone felt the loss when the tree grew too old and had to be taken down." See "Minder fra Little Iowa Prestegaard," in *Folkekalender 1933,* 11 (Minneapolis, 1933). This series of *Folkekalender* began in 1892.

that I am in danger of becoming melancholy, and must try to divert my thoughts by writing a little. Vilhelm has gone to Paint Creek and will be away more than a week, for he will also visit the settlements to the south. We were busy baking communion wafers this morning; I had forgotten that it had to be done. Ingebret was here before Vilhelm left and got a subscription list which he is to take care of. He said something about Nils [Katterud] having managed to obtain twenty acres of the parsonage land, to the great sorrow of Ingebret, who considers the action very wrong and is doing all he can to get it changed. It looks as if he might succeed. He is an unusual man, this Ingebret. There is something sincere and straightforward about him and he undoubtedly means well in all he says and does.

It was ten o'clock by the time Vilhelm had everything ready. He had a good deal of trouble getting under way. In the first place the horse was lame when he brought it out; next he discovered half a shoe missing on one of the hind hoofs. One of the wagon wheels needed to be replaced; it will be a stroke of fortune if it lasts this trip. At last the horse was hitched up and the miserable harness patched and tied together as well as possible. Now the question was, how to carry the wine with him. He had to take the whole jug along, lashing it fast, and his bag, too. At last everything was ready. If he went as slowly as he did while I could see him, he certainly did not reach his destination early in the evening; but I comforted myself with Erik's assurance that the horse would soon recover. I hope the wagon holds out.

I do not know why I am so much more reluctant to see Vilhelm go this time than before. I ought to be more accustomed to his leaving and should be satisfied with his having been home fourteen days. But the feeling is there; I can do nothing about it; and it is not something I can become accustomed to. But I shall manage to be in good spirits before he returns.

This morning I went up to my trunk for some things and ran across *Valdemar Seier*; I began to read a little, and soon found I could not tear myself away. Since Helene was scouring the floor below, I seated myself on the chest and read until the disturbance was over. Then I had to go down to the world below, which at times is unreasonably prosaic and has no savor at all for one who has just come from the company of knights and ladies.[10]

At the moment Helene is at Aarthun's, and the children are sitting on the table watching for her very impatiently, expecting her to return with a puppy. I was just interrupted by Ingebret, who had made the rounds with his list and wished to speak to Erik. He was well satisfied with the results. I hear many have subscribed, even though they do not belong to the congregation.

Sunday, February 26. It will soon be dark and the day will be over, for as soon as we have eaten and read a little, the family goes to bed, whether the clock says seven or eight. Today the same gray, monotonous weather as yesterday. We have not seen the sun, so I have no idea of the time; but I suspect I ate dinner at eleven o'clock. It has been a quiet day with nothing to enliven it. Erik left early in the morning, we knew not where; he came back a little while ago, smoked a pipe, and went over to Aarthun's. For the greater part of the afternoon Helene lay on the bed and complained of a headache. I have been reading all day; time drags, however, when one reads so uninterruptedly without speaking a word from morning to night; I get tired, even though I am interested in what I read. Thus I spent the day. My whole conversation has been confined to quieting Kari and Per, and that has not been often, for most of the time they sat, one on the table, the other on the bench, afraid of the puppy which Helene brought yesterday. At last they both took refuge behind the curtain and crawled into bed with Helene, where, to judge by the silence, all three have fallen asleep. So, for the moment, I am alone.

[10] Bernhard S. Ingemann's *Valdemar Seier* (Valdemar Victorious) was a Danish historical novel that appeared in Copenhagen in 1826. The chest that Mrs. Koren used for a seat was in the loft.

When I sit alone in this way and all is quiet about me, my thoughts naturally tend to cross the Atlantic and dwell on earlier days. But when Vilhelm is away, I am not always rightly disposed for such memories and would rather keep them away. When I get my own home, this too will change, I believe; I rejoice more and more at the thought of our home, and especially every time Vilhelm returns from a journey.

Now it is dark, and I see a man coming who is evidently Erik-on-the-Hill.[11]

Monday, February 27. I was awakened this morning, and also several times during the night, by Burman's (the puppy's) whining. This morning the children made a great racket, yelling and jumping up on whatever was nearest, to save themselves from the poor creature. It is certainly lucky that it came while Vilhelm is away; when they get used to it, there will be less noise. It is a source of pleasure, however, not least to Helene and Erik. Per has just now taken off both his stockings, placed the dog upon them, hitched them to his boots, and well content with his heroic deed, cries, "Don't laugh, now, ma, now the dog is going to have a ride."

We had unexpected guests yesterday, namely, Anne Aarthun, who had been over at Sørland's and presumably had talked her fill concerning the parsonage land and the subscriptions, which naturally are their topics for the present, and Knud, who accompanied Erik home; they stayed for supper this evening. Helene made corn cakes, which tasted very good both to the guests and me. Then we had a lively discussion about the Sørland cattle and the beauty of the calves, while I was busy talking with Knud about the best place for a garden next summer. I heard to my joy that I "cannot get finer land than what was planted to Indian corn there last year."

Now it is afternoon. There has been, as usual, clothes washing and floor scrubbing. I intended to write, but had to

---

[11] Erik Olsen Bakke (1824-1908) married Gunhilda Ramsey in Norway and came to this country in 1851. He settled in Section 5, Frankville Township, Winneshiek County; Bailey, *Winneshiek County*, 2:64.

leave my work every now and then to run and drive that impudent cow away from the washtub.

I have just returned from Katterud's, where I stayed for dinner. A young boy was there whose family intends to buy the remainder of the Kvale land — an old acquaintance of Nils from Muskego. I thought I was surely going to drown in mud on the first part of the road from Nils's house — where there is new "breaking" and the walking is dreadful in either snow or mud.[12] I actually had to walk with a stick in my hand and scrape off my galoshes to keep the mud from going over my shoes. Yesterday I walked down to the bottoms, as I intended, and saw Erik; I found a path which led me straight to [John] Dysja's, where I went in and visited the little child who was so ill, but is now better.

Today is already the last day of February. If Erik does not bring back letters from Decorah tomorrow, it will really be too bad.

Wednesday, March 1. So today we write March 1, and today my little goddaughter will be three years old; since it is Wednesday, it may be that Christiane is there and gives her goose coffee in my place.[13] Would that I knew a little better how all the dear folks at home are getting on! No one went to Decorah today, unfortunately, so I live in the same uncertainty.

This month is beginning with rain and thunderstorms. Just as I was thinking of taking a walk to refresh myself after ironing this morning, it began to patter against the windowpanes and has kept on ever since. It is well Vilhelm took his umbrella with him. But how is it with our baggage during such weather?

There is a bellowing and racket here by all the wonderful Sørland calves, which are running round the house and licking the windowpanes. The door is open and the children run back and forth, transported by the event. Then Nils Katterud came here to fetch them [*the calves*] home for Ingebret. I was

---

[12] "Breaking" is land newly broken up by the plow.
[13] Goose coffee was make-believe coffee.

standing in the door to enjoy the fresh smell of the rain, so he came up and greeted me with his peculiar, awkward bow and stopped for a little chat.

Yesterday we had a prairie fire near us. It was on Thorgrim's field and fairly violent, but did not last long.[14] I get quite frightened when I see them so close at hand, for I have not yet become used to fires of that kind. The other evening we saw prairie fires in four places at one time; they are spreading every day now. I think I shall have to give up my usual walk today, for the rain does not let up. Well, I am content to see it rain, if only spring comes soon. I long for it very much and rejoice at the prospect.

It does not look as though I shall get letters written to Mrs. Garrigues and Mrs. Lund while Vilhelm is away. I have no desire to write, and so I do nothing.

Anne Aarthun is here to talk to Erik, and therefore we are to eat supper, although it is hardly four o'clock.

Thursday, March 2. What weather we are having today! It is blowing as if it would break down the windows and doors. At noon the sun shone a little, but this forenoon it rained so hard that water streamed in the door. I hope Vilhelm is not on the road today.

Erik is in Decorah. I am sitting, as I have done many times, waiting for him to return, with a faint hope that he will bring letters. God grant we may not be disappointed this time, too!

It is getting toward evening. The day has gone quickly and agreeably with steady work and reading; it has been still and peaceful save for the noise of Per and Burman. Since tomorrow is Friday, it will not be long before Vilhelm comes, I hope. I wish I might have the joy of giving him news from home.

It is now our usual bedtime, but Erik has not come home. I am glad that Helene is not so anxious as she was last time, although she is uneasy and runs outside every few moments.

[14] By Thorgrim she means Thorgrim Busness.

But there is no reason for anxiety, for she knows the mill is not yet entirely ready, and moreover, is overfilled with grain. I spent the evening reading as usual; but it is so disagreeable today. The wind has increased in violence, and howls and whistles so frightfully that one hates to be alone in the evening. I only hope Vilhelm is not out in this. It is fearfully dark, too; one can scarcely see one's hand in front of one. I see Helene is going to bed. I thought she would sit up and wait, but I have nothing against going to bed myself and forgetting the storm and bad weather, if that is possible. It really sounds as if the house would be blown away.

Friday, March 3. Beautiful sunshine, but about the same wind today. I have no desire to venture out, but sit and wait for Helene to return from Aarthun's; she went there at last to seek comfort, for Erik has not yet returned. Suckow calmed her this morning by telling her that he had heard the mill had broken down again and that those who were there had had to wait for their flour. But now she thinks it has taken too long.

The sun is well on its way. I just laid aside my knitting and Irving's *Sketch Book*, with which I amused myself this afternoon. My attention was divided between them and looking after the fire in the stove (with which I have great trouble, running out time and again for chips), and finally, seeing to it that the children do not tease poor Burman to death. Now Per has tied his shoes to the dog's tail, his stockings to the shoes, and filled both of them with chips, and has climbed upon the table and now is laughing so hard he is in danger of falling as he watches the dog pull that load around the room.

Helene has returned without hearing from Decorah, but with a promise that someone would go down the road at sundown if he still had not come. She is now quite inconsolable, weeps, and does not know what to believe. I hope he comes before dark. I hope I shall not lose courage so easily if now and then Vilhelm is later than may reasonably be expected.

Saturday, March 4. Well, all grief and fright ended in joy yesterday, although it had looked as if Helene would have to take her anxiety to bed with her. After we had eaten and she had washed the dishes and put the children to bed, she went over to Aarthun's again; I sat here alone, which I did not like doing the last time this happened. This time, however, I felt no anxiety, but quietly awaited Helene's return. As the wind had died down, it was not disagreeable. The sunset had been beautiful, and now there was a peaceful, clear, starlit evening after the stormy day, which with its lovely sunshine and strong, gusty wind reminded me of that fearful day of storm on the Atlantic Ocean. Sooner than I had expected, Helene returned with smiling face and said that as she neared Aarthun's she heard Erik coming and so had hurried back that he might not see her. When at last he came, she received him as if nothing had happened. How strange they are, these people! The mill had been filled up, of course, and so he had had to wait.

No letters this time either, not even an *Emigranten*! The mail from Wisconsin had not come; very likely it cannot get across the river on account of the ice; possibly that is also the reason we have heard nothing of our baggage. But now it is all of five months since we heard from home. Not a line from anyone since we arrived here. I only hope those at home do not have to wait so long for our letters!

The first thing I heard this morning when I awoke was Anne Aarthun's voice; she had come to inquire about Erik. She stayed, of course, half the forenoon, and then Helene began cleaning. I took a brisk walk, clad in full winter dress because it was blowing lustily. I walked straight into the wind, with coat and veil fluttering in all directions, around the Sørland hill, over to look at my old oak; then, I thought, I should be able to realize what it was like on the parsonage land in such a wind. I turned off a little too soon and came upon two men who were chopping rails for Nils Katterud. I talked with them a little and rendered an accounting of when the "Father" was coming home, whereafter I continued my way toward the hill.[15] It was not very pleasant on the parsonage land today; the light was not advantageous and it was blowing hard, of course. I do not know where we can place a house so that it will be sheltered from the west wind, unless we set it in the midst of the woods. I went back and forth for a long time, hunting for a building site, and made very practical calculations for outhouses, garden, and all, and considered which vegetables should be planted this summer.

These household thoughts occupied me so completely that I walked right into a marshy spot; I leaped over very quickly, lest possibly some snake might have come out unusually early and been sunning himself in the warm mud, for "I am so afraid of snakes that it is dreadful." Really, I grieve every time I am on one of my excursions to think that soon I shall not be able to go about peacefully wherever I please, but must keep to the main road.

The sun is setting, and soon this week will be over. Helene has just come back from Aarthun's, bringing with her a chicken and a jug of beer as an addition to our larder. In honor of this, mush is being cooked for supper and Kari and Per are dancing around the stove for joy. Now I shall put this away and go outside and look at the evening sky, as I usually do; tonight is so lovely, I wish Vilhelm could be here to see it.

Sunday, March 5. I am so angry with the Decorah post office! Old Ola, the smith, and his son-in-law stopped by this forenoon to tell Erik that a letter was waiting for him at the post office; the smith had been there and had actually challenged the postmaster to show him all the letters.[16] Erik has been there almost every week and yet each time has had a chance to see only a couple of packs of letters, which were supposed to be all there were. The letter there now is said to have lain there a long time. This is certainly a fine post office! If Vilhelm has time, he will have to go himself, if that will

[15] The "Father" was the pastor.
[20] William Linnevold believes "Old Ola" might be Ola Nesheim, who lived about one mile southwest of the parsonage land.

help. We all agree that this post office simply will not do, and yet all our letters are dated from there.

My walk took me to Sørland's today; I had an errand to Ingebret, whom I found home alone reading his Bible. I sat there for a time and talked with him of this and that, likewise of our future home, which he has very little hope will be ready before autumn. It is said that subscriptions are coming slowly out in the western part of the settlement. That it will not be very soon, I understand well enough; we must be patient!

Sigrid Suckow was sitting here when I came home, talking of her favorite pastor, Dietrichson, and of Ingebretsen.[17] She also told a good deal about the suffering of the newcomers during their first years in America. If those coming later knew what was in store for them, they would no doubt think more seriously before they left the fatherland.

Monday, March 6. I have half a notion Vilhelm will be here today, although it is unreasonable to expect him so soon. Tomorrow, perhaps. This time he will certainly expect me to have letters for him, and he will be disappointed again. It is still early in the day. I have just finished two beautiful drawings for Per with all sorts of domestic animals, and I made a circuit of the fields in this lovely weather and fresh morning air. Now I must try to be industrious.

I have now taken my customary walk. I went to the parsonage land today, too. It was very lovely there this evening. I stood still, was filled with joy at its beauty, and cannot say how happy I am to have my wish that there might be natural beauty where we are to live. It is a mild, delightful evening, almost too warm to wear a shawl. All the time I kept wishing I might meet Vilhelm; but I suppose it was a silly wish, for I do not even know if he will come by that road. I passed

[17] The Reverend J. W. C. Dietrichson (1815-83) organized the Koshkonong, Luther Valley, and eight other Norwegian Lutheran congregations in Dane County, Wisconsin. Most of the Norwegian settlers on Washington Prairie east of Decorah came from Dane County, Wisconsin. Ingebretsen has not been identified.

through Sørland's woods and looked at Ingebret's split rails and had some trouble getting through all the felled trees. He has let a good deal of daylight into his woods since we arrived. When I got down to Erik's field I halted, quite alarmed at seeing three or four half rings of fire encircling the hills to the east, one beyond the other. They were the prairie fires, which rage everywhere now. These were far away. All day, indeed, there has been a strong smell from them, just as when the east wind blew at home and brought us the smoke from the charcoal pits in Yttersø on summer evenings.[18]

[18] Yttersø was a farmstead or estate east of Larvik, Norway.

12

From Egge's to Sørland's

Tuesday, March 7. Just after I had taken out my work and
we had lit the light last evening, Per cried, "There comes the
pastor!" and sure enough, it was Vilhelm who stopped at the
door. So I was not disappointed in my expectations after all,
although his coming was a surprise. I had every reason not to
expect him — but so much the better. The wagon, it seems,
had held together, and Charlie, or whatever the horse is called, had brought it safely through the deep mire. Vilhelm surprised me by bringing out one gift after another. First a
cheese, which is to be kept in the cellar until it is sufficiently
aged — it was from Gunhild Ederklep in the Norway settlement; then a big box of eggs, also from the same worthy Gunhild Ederklep; and finally a pretty fan.[1] It was the tail of
bird, just as nature had formed it. That was from a young

[1] Gunhild Ederklep was probably the wife of Thorkild Ederklep (or Eite-
klep) of Numedal, Norway, who in 1849 moved into the Norway settlement
near St. Olaf, Clayton County, Iowa. See Jacob Tanner, "En kort beretning
over 50 aars kirkelig arbeide i Clayton County, Iowa," in *Lutheraneren*, vol.
8, no. 45, p. 707 (October 25, 1901); and Bredesen, in *Symra*, 101 (1907).

*g*irl, Anna Gunderson by name.[2] It would have made a sensation at a ball back in Norway and would have given the gentlemen something to talk about.

Last night had an unexpected ending in other ways, too. The family had gone to bed some time earlier, and Vilhelm was reading my diary, which is one of the first things he does when he gets home, when we heard Helene begin to complain about not feeling well. Erik got up; and at last it came out that they could not very well house us any longer, for Helene was not well and found it too burdensome. This was very sudden and unexpected. Helene had not been very well for a couple of days, I knew; but it had not occurred to me that for this reason we should have to move. I do not believe she is ill because of increased work while we have been here, but rather because of carrying water and all the care of the cattle, which are too much for her now.[3] On the other hand, I find it very reasonable that she wants us to leave. But it will not be easy to get other lodging. Decorah will be the only solution, to begin with; but it will not be satisfactory to stay there all the time until our house is ready, and it will be very inconvenient, too, for Vilhelm. I have no desire to move there, but what are we to do? Oh, to have one's own home and do one's own housekeeping! Helene is feeling poorly today, too. I took a long walk with Vilhelm early this morning; it was well we went then, for the weather has suddenly turned bad, with snow and sleet.

Wednesday, March 8. Vilhelm rode to Decorah this morning to inquire about lodgings. This time he will probably be back early, although he will not be able to ride fast in the heavy snow which fell last night — more than I have seen at one time here. But it is melting very fast and the south wind has started to blow, so no doubt this wintry prospect will soon disappear.

[2] Anna Gunderson might be a daughter of Tallak Gunderson, who in 1849 took land in the Turkey River settlement in Clayton County; Tanner in *Lutheraneren,* vol. 8, no. 45, p. 706.

[3] A daughter, Magdalena, was born to Erik and Helene Egge on May 9, 1854. She married Gudbrand E. Sørland (later Soland).

We have lived here for some time now, but I have not yet described how our first home in America was arranged. The whole house is fifteen feet wide and sixteen feet long and consists of one room and the loft. About a third of the room is partitioned off by a shining chintz curtain with large, variegated flowers, which win universal admiration from those who visit Helene; they think they are "frightfully fine flowers." This curtained space is again divided by another, which thus forms the two sleeping chambers, with half a window for each; actually each has just room for a bed.[4]

One wall of our chamber is full of nails; on one of these hang a dusty little bottle and a big pair of sheep shears; above the head of the bed hangs the towel. Under the ceiling there is a shelf; Erik keeps his writing case on it and there, too, Vilhelm's clay pipes have their place, from which I should prefer they never descended, for there is a horrid smell from that molasses tobacco, with whose aroma Erik blissfully fills the room when he is home. On this shelf there is also a large box of cigars, from which I daily bring down a supply by crawling up on the bed. On this bed lie Vilhelm's dressing gown, toilet case, a cigar box which at present serves me for a sewing case, and such other articles as we have no place for.

Then we have the living room, which takes up somewhat more than a third of these sixteen feet. It has two windows, with white curtains, directly opposite each other. Beneath the one to the north is a large black walnut table, where Helene is usually busy. Beneath the other are Vilhelm's table and chair. Here I have my writing case and my work while Vilhelm is away; when he is home, on the other hand, I have to vacate the place and take my case away, for then the table is full of papers, certificates, and records. Near this window is the door that leads outside. Above the window Vilhelm has nailed a shelf for our books, which before lay on the bed.

[4] This cabin may be seen on the campus of Luther College in Decorah.

There is a similar shelf above the other window, where the library of the house is found in beautiful confusion next to candlesticks, an iron heater, a lamp, etc.[5]

In the little space between the curtain and the window hangs a mirror above which, among many other beautiful things, Helene's comb is displayed on weekdays; it is used only on Sundays and state occasions. Here, too, are found Erik's tobacco pouch and the unlucky clock, in it green case with large round gilded feet, which has now probably stopped for good. It amazed us a couple of times by moving forward an hour or two, until at last we discovered Master Per had climbed on the table and brought about that marvel. Directly in front of the curtain there is a chair; the rest of the furniture consists of three stools, also of black walnut, which are moved about as they are needed. That is the picture here since we got our table and two chairs; before that there was a chest which was pulled here and there for a seat.

The last strip of the room is the kitchen. Here is the stove; its appurtenances are distributed round about. On the walls hang all the pans and the coffee roaster; under the ceiling a row of kettles, coffee cans, a flatiron, a tin funnel with matches, and our candle snuffers; in addition there is a crosspiece where all their belongings hang, together with rags and I know not what else. Under the steps which lead to the loft (which also is hung with kitchen utensils) is a bench for dishes, with two small cabinets beneath. Right by our bed is the cellar trap door, very inconveniently located. The whole room is papered with all sorts of newspapers and prints, chiefly *Maanedstidende,* of which some are upside down and others sideways. The lowest part of the wall (it is of logs, as usual, with plaster in between) is not yet papered; but Helene is tireless in covering it with *Emigranten* whenever she man-

[5] An iron heater was heated and placed in a flatiron or box iron for pressing and ironing. "The lamp was a dish with melted fat and a piece of cloth for a wick. We had our first oil lamp given to us within my memory"; Mrs. C. A. Naeseth, daughter of the Korens, to the editor, undated.

ages to get hold of copies, although they are constantly being torn to pieces by some little meddler or other, of whom Burman is one.

The door leading to the loft is next to the door to the outside.[6] In the loft, which is not plastered, the wind has free play. It is full of all sorts of things: a large wheat bin, pork barrels, large and small chests, our valises, a bed, meal sacks, some clothes, and a great many tools; Per's greatest delight is to get hold of these and then drive nails into the floor. In short here are found all the countless things usually found in a loft, and a great many more. There are two windows, too, one to the east and one to the west, where I have often stood and watched the sunset or been on the lookout for Vilhelm. When we can no longer bear the smell of pork or of roasting coffee, we leave the door to the loft open.

The house has a poor location. There is a dreary view toward the road to Decorah with a few scattered trees; but on the other side, where there is no window, there is a very pretty wood. Such is the place where we have lived more than three months.

I wish I knew what news Vilhelm is going to bring from Decorah. There he is now. I scarcely recognized him in that hat he has acquired.

Thursday, March 9. God be praised for letters and good news from home, even though they are old! How good it was, nevertheless, to hear something at last from all our dear ones at home! But this is really extraordinary; this letter was sent from Larvik November 17, came to Boston December 10, left Preus's December 28, and then we do not get it until March 8. It must surely have lain a long time in that stupid Decorah post office. In this same mail Erik received a letter sent from Christiania January 24, so we know letters can come quickly.

I was so unprepared for these letters. When Vilhelm got home, I looked at him to see if I could read anything in the

---

[6] As one enters the cabin, the stairs to the loft are to the left along the wall and lead to a hinged trapdoor in the floor of the loft.

expression on his face; but no, it was the same as usual. I did not like to ask because I did not want the same disconsolate answer again, especially since I knew no mail had come these last days. "Have you Erik's letter?" I merely asked. "Yes," he answered quietly and went up and took off his things, came down again, and gave Helene her letter. I went over and closed my writing case, thinking, "Some time you will get something, too; you will have to wait patiently till then," and suspected nothing until Vilhelm said, "Eleis, come here; I, too, have received something." And then the joy and surprise when I saw the letter and recognized my dear father's handwriting! I am sure I could not have contained myself and kept from betraying such joyful news.

Vilhelm has ridden over to McKay's to inquire about quarters.[7] He had gone to every house in Decorah without being able to find anything. There is not much housing in these new, small, straggling towns. We shall have to hear what McKay finally says; perhaps I shall yet have an opportunity to practice my English, if we are to live with Americans. It is really comical that our stay here should end thus; we are just like two prairie chickens, as Vilhelm says. Meanwhile I hope there will be a decision soon so that we may get away from here.

Saturday, March 11. The chickens did find a roost, just the same, and it is a very good one. We are now living at Sørland's, where there is plenty of room, neat housekeeping, and a very tidy housewife, who excels at setting a table with cakes and pies.

Vilhelm did not go to McKay's Thursday, as his intention had been, but went to the Skaarlias instead. They wanted to move out of their own house and into the old cabin, so that we might have the neat little new one; they would not hear of our living in the old one. After all, they generally move

---

[7] John McKay had extensive land holdings, especially in Frankville Township. In 1851 he paid the largest taxes in Winneshiek County; Sparks, *History of Winneshiek County*, 117. See also chapter 9, footnote 4.

over there with their stoves in the summer. But I am still afraid that it is too cold for the old people, and so I would really rather remain here until it gets a little warmer, and as soon as possible get a cabin for ourselves. We have been invited to stay here until we get a stove and such other things as we need; how long that may be, I do not know.[8]

I came here yesterday forenoon, Vilhelm had been at the meeting of the congregation and did not get home until after supper. The meeting went well enough, but no final decision has yet been made about the parsonage, for the men who have that in hand were negligent and did not appear. Nils Katterud is really in a dilemma over the twenty acres, and has to listen to unpleasant things about it on all sides; he does not know what to do and has resigned as a member of the committee.[9] Erik Egge was elected, and that is well, for he is a good carpenter and knows more about building than the others. I hope now that they will not argue and talk too much, but just begin something, so that we may have a house by winter at least; it will certainly not be sooner.

Services are to be held tomorrow at Rognald's, and on Monday and Tuesday west of here. It is too bad Vilhelm has so much to do next week, for he surely will not find time to write home, and I want so much to get a letter off soon.

It is attractive here; it is good to have something pretty to look at again. Then there is so much life with all the cattle, and we have a view of the stable and all the sheds and the haystacks from the window. Eli spends most of her time there when she is not busy baking one of the many cakes which are so common here, all of which taste much the same.

Sunday, March 12. Today services were held at Rognald's. Sundays are far more pleasant when Vilhelm is home and

---

[8] "Here" is Sørland's, where the Korens moved from Egge's. Later they accepted the invitation of the Skaarlias, moving to their cabin May 2. "The old people," that is, Erik and Guri Skaarlia, were then in their fifties.

[9] After the original eighty acres for the parsonage land had been purchased, some changes were made. About twenty acres from the north end of the tract were sold to Nils Katterud and approximately the same amount of land was added to the eastern portion of the property. The parsonage was built on the added portion; information received from William Linnevold.

preaches in the neighborhood. There was a large gathering; people came from far and near. We did not get home until after three. The service took a long time, for today there was catechizing of candidates for confirmation.

We did not stay for dinner as usual, but drove directly home, and afterward took a walk to the parsonage land, where we wandered about and pictured our future home. There is perfect spring weather today — a fresh smell of buds and that delightfully hazy air that throws a lovely blue tinge over all distant objects. At such times it is especially pleasant on the parsonage land.

Monday, March 13. Vilhelm has started at last for Whisky Grove, where he is to be today. He wanted to get away early of course; but it was impossible to get him awake this morning. It is not more than half past eight, it is true, but he will hardly go faster than a walk in this mud and with that miserable wagon. When I came down this morning Thore Skotland was sitting here; he went with him.[10] It is raining pleasantly and is as mild as a summer's day. Vilhelm lost his sou'wester on his last trip. He will miss that today, I imagine. I really should go to Suckow's on an errand for Vilhelm, but the way the rain is pouring down, I had better wait and begin a letter home.

We are indeed comfortably settled here; everything is pleasant and attractive, and in addition we have a room to ourselves in the loft, where Vilhelm can have peace. He will certainly not be disturbed by the people here; they are very quiet and always speak in a low voice when he is studying. One really learns to appreciate that. Here, too, I shall not become moody in gray and rainy weather because of the melancholy view, as I sometimes did at Egge's when Vilhelm was away. It is always beautiful here. But I am really afraid Vilhelm will be spoiled by both the food and roomy quarters, so that it will not be so good when we move to Skaarlia's and

[10] In 1850 Thore Skotland took land in Sections 22 and 27, Calmar Township, Winneshiek County. He was one of the incorporators of Luther College; T. L. Rosholt, *Life Histories of the Descendants of Peder and Gjertrud Sandager,* 106 (Decorah, 1954).

have our own ménage. Oh, well, it is good to get used to a little of everything, I believe.

It will soon be pitch dark and it is still raining as hard as ever. I wonder how Vilhelm got along today; he must have been soaked, for he had nothing to cover him. He really must get a raincoat soon. I have kept busy writing home today. Now I can no longer see and I am getting very tired of writing.

Tuesday, March 14. After all the rain it was pleasant to wake up to beautiful, warm sunshine this morning. Vilhelm will have fine weather for traveling today. As soon as I had eaten breakfast, I went over to Suckow's. It was fresh and delightful, and I was surprised to find that it was not muddier. I met Suckow on the road, and afterward went in to Helene's; she seemed to be well and was washing clothes. Erik had received a new *Emigranten;* but it was very dry, containing only the school laws. From Turkey news of a couple of victories over the Russians. The emperor is going to cross the Danube, has sent agents to the United States to buy ships and weapons. This news was from January 14. *Emigranten* urges its readers to consider that Europe in all likelihood will need much wheat from America this year. God knows what the end will be! If one could only get recent news from Norway! "Well, it is a good thing we are away from there when it looks like that," say many here, although under such circumstances most people would be much more reluctant to be so far distant from those they hold dear.

While I was reading the paper, a girl came in. After she had sat for some time, she asked if there were not to be services today. She had walked twelve miles yesterday from up north under that impression, for she, too, wished to be enrolled for confirmation. She was a grown-up girl and one of those who have been waiting a long time for the pastor. Now she was at a loss for a place to stay, being a total stranger here. It occurred to me that Thorgrim's wife, who is alone so much, might like to have someone in the house. I asked her to wait at Erik's and went over to Thorgrim's; but they did not care to have her, for they had no bed. That settled that. The best plan I could think of was to send the girl to Aarthun's; he, according to Thorgrim, had promised her father that she could stay there. At least she can stay until Koren returns.

The first thing I heard as I stepped into Helene's today was "Molasses, we have got molasses!" from Per and Kari, who came toward me, each licking a piece of bread, their faces all smeared. Then Per brought paper and shears and began his "Cut me ships and sleds," although he had found a new comrade in the cat, which our arrival had driven away.[11]

Now we are to eat dinner; the whole forenoon is gone and I have not yet written home.

Wednesday, March 15. Yesterday afternoon I sat upstairs and wrote steadily, for Eli was busy washing floors, hanging curtains, arranging and baking, and getting everything ready for the pastor's return, which she got into her head should be yesterday. But nothing came of that; he is hardly likely to come this forenoon either.

What lovely moonlight there was last night, and how mild and peaceful! I sat knitting by the open door. Eli was inside washing potatoes; the cattle were in the stables; we did not hear a sound save now and then the baying of the dog. It is very beautiful at Sørland's when the moon is above the trees by the brook. I could easily have sat there all evening, but had to close the door at last and take my place at a well-provisioned supper table.

Today is a perfect summer's day. It is very warm, although it is blowing fairly hard. While I was writing, a little while ago, Eli called down from the loft, "The fire is right up to our field now." I went upstairs to look at it and then ran out to the road to see where it was. I soon stood right by it and

[11] Pastor Koren's aversion to cats is said to have been the cause of the cat's departure.

saw how it advanced with each little gust of wind. Since there is not much grass, it does not travel fast; otherwise it might easily be dangerous to the woods, which are not many steps from the house. I stood and looked at it and heard how it snapped and crackled in the dry grass, how at times it shot up a tall tuft of grass and caught in the tops of the withered flower stalks when the wind bowed them down. At last the smoke was so strong that it put me to flight; but now at any rate I have had a chance to see a prairie fire at close range.

I have just had an interesting little visit from Mari Katterud and a sister of Ola Hegg. The former does not say much and the latter was as talkative as a mute and looked as if she were asleep. But I am no master conversationalist, either. Eli went about her work as if everything were as usual; nevertheless, they sat here a terribly long time before it occurred to them to get up and go.

The fire continues its way through the woods; it burns only the grass and leaves without setting fire to trees or twigs. I have been far up in the woods with Eli to investigate, accompanied by the dog, the cat, and the sheep, who now and then come bounding over the fence in one leap and gallop right into the house, so that we have to block the door with a chair when we wish to have it open.

There were many people here today. Just a moment ago there were the two delegates from Clermont for the meeting tomorrow; scarcely had they ridden off before the two from Paint Creek came — Møller is one of them.[12] They are putting their horses in the stall, I see, so they will no doubt spend the night here. But it does not look as if a pastor is coming to this meeting. I wanted to go to meet him, but this entertaining group came and prevented me. The sun will soon be going down, so he should be here before long. There, the dogs are beginning to bark; I wonder if that can be he?

Thursday, March 16. Quite right, it was Vilhelm who came

[12] Clermont is a town in Fayette County thirty-five miles south and slightly east of Decorah.

driving along the road, step by step, so very sedately. So I went to meet him. The first thing I heard was, "Why, how tiny you look when you come walking like that!" He could not forget it, just as if everything does not look smaller at a distance. Why, he himself, the wagon, Charlie, and the whole glorious procession almost vanished in the grass while I watched them coming! "Here is something for you," he said and gave me a bundle of cotton and a quantity of goods with which to start quilting. I was glad to get it, though now I shall have plenty to do. He was very tired yesterday but had to go ahead with preparations for the meeting today just the same, poor man.

That meeting is now under way downstairs, so I had to retire up here. I hear Vilhelm reading something aloud without interruption. I sit and laugh because of the hearty laughter I hear below; I suppose Vilhelm has made some witty remark. Now I have been down to help Eli set the table and serve coffee, and have watched the men come in one by one to take their places; and every last one of them before he crossed the threshold very audibly blew his nose with that nature's handkerchief they customarily use. Now they are leaving the table, and there comes Vilhelm rushing up the stairs. He is after cigars, I imagine. Now I had better go down and have a little to eat.[13]

That is done. I was introduced to Thorkild Ederklep, and had a conversation with Evenson, a stiff-appearing person, so stiff he looks as if he were afraid to move his lips when he speaks.[14]

Now the deliberations are in full swing again. I found a pretext for going downstairs to see what it was like. Vilhelm

[13] The meeting was called to draft rules for the several congregations in Pastor Koren's call and to recommend what their future relations should be to other Norwegian Lutheran congregations in the United States; minutes of the Little Iowa congregation for March 16, 1854. This minute book is filed in the Koren Library at Luther College in Decorah, Iowa.

[14] Johannes Evenson was a member of the Little Iowa congregation; in 1850 he had taken land in the northeast quarter of Section 32 in Madison Township, Winneshiek County; Sparks, *History of Winneshiek County*, 27.

is sitting at the table with a map before him, the others about him, old Thrond with folded hands and a very devout look, several smoking tobacco and spitting on the clean white floor. When they are through, the whole committee will go over and look at the parsonage land. Meanwhile I must be industrious and write while I am banished up here, where Eli, too, has taken refuge. The noise is very loud below, as if they were all talking at once.

Friday, March 17. The meeting began and ended in complete peace and harmony. The whole group visited the parsonage land, Vilhelm and old Thrond, deep in conversation, bringing up the rear. They returned well satisfied, and all went home except our guests from Paint Creek.

In the evening I watched the prettiest fire I have yet seen. It began quite near us but gradually drew farther away and took on the appearance of a distant conflagration which had sprung up not in one but in many places; here flames, there smoke, farthest off a sudden puff of flame, only a weak reflection in the sky, and in the center a great sea of fire. The whole thing cast a magic illumination on the landscape and formed a rarely beautiful scene. Hardly an evening passes that we do not see a prairie fire; but today I hope will be the exception; a fire would be dangerous, for there is a regular storm outside.

The Paint Creek people rode away this morning. This forenoon Vilhelm has had candidates for confirmation, fifteen in all. Unfortunately he does not feel well today, and tomorrow he is going away again if he is better. He went upstairs some time ago to lie down a bit. Since he is sleeping soundly, I shall not disturb him yet; but it is not wise for him to lie up there while it is blowing hard, there are so many drafts. Oh, well, I need no longer have any doubts whether he is awake or not, such a racket as there is up there with the table and chairs. I had better pay him a visit — I hope I shall be graciously received and will not disturb his reverence.

Saturday, March 18. It is now that time of day when the

sun has set and the twilight is deepening. I am alone in the house, Eli is milking the cows, and Ingebret, very erect, is marching back and forth on top of a haystack, throwing down hay. It is pleasant here; the fire burns merrily in the stove. Eli churned this afternoon and so we shall have buttermilk mush this evening; it is already on the fire and has been left in my care.[15]

I hope Vilhelm is in Paint Creek by this time, for he got an early start. It is delightful outside this evening. I hope he keeps well while he is away. He is not coming home before Tuesday or Wednesday.

I have been busy sewing for Eli today. The old man from McKay's was here to say there were no letters; he had promised to inquire. I hope Vilhelm may be luckier. Preus surely must write eventually and give us some news of our belongings.

Monday, March 20. It is already March 20 — I do not know where this month has gone. Time certainly passes much faster here at Sørland's than at Egge's. That I feel much better here is doubtless due not least to the more beautiful natural surroundings. Today we have once more that lovely summer weather which threatened to leave us; this is a delightful morning.

We have just eaten, and had some chickens in to visit us, and afterward watched Ingebret let the little pigs out for the first time. There was certainly a running and grunting, in fact there is almost a concert here by all the animals.

Yesterday forenoon we went over to Skaarlia's, ate dinner there, and talked with the two old people until late in the afternoon. They, especially Guri, were very much dissatisfied because there was so little progress with the parsonage and because people, once they had sent a call to a pastor, were not more conscientious in meeting the conditions agreed to. When we went home, we took the road past the parsonage

---

[15] Buttermilk mush is made by boiling buttermilk and adding flour for thickening and salt to taste.

land so that Eli could see where the house was to stand; while we were there, two beautiful deer went leaping across the meadow into the woods. Fido, who was with us, ran after them; but they were too swift for him. It is pleasant to know they are there; I hope we do not drive them away by building our home there.[16]

The rest of the day passed quietly. I read. Ingebret is quite English in his idea of Sunday — sat the whole time and read aloud in a book of family sermons. But there is little comfort in reading one sermon after another without a pause; he hurries on without even being able to wait until all have eaten before he begins again.

It is evening and will soon be bedtime. I have been busy today; I ironed and cut out some things for Eli on which I am now sewing. It began to blow disagreeably outside, so I did not take my intended walk this afternoon. I have neglected my walks since I came here; I must see to correcting that. I have just been down to the cellar and watched Ingebret sitting there singing and cutting up beetroots for the cattle. Now I shall put this away for the day.

Tuesday, March 21. What weather! It blows and rains frightfully, and lightens and thunders now and then. I hope Vilhelm is not out in this weather! He would be completely soaked, for it certainly is blowing too hard to hold an umbrella. I so much wanted him to come today, but now it would be better for him to wait until tomorrow.

The rain is forcing its way through the walls here and there all over the room. I do hope we get a tight house so that I will not have to go about with a rag in my hand and mop up, every time it rains. Yet, if we only get a house, it will not matter what it is like.

I have been busy all day trying to finish my sewing. Since it will be dark in no time now, I do not believe Vilhelm will come. Eli has gone after the cows and left me to take care of her biscuits, which I must put in the oven.

[16] Guri was the wife of Erik Skaarlia and the mother of Eli Sørland.

Wednesday, March 22. I had no more than put the biscuits in and tidied up the room a little before Vilhelm, with water running off his hat, stuck his head in the door, handed me my old cloak, which is useful for almost everything and this time had served him to sit on, and said, "Throw this upstairs, it is so wet and dirty," and dashed off. I did as he said and then went over to the window, where I stood wondering what they were fussing over down by the wagon, something which moved and which Ingebret carried away. It turned out to be a puppy which Vilhelm had brought along from Paint Creek and of course had had trouble enough looking after on the way. Vilhelm was not as wet as one might have expected, however, although he not only had to drive in the pouring rain, but also had to hold the umbrella and take care of his restless traveling companion. While he was standing in the door recounting his adventures, Ingebret called to us and asked what had become of the horse. Well, we knew nothing about that; Vilhelm had walked away from the horse and now it was gone. Mr. "Challe" (of course it should be Charlie) had found it most reasonable to look after himself, since no one else would, and had gone his usual way to the stable with the wagon behind him, and there at the stable Ingebret caught up with him.

I went with Vilhelm and fed the dog and named it Vige. It is a nice golden-brown puppy. So now we have obtained one of the two much-talked-of dogs. The weather is disagreeable and raw and keeps us inside. Vilhelm is absorbed in his certificates, smokes cigars, and talks to himself. I must finish my letters and would be glad if they were safely started on their way.

Monday, March 27. It is too bad I have let four days go by without writing a word; it is only laziness or, more properly, industry, which is to blame. The fact is, I have been so busy sewing for Eli that I did not take time for anything else, or I have been writing letters home and was so interested in them that I did not even think of the diary. Now these matters have been taken care of and I shall be able to think of other things.

Saturday Vilhelm was to go out to the settlements west of us but was in a dilemma for a suitable means of travel, for he has no horse collar and, if he rides, no knapsack for his gown. So he rode over to Knud. Knud and Erik were to go with him so that they might finally reach an agreement about the parsonage, which haunts the heads of all the people. I hurried to bake communion wafers and get his clothes ready in case there should be an order for a hasty departure. They decided to put their horses together and get a wagon and start as soon as Knud could get ready. Knud, good soul, who does not know what it is to hurry, did not get here until half-past four, which was rather late. So they left Sunday morning — at eight instead of seven.[17]

Eli asked me to accompany her to Andrew's — her family; I agreed and we set out with Guri [Skaarlia] and little Embret.[18] The latter ran ahead and played with Eli, while I walked like a grave and sedate matron and talked soberly with Guri. Since we had three miles to go in raw gray weather and a fairly strong wind, the walk was not particularly pleasant and I was glad when we reached the house. Before anyone heard us, we were inside, finding them in the midst of their family devotions. It was very pleasant to come into that room, where everything was arranged neatly and without crowding. Bjørn sat in a rocking chair and read aloud from the Bible; by his side sat his young wife, a handsome woman with attractive features and a pretty little child in her lap. Two old women, a grandmother and a maternal aunt, their gray hair tucked up under their caps, sat on stools with their hymnbooks; on the bed lay an old man reading. The

---

[17] The western settlements or western district served by Pastor Koren comprised the areas west of Trout Run, a stream that runs northeast from Conover in Calmar Township to the Upper Iowa River at a point just east of Decorah.

[18] Embret was Guri's son, then about nine. Later he stayed for a time at the parsonage with the Korens. He eventually married Kari Egge, daughter of Helene Egge by her first marriage; Bailey, *Winneshiek County*, 2:444.

whole scene seemed to be very Sabbath-like and comfortable.

We had dinner before we went on to the other brother,
who lives nearby. It was pleasant there, too; both wives had
worked for Americans, and where this is true one can be sure
to find things tidy and clean. Of course it was impossible to
leave without having something to eat and drink, although
we had just come from the table. Guri and Eli went out and
looked at the calves and livestock, which are among their
chief interests and positively have to be inspected wherever
we are before we can leave.

Many plum trees had been planted on these farms, and at
one, a vine on the side of the house. "What kind of a plant
have you there?" I asked the man. "Oh," he answered, "it has
leaves and such like on it in the summer, so it is green."
Well, now I know what kind of a vine it is that has this remarkable quality of being green in summer.

I was glad to get back to the Sørland valley, for the wind
was biting all the way home; but there it was spring and
summer, so I sat down on a stump and rested, a large stick in
my hand to keep off the dogs.

Some time after everyone had gone to bed and just as I
was about to fall asleep, I heard someone open the door
downstairs. Thinking it was Embret, I calmly turned over to
go to sleep, but a moment later was disturbed again by someone stealing up the stairs and taking hold of the door. "Who
is there?" I cried, quite terrified. "It is I," said a voice, which
I gradually convinced myself was Vilhelm's. Who would have
thought that, after setting out this morning, he would return
the same day? And who would have thought that, coming
from the western settlements, he could possibly bring letters?
Yet he so distinguished himself this time. He isn't bad — at
times! I received the letters we had been expecting so long
from the "Buonovento." It was wonderful to get Christiane's
letter; now I know the news of Christmas at home too and
have had an account of the wedding, which I have longed for

since I was aboard the "Rhein." Christiane is very good about writing fully and telling me everything to the last detail. God be praised, all is well at home.[19]

Vilhelm received a letter from Mr. Solmer with the joyful news that our things are on the way.[20] He also received a letter from Consul Bech, who is certainly very kind to us. He offers to send us American newspapers and says that he has forwarded another letter from Larvik, which I may now expect soon. Mrs. Bech has received my letter at last, so I know one at least has gone through safely. Now the letters are beginning to stream in.

[19] No doubt the Korens watched for news of ship arrivals, if the papers carried them; they might also have had word from home that the "Buonovento" carried mail. Christiane was Mrs. Koren's sister. The wedding here mentioned was that of Johan Koren, the pastor's brother, who was married in October, 1853, to Marie Louise Münster. See chapter 1, footnote 10.

[20] Jørgen Ziølner migrated to the United States in 1851, crossing the Atlantic on the same ship as the Herman A. Preuses. He lived with them at the Spring Prairie parsonage for two years; later he changed his name to Solner; Mrs. Koren spells it Solmer. He is mentioned frequently in *Linka's Diary*. He married a sister of Mrs. Adolph C. Preus.

13

The Baggage Has Come at Last

Tuesday, March 28. Winter is coming again, I believe. I awoke this morning to windows wholly frosted over; it is very cold, although outside it looks as if there were only sunshine and summer. And yesterday I had to leave my husband on the prairie and hurry home because of the horrid wind. We had taken a walk through Ingebret's woods over fallen trees and broken branches, high grass and the like, and my poor blue dress was quite torn at the bottom. But it was wild and lovely in the woods and delightfully sheltered and warm.

I have been passing the time watching Erik Skaarlia fell trees — logs for the parsonage. I have never seen a tree felled before. Eli is baking cakes — small hearts. Naughty Vilhelm steals the ones Eli gives me and excuses his bad manners with a poor witticism. He has completed a list of all the letters he is to write and at last has started on them. Well, now it is time to eat dinner, but I have no appetite.

Wednesday, March 29. I am so tired after a long walk that I shall very likely soon fall asleep. I had better try to rouse myself a little and describe our walk this afternoon so that I shall not sleep away all its interesting features.

I have been sitting a long time watching the pretty prairie fire just outside our windows; Ingebret is burning the field between the brook and the woods. Vilhelm went down and helped set the fire; it was interesting to watch them take burning grass and set fire in circles over the field. The flames quickly licked their way up the grassy slope; now they have spread out and have gone through and behind the woods, which look magnificent, for we see not the flames but only the strong reflection, shading from bright gold to dark blood-red, and the dense smoke rolling over the trees. The trees along the brook are brilliantly lighted by the reflection. And now Ola Tollefsjord has set fire to his field, too, so there is a whole sea of fire. Here in the house one could see easily, even before the light was lit. Vilhelm came in and ate, but went back again at once. It looks strange to see his figure and Ingebret's, followed by all three dogs, now quite shadowy, going ahead of the fire with hazel switches in their hands, striving to put it out, for the flames have already reached the top of the hill. If uncontrolled, they could easily start in on the house, now lighted brightly by the flames. This is a very large fire. Ingebret is likely to be watching it the greater part of the night.

But it was our walk I wanted to write about. Well, it was remarkable enough, for first we headed down the large hollow by the brook, which is quite dry except for a stream of water which flows to the bottom over some natural stone steps and vanishes through a little opening in a wall of rock. It was rather strange to stand in that deep ravine with all the big trees along the sides. At last we had our fill of gazing at this and turned back, Vilhelm starting straight up the steep wall of soft, slippery clay. I must certainly have thought I was Vige, since without further ado I followed at his heels; but when I got halfway it dawned on me that I was only a frail woman, not adapted to such undertakings, and with as good grace as possible I made my way carefully down the slippery clay wall and kept to the road by which I had come.[1]

From there we continued on the road which leads to Katterud's, and came to a region where I was a complete stranger. It was not pleasant — rocky bluffs, their scattered gray trees made even more melancholy by the raw gray weather. We followed a little wall of rock which rose higher and higher the farther we advanced into the valley, then we jumped over a stream, and stopped at last before a bluff which looked very interesting. It formed wonderful ruins of all kinds and in places was overgrown with vines and countless other delicate creeping plants, besides all the other growths which had taken root. There were ever so many plum trees on the level ground and here and there a half-burned, charred tree which sought to hold itself aloft a little longer by leaning against the bluff. This valley had a remarkably wild aspect and I was glad I had not let my fatigue deter me from going.

It was a long jaunt, indeed. We got home late, for we had to stop to chat a little with Erik Skaarlia, who was building a hog house; and besides, we were curious enough to walk over to the parsonage land to see if any more logs had come. But we might as well have spared that effort; there are not very many, I dare say, as conscientious as Embret [Sørland] and Erik Skaarlia.[2] There, I hear Vilhelm returning from the fire. Poor Vige, who is supposed to be trained to be a model of virtue! Vilhelm is really romping with him now.

Thursday, March 30. Ugh, I have been so lazy today — written only part of a letter to Lotte and listened to Vilhelm and Erik discuss the parsonage, which is very difficult to plan if it is to be as we wish it.[3] All the rooms will be too small, I suppose; if we are to have them larger, then the house will not

[1] Vige was the Korens' dog.

[2] Logs for the first parsonage were furnished by the parishioners, cut and hand hewn by them. For the present church edifice, which was begun in 1869 and dedicated in 1873, the parishioners quarried native limestone and built the structure. They followed the same procedure in making an addition to the church, in 1949, in the form of a parish house.

[3] Charlotte Amalie Koren (1831-1910), a cousin of Elisabeth Koren's, was a teacher and author; Johnson, *Slekten Koren*, 1:196.

be so comfortable. One alternative must now be chosen. I am tired of it all and shall try not to give it another thought before the house is ready, and then do my best to arrange it. This is a very sensible resolution if I can keep it.

At times my lord husband is afflicted with sleeping sickness, and such was the case today. Then I can shake him as much as I will, but he only blinks his eyes a little and looks about him with a more languid gaze, until at last I give up, thinking that if this lasts altogether too long, I shall have to go up again, as always happens, too. Now to my joy he has sealed a number of letters — I rejoice over every letter that gets written — and now he is outside chopping wood, an operation at which Vige is a greatly puzzled spectator. Of course he left the door open as he went out, so the sheep came galloping into the room and I had a hard time getting it out again.

It is evening. Vilhelm has gone over to Tollefsjord's to get a messenger to take the letters. It is too bad the post office is so far away; we cannot get a messenger whenever we wish and so must wait longer than necessary for letters. Eli has hurried supper so that I have hardly time to write what I want to; no doubt it is because of Erik, who is here building a summer kitchen. We shall eat by daylight this evening and Vilhelm will have to eat later.

Friday, March 31. How disagreeable it is to see snow and winter when one is waiting and hoping for spring! It is so wintry inside, too, this afternoon. Vilhelm has just returned from Aarthun's, where he instructed the candidates for confirmation; now he is writing busily. I have written to Sellø — it is very well to keep busy writing letters, provided they do not cause me to neglect my diary; but I write and write and still don't want to lay the letter aside. So it will be dark before I get what I want written here.

Eli is weaving a floor mat of cornhusks; the latter have many uses and are said to be better than straw for filling mattresses. The teakettle is simmering; the cat is sleeping under the stove; Fido, too, has stolen into this warm room and has stretched out in the middle of the floor.

All forenoon I waited, expecting that the boy who took our letters would return and bring at least a newspaper. He was here just now, bringing neither paper nor letter. I hope he was able to make himself understood.

Tuesday, April 4. Now all of Saturday, Sunday, and Monday have passed without my doing any writing; that is too bad! I believe it is because Vilhelm is home; when he is, I never care as much about writing as when he is away. Then I always regret not having written, for I know he is eager to read what I write. Since he is to start out tomorrow, we shall see if the inclination returns.

God be praised for all the happiness we have had these days! Letters from Norway and Wisconsin, and imagine, the baggage — the baggage which has been awaited with so much longing and anxiety — has really come at last! I was writing to Mrs. Bech yesterday afternoon, when Eli, who stood by the window, washing, cried, "That surely must be your baggage coming!" I answered, "You must be mistaken. Don't you see that woman with a red scarf on her head sitting in back?" But Eli was right, though I could scarcely believe my eyes when the wagon came nearer and the woman changed into the red New York trunk. Yes, God be praised, it really was our baggage! I was very happy, but also sorry that Vilhelm was not home to enjoy it; he went to Andrew's this forenoon and was not to be back before evening.

I sat by the window for some time, glancing out every now and then to see if he were coming, but soon became too impatient to wait quietly at home. So I put on my things, called Vige, and hurried away, hoping to meet him and be the first to bring him the good news. I walked and walked without meeting anyone and became more and more disappointed as I went farther. Then I began to feel tired, especially since I had a good deal of trouble with Vige, who is very foolish and does not obey. "When you get to the top of that hill, you must turn back," I kept thinking, until I did stand on top of it and saw the next hill in front of me; then I thought the same thing again — and so it went until I was near Iver Johnson's.[4]

Here I met a prairie schooner with a large load of household goods, from which projected here a face, there the leg of a chair or some other article of household furniture. It was drawn by three or four pairs of oxen and led by a large, tall Yankee, who marched ahead with his gun on his arm and who halted me for directions about the road. I had not taken many more steps before finally I gave up hope of meeting Vilhelm and turned back, little as I wished to do so. I should have liked to walk as far as Andrew's, but I was so tired that I was afraid of being stranded halfway.

I turned slowly homeward and often stopped to look back. I had almost reached the bottoms when I discovered something dark coming on foot from far away. I stood still a little while and made certain that it was a man and that the man might possibly be Vilhelm. Then I stood still even longer and finally started forward very slowly, keeping my eye on the approaching figure. At last to my great joy I recognized Vilhelm coming toward me, waving his red handkerchief like a banner. Now it was his turn to be happy and surprised, and no one had taken from me the joy of being the first to bring him the news. Along the way Vilhelm still had to close a horse deal before we got home to tea and hot biscuits.

Then the man who had brought our baggage handed us a little package, which, I was quite touched to see, contained the old kerchief and half shawl which I had given Lars Møen to keep his ears warm. There were letters with it, too, some words to Koren and a very sprightly, gay letter from Linka, which I was very glad to receive. It was written early in February. It was stupid, of course, to send it with the baggage, which stood safe and sound in Dodgeville more than two months while we were worrying here. Well, I imagine that

[4] The location of Iver Johnson's farm has not been determined.

the Preuses will now understand why they have not heard ·
from us and do not get the things that we brought for them.
It is really too bad that Vilhelm did not get home earlier, so
that we could have unpacked their things and sent them back
with the man.

We were glad yesterday to get our baggage, but are still
happier today to find that our things are in very good condition; nothing is damaged. First Vilhelm opened the cases of
books; there were the books as if they had been put in yesterday. The same was true of the boxes; the things were not
even damp. Who would have believed it could turn out so
well? The least I expected was to see part of it spoiled. How
gay it was to unpack and see all our things again, both old
and new, but especially the daguerreotypes. God be praised
for all the dear faces we have with us!

How good it will be when we can unpack in earnest and
arrange everything in our own home and not, as now, be
forced to put it in that old room, which is full of hay, mortar,
and all sorts of rubbish! Now we take things out and look at
them, only to put them back again and leave them. It will
not be long before we move to Skaarlia's, I suppose, but there
we shall have only what is most necessary. The rest must wait
to adorn the parsonage. I long for that more every day, as
does Vilhelm, too. But as yet there are only twelve logs.[5]

Sunday a letter from Norway. Vilhelm got it, with an
Emigranten, at Rognald's after services. He also had a letter
from A. Preus, whose family has had much sickness.[6] That is
why I have had no letters; I thought there must be some good
reason. The letter from home was from my dear Christiane,
dated January 28. It was a good letter; all was well at home.
Christiane also is better, God be praised, and gives me detailed accounts of everything.

[5] "For a long time there were twelve log beams for the house; I used to go
up and count them. When Vilhelm came home, his first question was, 'How
many are there now?' " These words, to be found on page 171 of *Fra pioneertiden,* are not in the manuscript diary. Apparently they were added with Mrs.
Koren's approval when the Norwegian version was edited for publication.
[6] The Reverend Adolph C. Preus.

I am no longer homesick when I get a letter. I was not really homesick before, either; but I was quite depressed and out of spirits when I read their dear letters, especially the first ones in Hamburg and aboard ship. Now, God be praised, I can follow them more calmly in their pleasures and everything. But there was a time this winter, when Vilhelm was away, that I simply could not endure the thought of home at all; the contrast was altogether too great. But a longing to return or a wish that we had not come — such a thought I have never entertained. I have Vilhelm here — what more can I want? And whenever I thought of him, then I was happy again and could not understand how a moment earlier I could have been so downhearted. And how can I be really distressed when I am with him whom I love so much, and who I know loves me? In this I have the best of all possessions and am always happy, whatever the outward circumstances may be. I only hope I may be for Vilhelm what I so dearly wish to be.

I am very tired from unpacking this forenoon. It is so warm today. Vilhelm has ridden to Freeport.[7] I have made an effort to put our room somewhat in order. Now, despite my fatigue, I think I shall try to wash Vilhelm's knitted gloves, which I found in my hatbox, in case he should want them tomorrow. In my hatbox — well, there were many things, and I was quite touched to find so many reminders from the ship: Mr. Giering's "Present from Ryde"; our jars of preserves, of which we so often took a mouthful in our cabin — one of them is still full of raspberries. The sugar has crystallized on top, of course, but I think the berries will taste good on pancakes just the same.

Wednesday, April 5. Nothing came of my good intentions to write today; I found other matters to attend to. Vilhelm was to leave at seven this morning. I awakened him, too, very punctually before six, but he loves his pillow, the dear man.

---

[7] Freeport is a village on the Upper Iowa River two miles east of Decorah. In the early days it was a rival of Decorah.

He was so tired, too, that I would much rather have let him sleep, if I had dared. It was nine o'clock before he left with his Rosinante, which certainly is well matched to the wagon; the latter would fare ill, I believe, were it to follow a spirited horse.[8] But as it was, it all fitted nicely together and was in complete harmony with the gray, foggy weather.

I found Vilhelm's sheath knife sticking in the fence this afternoon. It is too bad he forgot it; it is indispensable to him, and perhaps may be doubly so this time, because he has such a rickety equipage. I wish I knew whether he got there without trouble and not too late. It is a shame, this difficulty he always has with a conveyance for his journeys; one can easily enough become sick and tired of traveling early and late in such rigs. I shall be very glad when he finally gets himself some proper driving gear, and poor Rosinante can claim another name. Where is Vige, I wonder? He has not been home all day; and yet I saw him shortly after Vilhelm left. I hope Vilhelm finds him if he followed him.

After Vilhelm had gone, I sat down and did some figuring, then took some money and went over to Erik's, but did not find him home. So I continued on to Aarthun's and confided to Anne how tired I was of all the soiled clothes; these she has now promised to take care of. Then it was agreed that I should have one of her daughters when I move, which pleased them very much. Anne thought I would have to take them one at a time so that they would not be jealous of each other. She wanted me to stay and eat *flødegrød*, but I wanted to get home and write; so I left. Oh, how warm it was! The fog had disappeared and the sun beat down.

Some time after we had finished dinner, Helene came to have a look at the parsonage land; I accompanied her there and walked back through the woods. Then I had to get my clothes together, since Anne was to come for them, and I found Kari Bergan sitting here when I came down. She has

---

[8] Rosinante, Pastor Koren's horse, was so named because of its resemblance to the famous steed of Don Quixote.

now had her coffee, which no visitor can escape having, and has just left, Eli going with her part way. She urged me strongly to visit her some time; I must try to do that, too, though I have no special desire to take that long walk with Eli, especially if it becomes very warm. It is not easy to make excuses for not going with them so long as I am here; when we have our own home it will be a different matter. I like very much to visit people, but it should be possible for me to go with Vilhelm now and then — it is so pleasant.

Tomorrow I must really see to getting something written. It seems as if I have so much to do, now that our things have come.

Thursday, April 6. I am very glad I am rid of all the soiled clothes. Anne left with them just now and took everything there was. I wish I knew how Vilhelm and Rosinante got along — whether they reached their destination with whole skins. No doubt there are many people at the services today in this lovely weather. It is as warm as a midsummer's day.

I wrote to Mrs. Linka today; I enjoy writing to her. I should like very much to visit her this summer. At times I wish so much there were a young matron in the neighborhood, one whose company I could really enjoy, otherwise it would not be worth while; but if there were one, that would be delightful. I keep wishing more and more for my own household; I get so tired of being always among strangers. It certainly is not good for me, either. I wish very much I could keep house and make Vilhelm comfortable and thus have some more interesting occupations than I do now. I can always find things to do, of course, but they are only little trifling things which do not satisfy, or I am merely helping Eli — but now it will be better, for I am to start quilting. I could find enough to do, now that we have received our baggage, it is true, but that had better wait until we have our own home. No, a young wife certainly is not benefited by being so long without a home of her own to look after. I am afraid I shall become lazy and lose some of my interest in housekeeping — but there is no real danger, I hope.

I have finished my letter to Mrs. Garrigues; tomorrow I shall write Mrs. Lund. I shall be glad to get these two letters off. Despite the beautiful weather today I did not take a walk — merely sauntered about in the yard down by the spring. I have been too lazy to go farther and am very tired because of the heat. What will it be like, this summer, if I am so tired now? I shall have to hope it is only that I am not used to it.

Friday, April 7. Who would imagine such changes of weather as we have here? Today it is raw and raining as hard as it can, and yesterday it was so warm. Well, it is April, it is true, but it seems to me that all the months here are like April in that respect. Just now there was a man here from Minnesota to inquire when the pastor would visit that area. I wish old Torkild would come so that I could dispatch my letter to Mrs. Preus and get an *Emigranten* in return, and perhaps learn how matters are in Norway in this dreadful time of famine.[9] Many here have a strange way of looking at it. Thus, the other day one woman told me she had heard there were many here who were willing to get together and send wheat to their families, but feared the "higher-ups" would seize it for themselves; and as for sending money, why, it was much more sensible to bring their relatives over here than to send a few dollars home. What good would that do?

I have now written Mrs. Lund and finished a good share of the letter to Sellø. Am I not smart? I also spent an hour in Barfod's poetical anthology and revived memories of early childhood, when I first learned all these songs and received my first impressions of them.[10] I recalled my old favorites, of which I remember especially the ballad about Christian II — for whom I always had a soft spot in my heart, bad as I thought he was — and a song about Eleanora Christine.[11] Yes,

[9] Torkild Hanson Holla, from Telemark, was a relative of the Dysjas; in formation received from William Linnevold.

[10] Povl Frederik Barfod, *Poetisk læsebog for børn og barnlige sjæle* (Poetical Anthology for Children and Childlike Spirits — Copenhagen, 1835–36).

[11] Christian II was king of Denmark and Norway, 1513–23. Eleanora Christina (1621–98), a gifted and beautiful woman, was the daughter of King Christian IV of Denmark.

that was indeed a beautiful time when, without disturbance from anyone, I could lose myself in what I was reading. How many times have I grieved that confirmation brought its passing! Then I was a grown-up girl, as they say, and had other things to do than pore over books. Of course I was not supposed to cease my earlier occupations entirely, but I soon had to leave most of them. There was not enough time for everything, at least not for me. But I wish I could have kept my childhood privileges a little longer. I did not find that becoming grown-up was compensation for giving them up, for what interested me most was then more and more lost to me, instead of being of real benefit. But it now seems that what was lost is returning.

Saturday, April 8. Would to God I knew where Vilhelm is now! It is impossible not to worry lest he be out in this weather — and it is Saturday, so he is almost sure to be on his way somewhere for tomorrow. I have never seen such rain nor have I ever heard such loud thunder.[12] I sat here alone some time ago sewing, at which I have spent the whole day, when a thunderclap made me jump from my seat. It must have been a loud one, indeed, to make me do that, for as a rule I am not afraid of thunder. It seemed as if the rain which followed would never let up, and it held Embret [Sørland] and Eli captive a long time in the cowshed, until Embret's patience gave out and he walked up here with the water bucket over his head instead of an umbrella. The rain is driving in from the north and east, so Eli has had to take down the dripping wet curtain and move everything that was next to the wall. One could take a little boat trip on the doorstep. I hope our house will be tighter, for it is really too bad that it never rains without water streaming in through walls and windows. Yet since the plastering here is supposed to be excellent, doubtless log houses are of that nature.

[12] Thunderstorms such as are common to Iowa and other parts of the Midwest are almost unknown in Norway, and hence were unfamiliar experiences to the Korens.

My, how it lightens! Although we have a light, I must close my eyes every now and then. But such a storm is interesting. I have not lost my old desire to stand outside and watch the lightning streak down the sky, which as a child I was often forbidden to do. I must stay inside like a good child today, too, and be happy over it. Alas for the poor people who have no roofs over their heads tonight! Vilhelm must surely be in some house by this time, if indeed he has been out today — for now it is already evening. As I started to write a while ago, it suddenly became so dark that I had to lay this aside. And now we are about to eat; Eli fried pancakes and Embret, pork; he wouldn't be satisfied with cakes only.

Monday, April 10. My dear, sweet sister-in-law's birthday. God grant it may find her as glad and happy as I wish and hope, and may its memory, bright and smiling, return many, many times to her and Johan! Ah, if one could be with them for only a little while in that pleasant little home in the new town! Well, I am not alone in that wish; I am sure Marie and Johan are wishing just as heartily that we might come, and are thinking of all the times we have spent this birthday together in the old mansion. Johan was always with us — but not Vilhelm, to be sure — and last year I wondered if possibly it might be the last time we should be together. I have spent the day prosaically enough, busily washing my fine linens, but that has not been enough to keep my thoughts from dwelling on Horten.[13]

Guri [Skaarlia] and little Embret were here all forenoon, and then Suckow was here, in despair because Iver Kvale does not let him work in peace, but prates about the unfortunate parsonage land that is still not fully paid for. Now he wants interest on the balance and comes to Embret [Sørland], who sends him to Katterud. Whenever it is a matter of money, or a question of borrowing anything, they all have a certain dread of dealing with Kvale.

I now have all my linens starched and dried. After that

[13] See chapter 1, footnote 10. Johan Koren and his wife lived in Horten.

was done, I went downstairs to look through the other chest and get some scarves for Vilhelm. In this chest everything was in just as good condition as in the other. While I was in the midst of unpacking our many tablecloths and napkins, Anne returned with the wash. She was no doubt well pleased to have arrived so opportunely as to be able to get a look at some of our things, and helped hold the pieces which were not to be put back again, while I packed and packed and forgot entirely what I was really after, namely, scarves; so now I must go through it again. But I cannot understand why I did not see them, for I went to the bottom. I shall have to hope for better luck next time, so that I can get Vilhelm a clean scarf for Easter. It was nice to get all the clean clothes, but it is annoying that Anne would not take pay for her work. I showed her the daguerreotypes, to her great delight. But to get her to admit that Marie is good-looking is impossible. "Is she pretty, really?" said Anne. "No, but these are elegant, indeed," she said, and pointed to the Lassens.[14]

I did not get much sleep Saturday night. The thunder stopped but not the rain, which beat against the shingles of the roof until it sounded as if it would come tumbling down upon me; and it is not easy to sleep amid such unaccustomed noise. This was another long bleak day — the same wind and rain. Embret did not even go to Thorgrim's, but took a nap in the middle of the forenoon instead (as did Eli, too). As their nap lasted until twelve, we did not have dinner until two; there was this advantage — the afternoon did not become so inordinately long. I read and enjoyed the pleasant book I had received, Theremin's *Abendstunden*, but just the same it was a dull day.[15] How I long for Vilhelm! For a time I enjoyed the book so much that I did not notice the bad weather, but eventually I no longer got any good out of

[14] Marie was Johan Koren's wife. Mariane (Mally) Lassen married Elisabeth Koren's younger brother, Johan Augustinus ("Stin") Hysing (1834–88), in 1864; Johnson, *Slekten Koren*, 1:188. The Lassens were friends of the Hysings.
[15] Franz Theremin, *Abendstunden* (The Evening Hour — Berlin, 1845).

what I was reading. I felt so lonely, and saw everything in such dismal colors; but, God be praised, the mood did not last very long. Then the depressing thoughts went away and I sat quite cheerfully and talked with Eli and Embret. Why can't I chase these depressing thoughts away at once when they come!

Today I sent a letter to Mrs. Linka. I had just picked it up with some money, intending to ask Magnus to take it to Erik, when Erik himself came and saved me the trouble.[16] I hope he will bring something back with him!

Wednesday, April 12. Maundy Thursday Eve — they are now ringing in the holy days at home. How I miss the church bells! I should so much like to hear them on Sunday mornings, and when they call people to work in the summer. How many times I have stood and listened to them in the garden at home! It was at this time, too, usually Easter Eve, that I could bring the first wreath of flowers to the grave.[17] Perhaps the small white flowers are already in bloom outside the windows of the yellow room. I am going to miss my walks to the cemetery; I have spent many of my best hours there. It was so good to be there in the evening, so quiet, peaceful, and solemn. I am thankful Vilhelm will be home for Easter Eve.

Yesterday was a busy day, but I was well satisfied, too, when I had all my clothes, to the last rag, ironed; it seems to me I did well. It was really a joy this forenoon to put away so many clean clothes and get them somewhat in order, though it is not easy when one has so little room. Erik brought me neither *Emigranten* nor a letter. McKay had not been home and his wife did not have the key to the letter drawer.[18] That's a way of doing things! I hope Vilhelm will go by there Saturday and be more fortunate.

[16] Magnus Arneson Linnevold (1805-97), a carpenter, lived in the southeast quarter of Section 7, Frankville Township, Winneshiek County; Linnevold in *Decorah-posten,* May 24, 1929.

[17] Mrs. Koren is speaking of a visit to her mother's grave.

[18] On McKay's post office, see chapter 9, footnote 4. The messenger was Erik Egge.

I am wondering what I should do — take a walk to the parsonage land and watch Suckow, or go out and ransack the chest for some scarves. Perhaps I had better pay the sheep a visit. I imagine Vilhelm will be home late, and naturally he will have both his scarves soiled. I had better be sensible then — doubly sensible — since it looks like rain, too.

Easter Eve, 1854. It is the eve of Easter, but no indication of it in my surroundings — nothing to distinguish this evening from an ordinary Saturday evening. Eli is roasting coffee. Embret is outside; he and Erik hammer away at the summer kitchen. Everything looks as usual.

And yet it is so pleasant when one can notice everywhere that it is a festal eve, when everything is polished and tidied and the daily work is laid aside; and thus it all had to be at home before the church bells began to ring. I remember so well how as a child I used to help Father rake and clean the garden; how often I hurried in order to be ready before the holy day was rung in — here there is nothing like that. But, God be praised, Vilhelm will be coming tonight — that makes me very happy — and will then stay home tomorrow at least; so we, too, will have a somewhat festive Easter. I know of course that I can observe Easter in my heart, it is true, but when Vilhelm is home, it is nevertheless different. I do not know why, but here the holy days always seem so long to me when I am alone. I get tired of reading all day and, moreover, I have no one to talk to. So the time seems very long; and the cold, raw weather we had yesterday and the day before makes it seem longer.

Maundy Thursday I wanted to go to the home where Gullik [Rønningen] was to read, but no one knew how to get there and, besides, no one cared to go. Embret went to Andrew's and Guri came to Eli's. I went alone to Thorgrim's to find out where the reading was to be. Only his wife was home, and I learned from her that at the last meeting at their house they had agreed not to meet this week because there were to be services on Sunday — a strange reason, but such it was. I sat and talked awhile, then left to take a little walk; but I was so tired when I got back to the brook I was glad to go no farther.

Guri was still here and stayed for dinner, for which she had brought some veal that tasted delicious to me after I had been without it so long.

I thought the Franckeans observed all holy days very strictly, but now I hear that they are harrowing and seeding for all they are worth and even had their meeting at Iver Kvale's on Wednesday instead of Thursday, simply because they have so much to do — such, at least, is the gossip.

Eli went for a walk with her mother to see how the logs on the parsonage land were doing — whether possibly the twelve had grown fewer in number. So I sat alone and read and waited for Embret, to see if he brought anything from the post office. "Do you have a letter?" I asked when he entered the door. "Yes, sir," he answered, smiling very contentedly, and I stood there with no small expectations while he drew forth the mail. I threw *Emigranten* on the table and seized the letter; but it soon suffered the same fate as *Emigranten*; it was only a tiresome business letter to Vilhelm. I wonder if there will be anything today. But perhaps the mail has not come yet. *Emigranten* confirmed reports of the increasing famine in our beloved Norway, for which help is being earnestly solicited in Wisconsin. Otherwise there was nothing new.

Eli returned and reported that the logs had neither increased nor decreased in number, and thereupon she began to fry pancakes. Embret expressed concern lest people be careless in paying up, and lest the land not be paid for on the date set and thus fall into Paulsen's hands.[19] From these dreary reflections (thus they always are when they concern the parsonage land) he was roused by a Minnesota man whom the pastor is to marry. The stranger stayed here until the following forenoon, which Eli and Embret passed in sleeping

[19] On Paulsen, see chapter 11, footnote 6.

until Per Haugen came and woke them. They are so tired, Eli and Embret, and do not stand severe weather well. It is the usual aftermath of that horrible ague, which was also the cause of their spending the forenoon as they did, but it seems to me that Embret is not so eager to read as he used to be.[20]

There is a disgustingly cold wind today; I do not like having spring begin so early, and then wait so long before it comes in earnest — it would be better for winter to last a little longer, I believe. I hope I may meet Vilhelm now; at least I am going to try to do so. I hope he does not come too late and that nothing is wrong with Rosinante and the wagon.

Thursday, April 20. Again several days have passed, during which this book has not been brought out; but this time I have been away on a journey. I went out to the settlements west of here with Vilhelm for a couple of days, and came home yesterday.

Oh, how warm it was yesterday! It was awful. I could stand it while we were driving; then there was a little breeze. But when we got home — well, I sat where I sat and could not lift a finger; the others were not much better off, either. The heat came so suddenly, too. I have never seen such thunder and lightning as we had in the afternoon. The thunder was not so loud, but the lightning was all the more frequent, flash after flash in every direction. Nor did it cool off, for it rained only a very little; and we sat with door and windows closed because of the lightning, and with a fire in the stove to warm the milk for the precious calves. No, I shall not forget that evening. I only hope it doesn't happen too often. Today is hot and oppressive, too, but better than yesterday, nevertheless; so I shall try to write. Vilhelm is at Aarthun's instructing the candidates for confirmation; think how hot it must be in that small room!

[20] Per Haugen was possibly Peter E. Haugen. Fever and ague, or malaria, was a dreaded enemy of early settlers in all the Midwest states. See Ludvig Hektoen and Knut Gjerset, "Health Conditions and the Practice of Medicine among the Early Norwegian Settlers, 1825-1865," in Norwegian-American Historical Association, *Studies and Records*, 1:1-59 (Minneapolis, 1926).

My expedition turned out well Easter evening. I had walked only to the beginning of the bottom when I saw something coming down the road which at last turned out to be a horse and wagon and two men. Someone had come with Vilhelm from Paint Creek and now was driving poor Rosinante, who actually had brought both herself and the wagon home without mishap, surpassing all expectations. Vilhelm was walking behind with a flower in his hat and three fruit trees in his hand. This beginning of our garden (a cherry tree and two plum trees, the latter of which will surely die, I regret to say) he had received from McKay, at whose house he had met Embret. Embret, in reply to his question as to how matters were at home, had said that I had lost my appetite, over which he was much concerned. Vilhelm always brings me something from his journeys, and this time he brought a spurtle, a real Norwegian one, from Gunhild Ederklep.[21]

First Easter Day services were held at Rognald's. The rest of the day we spent quietly at home. Magnus and a *tinndøl* and Gullik [Rønningen] were here part of the afternoon.[22]

The next morning we drove off to the west and of course had to stray from the road a bit before we reached Ola Bekken's, where we were to make our first stop. I very nearly became ill during the service, the little room was so crowded with people, and every other woman, I believe, had a small crying child with her. This was the first time I had been there, so the people were strangers. Ola's wife is lively and interesting to talk to, and so genuinely Norwegian. She told me at great length of her livestock, how many eggs she had sold, and what she had been able to buy with her egg money. She thought it was too bad that I was not used to caring for livestock. She was extremely busy running downhill to where she had moved her stove, and up to the house again for some-

[21] A spurtle, thivel, or pudding stick was an implement carved of wood, with blades at the lower end; it was used to stir porridge.
[22] A *tinndøl* is a person from the district of Tinn in Norway. Magnus is mentioned in footnote 16 to this chapter. On Gullik, see chapter 6, footnote 19.

thing for the meal. At last the pork and the coffee came and some fowl with a salty gravy on it. I, for my part, took the fowl, though it did not have much taste; at least I thus escaped the pork.[23]

We had now eaten and were to leave, as we planned to spend the night with Thore Skotland, who lived a little closer to where we were to be the next day. Aase was much dissatisfied with this. "At least you must have something to drink first," she said, and, climbing on a bench, stood there handing everyone who cared for it a large bowl of unskimmed milk with which to refresh himself.

The Thore Skotlands are a pleasant family. In their little cabin, which was as modest as it could be — there was not even a ceiling to partition off the loft — everything was clean and neat, even the children. We stayed there that night. Bedrooms are scarce wherever we are; there was not even a loft there. The farm folk do not feel embarrassed; it would be well if others could learn the art from them. Thore's wife set a very bountiful table and was quite in despair because we ate so little.

The following morning (Tuesday) we drove to Erik Gudbrandson's, where the service was held. It was roomy there and on the whole more pleasant; they took the crying youngsters outside when they became too unruly.[24]

Jørgen Lomen invited us to go home with him, and we did. He lives in a dugout, but that is not so bad as one might think. I like these people very much; his wife is a sister of Pastor Brandt, attractive and friendly; she did her utmost to arrange things for us, hung a fly net about our bed for bed

[23] Ola T. Bekken (later Bakken) and his wife Aase Kittelson Bekken lived in the northeast quarter of Section 5, Military Township, Winneshiek County; information received from Miss Marie Koren. See also George E. Warner and C. M. Foote, *Platbook of Winneshiek County*, 13 (Minneapolis, 1886). The stove had probably been moved outside the cabin to make room for those attending the service.

[24] Erik Gudbrandson Egge and his wife Berit Johnsdatter Egge lived in the southwest quarter of Section 33, Madison Township, Winneshiek County, ten or twelve miles from the parsonage land; Alexander, *Winneshiek and Allamakee Counties*, 577.

curtains, and made everything as comfortable as she could. Vilhelm and I took a walk with Jørgen in his woods; it was a lovely evening.[25]

The next morning the weather looked bad, but before we had gone far the sun was shining; we felt its warmth as we went up a long steep hill. Apparently there can be steep hills here, too. When we got to the top of that one, I broke my parasol. Then we discovered that Vilhelm had lost his whip. Jørgen, who was with us, immediately went back for it; then Vilhelm set out after him to tell him to go no farther. So they went all the way down the hill and back to the top again, where I was sitting and sunning myself. Luckily, the whip was found.

It is not beautiful in the western settlements; here and there the landscape is cheerful enough, but generally there is one great desolate prairie after another without lovely lines. The horizon at times looks so much like a distant, peaceful sea that it would be impossible to believe otherwise if one did not know the land's physical characteristics. We thoroughly enjoyed surrendering ourselves to the illusion for a little while. Some of the prairies are sprinkled with small stones, and such areas are now overgrown with a gray-blue flower which much resembles the crocus.[26]

Saturday, April 22. I wonder how Vilhelm is managing in this fearful heat! He went to Minnesota today. I moved the table from our room to the open window and worked steadily on the Sellø letter until I could bear it no longer and had to sit outside, where it was too windy to manage pen and paper.

The other day there was more discussion about the parsonage land. Nothing was decided; everything was postponed until today. Now I wonder how it will go. It is moving extremely slowly, it seems to me, logs and all!

[25] Many settlers built their first shelters, which were known as dugouts, in the side slopes of hills. The floor and three walls of such a dwelling were of dirt, the roof and front wall of timber.
[26] This was probably the windflower.

14

We Are Living at Skaarlia's

Wednesday, May 3. We are now living at Skaarlia's.[1] We moved yesterday. Embret set off with his wagon filled with our traps. (It's appalling, all the things we have taken out since our baggage came.) We followed, walking, Vilhelm with his arms full of clothes and his hands full of daguerreotypes, and I with a pile of newspapers, the umbrella, and the spurtle, while holding on to my hat, which threatened to blow off of my head. So we set out, climbed a couple of fences, and arrived here, where everything lay in disorder in the middle of the floor.

The coffee mill, spurtle, and four tin cups formed the sum total of our domestic equipment — nothing to cook in or on, and not a bite of food. True enough, we had forty dollars in gold, but of what use was that? Guri, however, had left two chairs, we ourselves had one — in other words, something to sit on; and so we sat down. Vilhelm lit a cigar, and as I had

[1] Pastor Koren states that he and Elisabeth moved from Sørland's to Skaarlia's for family reasons, just as they had moved from Egge's to Sørland's. The Sørland's son, Gudbrand E., was born July 15, 1854; Koren, in *Symra*, 33 (1905); Bailey, *Winneshiek County*, 1:210.

just that morning received a letter from my dear Christiane, written a couple of days after the former one, I now read it aloud to him. He sang and we made merry over the four-shilling banquet which Christiane had described. Then we read *Emigranten*, which had also come. I brought forth Giering's "Present from Ryde," we drank a little wine, and had quite a splendid time as we sat there in the midst of all the confusion.

Then it struck us that it might be time to bring some order out of chaos. We packed and unpacked, put our clothes in place in the loft, opened the boxes, and took out the books; so now the boxes are in use as bookcases and contribute materially to the adornment of the room. At last we were through, fairly well satisfied with our little room, and especially with being by ourselves. Now Vilhelm will have much more peace.

At this point it dawned on Vilhelm that we could hardly live on love and spring water alone, and so we went over to the old [Skaarlia] cabin, which stood open, to seek more substantial nourishment.[2] I climbed on a table for a little milk; Vilhelm found bread and butter and cake; and then we had our meal, standing in the middle of the floor, Vilhelm with his hat cocked on one side like a tipsy sailor, I in my white cap and violet dress, which could hardly be called clean, and my knitted shawl wrapped about me, a bit of food in one hand and a bowl of milk in the other.

Next I took the broom and swept the room and dusted, and then we were able to rest on our laurels. Vilhelm read aloud to me from Landstad's ballads, and soon afterwards the Skaarlia folk came home.[3] We had supper with them and stayed there awhile, then went back to our own house, sat up a couple of hours, brought down all the bedclothes from the loft, laid them on the floor, since everything is open in all

[2] The Skaarlias gave the Korens a small house that they had just completed and themselves continued to live in their old cabin for the summer This was the first home that the Korens had to themselves; Koren, in *Symra* 33 (1905).

[3] Magnus Brostrup Landstad (1802–80) was a Norwegian clergyman, hymn writer, and collector of folklore.

directions, and slept very soundly in our new home. Vilhelm had to go to the spring this morning for water to wash in. Today he has gone to the smith to get his wagon. If it is ready, I shall accompany him to Paint Creek tomorrow.

Imagine our joy! They have begun work on the parsonage! Today they are hauling stones and logs with all their might.

TROUT RIVER P. O., WINNESHIEK CO.

SKAARLIA'S, May 22, 1854.

MY DEAR, DEAR FATHER:

I have been so slow in writing because we have been away on a trip, and since our return Vilhelm has not been well. Now, God be praised, he is much better and is up again. He had a very bad cold and was confined to his bed for some time.[4] Pastor Clausen came here just at that time, spent nearly a whole day with us, and was a great comfort. He is friendly, sympathetic, and helpful. I liked him very much. He conducted services for Vilhelm on Rogation Sunday; his coming at that time was indeed fortunate for us. We have been invited very cordially to visit him this summer; he lives about eighty miles west of us. Well, there is no lack of invitations from all sides.[5]

We are now living by ourselves in this little house, which I feel sure I mentioned in my last letter.

Now you shall hear what it looks like. It is a little oblong room with a door in the middle of the long wall and two windows, with chintz curtains, just opposite each other. Under each window is a table; on one of them rests my writing case — where I am now writing — also a bowl of wild flowers; by the other Vilhelm sits in a rocking chair, reading. The bed is

[4] "It was a severe attack of bilious fever — no doctor. It took weeks before he recovered his strength"; *Fra pioneertiden*, 165 n.

[5] Claus L. Clausen (1820–92), pioneer pastor and colonizer, was a Dane who went to Wisconsin in 1843 with the idea of being a teacher for the Muskego pioneers. The settlers requested that he be their minister, and he was ordained that same year. He became a prominent and controversial member of the Norwegian Synod. During 1853–56 he had a congregation at St. Ansgar, Iowa. See Carlton C. Qualey, "Claus L. Clausen, Pioneer Pastor and Settlement Promoter," in *Norwegian-American Studies and Records*, 6:12-29 (Northfield, 1931). Rogation Sunday is the fifth Sunday after Easter.

in one corner; it occupies the long wall, together with one of Vilhelm's boxes for books, which is shaped somewhat like a bookcase and which, to our joy, stands upright, so that we can get at its contents. On the wall where I am sitting there is another box for books and likewise a closed stairway to the loft, where we keep our clothes and the hired girl sleeps. Finally, Guri has been so kind as to leave us a large shelf just opposite the bed; that is my pantry. And now you have a description of our present home.

These two, Erik and Guri, who have given us their cabin and are themselves living in the old one, are kind, excellent people, and very helpful and obliging to us. We get what milk and potatoes we need from them. We now have our stove, with which I am greatly pleased, and I have had a shed built in which to put it and prepare our food. It is out of the question, of course, to have it inside the cabin during the summer, since there is only one room.

I have one of Anne Aarthun's daughters to help me — she is one of the candidates for confirmation — so you may be sure that I begin to feel my dignity as a housewife. I have begun to bake bread, too. Something went wrong the first time and I was quite disgusted with my new stove, thinking it would not bake properly; but I found a man who taught us how to operate it — it is a new type, it seems. Now all goes well and the other day I ventured to bake white bread and rusks for Vilhelm's barley soup. They tasted good but gave Vilhelm a chance to laugh at me because of the remarkable shapes they assumed.

I was really at a loss to get some barley soup for Vilhelm while he was sick. Ground barley and oats are not found here; I hope they can be had in Wisconsin. Well, it was no use to stand there helpless; I got some barley, dried it, ground it in my coffee mill, and made soup. Then I had to find something to mix with it; the only solution was to cook some dried apples and use the juice from them — one has to do the best one can.

You should have seen me, Father, when I went to get salt for the dough for my rusks, walking to Guri's house and back to ours accompanied by two frisky calves, which run loose outside here, and Vige dashing on ahead.

We have received many gifts from neighbors — butter, eggs, cream, and flour. As long as we lived with others there was no pleasure, they thought, in bringing us anything; but now it is different. The other day I made chicken soup with dumplings and was very proud of it; it must have been an excellent chicken to make such good soup. It was given me by Mother [Anne] Aarthun, and I was happy to have a meat soup for my convalescent. The only way of getting fresh meat here is to kill a rooster or shoot a bird; as yet, people butcher only hogs. Not long ago we received a splendid gift when one of the candidates for confirmation brought us a fine mess of trout; they were really delicious. There are fish in abundance, mostly pike and other fresh-water fish, about three to four English miles from here; but it is so difficult to send for them. It will be good to have an errand boy, as we must have when we get the parsonage — one of the candidates for confirmation.

Here you have a little account of my household activities, dear Father; it is fun to have one's own home, you may be sure. It seems to me that I am very busy now, especially teaching my girl, who has never seen other housekeeping than that at Aarthun's and is quite bewildered by everything I undertake and by the new dishes she has never seen before.

We returned from Paint Creek the evening before Rogation Sunday.[6] On the whole it is more beautiful there than here, and of course everything then was in its spring glory. The scenery is marvelous, but wild; it is easy to realize that one is only five or six miles from the Mississippi.

We also made a trip to Columbus, a little beginning of a town, which lies right on the Mississippi — a delightful trip.[7]

[6] In 1854 the evening before Rogation Sunday fell on May 19.
[7] Columbus was a hamlet at the mouth of Village Creek just south of Lansing, Iowa.

It had just rained, so everything was fresh and full of fragrance from the newly leaved trees. The road was charming and interesting, the last part of it parallel to the river. As it lay fairly high, we had the beautiful river with its luxuriant valley and small, thickly wooded islets below us. The bluffs, most of which are covered with grass and are partly wooded, had here somewhat the form of a sugar loaf. It was the most beautiful summer evening we have had. The river was blue and clear; one rarely finds it so.

We took a walk along the bank — a road through the woods. The trees extend to the water on one side, and on the other there are bluffs thickly overgrown — such luxuriant foliage! There was a profusion of brush and bushes of every sort. The sun's last rays were falling on the thickly wooded islets dotting the river and up the heights of the opposite bank. It was lovely. In addition there was a fresh smell of verdure, large rocks overrun by creepers, many kinds of vines, bird-cherry thickets, plum trees in blossom, and more that I did not recognize, and many new wild flowers which I saw for the first time. So you may imagine, dear Father, what a pleasure it was. Ah, if you, too, could only have seen these flowers, bushes, and creeping plants! I thought of you, you may be sure.

Is it not strange that the wild cherry grows only as a shrub here? I have not seen a real cherry tree, though there are two kinds. The black currant grows wild — asparagus, too, Clausen told us; he had many at his place. They are good, but not so good as the tame. If the fruit lives up to the promise of the blossoms, there will be great quantities of strawberries, and raspberries too, I hope, so that I may get some for preserves.

The following day we rowed from Columbus to Lansing, quite near by, which is a town of more importance and is growing. Here one can get whatever one wants. The steamboats come here; yes, in fact, they go much farther — to St. Paul, I believe, in Minnesota.[8]

[8] Lansing is in Allamakee County, Iowa, on the west bank of the Mississippi.

It was my dear Lina's birthday. Greet her and tell her that I sat on a pile of planks down by the Mississippi and thought of her while I watched the beautiful birds that flew over the water.[9]

On the way down Vilhelm got out of the wagon more than once to bring me an unfamiliar flower. Although it is not yet really the season for flowers, I have found quite a number; for example, a yellow flower whose petals and leaves, especially, resemble certain wallflowers and smell almost like auriculas; a white flower, without fragrance, but pretty, which has much in common with the lily family; some fiery-red phlox, both in scent and appearance much the same as those in the garden at home, though they grow only in very small bushes. The ground has really been blue with violets, but they have no fragrance. Cat's-foot, as we called it, and pansies, somewhat different from those at home, were also here in abundance.[10] Rumor is slanderous in what it says about the fragrance of flowers in America — many are fragrant.

As to songbirds, rumor is perhaps more truthful, although there are said to be many that sing beautifully; but most of the time we must be content with chirping. There are, however, a great many beautiful birds, large and small, of all colorings. There are three kinds of swallows, some very pretty, blue with brownish wings. But the little bird of indigo blue wins the prize. I have not noticed gnats and mosquitoes yet, but most of May was cold and very stormy. We had spring in March. But this rain has done good; now everything is green and beautiful. The oak, however, which is very slow, is not fully leaved out yet.

As I mentioned before, we came home the evening before Rogation Sunday and heard on the way that Pastor Clausen had arrived. Vilhelm immediately went over to Katterud's, where he was lodging, and when he came back told me he had invited Pastor Clausen to dinner the following day.

[9] Mrs. Koren's sister, Caroline Mathilde Hysing, was born May 9, 1840 and died March 6, 1923; Johnson, *Slekten Koren*, 1:189.
[10] Cat's-foot is ground ivy.

"What are you thinking of?" said I. "We haven't a bite of food in the house except the ham." Well, he had invited Clausen on the strength of the ham — and there it rested. I wished that I had the five lobsters with which Marie had entertained Herr Bang.[11] Well, it was not so easy. I had to do my best with the ham and go to Guri's for boiled potatoes, and then we ate with good appetites. When the gentlemen had drunk their coffee and smoked their pipes, we walked up to the parsonage grounds and looked at the building, on which work was in full swing. The next day the trout came and I was glad to have something for the pastor which was a rarity even for him, though he lives, it is said, next to a river so full of fish, mostly carp and pike, that at times one cannot see bottom. One evening he himself caught a large mess of fish with his hands.

Thank you a thousand times, my dear, dear Father, for your kind blessed letter of March 9, which I received toward the end of April. At last you had received a letter from Iowa! God be praised for the joy it brought you, and because I am able to send you good news this time, too! You may be sure there is joy in Iowa when a letter comes from home.

You were in good health, dear Father, and now, I imagine, you are in the garden every day. Have your flowers stood the winter well? Here flowers often have a hard time, I think, for sometimes there is spring in March and winter in April. Has the ivy in the corner done well this year? My cherry tree is no doubt blossoming beautifully now. I am glad Marie has my garden; ask her to look after it well.[12] Was the beech wood beautifully in leaf for my birthday? Here everything is really well advanced.

We were at the parsonage land yesterday. It was lovely. The large wood and small groves were beautiful; during the last few days the oak has leaved out fully. The leafy trees are much larger than at home. The grass is very high. The foliage

---

[11] Marie was Johan Koren's wife. See chapter 1, footnote 10.
[12] Here Mrs. Koren speaks of her sister, Christine Marie Cappelen Hysing See chapter 8, note 22.

is luxuriant. The low hazel brush is dense, interspersed with raspberries, somewhat different from those at home and now in full bloom; the blossoms rather resemble apple blossoms, have a little fragrance, and are beautiful. We shall be in a wooded area. The house will have two large oaks in front of it, on one side an old gnarled oak whose branches reach the ground, and behind it the beautiful grove of oaks and poplars. It should be charming surrounded by a garden.

I think the whole population of Wisconsin must be moving west. A young man who came here yesterday with greetings from Pastor Preus had passed more than three hundred wagonloads of Norwegians, the greater part bound for Minnesota — some few for Pastor Clausen's.[13] There is no land for them here. Those who journey thus are either newcomers who have wintered in Wisconsin, or others who have sold their small farms to older Norwegians and now move to where they can easily pick up large tracts at a lower price. Many are migrating from the congregations of the Preuses, Stub, and others. In Minnesota people are so eager to get a minister that it can hardly be long before they arrange to send a call to Norway. Duus, I understand, has now been called to Waupaca; he will no doubt be the farthest from us of them all. I wonder, will no one apply for Blue Mounds?[14]

You ask about our chests and trunks. Yes, we have received them. We were unable to take them with us on the train on which we traveled; they were sent on another. When we got to Milwaukee, they were not expected for a couple of days, at least. We could not wait, and so left it to Preus to take care of them, and then made an agreement with a man in Dodgeville, [Wisconsin,] to forward them.[15] Finally in April they

[13] Clausen was at St. Ansgar, Iowa. See footnote 5.

[14] The Reverend Olaus Fredrik Duus (1824–93) migrated to America in 1854 and was a pastor in Wisconsin until 1859, when he returned to Norway. See *Frontier Parsonage: The Letters of Olaus Fredrik Duus, Norwegian Pastor in Wisconsin, 1855–58* (Northfield, 1947). Waupaca is a city in Wisconsin thirty-five miles west of Appleton; Duus was pastor there, 1854–57. Blue Mounds is near Madison, Wisconsin.

[15] The name of the man in Dodgeville was Solner; he was possibly the Solner who was a friend of the Herman Preuses. See chapter 12, footnote 20.

arrived after having stood in Dodgeville for a long time; the Mississippi was the barrier to their being forwarded. No, that little nutshell of a canoe could never have taken our heavy chests across!

Vilhelm greets you affectionately. He is making good progress and has a good appetite; he has not yet started on his journeys, for which I am happy. God bless you, dear Father.

Your own
LEIS

Monday, June 12, 1854. Now I begin this poor neglected diary once more; I sincerely hope I may keep at it and not let more than a month pass again without giving it a thought, I had almost said. But that would not be true. If thoughts had been of any use, I should not need to sit here annoyed at all the time lost — time, too, rich in material for a diary. Well, it is no use to regret. But what shall I do to make good my error? All the innumerable words, scenes, and small domestic events which must be seized at the moment or else vanish — they have now vanished, and I must be content simply to write the main outlines of that period which I should like so much to keep with every possible detail. I certainly think that the time when we first got some kind of a house and began our own housekeeping deserves to be remembered, does it not?

It is evening, the hired girl has gone to bed in the loft, and my lord husband and his wife sit very sociably, one at the window, the other at the table, with backs turned to each other, writing. I enjoy the honor of having the candle snuffers and of walking back and forth to trim Vilhelm's light. Complete as our household furniture is in other respects, we still have not been able to obtain more than one set of candle snuffers, and that had to be ordered from afar at an exorbitant price. The Yankees find they can use their fingers just as well — so why then procure snuffers?

I was cross this morning, for no reason at all, of course — but now I am happy as a lark, if only there were someone to appreciate it. I had just put on the gruel this morning when Magnus' daughter came. She was to help me for a couple of days, and I was cross because she came, for I did not care to have so many girls who were strangers to me. Vilhelm was on the point of becoming angry, but stopped halfway and broke into laughter at my genial mood. I hurried off with the girl to a large straw pile to get her mattress filled.[16]

There we had many tribulations. It was warm, even hot; the straw was so wet that we had to pull away a good deal and dig deep before we reached what was dry; in short, it was enough to make me more peevish than before. But, remarkably enough, that served to bring me to myself again. Just as we had finished, Vilhelm came and scolded me for undertaking such work and tiring myself out. So we came back, Vilhelm and the girl carrying the mattress. I hurried over to my gruel which, during this affair, had been left to itself, in consequence of which I was taunted by my spouse because of its excellence. So far as I could see, he found it very much to his taste, and I wish I could often set the equal of it on the table; but now the oatmeal is all gone.

In the afternoon the girl did the washing. After Vilhelm had heard Embret's lesson and I had finished my rug, we went out for a walk.[17] We had not gone far before we stopped to pick strawberries, for which I have a veritable passion. Wherever I go, I look for them; no matter if I have both hands full when I go to the springhouse, I have to set things down if I see a berry. We found our first ripe strawberries June 18, and the following day Embret came with a bowl of them; so we had strawberries and cream for dessert after a dinner of egg pancakes and sour milk soup. The latter was a new dish which fortunately won Vilhelm's approval. I am lucky when I find a dish like that in this land of pork, where they use only coffee — coffee for breakfast, coffee instead of

[16] Caroline, daughter of Magnus Arneson Linnevold, worked for the Korens for a time as a hired girl. She later married Ole Steen; information received from William Linnevold.

[17] Embret Skaarlia was the boy who was taking lessons.

soup for dinner and, when things are really topsy-turvy, coffee for supper too.

Now I had better write a little about the past month and its notable events, so that they will not be entirely lost. But it will be even better to put that off until tomorrow and go to bed now; it must certainly be past eleven.

When I last wrote in my diary, we were to leave the next day for Paint Creek. We did leave, too, but were so late in getting away that when we neared Waukon, the future county seat of Winneshiek, Vilhelm decided we had better spend the night there.[18] I had no great desire to do so; there is little pleasure in passing a whole afternoon in such a tavern. However, I was tired and we both were hungry; in a word, it was the sensible thing to do and we stayed. These taverns are laughable. We were shown into a fairly large, but very cheaply furnished room — there was not even a table. Well, there I sat. Vilhelm went in and out; during the setting of the table (supper was served almost at once) he picked up a book that he found and stalked noisily up and down in an adjoining room, the door to which I was not permitted to close, despite several attempts.[19]

Tuesday, June 13. I am very tired but must really write a few words before bedtime. I am tired as a result of having starched and ironed clothes this morning and prepared dinner; then I took a good afternoon nap, had coffee, and read "King Erik and the Outlaws" until Caroline came to scrub the floor, when we moved outside.[20] I sewed; Vilhelm read, as he has done all day, and was angry at not being able to write because we were ironing. I maintained that he could write anyway; but no, it was impossible when his surroundings were so disagreeable. To be really fair, I hardly dare in-

---

[18] Actually Waukon became the county seat of Allamakee County and Decorah, of Winneshiek County.

[19] Here follow sixteen blank pages which were set aside in the diary for an account of the preceding month; it never was written. In its stead has been included here the letter of May 22, 1854, which precedes the diary entry of June 12.

[20] Bernard S. Ingemann, *Kong Erik og de fredløse* (Copenhagen, 1831).

sist he was angry, for he did not say much; but he was, in all
likelihood, inwardly annoyed. Well, now that we have had a
scrubbing and cleaning, he will be undisturbed tomorrow.
The girl has gone home; she was a great help during the
short time she was here. Next week, or when Vilhelm is away,
she will return and we shall have a great washday. I wish that
were over. I expect a member of the confirmation class here
Friday. She is a large, stout Valdres girl, at least twice as large
as I. I am really afraid to take her, she looks so fat and lazy;
but there is nothing else to do — and perhaps I do her an
injustice.[21]

For the greater part of the afternoon I sat outside sewing;
Vilhelm sat inside singing. Now, probably realizing that
everything is peaceful about him, he has suddenly started to
write. I asked if we should not take a walk and added that
we would have to go soon, for rain was coming up and it was
thundering sharply. First he was going to hear Embret's lesson, and called for him; but instead of the boy a strange old
man came in, a newcomer from Wisconsin, who sat here for
some time and offered to sell Vilhelm a large snuffbox. But
V. has not started to use snuff, fortunately; at least not yet.
The man left and Embret came; but when he had gone, the
rain began to stream down and we had to give up the walk.

By way of compensation Vilhelm read aloud to me from
Asbjørnsen's fairy tales until it was time for tea.[22] After that
he sat in the door and smoked cigars and read until the last
glimmer of daylight vanished, while I sat in my rocking
chair, left to my own reflections, and watched the fireflies
darting in ever-increasing numbers through the grass, far and
near, and sometimes pursuing each other through the air. It
is a pretty sight, when darkness falls, to watch all these countless, lightning-like, bluish sparks in and over the prairie grass.
Fortunately for Vilhelm's eyes, he soon found it too dark to
read, so we sat talking for a time before we lit a light. It must

[21] The Valdres girl was Johanne Karine Kristiansdatter.
[22] Peter Christen Asbjørnsen, *Huldreeventyr og folkesagn* (Fairy Tales and
Folk Legends — Christiania, 1845).

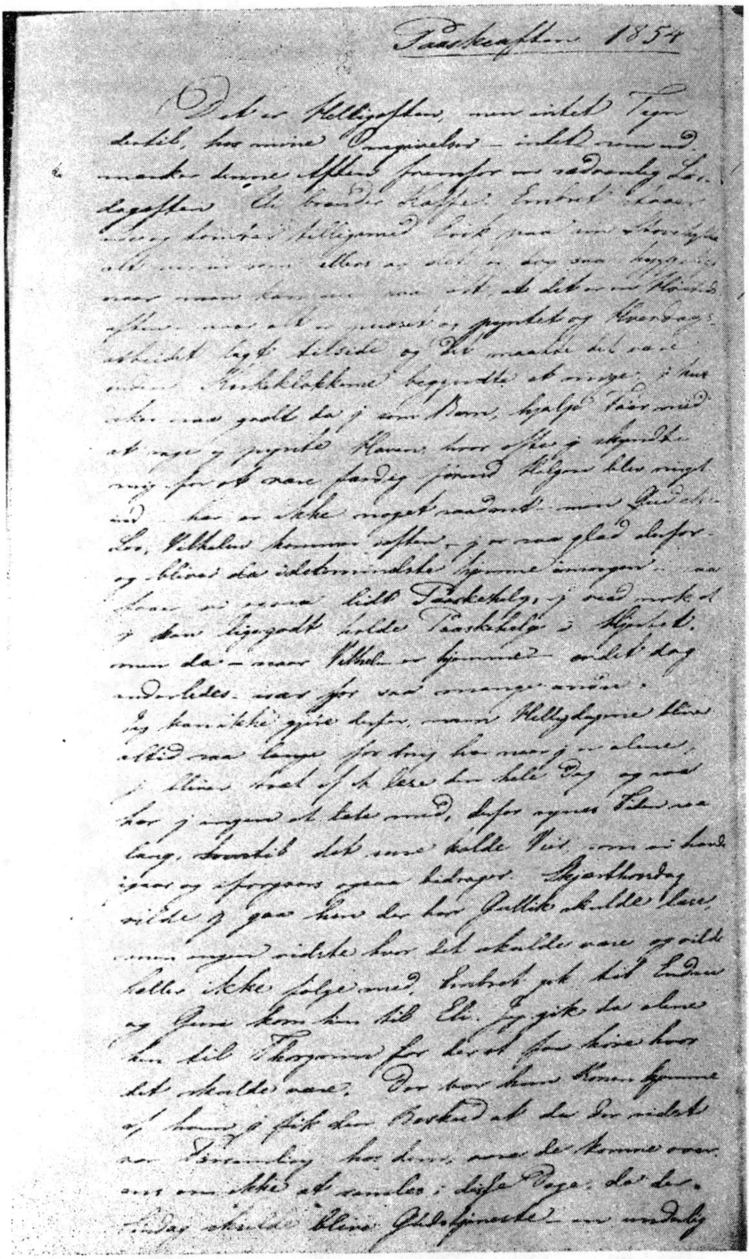

PAGE FROM ELISABETH KOREN'S DIARY, EASTER EVE, 1854

First Norw. Luth. Church West of Miss. River.

The Original Washington Prairie Church

be late now. I shall read a little and then go to bed. I hope I can get up fairly early tomorrow, too. Today I did not do so badly.

Wednesday, June 14. I shall now try to write a little, in the hope that I may be left in peace by Vilhelm. He is very naughty and has been teasing me all forenoon. While we were eating breakfast, he was still quite good-natured. I had been up fairly early and set the table and had everything ready by the time my lazy husband was finally dressed. (He really made his bed, too, Papa.)[23] As I stated, while we were eating, everything was lovely, and we discussed, among other things, whether our forefathers had had sugar with which to tickle their palates and, if so, where they had obtained it. To clear up the point, Vilhelm looked it up in — I know not what — and thereupon related what Plinius said on the subject. Of this Plinius, unfortunately, I knew only that he was a Roman, and so the teasing began. It became still worse when I called the man Pinius and asked who Pinius was. Vilhelm was so mean and naughty that I became angry and tried a dozen ways to make him be quiet. (She struck me, P.) It was not just the old Roman that made him so mean. Then I also had to hear that I was cross and ill-behaved. Yes, we have heavy afflictions, alas, not least at the hands of our spouses. This I surely experienced today; nor was it the first time. (She became angriest of all because, when she insisted that no woman's name ended in "us," I answered by naming "Rasmus.")[24]

At last I tired of him and sat down to write; this brought about a temporary truce, and now I think it will be converted into a formal treaty of peace, for Vilhelm has gone to light the fire in the stove for me.

The weather is beautiful today, almost too warm, but this is a cool room. It is remarkable how heavy the dew is at

[23] The interpolations in parentheses in this paragraph are in Pastor Koren's handwriting in the diary.

[24] Caius Plinius Secundus was Pliny the Elder (23–79 A.D.), Roman soldier, public servant, and author of *Historiae naturalis.* "Rasmus" is a colloquial term in Norwegian for a nagging, scolding wife.

night; late in the morning the grass is still very wet, and early in the morning the dew looks almost like rain. But despite the wet grass I have been out for strawberries several times.

It is now twelve o'clock by the sun's mark in the window, I see, so I must look to my dinner. We have a clock, to be sure, but nothing to wind it with, since the key lies somewhere on the road to Sørland's, and Decorah cannot furnish a new one.

Now it is late afternoon; we have had our dinner and coffee and had our siesta peaceably and amicably as behooves a well-behaved married couple. Vilhelm read *Ydale* and laughed.[25] I read "King Erik" — which interests me, though not so much as the first two volumes — until I was quite tired. Then Embret Skaarlia came with a saucer of luscious strawberries, which so refreshed me that I was able to defy the heat and fatigue and sit down to write. Vilhelm is now hearing Embret's lesson and is having great difficulty making him understand that Abraham had more domestic animals than are to be found in the whole county, that he had many goatherds and dwelt on a large prairie. It will doubtless soon be my turn to read with him.

We are not likely to get our walk before late today. There are so many roses here that we literally walk "'mid roses where we go."[26] Most of them are rather small bushes with pale red or red-streaked blossoms like our pinks in the garden at home; but there are also larger bushes with fairly dark flowers. The roadsides are often overrun by the small ones, but I have not seen a single large wild rosebush like those we had so many of at home.

Thursday, June 15. The day is really beginning very well. My consort and I are good friends today.[27] It is so hot, however, that the heat could easily reduce one to a very mellow mood.

[25] *Ydale: Et vinterskrift* (Christiania, 1851). This was volume 1, and the only issue, of a projected annual.
[26] Mrs. Koren may have been thinking of Hans Adolf Brorson's hymn, "Jeg gaar i Fare hvor jeg gaar," in which the fourth stanza reads, "Jeg gaar blandt engle hvor jeg gaar" (I walk 'mid angels where I go).
[27] After this word there is a line and a half neatly cut out of the diary with a knife or scissors.

I have really had to exert myself not to give in to listlessness; but it was helpful to wash the dishes, make the beds, sweep the floor, and dust, all in one stretch. If I had not done that, I should probably still be sitting on a chair without moving a finger, I imagine. Now, on the contrary, I shall try to be diligent and write. I wish I knew what we ought to have for dinner. That is a very difficult matter. I have almost no eggs left, and without them one does not get far here, where one has no choice but pork and dishes made of meal. And with pork I must have scrambled eggs or nothing. Oh, that I had some new potatoes and a little mackerel from home! It is really boring, this constant puzzling over tiresome food.

We went for a walk yesterday evening and picked a great many strawberries. We were hardly past the gate when we discovered a patch which held us enthralled a good while; so we picked peacefully until we turned the corner. But then it was no longer easy to proceed without constantly stooping and keeping a sharp lookout. Vilhelm was obliging enough to plunge through the thicket; I did not venture in there for fear of snakes, but . . . berries on which I feasted while I followed him to the end of the fence; then I turned back.[28] Vilhelm went on to the parsonage land. I picked a beautiful bouquet of roses, which I have discovered are fragrant, though not so fragrant as garden roses; but they smell sweet, nevertheless. Then I found a pretty flower I did not know, picked a couple of berries hastily, and hurried back to get tea ready before Vilhelm returned.

After I had been down to the springhouse for butter and had set the table, I thought it might be nice to have a little bacon, too, and walked back.[29] When I came out, I heard whistling on the hill; it was Vilhelm, who came just at the right moment and brought with him the most beautiful and

[28] The elision indicates two lines missing because of the cut mentioned in the preceding footnote.

[29] A springhouse was a small structure that the early settler usually built over a spring or well. Milk was cooled in it by setting the container in the running water.

wonderful flower we have seen here. He had found it in the parsonage woods. It is so delicate, so very delicate, that if Johan had seen Vilhelm coming with it, he would have had a good laugh. Yet he would have had to admit that it is beautiful, no matter how much he might have made fun of it.

I have written to Mrs. Linka — and now a few words here before I start a letter to Marie Horten.[30] Today our rest after dinner was especially welcome. I had had so much trouble with cream pancakes. The pan had rusted while hanging in the summer kitchen, where the rain often comes through, and the cakes would not brown. At last, after much hard work and some sweating on my part, they were ready and eaten. The coffee was made and brought in, and then we sat and read peacefully. At last, fortunately for our writing, we were interrupted by little Embret, who brought us a dish of delicious strawberries. He comes so faithfully every afternoon and today he surpassed himself. They are delicious, but I always have to eat them alone. Vilhelm hardly touches them, so that I may have the more. Oh, how peaceful and comfortable we really are! Now I must begin my letter to Marie if it is ever to be written. I wish that in the afternoon I were just a little more in the mood for writing.

Friday, June 16. I am alone in this little room this morning. Vilhelm is teaching his confirmation class. Guri sat here awhile with her knitting and asked my advice as to Eli's indisposition. I have gone through my medical book without finding anything. People come and ask for help, but those they come to are only indifferent counselors. Yesterday Iver Kvale was here for advice and medicine for his child. That medicine came in handy, indeed; I wish we had much more of it.

I did not get far with my letter yesterday. Nils Katterud sat here for a time, too; he came with a few words and a gift of a bottle of port wine from Paulsen, who must be very

[30] Marie Horten (Marie Münster Koren) was so called because she and her husband were living in Horten, Norway. Horten is a naval base on the Oslo Fjord.

thoughtful. It is raining so hard today that I do not know how I shall prepare dinner; my stove will no doubt be full of water. I wish Vilhelm would find some letters, or at least copies of *Emigranten*, when he goes for Johanne Karine.[31]

I managed to get some food ready just the same. The rain let up in time for me to tie up my skirts and go down to the springhouse for butter. I had just put the finishing touch to the *flødegrød* when Vilhelm came walking slowly, warm and tired. He had neither girl nor newspapers nor letters. The girl had not been there today. But I do not understand why we get nothing from McKay. I long so much to hear from home — at least a newspaper. I wonder if I shall not soon have a letter from Christiane; I have heard almost every month before. There comes Embret; I must hear his lesson now.

Saturday, June 17. It takes a long time for Vilhelm to return; he is either at Egge's or Sørland's. He planned originally to go before dinner. But it was twelve o'clock before we realized it, so we had one of our peculiar dinners: first, *tykmelk*; then, cold *flødegrød*; then, a glass of port wine to top it off.[32] Since I intended to bake bread and biscuits, I was well pleased not to have to prepare a meal, and set to work — my first attempt of this kind — when Vilhelm left. The baking is over, but it was warm work. I have washed the dishes and am quite proud when I survey the bread, which turned out well and is cooling on the table. Now Vilhelm shall see what a woman he has — if he would only come; it must be past five.

Yesterday we had a real strawberry excursion, and a very pleasant stroll it was. Vilhelm suggested that I refrain from picking any berries before we reached the appointed place, and that I keep my eyes off the ground so as not to be tempted. I succeeded in this and, when we arrived, was fully rewarded. Vilhelm picked great quantities for me. I was bold enough to leave the road, and found so many berries that my

---

[31] Johanne Karine Kristiansdatter was the hired girl.
[32] *Tykmelk* (thick milk), or bonnyclabber, is coagulated sour whole milk, frequently eaten with sugar and toasted bread crumbs sprinkled over it.

tongue became quite raw; at any rate it smarted very much. Then we walked on peacefully, and wisely omitted going to the parsonage land.

The wind blew hard and a storm gathered which broke loose after we had eaten and washed the dishes. It was a fearful storm. We sat without a light for a long time. The lightning became brighter and brighter and at times it seemed as if the thunder would topple the roof over our heads; rain fell in torrents. After a while we lit a candle, but though we had two candles in that little room, it was still lighted up by the lightning flashes. Vilhelm read to me. We sat for some time talking of old hymns and hymn writers before we went to bed; and before we fell asleep, the flashes became fainter and we were able to sleep in peace, undisturbed by the thunder.

This is a lovely Saturday evening. When Vilhelm comes, I shall go out and pick flowers for tomorrow. More than any other time, Saturday evening makes me think of my old home, possibly because that evening always had a character all of its own for me. On that evening I always gathered flowers for the bowls and vases, and now no doubt Christiane or Lina — or perhaps Marie is again home — now they bring the flowers to the grave. It is the seventeenth today, the day of Mother's death. Alas, how well I remember that first June 17 when I brought roses to the grave, and what I prayed for as I lay and decorated it — I was so distressed. I was then nine years old and the preceding year was the hardest I have ever lived through. Now it all remains with me in melancholy, if no longer sorrowing, remembrance.

15

Dear Memories

Sunday, June 18. Oh, that Vilhelm were home again! I expect him this evening, to be sure, and should be ashamed of my lack of patience, but I long so much for his return. I believe evening will never come. It has been a long day; I have been so alone, so completely alone, and have not seen a soul since they left (the Skaarlias are away). At times it became so quiet that I had to go outside just to hear the twitter of the birds. The interminable croaking of the frogs intensifies rather than diminishes the loneliness. It is beautiful outside, but so quiet and monotonous, green upon green, almost no color variations. Oh, for a mountain with a view of forest and sea!

No, now I fear I am really becoming melancholy. Yes, if this were a dreary, rainy day, I am sure I would become so. Ought I not be better able to stay alone? If not, it does not look well for the future — but it is something new for me to be completely alone and not see a soul. I must be a frail creature, however, not to endure being alone one day without becoming quite sad, instead of remembering how happy we are when Vilhelm is home and how comfortable everything is now. Oh, well, I am melancholy no longer. That was a mood of the moment, brought on by thinking of home and everything associated with it. And a quiet Sunday, when all work and bustle ceases, tends to intensify such a mood all the more.

I have walked about in the garden at home; seated myself in a corner of the summerhouse; lingered in all the rooms; wandered about on the mountain; tramped back and forth in the beech grove, down by Farris, in the Gople Valley, across the barren with its fir trees, and through all my favorite haunts in Treschow's garden and down by the waters of the fjord; and have seen and talked to all my dear ones.[1] I did not long to return; I did not for a moment wish that we had not come here — but these dear memories have made me melancholy. Even if they have caused me to grieve, I would not for any price be without them. Even the saddest memories contain so much that is sweet. I would not, if I could, make a visit home now — it would be too soon to make so long a journey again. But to stay here forever — I cannot think of such a thing, nor can Vilhelm either. There was a time this winter when I could think of the possibility of not returning, it is true; but no, no matter if we were ever so comfortable here, and even ever so contented, I would still return. Never to gaze again on what I have left behind — that would be too heavy a burden; I cannot see it in any other light, unless — God forbid — there should be too many changes. Yet, God knows what may happen. He guides all things, and we will confidently submit to His will.[2]

Now I have been outside, and I feel better. It was warm, so I went only just beyond the fence; I picked roses and ate strawberries and chatted a little with Guri, who had come home, bringing her sister and her sister's husband with her.

When Vilhelm came at last yesterday, I had to get busy at

[1] Farris is a large lake that extends northwestward from Larvik, Norway, for about seven miles.
[2] In May, 1870, the Korens made a trip to Norway with their seven children, returning to America shortly before Christmas of the same year.

once and make a plaster to send to Sørland's, as Embret had cut his hand. Then I took my knife and went to gather flowers along the little path past the springhouse. But I soon forgot to look for roses when I discovered one strawberry after another beckoning me; I found a lot of them, and it took a long time before I finally returned with a bouquet of roses and a dish of strawberries for Vilhelm.

Gullik Rønningen had come and left two copies of *Emigranten,* which I immediately pounced upon eagerly. The latest was from June 5 and contained no news from home later than the beginning of May, and nothing special except that Oscar will perhaps repeal neutrality.[3] I wish some letters would come soon; I wonder if Johan is away. There comes someone driving; it must be Vilhelm.

Monday, June 19. I am so lazy these days. What shall I do about it? "You shall write diligently today," was my first thought after dressing. But then we began to argue about the flower Vilhelm had brought yesterday. Was it a tiger lily or an imperial lily? I had to look it up in the "Nature Book" but did not find what I was looking for; on the other hand, I found other interesting things which kept us occupied until late forenoon. Vilhelm explained experiments in physics for me; we investigated the design of an air pump, sponges, and, not to be overlooked, the articles of food considered most digestible — all of it very instructive, of course.[4]

Well, it was Vilhelm who came so early yesterday. One makes good time with a good horse. I wish he had one himself; then it would take him only a couple of hours to drive to Ola Bekken's. He was so tired when he came that he could not get down from the wagon without help; he was really exhausted. I wish he would be careful and not drive too much to begin with. He brought some butter as a gift from Aase

[3] Oscar I, son of Charles XV, Marshal Bernadotte, was king of Norway and Sweden, 1844-57. The neutrality mentioned no doubt refers to that of Sweden-Norway in the Crimean War.
[4] P. C. Asbjørnsen, *Naturhistorie for ungdommen* (Natural History for Young People — Christiania, 1838-49).

Bekken. We are given so much butter. The first thing I must get is another butter jar. I had just started to work this butter again (the good women generally are accustomed to work it only once) when Suckow came, carrying a big box for Vilhelm.[5] I was very inquisitive as to what it might be, but soon grew correspondingly long-faced when it proved to be only books from the printer's.

We have just come home from a strawberry expedition which turned out very well. I walked about and ate the berries Vilhelm picked. I wonder if Johan and Marie have found a place in Horten like the Jordfald Valley, where they may pick strawberries at their ease?[6] But perhaps Johan has far different matters to look after. Vilhelm is outside washing his wagon, which has been painted and has now taken on a respectable appearance. While he is busy, I shall make use of these moments before I make tea.

We took our walk unusually early for fear of rain; it is sultry, and this evening, too, is not likely to pass without lightning and thunder. It storms nearly every other day now. This forenoon it thundered and rained so hard that we had to do the best we could for dinner. Well, it wasn't so bad after all. I was not permitted to go to the springhouse through the wet grass; Vilhelm went down to slice the smoked ham and I went to the summer kitchen and made scrambled eggs. Then Vilhelm had a dish of *tykmelk* and I had cold *flødegrød*. We ate with hearty appetites, well satisfied with what we had, then drank coffee and read. Yes, we are comfortable. God be praised for that and for everything! And now I must go to Guri's and make tea.

Tuesday, June 20. Such weather as we had last night! I woke up — I do not know what time it was; it was pitch dark

---

[5] After the butter has been churned and the buttermilk drained off, salt is added and the butter is worked with a wooden paddle to distribute the salt evenly and remove the water. The second working removes more water and makes the butter firmer. If the butter should become too salty, water is often added before the second working; the water carries the excess salt out with it.

[6] *Jordfald* means a sinking of the ground. The name "Jordfald Valley" was applied by the Korens to a spot on the parsonage grounds.

and very sultry and close. Vilhelm woke up too. I could not sleep. It stormed and rained frightfully. The rain drove through three walls of the room and formed a large pool by the door.

When I went to Guri's to get some hot water, I found her busy scouring her milk crocks and quite dismayed over the condition of the springhouse. The brook, usually so peaceful, had left its banks and formed a broad stream, with the result that the grass was laid flat on both sides.[7] Inside the springhouse, every drop of milk and cream had been spilled and all the tin pails lay in a heap by the door; the churn was overturned; all the cream gone; and everything was helter-skelter save a big vessel of sour milk and my jar of butter; the stream had kindly let them stand. It had never happened before, said Guri; and such weather, God be praised, comes but seldom, too. Now the sun is shining; it is fortunate that such storms generally do not last long.

Vilhelm has gone to the schoolhouse to teach his confirmation class; but as the English school is making use of the schoolhouse, I suppose I shall soon see him back with the children.[8] Vilhelm did come back, just as expected, and brought with him a letter from Sellø and a copy of *Emigranten,* but it was an old number from May. It was pleasant to get these letters from Vilhelm's mother and Laura; late in July Mother is going to visit Johan and Marie. Fortunate are they who can have her with them and look after her comfort. We just had the daguerreotypes out and looked at the familiar faces.[9]

Wednesday, June 21. Today is Brother Stin's birthday; he is very likely spending it at home in the old mansion — and it will probably be many years before he again rounds out a

[7] A small brook that takes its rise from a spring runs from south to north through the Skaarlia (now Clement) family's farmyard.

[8] The schoolhouse referred to is probably the one at the corner of Glenwood, Decorah, Springfield, and Frankville townships.

[9] Vilhelm's mother was Henriette Christiane Rulffs Koren (1794-1872). Maren Laurentze (Laura) Stub Koren (1824-1914) was his unmarried older sister; Johnson, *Slekten Koren,* 1:57.

year in his childhood home. May God hold His hand over him wherever he goes and let him return safe and sound some day! Stin and I, we are the ones, it seems, who will be farthest from the ancestral home.[10]

This morning I went on a hunt for little chicks with Guri. The large, ugly sow had taken two chicks and was at it again; Guri became very excited, dropped her clothes and soap and the whole wash, and circled around inside the fence with the sow ahead of her until she finally chased it out through the gate. I stood outside with the poor, panting little chick that the ugly creature had injured.

The day is over, though I do not know where it has gone, we live so quietly and peacefully and comfortably while Vilhelm is home. I don't like to see him leave on his next trip; moreover, I fear he will not be able to stand it. He leaves Saturday and will be gone all of three weeks.

Vilhelm had to go to Aarthun's this afternoon. I was bold enough to go with him part way on the "snake road," as I call it; it was there that I saw that big, horrid snake, and afterwards a grass snake. Some time after my return, Kari Katterud came with Magnus' two children and interrupted my letter to Marie. She brought word that Caroline's mother could not spare her more than a day now and then. Well, I shall not be able to get her, then. Meanwhile she will come Friday and help me a little.

The children brought us luscious strawberries, which we enjoyed when Vilhelm returned. Later we sat outside and read, even after sunset; it has been an unusually lovely evening. Then Vilhelm wanted me to sing — no, not sing; he does not make such high demands, but teases me by making the melody that I am to follow resemble singing as little as possible. But I am stubborn and will not do what he wishes, and so as usual it ends with my begging off sweetly and promising "some other time." And now it is time to snuff my candle and lay my head on the pillow.

[10] On "Stin," see chapter 13, footnote 14.

Thursday, June 22. There are not many who have so excellent a husband as I, so excellent in every respect. When I came in from the summer kitchen this morning after having washed the dishes, what should I see but the bed all made and Vilhelm standing in the middle of the floor, dusting with great care and with that diffidence that characterizes men in such unfamiliar womanly tasks. Later he helped me look through the cookbook to see what could be done with the two eggs I still had; he had many charming suggestions, which I nevertheless ventured to reject, deciding instead to save the two precious eggs and cook rice pudding. This was all well and good, especially since Vilhelm treated us to a little of his wine. Yes, he even wanted to help me clean the kettle, but since scouring pans was an unfamiliar task for us both, I finally took Vilhelm's advice and put it to soak till tomorrow. Then the girl will be here.

We wrote busily this afternoon, Vilhelm to Johan and I to Marie, until it was time for a walk. We agreed not to pick berries, but to go directly to the parsonage land. Well, we went. I pretended it was strictly in accord with the agreement to stoop down and pick a berry once in a while, despite Vilhelm's objections. Finally we reached the parsonage land and went into the woods; but the mosquitoes drove us out and we took refuge in our future house, sitting down in the living room, where we had the honor of receiving our first guest in the person of Iver Kvale.

It is evening and Vilhelm is at the other table absorbed in writing. Suddenly I hear a slap and a whack from that direction and see Vilhelm fencing with arms and hands against his tormenting spirits, the mosquitoes. They are rude to him; to me they are quite polite, only a little bite occasionally so that I may keep them in loving memory.

Friday, June 23. It is late and there is time for only a few words; I must also try to finish Marie's letter, so Vilhelm can take it when he leaves. Caroline came this forenoon, and we had a busy day — washed, starched, and ironed; then I mended Vilhelm's vest, and have accomplished more today than in all the past week put together. It goes without saying that I have racked my brain, too, to provide food for these people, Vige included. The last egg was used. But we had food, thanks to my clever head and my firmness with Vilhelm, for I did not let him eat *all* the cold rice pudding which I was saving for today, as was clearly his intention yesterday. Well, I am so sleepy now that I doubt I shall be up early tomorrow, as I should be. Moreover, I shall have that labor of Hercules, the rousing of Vilhelm, which is often a truly difficult matter; and I do it regretfully, too, for I could so cheerfully see him sleep longer.

Saturday, June 24. Yes, today is really Midsummer Eve![11] Just think, it is already midsummer! Time flies; these last days, especially while Vilhelm has been home, have passed swiftly. It is afternoon; the room is scrubbed and in order. I have been outside picking flowers and strawberries, the latter with Caroline's faithful help; I shall have them as a surprise for Vilhelm, whom I expect back soon from Aarthun's. He was to have set out today, but he has no horse; his own is sick and it is not likely that he can use it. I shall be very happy when Vilhelm finally gets a good horse and escapes all this trouble every time he is to go anywhere. We must get up early tomorrow. I am afraid Vilhelm will have a strenuous day, especially if it gets very warm. Thore Skotland had tea with us this morning; later I baked communion wafers and packed Vilhelm's things; when that was done, it was time to think of dinner.

Our dinners — well, they are certainly remarkable, quite in a class by themselves. If we live long enough, we shall surely often look back with amusement to the time when we kept house at Skaarlia's. Here is our dinner today, for example. It consists of *tykmelksuppe* (a very frequent dish), boiled potatoes, and ham. Here we sit then, we two, at Vil-

[11] Midsummer Eve is June 23. Mrs. Koren may have been thinking of Midsummer Day (St. John the Baptist's Day), which falls on June 24.

helm's little table (the large one is always littered with books and papers when Vilhelm is home), with a napkin for table-cloth, a tin dish for a soup tureen, and bowls instead of soup plates. All goes genially, with a little teasing now and then. A soup ladle is a luxury. When the soup is warm, we dish a little at a time into our bowls, each with his own tablespoon, very cozily. We have good appetites, and everything tastes delicious, even though my good spouse at times hums very softly, "Milk pottage they gave me, though porridge I asked for." We say, "Tak for maden," and then comes the delightful reading hour and coffee.[12]

I wish I knew what it is like at home this evening — whether they have as beautiful weather on Midsummer Eve as we and whether the small boys are busy with bonfires; today would be just the time, for it is Saturday. Tomorrow there will be a concert in the beech wood, no doubt; I wonder if those at home will attend faithfully this year? It is really very long since we heard from home; God grant letters may come soon.

Vilhelm has returned and we have made a very tasty meal of strawberries. Early tomorrow there will be a horse for him. So tonight, at least, I shall have him home; hereafter I am afraid there will be constant traveling.

Sunday, June 25. The quiet Sunday morning is over. Vilhelm is in the western settlements, but will return for a little visit tomorrow. So I am all alone — all alone — for I let Caroline go home. I spent most of the forenoon reading, until I became tired of sitting so still and had to stop. Sometimes when I am thus alone, everything becomes so oppressive and close about me that I have to go outside for a breath of fresh air. So it was today. I went out, therefore, and stood awhile talking to Erik and Guri through their open window; after I left them, I had my dinner. Cold dinner today, namely, sour milk soup, cold ham, and cold boiled potatoes. I ate with

[12] *Tykmelksuppe* is a soup made of clabbered milk. "Tak for maden," means "Thanks for the food," an expression commonly used at the end of a meal.

relish, took my afternoon nap, and began to write to Christiane. But I was very pleasantly interrupted by Erik Egge, who brought me letters from home — from Father, Mother, Stin, and even a few words from Smakke. How happy I was! If only Vilhelm had been here when they arrived! He will come tomorrow, however, and will then get the greetings from home.[13]

I almost asked Erik to leave — he sat here so long — so I might read the letters undisturbed. Afterward it dawned on me that it was the postage he was waiting for, since he had paid it, I suppose; but at the time I never thought of it. At last he left and I was able to read in peace.

Everything is well, thanks be to God, both at home and with our friends. The daguerreotypes had arrived, to their great joy, and have been on exhibition, of course. The hard times are not so bad as *Emigranten* states. While I was deep in my letters, Embret brought me a dish of strawberries; they were delicious. Then it was *Emigranten's* turn, but it did not contain much more news than Father's letter. The war situation is the same, it seems; and Norway and Sweden are already in it, or will be.[14] I must go out now and take a little walk and then have tea. Later I must write to Christiane and then say good night.

Monday, June 26. I have finished my letter to Christiane and am keeping a lookout for Vilhelm; but I dare say it is too early yet to expect him. I am thinking of going to meet him, but it is still altogether too warm. There is a strong wind, and yet it is so warm that I sit here with pearly drops on my nose. Today I finally succeeded in getting the mattress filled with straw. Caroline did the job alone; Vilhelm need not worry that I overexerted myself. The bed is so high now that I need a chair to get into it. Then I was lucky enough to find my ring, but not until we had gone through the mattress with the greatest care, straw by straw.

[13] Smakke, evidently a pet name, may refer to Elisabeth's younger sister Caroline Mathilda, who was then fourteen.
[14] The war situation is that of the Crimean War, 1854-56.

The one-eyed man from Dysja's was here this forenoon and asked whether "the mother" could advise him what to do for the neuralgia in his head. Well, "the mother" looked in her book and then put a Spanish fly plaster on him, and gave him a rag with salve on it for the sore, and explained how he should take care of himself. The old man seemed to have great faith in my skill in the art of medicine and left with many expressions of thanks.[15]

Now come quickly, Vilhelm, or evening will be here.

Wednesday, June 28. Here it is evening and this day will soon be at an end. It has been a busy day. Caroline has surpassed herself by finishing all that very large wash. And I — well, I have been so indefatigable as to embroider, patch, and resort to many expedients before I got·my things as I wished them; I also cooked our dinner, consisting of rice pudding, and went in and out occasionally.

"Is that all you have to say about this day?" Vilhelm will remark when he reads this. "Can't you really keep your mind on anything but the work you have in hand?" (He asked me that this forenoon.) Yes, I certainly can. I thought of a great many other things besides how this or that patch should be placed. My thoughts flew to Europe and America, to the past and the future, to new and old authors; but they were of no real advantage to me, for they were far too unruly and ungovernable, and flew from one subject to another. At last they became quite melancholy, calculating how often Vilhelm was away and how little he stayed home. But then one of the sweet little yellow birds came flying past the window and fluttered from stalk to stalk in the high grass. It brought life and cheerfulness to my thoughts, which had begun to be alarmingly subdued.

Vilhelm did not get started until today, but he left early enough, and now I hope this trip may be less strenuous than the last. I am glad today has not been so dreadfully hot for

[15] The Spanish fly is a beetle common in southern Europe, used, when dried and powdered, for raising blisters. The one-eyed old man was John Dysja's father.

driving. The weather has been far different from that of the preceding days; and the rain, too, very kindly held off until evening, when Vilhelm no doubt had reached his destination and we were through for the day.

All yesterday was wasted because, although Vilhelm should have started, he could not get a horse. At last, late in the afternoon, a man came with a letter from Pastor Stub, who had a horse to rent; about the same time an old *tinndøl* appeared with greetings from Stub.[16] Vilhelm went to Freeport and brought the horse here yesterday evening. Then he had supper and we sat up as long as possible with doors and windows open. There was sharp lightning and it was exceedingly sultry; yet, fortunately, we were able to sleep better than we did the night before.

Just as we had finished tea Monday evening, I saw someone driving down the hill; I hurriedly put a kerchief on my head and went to meet him. I could easily tell it was Vilhelm, despite his white hat and all the packages. I knew very well I had an excellent husband, but I should never have thought him so clever. Does he not come home with all the things I need and more, too? And even though I have not mentioned them to him, is he not able to think of them? This time I got little tin containers for coffee and tea, and material for a quilt, so now we shall have work to do. I must remember all my ironing for tomorrow, too, and say good night. I don't like being alone here in the evening.

Friday, June 30. Last night I was so tired I was unable to write, and hurried to bed. Tonight I am tired, too, but first I must nevertheless tell my diary — or rather him who reads the diary — that I am so well pleased I almost forget my tiredness. I am pleased because I now have all our clothes and linens clean and in order, and it is a long time since that has been true. Everything is in order in the trunks, the last piece folded away, and I have both my trays full of clean clothes.

[16] The Reverend Hans A. Stub migrated to America in 1848; in 1854 he was pastor in Muskego, Wisconsin.

Caroline and I have been very industrious. This afternoon, moreover, I set my hand to the great task of pleating a clergyman's ruff; it came out — well, fairly well; I had not expected better. But I must certainly wash it again before Vilhelm can use it. Thus the day has gone. The greater part of the day I ironed collars and laces and busied myself with all the different memories that are associated with them.

Yesterday — let's see what happened then. We were to get the clothes rinsed and dried, but had scarcely started when rain hung threateningly over our heads. (How violently it had lightened and thundered the night before! The sound awakened me, and it takes something to do that.) Finally I said, "Well, we will go ahead with the rinsing, anyway." And we were actually fortunate enough to escape rain. Then I taught Caroline how to wash the woolen things; none of the girls know that. Well, one piece of work that was to be completed during Vilhelm's absence has been finished; I hope the other can be, too, if I can just get a quilting frame.

Where is Vilhelm this evening, I wonder? Is he well and not too tired? I hope he may get a good night's rest. I think of that every evening. After all, it is a good thing that I have plenty to do while he is away. I am much better now at getting up in the morning than when we first came here. Just think, tomorrow will be July 1! On Sunday I must be sure to write home. And now away with all writing this evening.

Saturday, July 1. It is always late in the evening now before I begin to write, a sign that my industry continues. Today my task was to sew the material for the quilt together. And I have now hung the curtain in front of the shelves. Vilhelm will be pleased with that, I think. Caroline has gone from farm to farm and at last was fortunate enough to get a frame. Monday the work begins.

While the floor was being scrubbed today, I went outside in the shade with my work and was glad it was blowing hard, for it would have been frightfully hot otherwise. Then we made ourselves a ham omelet with onions. It did not want to stay together, it is true, but that made no difference. (I really ought to write down every day what we have to eat so that Vilhelm can see that we do have regular meals). Well, we ate the unsuccessful omelet and followed it up with *tyk-melk*. Then I took up Landstad's "Folk Ballads." [17] While I was reading, I became aware that my neck was strangely hot and sore and therefore picked up a mirror to investigate. Then I saw that it was fiery red, quite sunburned. I must have gotten that sitting in the wind this forenoon; now it will be beautiful — first dark brown, and then off peels the skin. But it is ridiculous, too, that one cannot sit outside even in the shade without covering oneself! I have never had such an experience. I found it so pleasant to have the wind blowing on me. This is really a disgusting climate. What will Vilhelm say, I wonder? And how is he faring? He will certainly be tanned.

After it became somewhat cooler, that is to say, after we had eaten, I went out for a little walk and took the road past the springhouse. It was beautiful on the hill. The light effects were lovely. But the grass is now very high, the dew was gathering, and it was growing dark; so I did not venture farther. I am afraid there will be no more walks this summer; during the day it is too hot and, when it cools off, it becomes dark and dewy — and besides I am afraid of the high grass. The most beautiful part of the summer must be over. Ah, the lovely summer evenings at home, so refreshing after a hot day! I have promised Vilhelm to take walks; yes, but I surely cannot keep the promise. I shall stir about all I can, but I am very loath to walk alone when it begins to grow dark.

This evening I sat for a while on the chopping block and talked with Guri and Erik, who had much to tell me about a girl who is said to have been stolen by the Indians near Lansing.[18] And in Minnesota the Norwegians are living right next to the Indians; he thought that was dreadful. It was a quiet,

[17] M. B. Landstad, *Norske folkeviser* (Folk Ballads — Christiania, 1853).
[18] A chopping block was a large block of tough-grained wood, used when splitting wood.

beautiful evening; I was reluctant to be driven inside by the increasing dew. What should I see when I came in but a large disgusting toad, which had ventured to hop clear over to the bookshelf. We had left the door open; we will have to be more careful.

This week and this month are now past. Vilhelm has been gone four days — four out of fourteen; that is not much — but let me not start on that calculation again. I have promised myself not to do it; it is still too early. God grant him a good trip; then there will be joy when he returns.

Sunday, July 2. How is Vilhelm in this heat, he who has to preach today? Possibly it is not so hot where he is. I do hope so, but here it is frightful. Early this morning I closed the door to shut out the sun, and opened both windows. There is a strong wind, too, but nothing helps. I went upstairs and found my lightest shoes, and am clothed as lightly as I have ever been — and it will be still warmer later in the day.

This morning has not seemed so long as those of the two previous Sundays. I read, and went over to Guri's on an errand; there I sat for a time chatting and told them of our trip across the ocean. At length the talk veered round to the heat, snakes, and vermin; and I became quite embarrassed to hear that they had to think of getting a summer kitchen. They had not been able to sleep the night before on account of the heat, for she had baked bread in the evening.

And when they talked of snakes, Erik said, "Well, we can never be safe here; this is only a dirt floor and is not properly boarded up along the sides; therefore we have never dared to sleep here, but have always slept in the upper room."

"Yes," Guri added, "we can stand it now, but later, in July and August, it will be impossible."

This was not very pleasant for me to hear, for of course I had my share of responsibility for what they complained of, and it is an awkward situation, that is certain — it looks as if we shall be moving to still a fourth place. I should not mind that if we were not everywhere in other people's way. They

257

have not yet begun the roof of the parsonage. The frame was to have been up May 20, it is now July 2, and the time is coming when everyone will have more and more work of his own to look after. But in what a pitiful and complaining manner I am writing, and I wish least of all to complain. What have I to complain of? I am well and active and have Vilhelm. But what was said at Guri's made me a little out of sorts. Now the mood is past and I shall be cheerful; there will be a solution for this, too.

Yesterday I suggested to Guri that we take a walk to the parsonage land; she thought it too warm, however. But she did want to go berry picking. Now, if anything is warm, berry picking is. I have not picked any since Vilhelm left; no doubt the season is over. Nevertheless, if it could be managed, it would be fun to go up to the parsonage site this evening and on the same trip make sure the raspberries do not get away from me.

What does Vilhelm think of Vige, I wonder, who has run away from him? I was certainly surprised this morning when he ran up as soon as I opened the door — as hungry as if he had not eaten for several days. Where did he leave Vilhelm? Perhaps after this he will prefer to guard the house instead of the wagon? I am glad he is home; he is a very good watchdog.

If I am to get anywhere with my letter home today, it is high time to begin; but I am not quite in the mood for it. I let the girl go home today, too, so I am all alone.

Monday, July 3. No, this is really too much! Toads — one could stand them — but a snake, ugh! A snake in the house! That is what we had here today. As I was sewing this forenoon, I heard Caroline, when she got up to go outside, cry in great fright, "Ugh, just see what's here." I looked over to the door where she pointed and became even more frightened to see a snake just inside the doorstep. When Caroline spoke, it took alarm and hurried out the door and disappeared right under the threshold. That was an unpleasant visit. It was probably one of those harmless grass snakes, but it was at least two feet long, and it is horrid that such visitors can get into the house. I put Caroline to work at once stuffing chips and whatever she could find under the threshold, and stopping up the openings along the wall, where there are no moldings. Guri laughed heartily at our fright and at the chips under the threshold. Grass snakes are almost domestic animals with them. I hope we shall have none of them at the parsonage; there is a foundation under the house, at any rate. I wish Erik would cut the high grass outside here; one cannot tell what to expect.

While I was sewing on the quilt today, I found a special pleasure in thinking of our future home — in arranging it and picturing to myself just how everything will look. Yes, indeed, how nice it will be! I rejoice so much at the thought. I wonder if Vilhelm will be home next Monday. No, he is not likely to come before Tuesday.

On my walk today — for today I walked across the strawberry patch to that hill, the secret of whose fragrance we can never discover — well, on this excursion I found a new yellow flower, which resembles the others, but smells very much like the wallflower. There was a profusion of them. I found a couple of other flowers strange to me, but no strawberries; that pleasure is over. Then I looked for raspberries and discovered it must have been blackberries we had seen in bloom. The hazel bushes are loaded with nuts. There is surely an abundance of fruit here, if only it is possible to gather it. During my walk the sun was just setting. The evening sky was beautiful, but there were indications of sharp lightning and thunder. It has already begun; we shall have a storm tonight.

Shortly before I went out, a man, neatly dressed, came in, greeted me, and sat down as if he were an old acquaintance and began to talk about the hot weather and other things; he said he came from Chicago and was here to look over the country; and he had such an impertinently familiar manner that I had considerable difficulty in being polite. He soon grew tired and left. Later I heard from Guri that he and others were here with Dillson and wanted to buy Jul's land.[19]

Tuesday, July 4. There was a bad storm last night with lightning, thunder, wind, and rain. But what a beautiful fresh morning we have in return! Because the sky was largely overcast and there was shade, I sat outside until we were ready for breakfast. After I had read, had breakfast, and puttered around a little, I went over to Guri's and found it was not yet half past six. Yes, I was industrious today, and how much better it is to get up early while it is still cool. The air has cooled off very pleasantly. I hope the same is true where Vilhelm is!

I sit here annoyed because I cannot get a messenger to send to Decorah or some other "store"; we have one quilt ready now and cannot begin the other for lack of cotton. I had relied on Gustaf, who was to go there for the day's celebration, but was disappointed.[20] Today, indeed, is the Americans' Seventeenth of May. It is also our king's birthday. I can continue with my letter home, to be sure — that is all right, too, but I wanted so much to finish these quilts. Today Guri supplied our dinner. She came over this forenoon with soup, very much like Norwegian sweet barley soup with onions and grits; it tasted delicious. Meanwhile, since it is so early, I think we shall eat the cottage cheese that I had set aside for today and which we are to try for the first time.

We have now closed the door and windows on the mosquitoes and the night air, drawn the curtains, and lit the light — to prolong the evening a little. The day has been delightfully cool and it was most enjoyable to sit outside as the sun went down. I was reading in Asbjørnsen's "Fairy Tales" about the beauties of nature at home. When at times I

---

[19] Dillson was probably a real-estate dealer. Jul Kvale from Valdres, Norway, and his wife Gro Egge Kvale lived on the southeast quarter of Section 34, Decorah Township. Their son, O. J. Kvale, served as a Lutheran pastor and later became a congressman from Minnesota; Malmin, Norlie, and Tingelstad, *Who's Who among Pastors*, 321.

[20] Gustaf was the son of one of the neighbors.

glanced up and contemplated the scene before my eyes, it all seemed very strange.

I had no desire to take a walk this afternoon; but when I had written until I began to tire, I took my knitting, put my kerchief on my head, and sauntered off. I talked with Guri and continued down toward the stable, where I found some beautiful poppies. This is the prettiest spot at Skaarlia's, really very picturesque — in any event so thoroughly rustic with its outbuildings, haystack, and the little pond which the brook makes here, and over which the swallows fly back and forth incessantly. From there I went over and watched Guri milk and tend her cows. I pictured myself going about the parsonage in this manner some time in the future — an unsteady old matron, knitting and looking after her property. The scent of new-mown hay hung delightfully in the air. Erik had cut a path to the spring house; I wish he would soon turn his attention to us.

Wednesday, July 5. It is early yet, but not so early as yesterday. After lying awake during a storm, the like of which I have never seen, I had a good sleep just as day was breaking. I have thought on other occasions that it has lightened and thundered sharply, but all was as nothing compared to last night. I awoke with a start — thunder, no doubt — and sat up in bed frightened, for it seemed the whole room was ablaze. The lightning was frightful, one flash after another; one could hardly catch his breath between them. The dark curtains seemed entirely white; I could distinguish every little object in the window, and the light shone in under the door as it does when the sun comes up in the morning. Moreover, it thundered so violently that it seemed to me the bed shook. The rain poured down. Every moment I expected the girl to come down, for I thought she must be nervous in the loft, where doubtless everything seemed doubly violent; she had been on the point of coming, too, but then the storm began to abate. How I wished Vilhelm were home! The storm drew away as dawn was breaking, and I fell asleep at last.

A beautiful, fresh morning followed. I am writing by the open window, now and then greeted by my little yellow bird friends. But it looks as though the air contains more electricity, which will break loose this evening. It is also warmer today than yesterday, but delightful compared to what we have had. I hope Vilhelm, too, is now sitting in a cool room and not traveling, all hot and worn.

A few words more before I close my writing case today. I wrote home very diligently and took a little exercise now and then — during the afternoon, since it was so warm this forenoon. I hope I shall finish the letters by the time Vilhelm comes. This afternoon I all but believed it was he I saw coming, the horse and wagon so resembled his. It was an absurd idea, of course, and Vilhelm will certainly not be flattered to hear I mistook a peddler for him. The peddler has now gladdened Guri's heart with yeast, and Caroline's by spreading out his wares. I wondered today how I might get someone to go for the cotton. I just now sent Caroline to Andreas to see if he can go.[21] It will certainly be a relief to have an errand boy. I had a visit from Ola Berger [*Bergan*], who asked my help for his sick child and took an emetic powder back with him. Well, shall we have the same sort of weather tonight? Look — I can no longer see; we shall now have supper.

Thursday, July 6. How merrily it rains today! Let it rain, if Vilhelm escapes it or at least is not out in it. I am writing by the open window, as I did yesterday, hoping Andreas will bring my cotton. But it will probably be wet — and so am I, almost. Since today is Thursday, I hope it will not be long before Vilhelm returns. How good that will be! It is evening after a day of almost uninterrupted writing. The long letter to Father is ready, one for Stin, and a greeting for Christiane. The rain has stopped.

Erik swings along with his scythe outside the house and mows down flowers and grass without mercy. The grass is so heavy and high that he has great difficulty with it. Guri was

---

[21] Andreas is believed to have been a neighbor's son.

just here; she could not resist coming to announce that a group from Norway had arrived at Sørland's; namely, Embret's mother and relatives. She also related many things about their hardships on the journey and of how several had died in Chicago.[22] Tomorrow she will no doubt go over there and get more details. I did not take a walk. I should have done so, but did not feel like it, for it was very wet — suffice it to say, I was lazy and stayed home.

Friday, July 7. Today is Mother's birthday.[23] If all is well, I am sure there is a hot-chocolate party at home. At this moment a group of voluble women are seated about the table, busy with their chocolate and talking all at once, one faster than the other. And if the weather is as fine as it is here, the party is being held in the cherry arbor, or in the larger one. How well I can see them, and Christiane and Lotte serving! I shall be happy if my last letter has reached them for today.

I must now take up my sewing; that is my task this morning as I glance continually up the road to see if Andreas is coming. If this day is to be wasted, too, Vilhelm will surely come before the quilt is ready. After breakfast, a messenger came from [Ola] Bergan's to get help for their child, and later one from Suckow's asking for some Hoffmann's drops. I am glad I could help them.[24]

Just look! There is that beautiful little blue bird outside the window; I have never seen it so near.[25]

I hear such cries and shouts from Ola Katterud's; they are breaking sod. It is shameful the way they whip the poor oxen.

We have lit the light at last — I was loath to shut out the moonlight. This afternoon I took a walk, for which I am very glad. I had no great desire to do so today, either; I did

---

[22] For a description of the ravages of cholera and other illnesses in arriving immigrant groups, see Gjerset and Hektoen in *Studies and Records,* 1:1–59, and a chapter entitled "Frontier Ordeal" in Blegen, *American Transition,* 55-68.

[23] "Mother" is Elisabeth's stepmother.

[24] Hoffman's drops are spirits of ether.

[25] The bird was probably the indigo bunting.

it as a duty. But it turned out to be a pleasure when I got up to the road (the strawberry road, naturally) and saw the beautiful evening sky and found a couple of new flowers. I wonder if Vilhelm sees many on this journey? If he does, he would like to show them to me, I am sure. I walked over to — well, over one hill and up another, cracked nuts to see how well filled they were, watched the men breaking sod, came home and had a bite to eat, then took my knitting and sat for a while on the chopping block at Guri's. It was the most charming evening we have had for a long time, lovely moonlight, and even well-behaved mosquitoes. In here it is not very cozy this evening; the room is taken up by the quilting frame and there is a smell of cotton. I was fortunate enough to get the cotton this afternoon — therefore I am going to bed and will get up early tomorrow.

Saturday, July 8. I do not understand why all at once I can become so sad, or depressed, or whatever I should call it. It starts with a longing for Vilhelm, then everything about me seems so empty; I become rather faint and have to take a little walk and look around. That helps sometimes, especially when I happen to see something beautiful, as when today I saw a new kind of bluebird, with white underbody and light-red breast — that helps. And then when I can, I avoid thinking of Vilhelm (at least when I begin to long for him, you know) or of anyone at home or in Norway. Sometimes it helps to read — when I can persuade myself to pick up a book. This mood is sometimes of long, sometimes of short duration; but I simply cannot understand why it comes so suddenly while I am sitting here in good spirits. If only Vilhelm were home! But tomorrow is Sunday. Perhaps Monday he will come. God grant it!

Now I am in good spirits again; but that was not true when I took out my writing case. In the meantime Kari [Katterud] came before I had begun to write and asked if she might bake bread in the oven. So I took a little walk with her. That helped.

I believe the new-mown hay attracts the birds. The place is filled with them and there are many pretty ones, despite the fact it is a cool, rainy day. I am wakened almost every night by thunder and rain. This morning I was not yet up when Ola Bergan was outside my door to talk to me again about his child. We were industrious this forenoon and finished the quilt. After that was done, Guri came with *flødegrød.* She had made some to take to Siri Suckow. Today many newcomers passed here. They are reported to have said that fifty died in Chicago and that they themselves bitterly regretted having come to this country. I can believe that, too, especially at the outset, when they do not know where to turn and have trouble of all kinds.[26]

Sunday, July 9. The quiet Sabbath has come again and I sit here in my loneliness without seeing or hearing a thing save the rare chirping of a bird. I took a little walk, looked at the melons, and sat on the stoop behind the house sunning myself, for it is a little cool today. When I have written a little — I ought to write a little more to Mother — I am going to see if I can find a bouquet of flowers; perhaps I shall go as far as the parsonage land. But I hardly think so; it would be too far, and I don't want to see how pitifully slow the progress of the house is. Yet perhaps they have accomplished something this week. I do not know. Last Sunday a start had not yet been made on the roof.

I spent the forenoon reading, seated as usual in the open door. Then Vige and I had our simple dinner, consisting of bread and butter and milk. I am not particularly cheerful today, either; I am quite subdued by the solitude about me. But I am not downcast. I was far from that this forenoon; my mood corresponded so well with the peace and quiet which surrounded me — and soon Vilhelm will come. If it can be done, I should like to go to Wisconsin with him; that will do me more good than staying here.

I was just interrupted by Guri, who brought Embret's

[26] See footnote 22 to this chapter.

mother over, apparently to get a look at me. "Why, she looks like a mere girl!" she exclaimed as she came in the door. She then gazed about curiously and drew back the curtains from the bookshelves to see what they contained. They were here only a moment. Guri was going with her to Sørland's.

More new birds. I have gone out several times to get a look at a fairly large bird, blue, with white breast and purple-red head and neck; but it is so swift in its movements. At any rate there are several varieties of the blue. I am happy at having these beautiful little birds.

16

The Same Loneliness

Wednesday, July 12. Naturally I did not write either yesterday or the day before, for Vilhelm is home and then the
diary always fares badly. He did not get here for dinner, as I
had faintly hoped he would. Late Monday afternoon I was on
the lookout, and was just thinking of taking my knitting and
going for a walk when a woman came to ask advice for her
husband, who had an inflammation of the eye; so for one day
the medicine books took the place of the walk. They were
consulted a good deal while Vilhelm was away. While I stood
mixing a blister plaster for her, Caroline ran up and said the
pastor was coming. There he was, too, outside the fence, letting down the rails — strong and healthy-looking, though
tired from driving all day. But God be praised, he had had
no ill effects of the trip, strenuous as it must have been, having preached, as he had done, every other day — and then the
journey itself, and on top of that being wringing wet with
sweat several times a day.

Now he was home, and happy was he and happy was I.

Nothing is so pleasant as to have Vilhelm return. Soon after he got home, he had a bowl of cottage cheese; then we ate a dish of raspberries which Caroline had picked, and visited and had a cozy time. He was lucky that he arrived when he did, too, for a little later the rain began to pour down with might and main. Yesterday, too, we had a cozy time. Vilhelm read my diary and letters.

Announcements had been made for five o'clock services at the schoolhouse; we went there at that time and found a number of people gathered, mostly from the neighborhood. Helene's baby was baptized. These people with their broken English! When the name of the child was asked, Anne answered, "Melleen," which was supposed to be the English translation of Magdalene, as the child was named.[1]

I wish Vilhelm could hold services oftener in this way — I mean in the middle of the week, when people are coming from their work; it is so pleasant. The evening, too, was very beautiful — quiet and peaceful. When the service was over, we visited a while before going home. According to arrangements, Vilhelm was to have been at East Prairie today, but I had not sent them direct word, as indeed I should have done; and everyone said they undoubtedly had not heard about it.[2] So Vilhelm stayed home today. This was much better, for he certainly was in need of at least one day of rest.

We sent a message this morning to Magnus [Linnevold], whom Vilhelm has engaged to finish one of the rooms of the parsonage. I hope something comes of it. This afternoon Vilhelm was to meet him; so he took his new horse to drive to the parsonage. He wanted to try it out. He had bought the horse down at the Turkey River — a young one which has not been hitched to a buggy. Therefore I was not permitted to go along on this first trip.

I have accomplished nothing today, which generally hap-

---

[1] Magdalena Egge was born on May 9, 1854. The form "Melleen" is more likely an Anglicization of "Mallene," a popular shortened form of Magdalena.
[2] East Prairie is now Glenwood Congregation.

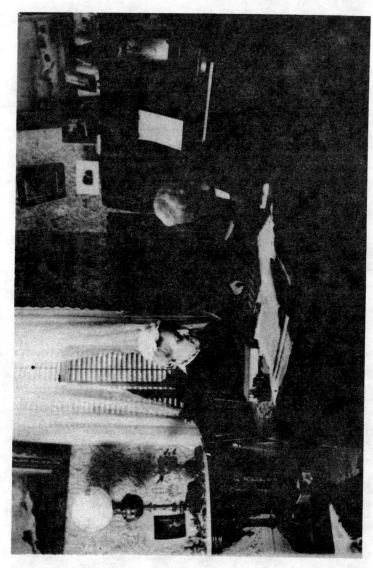

THE PASTOR AND HIS WIFE IN THE PARSONAGE, IN OR ABOUT 1903

THE PRESENT WASHINGTON PRAIRIE CHURCH
[Courtesy of Donald Severtson]

pens when Vilhelm is home so short a time. After Vilhelm had driven off I took out my work, but had not been at it long before I had a strong desire to go to the parsonage land, and hurried off, too, half fearing I should not find Vilhelm. I was glad when I saw his horse standing there and Vilhelm busy filling the box of the wagon with kindling for the stove. Magnus was not there, nor anyone else. We waited a while, talking about the house and its arrangements. Still no one came. Finally the pastor and his wife seated themselves on the load of wood and drove home in gallant style, racking their brains fruitlessly to find a name for their new treasure — the horse, I mean. On the parsonage grounds I found two very fragrant white flowers, one of them very unusual in appearance. Now Vilhelm has gone back to the parsonage land; Magnus and Erik came shortly after we had left.

Thursday, July 13. Vilhelm has set out again [for Paint Creek], but this time I hope he will be back sooner, God be praised; and so I shall be cheerful and think of how pleasant it will be when he returns. He left this forenoon. It is already Thursday. How swiftly these days slipped away! But Monday, Tuesday, and Wednesday were really good days. Now I have the memory of them to cheer me, and the hope of several similar days next week when Vilhelm returns. When Vilhelm is home, everything is different and everything is good. I shall always try, as far as possible, to be well occupied while he is away and to have no work that presses while he is home. And the evening hours after we have lit the light, how entirely different they are when Vilhelm is here and can talk to me and read to me as he did yesterday from the beautiful German hymns! God grant that when we are fairly settled in our own home this winter, he may often have a free hour and be able to spend an evening with me. What a cozy time we shall have!

Vilhelm took my letter to Norway with him. I am glad it has been sent. I hope he brings something from McKay when he returns. I am waiting for Caroline to finish so I can iron

269

some clothes. Meanwhile I shall take an inventory and make a list of what we need, should Vilhelm ever get over to Dubuque.

I have just had tea. After I was through with the ironing, I went promenading up the hill to the fence to get a good view of the beautiful sunset, and then through the brush to get some raspberries, but returned with a long face. I circled around the field, which is pleasant now since the grass has been cut, and there I found a dead baby bird, one of the small yellow ones, hanging from a rotted tree.

Friday, July 14. Vilhelm would be happy if he knew that I have been, and still am, in such good spirits today — really a cheerful mood; not exactly gay, but so quiet, peaceful, undisturbed — so bright — I do not know just how to express it. I am alone today. Before I was up, Caroline left to go to some store or other. It is now early afternoon.

I have spent most of my time sewing and thinking of I know not what — of Vilhelm and of everything that concerns us, of the home we are to have and of all that I, especially, will busy myself with; and all these pleasant, happy thoughts made the time pass very quickly. Then I thought, too, of the house, of housekeeping, of pigs and butchering, and became so alarmed at picturing to myself what will happen when once I start in on it all that I went straight over and took down Mother Winsnes to see if I could possibly find any comfort there.[3] But it seemed to me that with all the things to be done, everything became even more awkward and difficult; so I thought, "That time, that sorrow," and put the book away.

But thoughts of housekeeping continued to occupy me, and many important things occurred to me which I ought to talk to Vilhelm about. But I fear all these sensible ideas will have vanished before he returns. I ought to write them down, but that is so tiresome. Today I read in the *Kalender* "The Spirit

[3] Hanna Olava Winsnes, *Lærebog i de forskjellige grene af husholdning* (Textbook in the Various Branches of Housekeeping—Christiania, 1845).

of the Life of the Norwegian People" by O. Vig. I am certainly going to study the *Folke-kalender*; I can learn many useful things there concerning sun, moon, man, and beast.[4]

I am very glad Guri is now just as friendly as she always has been. I hate to believe there was anything she was displeased with; it must have been something else that depressed her. This morning, when I went to get some warm water, she was as pleasant as ever. She is now sitting on top of a load of hay. They are in full swing, putting up large stacks of hay for the winter. I have had my place in the open door today; it is something of a change to watch the people and oxen at their work in this meadow, which is otherwise so peaceful. Besides, there is such a pleasant fragrance in the air today. The birds and the gophers are extremely busy. The latter are certainly amusing little creatures; one of them ventured as far as the threshold and surveyed the room.

Is Vilhelm on the road to Paint Creek now, I wonder? I hope he is not caught in the rain. A few drops are falling here and it has looked all day as if it were ready to thunder. I think I shall start a letter to Sophie this afternoon.[5]

Saturday, July 15. It was a pleasant surprise yesterday to get those letters. I had been writing to Sophie for a time, had stepped out to get a little exercise and stood talking with Guri, when Mari Katterud came over and gave me a little book which she had received from one of the children at school; she knew nothing more about it. I opened it, greatly surprised to have Elias Stangeland's book for emigrants sent me, but saw immediately from the opened envelope in it that Vilhelm had sent it. It was kind of him to send it before he came himself; it was like getting a little greeting from him. In the envelope were letters from Aunt Koren and Marie. How happy I would be if Vilhelm should be sur-

[4] *Norske folke-kalender* (10 volumes, Christiania, 1846-55). The *Folke-kalender* (Folk Calendar) contained articles on a variety of subjects, besides the usual information found in almanacs.

[5] Karen Sophie Reusch Koren (1832–1933), younger sister of Vilhelm Koren, married F. W. Schiertz, architect and landscape painter; Johnson, *Slekten Koren,* 1:69.

prised, upon his return, by letters from Stin or some of his other friends![6]

I have just returned from my walk. I enjoy my walks more now and also walk much more briskly. Yesterday I was at Kari [Katterud's], stopped for a few moments, and came home through the little woods. Today I took the lane and turned off to Sørland's, flushing prairie chickens at almost every step. I did not venture very far, for a storm was gathering and it began to lighten and thunder. There were some beautiful clouds in the west above the wood. I reached home safely, but I fear now it will break loose. It has become so dark I cannot see.

What a storm it was! We have a light now, and the storm has passed, God be praised. The lightning still flashes, but it is farther away. I am glad when the storms come by day and do not wake us in the middle of the night. I wonder when I shall stop saying, "That was the worst storm we have had so far." It seemed to me I must have seen the worst; but that this last storm surpassed all others is certain. The heavy black clouds suddenly made it so dark that I could no longer see to write. Then the wind came, followed by a downpour of rain so heavy that in a moment the floor was covered with small streams of water. The rain beat in, driving from every direction. We pulled the bed away from the wall; when we got up to the loft, there was already a large puddle on Caroline's quilt; water was dripping through the roof in several places and beating in through the walls.

After a time it grew light very quickly and the rain let up so that we could open the door and gaze out on a truly beautiful sight. Directly opposite us was a full double rainbow; and the setting sun, piercing the clouds, cast its broken beams over the landscape that so shortly before had been darkened,

---

[6] Strangeland's book, *Nogle veiledende vink for norske udvandrere til Amerika* (A Few Hints to Guide Norwegian Emigrants to America), appeared in Christiania in 1853. Aunt Koren was Margrethe Christine Reich Koren (1797–1873) wife of Jess Didrichson Koren and familiarly called "aunt." Marie Jessine Margrethe Koren (1826-1901) was her daughter; Johnson, *Slekten Koren*, 1:182, 185.

and tipped the treetops with gold. Unusually blue lightning was still flashing here and there. It was all very solemn, but very beautiful. The air was pleasant, the grass and all green things now fresh and lovely. To see a rainbow, peaceful after so violent a storm, arch in all its splendor across the sky, leaves a wonderful and comforting impression. Has Vilhelm had this storm, too, I wonder? I hope in any event that he was safe in Thomas Anderson's cabin.[7] I pity those who were out in it. Now I shall go to bed; I am tired and sleepy. It must be past bedtime, although I was not up very early this morning.

Sunday, July 16. As I was reading by the open door this morning with a copy of Claudius in my hand, I kept thinking how completely changed my mood is today from that of former Sundays when Vilhelm has been away, and how on the whole there has been a difference since he left this time.[8] There is no outward occasion for it; the weather was just as pleasant before, the surroundings are the same, there is the same loneliness. The change must be in me. Several times in the past I have been quite disheartened, could not keep my mind on what I read, could not feel myself drawn to read a religious work or edified by it, found it so lonesome here, tried by walks and other devices to cheer myself, but usually in vain, and longed above all for Vilhelm. I do that now, too; I long just as much, just as fervently for him, but in a different and much better way. I feel so calm, so happy, so content — as if the same peace which rests over nature today, rests over me, too.

This mood reminds me so vividly of an earlier day when I was a child, growing up. I was fifteen or sixteen. Then I often felt as I do now. But a time came when these moods became more and more rare. There was so much that troubled me; I was no longer so happy as before. There were per-

---

[7] Thomas Anderson lived in Section 12, Paint Creek Township, Allamakee County; Alexander, *Winneshiek and Allamakee Counties,* 466.

[8] Mathias Claudius (1740-1815) was a German writer known as the "Wandsbecker Messenger." See *Asmus omnia sua secum portans, oder sämtliche Werke des Wandsbecker Bothen* (Karlsruhe, Germany, 1791-1804).

haps many moments when the old happy mood returned, but things were not as they had been in the past. I seemed to be changed, and was troubled. Nevertheless, I always felt that some day I should again be as happy as I had been; and this will surely come to pass. God grant it! And when should it come to pass, if not now?

I have been sitting for a time behind the house, where there was still some shade; I read a sermon and continued there, enjoying the beautiful day. This is surely a quiet, peaceful Sunday. At this hour Vilhelm is conducting services in Paint Creek, and at this hour they are in church back home in Norway.

The day will soon be over. It finally became very warm. I had thought of taking a little walk as far as Katterud's, but was glad to escape going anywhere. At dinnertime I visited with Guri awhile and ate a couple of the cookies she was baking. After that I read and, whenever I became tired, I took a walk outside as far as the grass was cut and watched the birds — one of my greatest pleasures.

Monday, July 17. Today is one of those hot days; one in which a person sits and perspires no matter if he takes it ever so easy and does not lift a finger. At any rate so it was with me this forenoon. I opened the door and both windows as far as I could, took my knitting and the "Nature Book," and tried to forget that it was hot — and succeeded fairly well. By the time I had read the book's preface and introduction, however, I was too tired of sitting still to start the section on astronomy, as I had thought of doing, and decided to sit outside on the stoop behind the house, where there was still a little strip of shade.[9]

So I sat there and watched the flock of quail that hopped about on the hay with their strange cry, and thought of the influence of nature upon character.

It is impossible not to be influenced by the natural surroundings in which one lives for a long time. Very few are

[9] On the "Nature Book," see chapter 15, footnote 4.

not affected to a greater or less degree, oftentimes without their being conscious of it. Especially must this be true where natural surroundings have a more positive character, as in a narrow, dark mountain region or at the seaside with the great ocean and the marvelously formed barren cliffs. The natural scenery here, though not on so grand a scale, may also exert a strong influence upon the mind — in general, a mild, peaceful influence. Vilhelm has remarked several times during sharp lightning and thunderstorms that he did not see how any person could think of doing evil at such a time — but I can understand even less how anyone could do it during a restful and solemn evening hour of moonlight and starlight.

After dinner (what a splendid appetite I have at present!) I began to read Lessing's *Minna von Barnhelm*.[10] This is now to be my reading at noon, for I am afraid the "Nature Book" will be too difficult to master. I am glad we have so many books from the "pocket library." Later I sat outside the door with my sewing and let the breeze cool me. The shadows are becoming so long that it must be time for me to start my walk. It would be nice to get as far as the parsonage land and very nice to see where the garden is, just in case there should be a carrot. I should like one very much.

Tuesday, July 18. Today I was up with the sun; consequently I cannot quite understand why the clock shows only ten. My appetite informed me it was time for dinner, so I had to eat a little *tykmelk*. Caroline looked quite astonished when she came down this morning and found me almost dressed, for this does not usually happen. It was certainly very warm last night; and it was doubtless because of the heat that I tossed in my sleep, awakened very early, became tired of lying in bed, and got up with the first ray of the sun. Nor did I regret it. When it sometimes happens that I am so smart, I find myself wishing I were so always, for at that time of day it is fresh and lovely and delightful to be outside.

As soon as I was up I took a chair and a book and sat in the

[10] Gotthold Ephraim Lessing, *Minna von Barnhelm* (Berlin, 1767).

shade until the dew began to disappear. Then I walked about and picked flowers and went down to the brook, until Caroline came back from Katterud's with the milk and made tea. After that I sat behind the house until the sun chased me away; then I ironed, and read Claudius, which I enjoy more every time I read it. The "Nature Book" will probably have its turn on some later day; now I am going to write to Sophie.

Tomorrow Vilhelm will come, God be praised! But I really feel sorry for him, it is so warm; and he is probably either driving or conducting services. It is a strange kind of heat, too. While I was sitting outside in the breeze, I did not find it very warm after all; now while I am sitting at my table, it is also reasonably cool and there is a draft of fresh air. Just the same, it is like sitting in a continuous steam bath.

Yesterday I was ambitious enough to walk to the parsonage land, where the only change I saw was a pile of shingles, some boards, and a planing table. Not a man there. Nor will anything come of Magnus' work; he has arranged for someone to take his place and has said it is useless to do anything until the roof is ready.

It was very beautiful there yesterday. The sun was just setting. I risked going through the grass to see if there were any raspberries; but no — I shall have to be content without them this summer. Nor did I get a carrot. The grass was very wet and I could not find the garden. Then I picked some flowers and went home. I met Knud [Aarthun] hauling a load of shingles and asked him why the carpenters were not there. Oh, they had not sent word to them yet; but he thought it would surely be soon. Ugh, how slow they are! It does not look promising at all. Knud talked about doing some "breaking" there. That is surely something.

Wednesday, July 19. No, Vilhelm apparently is not coming. I have been on the lookout, gazing in every direction all afternoon, but in vain. Still, it is hardly half past seven, so he may come yet. I hope he was not too thoroughly soaked by the heavy rain. It rained here nearly all day. It let up long enough for our dinner to be cooked without floating away, but then it started again. I had looked forward to walking to meet Vilhelm and then riding home with him; but nothing came of my plan. Probably the walk would have been in vain, even if the weather had permitted it.

Yesterday, after the heat had become a little less oppressive, I set out on the road past Kari [Katterud's] leading to the schoolhouse, not without a faint hope of possibly meeting Vilhelm.[11] I had not gone far when it began to thunder and lighten, but in this short distance I found three new flowers. True, I had seen one of them before, a violet; it smells like curled mint. I picked that first and then stooped down for a very insignificant white flower with a strong odor much like a peppermint drop. The best find, however, I made down by the brook, where some large plants were growing with a peculiar yellow flower and a strong, pungent smell as of curry or cayenne pepper. These have now found a place in my flower bowl for Vilhelm to see; otherwise they would not be permitted to stand there and overpower the more delicate and pleasing fragrance of the flowers from the parsonage land.

On my way home I stopped to talk with Kari, without noticing how fast the rain was coming up; so I hurried home posthaste and escaped getting really wet. This forenoon I read peacefully and worked; I knew it was useless to expect Vilhelm then. But I spent the afternoon going from window to door and, when the rain forced us to close the latter, from door to window. Vige, the tiresome rascal, fools me so often; he dashes off barking like mad, and of course I rush out every time, too, only to find it is a pig or something of the sort.

Oh, what beautiful light effects! I happened to glance out, threw down my pen, and ran out so as not to miss any part of the lovely scene. The light and shade which the sun cast over the prairies tonight, especially over the scene nearest us, were surely something for an artist.

[11] The schoolhouse was in the southwest corner of Glenwood Township.

Here is Caroline to ask if I am not ready for supper. I suppose I may as well eat; it is useless to wait longer.

Friday, July 21. Well, now he has already gone again — Vilhelm, of course, for he did come home day before yesterday. Consequently I forgot, as usual, to write in my diary yesterday. After sitting a long time without a candle, I had quite given him up Wednesday; and after I had lit one and read awhile, I thought it could hardly be reasonable to wait longer. I had already thought of going to bed, when Vige began to bark. So I went out, but could neither see nor hear anything. I stood and stared toward the gate, hoping I might distinguish him and his horse by the lightning flashes, but was utterly unable to do so. But as Vige continued to bark, I felt there must be someone. I went inside for a light, therefore, and had scarcely more than got out the door before Vilhelm stood before me, wet through and through, with beads of sweat on his face. I was very happy but quite frightened, too, when I saw how he looked and heard how, missing the road in the darkness, he had got into a thicket where the wet bushes struck him across the shoulders (how easily he could have walked straight into the brook!), and how at last he had come through down by the springhouse. His horse and wagon he had left at Aarthun's, because it was too dark to drive.

That day he had been at East Prairie, where he conducted services. The rain made him very late; moreover, the creeks, even those which are dry ordinarily, were so swollen that the water at times streamed into the wagon and poured out behind like a waterfall. And thus he had journeyed, mostly for my sake, my dear, kind Vilhelm. He had refused to wait until the following day, as his friends everywhere had begged him to. But he must promise me not to be so considerate another time; I would much rather be anxious.

This time, God be praised, he will suffer no ill effects, I believe. How wet all his clothes were! But how happy we were, too, that he was home and had got through safely! And yesterday morning, when the same rain continued, we

thought it fortunate that he was home and had not needed
to start out early in such weather to meet with the candidates for confirmation. By the time they left, the weather
had cleared just enough for us to cook dinner and bring it in.
Then the rain poured down. It was the kind of weather in
which it may be very cheerless to be alone, but just the kind
in which two can be very comfortable and cozy indoors — and
such were we two yesterday in this nest of ours, although the
rain streamed down the walls and in through the door. Vilhelm read aloud to me from Claudius and *En fjeldbygd*,
while I tatted.[12] Yes, it is cozy when Vilhelm is home!

Today there is a meeting of the congregation at Thrond
Lommen's. V. got a late start, for Knud Aarthun, who promised to bring the horse and wagon yesterday, did not come
until half past nine; then the two drove away. The weather
is clear again. I hope now he will speak to the members in
such a way that they will take it to heart, and that there will
be good results for the parsonage.

That man from Coon Prairie who talks of becoming the
schoolteacher came while we were eating breakfast and, if
Vilhelm had not left, would no doubt have been sitting here
at dinner. That is his usual custom.[13]

One year ago today Vilhelm was ordained; at this hour we
were then in church. Father and I had come to Christiania
the afternoon before. I can see Vilhelm upon the wharf,
searching the "Halden" with eager eye to discover if we were
on board or not. It is very strange to think back to those days
in Christiania. I am glad I was able to be there. I wish we
might soon hear a little from Vilhelm's acquaintances whom
I met on that occasion.

Tuesday, July 25. I am an incorrigible sluggard when Vilhelm is home and I show no promise of improvement, certainly not while each visit is such a short one. This morning
he is somewhere near Thrond Lommen's for a wedding — an

[12] Nicolai Ramm Østgard, *En fjeldbygd: Billeder fra Østerdalen* (A Mountain District: Sketches from Østerdal—Christiania, 1852).
[13] The Coon Prairie settlement was in Vernon County, Wisconsin.

occasion which gives me a chance to take up my pen again; but I am not likely to write very much, for today at last I intend to finish a couple of dresses I am sewing for Eli. Vilhelm and I visited her Saturday and I promised then to take charge of young Master Sørland's wardrobe.[14] Eli is now stronger, so Guri has come home and begun her familiar walk between the springhouse and the cabin, greatly to Erik's satisfaction. He just cannot get used to not having her with him. He cannot even stack his hay unless he has Guri in the wagon treading down the hay. Today they are busy driving from one haycock to the next.

We took a different path to Sørland's Saturday, a path I had not been over before. They have fenced in their land. So we went straight through the woods, I clutching my dress, and Vilhelm building bridge after bridge by gathering all the dry limbs and branches he could find and throwing them into the brooklets and small draws we had to cross. We got through, dry of foot and whole of skin; nor did we neglect to take with us such raspberries and pretty flowers as we found.

Saturday was sister Christiane's birthday. May God bless her and let her regain her health this year! I wonder how her birthday was celebrated this time? I remember it well six years ago when I went riding with Vilhelm as far as the bridge over the Laagen.[15] And last Sunday was the twenty-third. It was the third July twenty-third. The first one — yes, I remember it well; the second in Christiania; the third here in Iowa; and each time we have been together, God be praised![16]

There were services at Rognald [Belle's] last Sunday. It was a warm drive to his place; but we managed to get safely through all the creeks, which were still high. "What a crowd there is today!" said Vilhelm, as we came closer to the house, where people were camped outside on every available stump and piece of timber. At first I thought there were not so

[14] Gudbrand E. Sørland was born July 15, 1854.
[15] The Laagen River is just east of Larvik, Norway.
[16] July 23 was the date on which Elisabeth and Vilhelm became engaged.

many, but soon learned otherwise. When we came inside, every place was taken. A chair was immediately brought for me, however, and I did not have such a bad seat — just opposite the open window — until the communicants had to come forward. But then, with many others, I had to give up my place and go outside.

It was out of the question to think of getting in again and without doubt it was best to stay outside anyway, for, although it was hot, there was fresh air instead of the stifling atmosphere within. There were many more outside than in; they crowded about the windows and doors in order to hear. I could not stand the sun and found a little shade back of the house, where I sat on a stone but could not catch anything of the service. Others doubtless had a similar experience. I was much worried over Vilhelm during the long service, fearfully hot as it was inside; furthermore, he certainly exerted himself to speak loud enough for those outside to hear. I wish the next services could be held in the open air; that would surely be better.

I had let Caroline go home; so for dinner we ate what there was, without standing on ceremony and without starting a fire in the stove. *Tykmelk,* cold rice porridge, and bread and butter made up our meal; and they were enough to satisfy a good appetite. Then I went over to Erik's and made coffee. We drank it and talked of this day two years ago and what had happened since. When the air became cooler, we went outside and sat on a pile of logs. The clouds began to gather, the thunder to roll. We were interrupted by Guri and some friends, who came to ask Vilhelm to read a letter for one of the newcomer girls, and soon afterward by Caroline, who announced that tea was ready.

I shall not easily forget such a day as yesterday; I have never seen such a storm on land. The forenoon was fair, but hot. Before Vilhelm was through dressing, a newcomer came to ask him to write a letter for him; and while we were eating breakfast, the Coon Prairie man came again — it looks as if he might become a regular guest while he is in the neighborhood. There were more candidates for confirmation than usual — two new ones. A Yankee was with them and sat here for a while. I do not know what pleasure he found in it, for he probably did not understand a word of Norwegian. It was warm with so many people in this little room. I had to sit still, completely hemmed in as I was.

They were not through until late, and I hurried out to the summer kitchen, where to my surprise I found a dish of new potatoes which Guri had sent. They were doubly welcome today, for the C. P. man sat here all morning, of course; and consequently stayed for dinner, too, and for some time after coffee before he finally, apparently because of the heavy storm coming up, found it advisable to leave. It was lucky he left when he did, for soon a heavy storm blew up and in a few moments completely changed daylight to dusk and brought rain and heavy thunder.

It was a frightful storm and came with unbelievable speed. The rain, which for a time turned to hail, was driven across the fields as if it had been snow, and formed large streams wherever there was a depression. The little brook, which usually flows unnoticed, was swollen to the size of a river with many branches. In the springhouse everything was thrown helter-skelter; milk and cream joined forces with the brook. A large tree was snapped squarely off; a board was blown off the roof of the summer kitchen and in falling carried the stovepipe with it; all the boards lying outside were hurled hither and thither; the horse, which was staked outdoors to graze, broke loose and dashed away; and the poor wheat field was rather badly whipped.

Our place was a sight! The floor was a pond, so I had to tiptoe about with great caution, holding up my dress and finally sitting down in the rocking chair; I was fortunate enough to find a somewhat dry place for my feet. The hail beat so hard against the windows that we expected them to be broken at any moment, and the rain streamed in through the curtains and across the table, soaking them thoroughly. We had to pull the bookcases and bed away from the walls and cover them with towels, for the rain came through the walls and ceiling. In the loft, too, rain penetrated both walls and roof and soaked the bedclothes and other clothing. The storm lasted a good hour; then it let up and the wind subsided, though the lightning was as violent as ever.

We opened the door, glad to get a little fresh air after the oppressive heat. I took the mop and began to tidy up, but it was no light task; I really needed a pump. Erik came with a spade and axe on his shoulder and waded through the brook to the springhouse to bring back a semblance of order there. A little later the horse came back, galloping about before it could be caught. Vilhelm went upstairs and pulled on his large boots to go outside, but the rain continued and the thunder likewise. In the midst of all this came Caroline afoot, soaked through and through; she had been at Kari's when the storm broke. There they had all fled to the loft — the house is not plastered yet.

When at last the rain let up and we could go outside, the sky was aglow with a brilliancy of color hard to match. There was not a color or shade missing. The cloud formations were most wonderful and beautiful; no matter where one looked, there was endless variety. The lightning, which still continued, was blue and very sharp. No, I shall not easily forget that afternoon. Those who are old-timers in the country say they have never had such a storm. This is the first time I have experienced such a storm on land. On the Atlantic we undoubtedly had worse storms several times, but how different it is on land from on sea! Here at least one is free from the fearful creaking and whistling in the tackle and ropes and woodwork. God be praised Vilhelm was home! How glad we both were for that! Just think if he had been away and I had not known whether or not he was under shelter!

Wednesday, July 26. It is evening. We lit the light earlier than usual. Vilhelm had to do some writing and so I wrote, too, much as I preferred to sit longer in the twilight; it is so pleasant then — one of the best hours of the day, especially when Vilhelm is home. Vilhelm has been hard at work all day. In the forenoon I sat quietly at my work, too; but in the afternoon I do not know what was wrong. I was really out of sorts, had no desire to undertake anything, not even to go for a little walk in the beautiful weather; in brief, I sat there and was very disagreeable, and do not understand why Vilhelm did not scold me roundly. He did say I was annoying, but was much kinder than I deserved. He ought to give me a good scolding when I get such notions. What do they mean? It should be possible to drive them away, especially when Vilhelm is home.

Later in the afternoon we went for a walk. Then, fortunately, my charming mood had left me; so we had a pleasant jaunt. We wanted to visit the valley with the unusual bluffs, where we had been early this spring. To get there we first went over Ola Katterud's newly broken field and then through high grass along the brook, which we could not cross. Here we found beautiful white trailing morning-glories in bloom. It was pleasant to get down into the valley; it is so luxuriant; there are so many grapevines and other climbing plants. We had to stay well up on the hillside most of the way, for the valley was almost filled by the brook, which, like all the others, had left its banks. I would not have ventured alone through the high grass on that path for fear of snakes; but with Vilhelm ahead of me, I was brave. We took a much shorter road home and returned, well satisfied with our walk, while the last lovely rays of the sun were lighting up the various hues of the wood. Tea was waiting for us and we did not lack good appetites.

Vilhelm took a walk with me yesterday, too, after he had returned from the wedding. We went to the parsonage land. He had to build a large bridge of fence rails first before we could cross the creek; the storm had swept away all our bridges. It did not look very promising at the parsonage. The carpenters, those tiresome people, had not yet come! The cabinet-maker was not there, either — only the man who is to do the masonry. He was hauling stone. (But he came to see us this morning and said that since there were still no workers, he could do nothing, for he could not get into the cellar until a door was dug. "The window is too small," he said, "I cannot get through it." Isn't that management?)

Erik Egge's boy was up there; he came over to us and said, "Things really went crazy at Erik's yesterday; the roof of his cabin flew away and sixteen hayricks." That was a storm, indeed, to take the whole roof. Fortunately no one was hurt, although they were in the loft when it happened. Nearly everyone's fences are down.

Vilhelm went into the little grove to hunt for a cluster of grapes for me. He brought back several different climbing plants, plums, flowers, and a specimen of whatever was to be found. It is very wild. It will be interesting when a path is cleared so that I may walk there.

Thursday, July 27. If only Vilhelm could look in on me now, for I know he would be happy to see me sitting here so calm and cheerful, writing and thinking of him! I kept my word and remained calm and in good spirits after he had gone. Nor was I in low spirits earlier, though I was greatly distressed because he was going to leave. I could not help it. He goes away so often, and I am so often upset when he leaves; and this time it seemed as if I could not let him go — and then I was disgusted because he could see my distress. That made him unhappy, and he may perhaps think of it often and be uneasy on my account. God grant he may not, that he may believe my mood will soon pass away! I shall really be in good spirits. I will take great pains — I will be cheerful and think of how pleasant it will be when he returns. Nor was I really in low spirits; the mood was good for me. I became so calm and peaceful afterward, although tears often came to my eyes. I was strangely affected, but happy, nevertheless.

After Vilhelm had gone, my first impulse was to sit down and let my thoughts follow him; but that would not be wise, I felt, so I went to work to prepare dinner. This task, little as it interested me, was just enough to divert me. Then I proceeded to read the passages Vilhelm had suggested. And then my one wish was that Vilhelm might know just how I was and not be anxious on my account. At first I was troubled because I had not been strong enough to conceal my distress — at least until after he had driven away. But now I am troubled no longer. I know that Vilhelm would like it much less to have me upset after he had gone and while I am alone than to have me calm and collected, as I am now, because he was so kind and loving toward me and made me cheerful again. But if he had gone at once and I had been left alone, I would surely have been distressed for a long, long time.

It must be late afternoon now. Because the sky is somewhat overcast, I cannot calculate the time; but, God be praised, nothing more came of the rain and thunder that delayed Vilhelm this morning. I hope he reached his destination long ago; perhaps the services are not yet over.

I have now lit the light. I have been outside for a little exercise, I walked as far as the grass is cut and into the corn, which I examined very closely to see how far the ears have developed. I am sitting here alone. The girl has gone. I shall read a little and then go to bed. I wish Vilhelm could know that I am all right — quite all right.

17

A Trip to Wisconsin

Friday, July 28. I am seated near the door, writing. I moved the little table outside and have spent all afternoon here. It is so close indoors. A little while ago I came back from a ramble with Guri. I took advantage of a time when it was cloudy and not so warm to take a little walk, and met Guri on the hill. She said she would like very much to see the reaper in operation at Katterud's. I was eager to see it, too, and went with her over several fences and across considerable "breaking" to the Katterud field. There we sat on a bundle of wheat and watched three or four people bind grain, until at last the machine came and satisfied our curiosity.

I was ready to go right on to the parsonage land, since I was already so far on the way, but it was much too hot and sultry; moreover, I heard from Guri that the carpenters had not yet come. There must be something wrong with them. I wish Vilhelm had had a chance to talk to them yesterday. It is the twenty-eighth and no start has been made on the roof! Today it must have been terribly hot for Vilhelm to travel.

I have been busy sewing some things for Guri. At noon I started to read *Emilia Galotti*.[1] I have been in good spirits, calm and undisturbed, all day. The sun must be setting, it throws so lovely a splendor over the trees — I must go up the hill and get a good view of it.

Now I had to shut the door and windows, to avoid letting too many mosquitoes in, and had to kindle a light, even though I would have liked to remain in the open door dreaming of past and future. In memory I went over the events of two years ago, from the twenty-third until after Vilhelm had left and I was in Sandefjord.[2] Twilight is the time when I like most to have Vilhelm with me; it is such a pleasant hour.

When I came down from the hill (how glad I was I went up there, it was so beautiful!) I walked back and forth along the brook and listened to its rippling — it foams down from a little elevation — and remembered the locks and our walks there [in Larvik] in winter and in summer. How beautiful it was! My memories this evening turn back so often to the time Vilhelm spent at our home in Larvik. But now I shall lay this aside; perhaps I may continue my recollections in my dreams; I should like to do so, I cherish them so much.

Saturday, July 29. Now the light is lit and I am sitting alone once more. Alas, if Vilhelm were only here and sat now, as he usually does, at the other table, and I could walk over now and then and trim his wick! There are just three days left. Oh, I hope he will come Tuesday, and not too very late! He longs to get home just as much as I to have him here, I know. I do not sit up very late when Vilhelm is away. I am not afraid and do not really find it unpleasant, but just the same I would rather go to bed early — and God be praised, I sleep very well. Then I awaken early and get up earlier than I would otherwise. Caroline went to bed long ago; she is not well. She will probably come down with measles.

I have been very active today and I took a long walk with-

[1] Gotthold Ephraim Lessing, *Emilia Galotti* (Berlin, 1772).
[2] Sandefjord is a city about twenty miles northeast of Larvik, Norway.

out getting tired. I had been thinking since morning of walking to the parsonage land, but it looked as though the dark clouds which had hung over us all day would defeat my purpose. Meanwhile I took courage and set out over the fence and through a field, in hopes of finding the garden that I have looked for for so long. I marvel that I had the courage to walk through the grass; I walked about, back and forth, here and there, without finding what I wanted. Since I did not succeed, I picked some nuts and sat down on a pile of lumber near the building to eat them.

There was no one at the parsonage; the masons had been there, however, and had caulked the logs on the outside, and that poor man had begun the masonry work in the cellar. It could not have been very easy to crawl through the window! I sat and planned a garden and what I should like to have outside the windows, and conjured up a vivid picture of how pleasant and cozy we can be there, with God's help. It was very beautiful there this evening, too. I walked about a little and, when I came back, the carpenter was there with a helper; soon he will be unable to do more until the roof has been put on.

When I sit alone in the evening with my writing case and my diary, I very often think of all the evenings when I have sat up, writing to Vilhelm. While everyone was fast asleep, I used to sit a long time — often with my hand beneath my chin, thinking of him instead of writing. That is what I wish to do now; only there is this difference, that I close my case and lay my head on my pillow.

Sunday, July 30. Sunday morning once more, the same as it usually is when Vilhelm is away—the same peace and quiet, the same beautiful weather; and I — I am almost in the same mood I was in the last Sunday I spent alone, God be praised. Earlier this morning I began to be quite melancholy and to feel very lonesome (on Sundays I am more inclined that way). I wanted so much to have someone to talk to or, at the very least, some human being to look at. But Guri and all her family had gone to Sørland's. So I sat in the rocking chair and thought of Vilhelm and wished fervently I might become bright and cheerful again, and was willing to do everything I could to that end.

It was really shameful of me to be in such a mood. I realized, too, when I thought of Vilhelm, how good God is to us, and how well off we are. And little by little I became happy and light of heart, and felt only gratitude for all the goodness I have enjoyed, and was distressed to think I had so easily let my mind stray, I, who have so much to rejoice and thank God for and who nevertheless felt upset and in low spirits because I was a little lonely — because Vilhelm was not here. Indeed, with God's help he will be here in a couple of days, and even if he does not stay long — why, a couple of hours can often be a great deal. So I shall be cheerful, and if these vexing thoughts of loneliness come again, God grant I may succeed in banishing them as quickly as they come. Later I read several of Brorson's beautiful hymns and a sermon.[3]

I was interrupted by one of Kari's little girls; she wanted to talk to Caroline, who had gone home long ago; she was not well today, either, so she is hardly likely to come back this evening. I had thought I might get Kari's grown daughter to stay here tonight and help me a little in case Caroline became ill, but now I learn she is going to Lansing tomorrow. That is unfortunate, for we were to iron tomorrow and get our clothes ready, in case our trip to Wisconsin should materialize. I hope Vilhelm will know for certain on Wednesday!

Embret was here with a dish of hot potatoes from Guri; so they are back. The potatoes will taste good for dinner. I had already eaten a couple of cold pancakes from yesterday, but this is better.

I went over to Guri's and visited a while; later I wrote a little to Sophie and ate a dish of nuts that Embret had

[3] Hans Adolf Brorson (1694-1764) was a famous Danish hymn writer. See chapter 14, note 26.

brought me; and now I plan to take a little walk — over to Katterud's perhaps.[4] It must be a little cooler now, though today has been very hot in spite of the wind.

Monday, July 31. I have just returned from a good, long hot walk. I went over to see Eli, who I had heard was not very well. I took the path through the woods; it was a little cooler there. Vilhelm's bridges were still standing, but today they were not needed. The last storm had toppled several large trees. Eli was not very sick; she lacks strength. She has now promised to prepare a chicken. How can she regain her strength by eating only potatoes and cream gravy? And then it is so annoying that she wants to start right in with her usual work. If I had not come, she would have gone down to the springhouse and busied herself with the milk. Well, she does have a hired girl. I stayed awhile and promised to send over a soothing powder for the baby. I went home by way of the parsonage land. Yesterday Liv Katterud talked to one of the carpenters, who said they now were going to get the roof on the house; but I did not see a trace of them.[5] There was neither joiner nor carpenter, and yet it was not quite six-thirty.

Today I have been gay and happy all day. This forenoon I was making a cushion for Vilhelm's wagon; just as I was wondering whether I should go to the trouble of lighting a fire in the stove and cooking some food for dinner, Guri came over with hot potatoes, pork, and a bowl of delicious *tykmelk*. She is far too kind. I ate with relish and had just finished when Vige came running. I was so glad to see him that I jumped up at once and petted him, while he showed his delight in every possible way. I wonder where the poor creature left his master; he looked very hungry and worn.

I am all alone now; Caroline, as I had surmised, had to stay home. Kari asked me yesterday if I wanted one of her children to stay overnight, in which case she would send her

[4] Sophie was the pastor's younger sister. See chapter 16, footnote 5.
[5] Liv was the wife of Nils Katterud.

over when she returned from Magnus'. I answered yes, but gave up waiting for her when it became so late and was thinking of asking Gro to come over if she had not already gone to bed.[6] On my own account I was not afraid to be alone, but I knew Vilhelm would not like it. While I was considering the matter, Guri came to ask if I did not want someone from their place to come over; it was Erik, it appeared, who thought I should not be alone. So Gro came. And this morning when I went outside, I found Kari's daughter here; she asked if she could help me with anything. But for the time being I need no help. The ironing will have to wait until Vilhelm comes and Gro can stay until then.

Tomorrow I must be industrious and write home. It will be the third letter without an answer — that strikes me as somewhat annoying. How hot it must be for Vilhelm! I wonder if he is enjoying the beautiful weather we are having this evening. Next time he will have lovely moonlight on his journey. Yesterday I wanted so much to go with him, no matter how hot it might be — but it was out of the question then; I had to stay home and get everything ready for a possible trip to Wisconsin.

Tuesday, August 1. I have written nearly all day and am very tired. The letters to Laura and Sophie are ready, but I did not get further.[7] Now I must go outside for exercise. I have really done well with my walks during this absence of Vilhelm's. Tomorrow, God be praised, I can expect him. Tomorrow at this time I shall be on the lookout or perhaps will walk over to the road to gaze up and down, although that will hardly help, for he is not likely to come until late. Well, just so he comes. I long so much for him and am so happy at the thought of his return. No, I must go out now or it will be too late, for it is threatening to rain.

I have been outdoors a little; I looked at Erik stacking wheat, had a message from Andrew asking what to do for the

[6] Gro was the daughter of Erik and Guri Skaarlia.
[7] Laura was another of Vilhelm Koren's sisters.

baby, sat talking awhile with Guri, and now I am going to go to bed.

Thursday, August 3. Yesterday was a red-letter day! I sat behind the house all morning — read, sewed, and watched the men load wheat. I was lured away from this by Guri, who beckoned to me with a soup plate in each hand. These soup plates contained sweet barley soup, meat, and potatoes, which she wanted to share with me. Although it was scarcely half past eleven, I relished the dish immensely; I had just finished, and was sitting with some sewing that I wanted done before I took my midday nap, when I happened to glance out the window and see Erik taking down the gate. Then I saw a horse's head and a hat, but I could scarcely believe my eyes, that it was Vilhelm I saw coming so early. But he it was, to my great joy. He had traveled hard the day before and had been on the road early today to get home in good season, had my dear Vilhelm, and that was delightful. Now we had the whole day before us, whereas otherwise he would have come late at night, worn out by the long drive.

Nothing is so good and no day so pleasant as when Vilhelm comes home. He is traveling entirely too much now; yet a trip now and then followed by his return home — that I would not want to miss. Then, too, his homecomings were never so pleasant before we moved here; we were never alone before — well, except in the loft at Egge's and in *himlinga* at Sørland's.[8] But certain it is that his homecomings are delightful, and when we are in the parsonage and I can make him more comfortable, they will be even more so — but no, they cannot be better than they are.

After we had visited for some time, it finally occurred to me that Vilhelm might need food. Vilhelm built a fire in the stove, I washed potatoes (he had brought a sack of excellent new potatoes with him), put them on the fire, heated the rest of the soup, and went down for fresh butter. Meanwhile Vilhelm ground the coffee; I am never permitted to do that.

[8] *Himlinga* is dialect for "the loft."

The meal was now ready. We had a bowl of *tykmelk* for dessert; and I, who had already eaten a scant hour earlier, went ahead as if I had had nothing at all, keeping pace with him throughout the meal and doing full justice to the fine potatoes.

Then we had coffee and talked, giving each other an account of the time we had been separated. Vilhelm read my diary. He then told me that quite by chance he had met Pastor Clausen on the road.[9] He also said that he had now decided to take a trip to Wisconsin; that he was going to tell those who are in charge of the parsonage we are leaving; that if they do not have the house ready when we return, we will then take a trip to some other place. I hope that will help! It is really too bad — still no carpenters! Well, God willing, we are leaving for Wisconsin Thursday morning by train and steamer.

I hope Vilhelm will return Tuesday evening from Paint Creek, where he is now; meanwhile I shall be busy getting everything in order. Vilhelm went to see Guri about arrangements for the house during our absence. A little later I saw them down by the haystacks; I walked down there, too, and sat on a long sled and visited. When we came back, Vilhelm, who had brought home a lemon, made some excellent lemonade. I had gone out after the first mignonettes, and now we sat there and felt we were quite European and civilized with our lemonade and the fragrance of the mignonettes. But I wonder if a glass of lemonade would have tasted as good to us over there? Later we went up to look at the corn, and had a pleasant evening after a happy day.

Vilhelm did not leave until after dinner. How good these dinners of ours taste! Today the dishes were potatoes and butter and cottage cheese, with a good appetite to take the place of seasoning, dessert, and all the rest.

After Vilhelm had left and I had washed the dishes, I had intended to go over to Kari's to see if I could get someone to

[9] On Clausen, see chapter 14, footnote 5.

help with the washing. But I found Kari at Guri's. Vilhelm had already spoken to her. So that was why he had stayed so long over there. One of them will come Monday; until then I must keep busy with other things.

Since I did not go to Kari's, I went with her along the strawberry path in order to get a little walk, and arranged for her children to gather nuts for me. Going home I met [Dysja,] the man I had given medicine for his eyes; he was coming to thank me and get help for his daughter, who also was having trouble with her eyes. To judge by what he said, people believe we are skilled in medical matters; he also said he had heard that "the pastor had been trained as a medical doctor."

I began a letter to Father this evening; I hope it will be ready before we go. I have now been sitting here a while, reveling in the moonlight. I wonder if Vilhelm is on the road this delightful evening. It is well that it is fairly light if he has had to travel late. Tonight he will stay at a tavern. Vige has returned already; he is back soon. Tonight he howls and barks, whatever the reason may be.

Saturday, August 5. What beautiful weather this evening! If it had not been for the horrid gnats, which I could not drive away, I would still be sitting in the moonlight. I wished so much Vilhelm were home — because — well, because I always wish he were home, and tonight it was so beautiful, and I wanted so much to talk to him. Every time he leaves, I realize more and more that he is home far too little. There is no time for anything; the few hours go so happily, but so swiftly. And when I sit here alone, I so often call to mind something I wanted to talk to him about or ask him; and then I think, "Well, it will have to be next time." But when the next time comes, I am so happy that he is here that I forget it completely or else pay not the least attention to all the things I wanted to talk about; and so that opportunity passes, too. Surely this winter we shall occasionally have some good long evenings, with time for everything.

Diary of Elisabeth Koren

Today I have been very busy. All our things are ready. When we have washed and ironed, we need only pack and I am ready to go — if we really go. I do hope Vilhelm comes Tuesday. He certainly cannot get ready for Thursday otherwise. I really wish we could get away! To begin with I wished it only for Vilhelm's sake — my own inclination was not so strong; but now I, too, long eagerly for it, both for the trip (it will bring back many memories from last year) and for a chance to see Mrs. Linka and the others. I am afraid this trip will be at the expense of the parsonage. I have little faith that it will result in progress. The carpenters, of course, have not come yet — and then they do nearly everything backward. But that will have to be as it may.

Yesterday — yes, what about yesterday? I was busy all the time dividing my energies between my sewing and the "emptyings."[10] Then the eggs came from Lommen's; then I baked bread and boiled potatoes and eggs for dinner.[11] This is the first time that I have cooked a meal when I was alone. It was very strange to cook and then sit down alone to eat; it is far more interesting when Vilhelm is home. But since it probably agrees with both Vige and me to live in a somewhat civilized manner, I cook faithfully every day. But I am hardly likely to make discoveries in the art of cookery these days.

Later in the afternoon, after I had been sitting for some time outside the door mending my gray coat in case it, too, should make the trip, I decided to walk over to Magnus' at once and find out if we could keep Caroline. The sun was not very high and I strolled along, rejoicing because it was so cool. At Tollef's place I got a guide to show me the way, so I reached there safely. But I had not realized it was so far. I was not tired, however, and stood outside and talked to the children while one of them ran to the field for his mother.

[10] Mrs. Koren used a Norwegianized "emptien," referring to the "emptyings" from a pitcher of leaven for salt-rising bread, of which Pastor Koren was very fond. See *Tried and Approved Buckeye Cookery with Hints on Practical Housekeeping*, 26 (Minneapolis, 1885).
[11] By "Lommen's" Mrs. Koren meant either Thrond Lommen's place or that of his son Gudbrand.

It took a while before she came. Then I went in and talked with Caroline, who is still in bed. I got no definite answer; she is probably going back to her dear Yankees, I suppose. After this I drank a little milk and got an immense carrot by way of provision for the homeward journey.

As the sun had just gone down, I had to hurry. When I got to the parsonage land it was so dark, despite the beautiful moonlight, that at first I could not find the path and had to walk right through the wet grass until I located it. But, aside from that, it was very beautiful there; and I found the walking pleasant enough, save that it was so damp, and the path which leads across the fence and into Erik's field is so difficult. I reached home without mishap, however, and with a beautiful wet border on my skirts.

But here they had become much alarmed over my long absence, for they did not know where I was. Gro had gone to Katterud's to look for me, and Guri somewhere else. Just as I returned, Gro returned, too. It was not quite nine at Guri's, where the clock is always fast; but it is true that here nine o'clock is late to be out. If I had known it was so far to Magnus', I should certainly have thought twice before leaving so late. But now I am glad I went; today I could not have gone. I suppose I ought not write this — when Vilhelm reads it, he will say I am careless and the like. But I have now told it to him just the same. Aside from that, am I not smart to have walked so far without becoming tired? I have not done so well since this winter. I have written so long that I am tired and Ole Shut-Eye is approaching.[12]

Sunday, August 6. It is a long time since a Sunday forenoon has passed as quickly as this. Were it not for the sun, it would never occur to me that it is already late afternoon. True, I got up late; it was very dark and rainy and there was nothing to let me know that it was morning. I did not go over to Guri's to make tea, but drank milk for breakfast, and sat very calmly and read until I was interrupted by Guri,

[12] In Hans Christian Andersen's fairy tales, Ole Shut-Eye is the sandman.

who came in with a bowl of good barley soup. It was very nourishing and was good to get in this raw weather. I had dinner, although it was only half past eleven, and sat down again to read. Then Gro came and asked my advice concerning her hand, which pained her. Meanwhile the rain and thunder stopped, and now the sun is shining its friendliest again; so I have been out for a little walk. I hope we shall have good weather for the washing tomorrow, but where shall we get wood? I had quite forgotten about that. Erik probably will not have time to chop any. It will really be a relief when eventually we have order in such matters. Vilhelm is conducting services in Paint Creek; they are no doubt over by this time. I hope he comes Tuesday. I wonder if there should not be a letter at McKay's now? But I, who do not write home — what do I mean? There will be no time later.

Monday, August 7. Last night I wrote to Christiane and now I have sent a letter to Father. I hardly thought I should accomplish so much, for we are in the midst of washing. I am the cook and run in and out quite in despair over those tiresome "emptyings" which will not rise, and it is now late afternoon. I hope we may finish the ironing before Vilhelm comes tomorrow — if he does come, as I hope he will. I long very much to know whether or not we shall make the trip. I am more and more eager to go. I was up very early this morning, for I expected a woman to come to help me; but I could have spared myself the trouble. She did not overexert herself. It is extraordinary how cold the mornings can be.

Wednesday, August 9. Vilhelm has come, and we leave tomorrow, Vige and all. I hope the weather will be good and not too hot! If so, I expect a very pleasant trip. And so farewell to this part. Now I must pack.[13]

---

[13] The diary is in six parts, each stitched by hand. The part that ends here is the next to the last. The chronology for the Koren's activities from August 10 to September 30, 1854, is as follows: Thursday, August 10, left Washington Prairie for Spring Prairie and elsewhere in Wisconsin; Wednesday, September 6, left Spring Prairie for home; Wednesday, September 13, arrived at Washington Prairie; Friday, September 15, left for Paint Creek and Clermont; Friday, September 29, back to Washington Prairie; Saturday, September 30, moved into the parsonage.

A Trip to Wisconsin

THOMAS ANDERSON'S CABIN
IN PAINT CREEK,
September 18-20, 1854

MY DEAR FATHER,

Our outing is over. It was a great success and we are safely home, Vilhelm fully occupied with his usual activities. This forenoon he is at Sven Hesla's teaching his confirmation class; and I, meanwhile, shall return to my dear old task of writing you, my dear, kind Father.[14] "But why are you already on the move again?" you will ask when you read the heading. I may as well tell you at once why we are here with this family, who are among the best members of the congregation and with whom I am very happy to stay. You thought, no doubt, that when we returned from our trip we should be able to move into the parsonage. That was our idea, too, when we came home Wednesday and drove directly to it. But we were disappointed; several things were still lacking. So Vilhelm decided it was better to make the circuit to Paint Creek and Turkey River at once rather than a week later. After having been together so long, we were eager to be together a little longer, and so I went with him; besides, the weather had turned so comfortably cool.

Upon our return, which is to be in ten or twelve days, we are to move in at once. I should like very much to finish this letter at the parsonage, but I am afraid it will be too long a wait. But you may rest assured that by the time you receive this letter I shall be in full activity there. In less than a week everything is to be ready for our moving — and now they will really hurry, you may be sure.

We stayed Thursday at Skaarlia's and left Friday, I with a huge watermelon in my lap, also bread and butter for our lunch. We stopped to eat in a grove. How I wish I could picture the scene for you! We sat in the wagon while the horse grazed peacefully and circled slowly and contentedly

[14] Sven E. Hesla lived in Paint Creek Township, Allamakee County; Alexander, *Winneshiek and Allamakee Counties,* 497.

about us. I had the paper bundle of food and Vilhelm was steward of the melon, which he hollowed out, drinking the juice, as it gathered, to his heart's content. Do you know the watermelon? It is extremely juicy and refreshing — bright red inside. We eat the very part that in the yellow ones at home we throw away. The latter, which are called muskmelons here, are superior, I think, in flavor and fragrance; they taste good without sugar, but they are not so refreshing in warm weather. You should see how people here eat one big melon after another.

At the post office we were made happy by letters from home; you may be sure we longed for an opportunity to read them. It came in Waukon, where we had to put up for the night at the tavern; Vilhelm had been delayed by callers, so we were late in leaving. We spent the evening reading and talking about these dear letters. Greetings and thanks to all who wrote.[15]

When I mentioned our journey to Wisconsin in my last letter, I supposed we would travel by railroad and steamer. We gave up that plan, however, and for various reasons decided to use our own transportation. As it was very warm, there was little comfort in traveling on the hot, dusty railroads or upon the hot Mississippi, where some of the steamers are reported to be very dirty and disagreeable. We knew, moreover, that there was much cholera and sickness in Dubuque and Galena. In any event, Vilhelm had to have a means of getting to Brandt's; in short, there were many things that persuaded us to travel in this manner and we are glad we did.[16]

We left, then, August 10, Vilhelm with all his possessions — horse, wagon, dog, and wife — in pleasant weather. It was

[15] The family letters from this period that have been preserved are all written in a very fine hand; thus they would be extremely difficult to read without a good light. The post office was probably the one at McKay's, which would have been two or three miles from Skaarlia's.

[16] Dubuque, Iowa, is on the Mississippi one hundred miles south and east of Decorah. Galena, Illinois, is seventeen miles southeast of Dubuque. Brandt was then pastor at Rock River, near Oconomowoc, Wisconsin.

interesting to retrace the road we followed last year in coming here. What a difference crossing the river, then all snow and ice, and now so warm that the ferryman himself groaned and complained! There are horse-driven ferries over both the Mississippi and Wisconsin rivers.

We were to spend the night in Prairie du Chien. Just at the edge of town we noticed a hotel which lay, very rustic and inviting, behind a group of locust trees. Investigating, we found a very large, solid, white stone building, surrounded on all sides by a veranda, or whatever you might call it — very much like the porch outside Münster's. We were well pleased with our discovery. It was one of the buildings of the old Indian fort, now put to this use. This section had formerly been the infirmary. But in the evening, when I saw the large long room with a row of massive beds and a large fireplace full of iron utensils, it seemed more like a torture chamber than a sleeping chamber. Apparently it was the old dining hall, with an entrance to the buttery on one side and to Guard No. 1 on the other.[17]

It was pleasant at the fort. We sat on the veranda until late, enjoying the beautiful view over the Mississippi. These acacia trees — they are called locust trees here, but have leaves like those of your shrubs at home, and the flowers are said to be white and fragrant like those of the acacia tree in Treschow's garden — of these there are great numbers in Wisconsin, but not so many here. They are always planted, and grow very willingly and rapidly. They are used a good deal for hedges, and as soon as I can, I am going to plant an arbor and hedges, too, along the borders of our garden.

Next morning we journeyed from the fort up the long valley to the Wisconsin River. The road is poor in places. I

[17] The Münsters were friends of the Korens in Norway. On Dean Münster, see chapter 9, footnote 1. The hotel was the hospital building of the second Fort Crawford, which had been evacuated in 1849. Although the fort was reoccupied later, it was finally abandoned and the site is now occupied by a private school for girls; Bruce E. Mahan, *Old Fort Crawford and the Frontier*, vii, viii (Iowa City, 1926); Peter Lawrence Scanlan, *Prairie du Chien: French, British, American*, 136, 143, 154 (Menasha, Wisconsin, 1937).

had never dreamed it could be so hot as it was in that narrow valley. I do not understand how people can live there in summer — there are a couple of huts — and even less how the man I saw could stand to cut hay. It was very interesting, if only it had not been so hot. There were many grapevines, but there will be few grapes this year. How refreshing it was to come to a clear, cold spring which gushed out of the wall of the bluff, where the horses were watered and where we also wet our lips! We did not dare drink to our heart's content then. "When we get up on the prairie, it will be better," said an American ahead of us, to reassure us. But the change was not great. I have never experienced a hotter day; and wherever we came, we heard that no one could remember such heat. At the tavern where we had dinner it was so dreadfully hot that I asked only to get away as soon as we could. Outside it was a little better.

The following day was cooler. We had a good road and reached Dodgeville in the evening. We had to travel slowly, you will understand, in such heat and with our own conveyance. Bucephala (that is the name of our horse for the moment, though Vilhelm will not hear of it; it seems to me it is just as good as Sleipnerine or Pegasine; and since, unfortunately for the name, the horse is not of the masculine gender, the case is a rather difficult one) now this Bucephala is an excellent young creature who acquits herself very well.[18] We spent one more night at a tavern; at times, in these, one is received like a familiar guest. The landlady carries on a very lively conversation and inquires about our health; the landlord likewise. A landlady of this type, just as talkative as most of them, kept up an incessant conversation with me. I thought to myself, "Go ahead and talk with her; it will do you good to get the practice," and chatted as best I could about every sort of household matter; at last she showed me her home, her bedding, etc.

[18] Bucephalus was the celebrated war horse of Alexander the Great, and Sleipnir was the Norse god Odin's swift eight-footed steed; hence these feminine forms of the names. Pegasine is a corrupt feminine form of Pegasus, the winged horse of Greek mythology.

On Tuesday [August 15] we came to Spring Prairie and surprised Mrs. Preus, whom we found seated on a tree stump in the farmyard in lively conversation with a Vossing woman. We were received very warmly, you may be sure, though they had not expected us. I suppose Vilhelm's letter to A. Preus had not yet reached him. The pastor had already left for Brandt's, so Vilhelm set out early next morning and I remained with Mrs. Linka. She is a sweet woman and my favorite among the ministers' wives — cheerful and lively, too. We had a very pleasant time during the days we were alone.

On Saturday [August 19] we expected our husbands and Pastor Ottesen and his wife, and when they came the house was filled indeed. Nor were we entirely alone before; besides a man named Petersen, who manages Preus's farm, that Ziølner, who came over at the same time as the Preuses, was there visiting.[19] You may be sure it was very strange to mingle with educated people again after having seen, Vilhelm excepted, only farm folk for more than seven months.

They are of the opinion that Munch will now be our nearest neighbor; it will take us more than three days, however, to reach his home, but then we shall not have much more than a day's journey left to Spring Prairie. It will probably take at least five days from here to Spring Prairie; by railroad one can do it somewhat faster, to be sure, but by a very circuitous route. No, wait until the railroad reaches the Wisconsin River; then we shall be able to go there quickly. We shall need two days, it is true, perhaps more, to travel to Coon Prairie, where Stub will come as pastor in the spring.[20] Our nearest neighbor, however, will be the Minnesota pastor. He will be only a day distant, and if you can find us an agreeable man to go there next summer, Father, I shall be very

[19] The Reverend Jakob Aall Ottesen (1825-1904) was then pastor at Manitowoc, Wisconsin. Petersen has not been identified. On Ziølner, see chapter 12, footnote 20.

[20] The Reverend Johan Storm Munch (1827-1908) migrated to America in 1855 and became pastor at Wiota and Dodgeville, Wisconsin. Pastor Stub was at Muskego in 1854; he did not move to Coon Prairie, Wisconsin, until 1855.

thankful to you. But he must be married; that is one of my conditions. Yes, Pastor Brandt is available; he has a fine large parsonage, rooms all papered, and all that belongs to a house, but no wife. Of course it all depends on what he prefers, a house without a wife, or a wife without a house.[21]

Mother asks how we spent the eighteenth. Since Vilhelm was at Brandt's, we were not together on our first wedding anniversary. But Mrs. Linka and I celebrated it as best we could. In the forenoon we sat on the floor with a large paper of raisins and almonds between us, likewise a hammer, and cracked and ate, while little Christian crept about on his stomach from one to the other. Mrs. Preus wondered what she should give me for dinner in honor of the day; but we decided discreetly not to disturb the bill of fare which had been so nicely arranged for the guests, and confined ourselves to smoked ham, potatoes, and *tykmelk*. The day before, we had baked cookies; we helped ourselves to these in the afternoon and then strolled along the charming paths in the grove of young trees about the parsonage. Thus we spent our first August 18 in this country, and my thoughts were often with you in the old mansion that day! [22]

Sunday [August 20] the men came from Brandt's; that was fun, and it was a surprise to meet Mrs. Ottesen.[23] Those were pleasant days at Spring Prairie. The house is certainly the least attractive and the most modest of parsonages in comforts and otherwise; they still have the same sofa (of poplar limbs with the bark on) which Ziølner and Preus nailed together when they first arrived; but one feels so comfortable and thoroughly at home. They are very amiable, both he and she. Sunday Ottesen preached, Monday we spent at Preus's, too, and Tuesday [August 22] we left for Madison — Ottesens, Vilhelm and I, and Pastor Preus.

We were bound for Dietrichson's at Rock Prairie, where

[21] The Reverend Nils O. Brandt married Diderikke Ottesen in 1856.
[22] The Korens were married August 18, 1853.
[23] Pastor J. A. Ottesen was married to Cathinka Tank Døderlein in 1852.

the pastors were having one more meeting.[24] We had dinner in beautiful Madison, the most beautiful city in Wisconsin, and then took a train to that pretentious little Milton with its black suns on the houses. The first part of this trip was the strangest I have ever taken. The road was under construction, or something had broken down — at any rate, we had to travel in the freight cars with the locomotive behind us.[25] We whizzed along, seated in the last of these, which were open at both ends and without railing of any kind, over a long, narrow bridge across a lake. Soon, however, we got a regular train. Since we should have had to wait several hours in Milton for a train, we took a stage and drove to Janesville. That is not such a bad town; one can get what one wants and at a fairly reasonable price. The pastors down there are fortunate to have towns near them.

We had just finished supper when Pastor Preus, then Brandt, and then Clausen arrived from Dietrichson's with their horses and buggies; so we had six pastors in all. When the late arrivals had had a little food, the whole group started off, Ziølner in the lead, to have the ices which had been promised Mrs. Ottesen and me for our refreshment after the hot day. Then we went into a large bookshop, on which occasion Pastor Clausen enriched my English library with *Passages from the Diary of a Late Physician* by Samuel Warren, an interesting book, which you probably know.[26]

The next morning [August 23] we drove to Dietrichson's [at Rock Prairie] — a warm, dusty trip. There is so much dust in Wisconsin; here we are relatively free of it. I think nothing has ever tasted so good to me as the glass of cold lemonade with which the pastor met us. The Dietrichsons have an attractive stone house to live in. To come into the light, cheerful living room, with vines outside the door leading to the

[24] The Reverend Gustav Fredrik Dietrichson (1813-86) was then pastor at Luther Valley, Wisconsin. Rock Prairie is about five miles east of Janesville, Wisconsin.
[25] They were probably riding on flat cars.
[26] Warren's book was published in London in 1832.

garden, reminded me of a country house in Europe. I like Mrs. Dietrichson; she is no doubt the oldest of the pastors' wives, of whom I am now the youngest.[27] Here we also found Pastor Unonius and his wife, who appeared to be a quiet, friendly woman. During the summer she and the children live only a few steps from Dietrichson's. Fleischer, who manages the bookshop, and his wife live here, too. Pastor Stub was not present, either at Brandt's or here, as his children are very ill. Otherwise, all the Norwegian pastors were here. How fortunate that Vilhelm came! Now I have seen them all, too.[28]

We had breakfast and then the pastors took up their affairs. After dinner we were all invited to Pastor Unonius' for coffee and the evening. It was very pleasant. Since nearly all the pastors sing, there was much singing in the course of the evening; it was just like being in Norway to be together with all these people and hear the familiar songs. A few steps from Unonius' home is located the printing shop with which the storm I described in my last letter played such havoc. The roof and a portion of the wall were torn away, and most of the tools and types were destroyed, so that they are having a hard time to put it in running order. It stands now like a ruin; and there supper was served. It was rather romantic with the festive, brightly lighted table inside those ruined walls, and the dark, starry heavens for a roof. I must not forget that Mrs. Unonius served us oyster stew, just as great a rarity here as dinner in a large restaurant. Services were held the following day [August 24], which we spent quietly at Dietrichson's. We did not undertake a walk or other excursion, for it was much too hot.[29]

[27] The Reverend Gustav F. Dietrichson married Pauline Preus in 1845.

[28] On Unonius, see chapter 5, footnote 18. Knud J. Fleischer was editor of *Emigranten*, 1854-57.

[29] "In addition to the stone printing office, were a frame house occupied by Editor Fleischer and family and the Dietrichson parsonage. . . . In June, 1854, the printing office was wrecked by a cyclone, the roof being blown off." The demolished printing office had been the home of *Emigranten*. See Albert O. Barton, "The Norwegian Press in America," in State Historical Society of Wisconsin, *Proceedings of the Society at Its Sixty-fourth Annual Meeting Held October 19, 1916*, 201 (Madison, 1917).

Friday [August 25] we left Rock Prairie. Mrs. Ottesen and I drove with [Adolph] Preus; the others came behind in a large surrey. In Janesville we separated; the Ottesens and others went to their own homes; Vilhelm and I accompanied Pastor Preus to Koshkonong, where we remained till the following Thursday [August 31]. Sunday we partook of holy communion. There had been great renovations at Koshkonong; the house was very much cozier than last winter. Mrs. Preus is attractive; it was very pleasant to be there. But there, too, we had the same heat nearly all the time. Not only do the oldest Norwegians here say they have never experienced such heat, but even the Americans cannot remember such a summer. So they congratulated us, as newcomers, because we had not been sick. Yes, God be praised, we have stood the summer well. Now the worst heat for this year is past.

We made use of one rather fresh morning to take a little drive. There are many beautiful places near Koshkonong, but I would not trade the site of our parsonage for any of those I have seen. Pastor Duus, who by now must have arrived safely at Koshkonong with his family, will get a very charming location, close to water, I believe; a good house of fir, built in the Norwegian manner, is waiting for him. He, too, is likely to be somewhat isolated; Ottesen will doubtless be his nearest neighbor. The Ottesens live in a large wood among trees (the like of which apparently are not to be found here) so high and so large that they seem to shut out the sky. They can hardly stir because of tree stumps and are having great trouble clearing a spot for a garden. They have often wished for a bit of prairie or some young trees and underbrush. They, too, have an isolated location, but it is easy for them to come down by steamer; and the pastor has no extensive journeys to take, the longest only eight to ten miles, so he is always home.

Our last days we spent at Spring Prairie. We had thought of leaving on Monday [September 4]; but if it had been hot before, it was even worse then, and we did not dare start. We were lucky enough to get a heavy thunderstorm and rain, bringing cool weather, which we still enjoy. Tuesday was your birthday, my dear, kind Father. We drank your health in Madeira, the last bottle of the supply [Herman] Preus had brought with him from Norway. Wednesday [September 6] we started home. Pastor Preus went with us to Madison. The following day a steady rain held us in a tavern, where the daughter of the house was very considerate and brought us melons. The rest of the way we had good weather, fortunately.

The road down the valley to the Wisconsin River is disgusting. Often I preferred to walk. Ought not something be done about it, I wonder? When we were almost through the worst of it, we noticed that one wheel was about to fall off the wagon. By good fortune an American was driving behind us; Vilhelm walked over to him and asked if he would "please take the lady down to the ferry." The American was very polite; I seated myself on his buffalo robe and we drove away. Meanwhile Vilhelm, behind us, kept his rig steady, and by one or another lucky and incomprehensible maneuver, probably one jolt up and another down on that uneven road, managed to get the wheel back in its proper place so that we could continue our journey unhampered on the other side of the river. There we were surprised to find the last portion of the road, which had been so bad, much improved. No other misfortune befell us, and five weeks to the day after we had driven away, we were on the parsonage grounds again, and since then you already know what we have done.[30]

We are now back to our solitude, and Vilhelm to his work-filled days. We are both immensely pleased with the trip. Vilhelm has certainly benefited greatly from the outing; long as the journey was, back and forth, it was nevertheless

[30] Because the parsonage was not yet ready, the Korens left at once for Paint Creek.

a relaxation from other duties. And he was greatly in need of such a trip. And it was well that the relaxation came during the hottest part of the summer.

Here in the settlement health conditions were good, thanks be to God! Down in Wisconsin cholera was bad, especially at Rock Prairie. It abated somewhat while we were there, but then began at Spring Prairie. Our friend, Lars Møen, who drove us last year, lost his wife, poor man; she left a large flock of children. I was afraid people here might not escape, for earlier this summer there were a few cases, and there have been some in towns along the rivers — and how unfortunate it would have been if Vilhelm had been away then. There has been much rain here, too much, so this will not be as good a year as usual.

Well, when we move into the parsonage, which will certainly take place to the crashing of brass and cymbals, as you say, it will be as if a new life is beginning, a new sphere of endeavor for me. How I rejoice at the prospect! Next time I hope I can tell you all about it. It will then be amusing, too, to stroll down to Skaarlia's and sit on the chopping block and talk about all the happy hours we spent there — our first house! I am now going to take a walk. It is beautiful here. I shall not have Vilhelm's company, for he will probably return from services late. I shall visit one of the neighbors and have a good talk with Ola Storla's wife about the care of chickens and calves or churning butter, whichever it may be.

I have now returned from my walk. I went as I had planned, gnawing as usual on a big carrot, and came back, richer by the seed of a new kind of watermelon. I gather seed wherever I go. At Spring Prairie I got parsley and string beans; I cannot get these here. I wonder if it would not be possible to obtain lily of the valley pips and white narcissus bulbs from home, as the opportunity offers — if Munch comes over, for example. I should like very much to have some domestic flowers. The auricula is not to be had here. I shall not succeed in gathering seed from wild flowers this summer, I am afraid. I was away during the best time for it. It is hard to find the spot where they grow — and then they are cut down with the hay. Perhaps I shall have better luck next year.

Vilhelm sends you loving greetings and thanks for your letter. He wanted to write a good letter this autumn, but that is now impossible. The way his time is taken up, he does not have half a day at his own disposal. Journeys and more journeys, and all he can take care of during the short time he is home; but he hopes to write you for Christmas. He must also go to Minnesota this fall and make arrangements for calling a pastor from Norway. There he will probably meet Pastor Brandt, who is looking after Coon Prairie for Stub and who also wants to visit us and his sisters here.

Day after tomorrow we shall go to Clermont and then to Norway.[31] When I have been there, I shall have been in all Vilhelm's congregations. I am glad I shall get there this autumn. God bless you, dear Father, and may this letter find you well and contented.

LEIS

[31] These parishes were about twenty-five miles south of Decorah.

18

Our Own Home

Sunday, October 1. I now begin my usual task again — my dear diary has lain here for two months while I have been roaming about. And best of all, I begin in our new home. Yes, praise and thanks to God that I am now sitting in the bright, cheerful living room of the parsonage; and God grant I may be able to write very often with just as much joy and gratitude for all benefits as I feel at this moment!

There are services at [Rognald] Belle's today, but I did not go with Vilhelm. It was raining and threatened to storm but now has changed to beautiful sunshine.

Friday afternoon we came home from Turkey River and took the road direct to the parsonage, half hoping to get the bed up and move in that same evening. We were naturally full of expectation and wanted to see what progress had been made. According to promise, everything was to be ready this Friday. We had already learned how much we could rely on promises; yet I was not only disappointed, but also disgusted and provoked to find only one room sufficiently finished so that we could move into it. The plaster was not dry and there were no thresholds. That was all that had been done. The plastering was only half finished, no plowing had been done around the house, neither had any beginning been made on the well.

I became really downcast when I saw how things were; it hurt me. But I was also angry, ill humored, and unmannerly and began to complain as we were going over to the Egges, who, we were told, were awaiting us. We decided to stay there overnight, as it was very late. So I sat and complained and expressed my dissatisfaction, without stopping to think that I must have made Vilhelm even more dejected; but I soon regretted my action and was sorry I had taken it so hard, instead of remembering how much we had to be thankful for — we so often forget that when we experience something disagreeable.

When we got there (Egge's) we found the house full of lodgers (three or four carpenters). That was not so pleasant, and if it had not been dark we would have turned back; now we had to stay. Helene welcomed us very kindly and gave us the loft for our private sleeping room. Now that it is over, I would not give up that evening at Egge's, even though it was rather discouraging; nor would I give up the moments when I sat alone with Vilhelm outside the cabin, nor the cold, drafty, sleeping room where we had to stop the cracks in the ceiling and walls with our clothes.

We were up early next morning to get a good start with the moving, but the heavy rain, which had fallen during the night and still continued, threatened to hinder us. It cleared somewhat, however, and we set out, supplied by Helene with fresh pork, carrots, and beets. We drove for the last time to Skaarlia's, this time actually to move our things. Erik brought out his oxen, Gudbrand Lommen came with his, and now the moving began. I remained at Skaarlia's to supervise the loading. Vilhelm went with the loads, put up the beds, and got the chests from Sørland's. He came back for dinner at

Guri's. Then we were to leave for good. Guri was thoughtful and gave me a leg of pork, a head of cabbage, and some onions, besides bread and the cookies with which she has so often regaled us. Erik and little Embret drove ahead with the little hut for the stove. Then we followed, Vilhelm holding the umbrella — it had begun to rain again — and I with the head of cabbage in my lap, the bag of bread in my hand, small bottles and personal effects on all sides, and the bottom of the buggy filled with roots and pork and Madame Pompadour, our most troublesome baggage.[1] It was too bad Vige was not along when we made our entry! Happy we were, despite the rain and everything, to have come so far at last.

What a sight the parsonage was! A confusion of trunks, bedclothes, and packages everywhere, and the floor disgustingly dirty because it was so muddy outside! Gudbrand [Lommen] and Gullik [Rønningen] were here and wanted to set up the hut for the stove. They had not had dinner yet. "Have you a little food, Eleis?" called Vilhelm from outside. "Yes, of course, but nothing to drink," was the reply. Thereupon, with much difficulty, I managed to get at the plates and the knives, which lay hidden under all the clothes — these men, they have no understanding in such matters. Then I set the table with a large plate of butter, a loaf of bread, and the *mysost* that we had with us. That was the first meal in the parsonage, dry enough![2]

Then I went inside, wondering what I should tackle first and how I should manage everything. My compliments to Vilhelm — he is really a smart man! Who would have believed he could think of it? He had set the carpenter to work at once on a shelf, which was put up that same evening next to where the stove will be — and that is now my pantry.

While I was busy with this, I was called upstairs to be present when the boxes were opened. I stood there rather anxiously, waiting for the lids to be removed; I expected to

[1] Madame Pompadour was a dog that had been given to the Korens.
[2] Norwegian *mysost* is a brown cheese, firm enough to cut, made of the whey of milk. It is approximately the same as *primost*.

see one thing more damaged than the next. But no; not a single thing was broken. What a joy that was! How pleasant it was to unpack here at the parsonage! It was different from the old shed at Sørland's with all its whitewash and the sheep bleating around us. We hung out the table linen, carried the books and silver downstairs, and then, perhaps most delightful of all, put up the bookshelves and arranged the books. Oh yes, I forget; first we ate bread and butter, washing it down with water, which Sven [Gullikson] had been good enough to get. God grant we may have many meals just as happy as this first one! Many people had been here all this time; now at last they had gone, and we were alone — alone in our first home! Now for the first time I begin to understand rightly what "home" means, our own home, which becomes dearer to me day by day.[3]

We had managed to get things into some sort of order, curtains at the windows, the lights lit, and then we spent most of the evening putting the books in order. How pleasant it is to see the shelves upon the wall, one on each side of the window, and all my English books arranged in their accustomed order! Old Sagen and Christie also found places on the wall, with Lund, Berle, and Lassen between them.[4]

How wonderful it was to wake up this morning and realize that we were really here! I had just dressed when I heard a knocking at the door. It was Aadne, the carpenter, who brought us freshly strained milk and a copper pot full of

[3] Sven Martin Gullikson was a member of the confirmation class; he had been sent over to help at the parsonage. The completed parsonage had a bedroom, living room, kitchen, and loft. The original building was finished in 1854; it burned in 1872.

[4] Overlærer (Headmaster) Lyder Sagen (1777–1850) was a prominent educator and author who taught at the Bergen Cathedral School, 1805–50. Wilhelm Frimann Koren Christie (1778–1849) was a cousin of Paul Schonevig Stub Koren, Pastor Koren's father. He was secretary of the Eidsvold consttutional assembly in 1814, president of the Storting, civil governor of the Bergen diocese, and founder of the Bergen museum. See *Aschehougs konversations leksikon*, 2:705, 8:841 (Christiania, 1920–25); Johnson, *Slekten Koren*, 1:28, 188, and *Oversiktstavle* (genealogical table) I. The Reverend Jens Michael Lund (1821–1906) was present at the wedding of Elisabeth and Vilhelm. He was parish pastor in Old Oslo, the portion of the city on the left or east bank of the Akers River, where medieval Oslo was built. For a note on the Lassen family, see chapter 13, footnote 14.

coffee, because the summer kitchen was not yet ready.[5] It was a kind and welcome gift. While I was talking to him, some milk came from Magnus, too, so we had enough to drink in case we ran short of water. I have just had dinner (bread and milk), then I sat outside on some logs sunning myself, and now I am seated inside rejoicing at how light and cheerful our living room is and wondering why Vilhelm does not return.

Wednesday, October 18. Alas and alack for my inconstancy! I do not know what will finally become of my diary. I really should have kept a travel diary of our visit to Wisconsin, and especially of our return, when we came driving up here and discovered how many or, more correctly, how few of our conjectures concerning the progress of the building were confirmed. That was not a cheerful moment.

"Do you think it is plastered?" asked Vilhelm.

"Yes, some of it," I ventured, "but it is hardly likely that all the windows are in yet."

"No, there are no windows upstairs," said Vilhelm when, after keeping a long lookout, we got our eyes on the house. "No, really, I don't believe there has been any plastering," broke from him next.

And so it was, too; the house was open on every side — no windows, not even a finished roof, nothing. The floor in the kitchen had not been started. The carpenter came before we drove away. I do not understand how Vilhelm could be so — I don't know what I should say — so calm. That he was exceedingly displeased I knew, and I could read it in his expression, too, but that he still could talk so discreetly! I could not have done so. I doubtless would have blurted out something; as it was, I had trouble enough holding my tongue. When we came back the second time, it hurt me to see how little had been done; but the first time, I was provoked.

We were puzzled that first time as to what we should do — go to a tavern and stay for the time being? I did not care for

---

[5] Aadne Aadneson was married to Johanne Kristine Jonasdatter.

that — to sit there alone while Vilhelm was away. We decided to go down to Skaarlia's first and see if there were any letters. We left the horse on the hill and walked down. We saw no one. Vilhelm went to the field to look for them and I sat down on a bench in the summer kitchen, tired and far from cheerful. At length Erik and Guri appeared with a great load of hay, and it did us good to see the evident joy with which they greeted us. They had not yet moved into their [new] house and wanted us to stay on there. We agreed to stay overnight, and so we found ourselves once more in that little room, which is really dear to me in spite of its musty smell.

After some talk and deliberation it was decided that Vilhelm should visit the rest of his congregations and not return until the parsonage was habitable. My one request was to go with him, for there was nothing I wanted less than to remain behind or stay at a tavern. Much better go with him, no matter how embarrassing it might be in the cabins where we stayed. And so it was decided; and the next day, after we had driven some distance, we were both quite cheerful. In Paint Creek we stayed with the Thomas Andersons, splendid people; and at Turkey River visited Gunhild and Lise Brorby and others,-fine, attractive people. I was given a large bundle of wool, a large *mysost* that is now on our table every day, and likewise stout little Madame Pompadour, who caused us not a little trouble on the return journey.

Loaded with this baggage, then, we came driving home fourteen days later, this time with better grounds for our expectations, and began from afar to guess which grove was the one on the parsonage land. And when we came near Tollef's farm, we looked to see if we could not spy the house from there, and were happy to note the beautiful approach from that quarter, while all the time asking each other: "What is your opinion — do you think the plastering is ready? Do you think all the windows are in?" Yes, we thought so, and although we had not expected more than one room to be

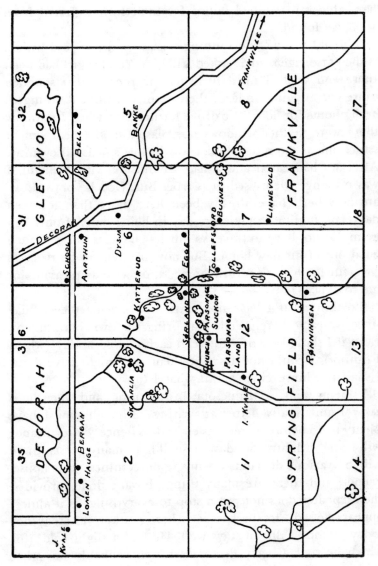

The Washington Prairie Church Land and Vicinity in 1854

habitable, still we had hoped for something different from what we found.

The old uncle came running out as we drove past. "Well, is the parsonage ready?" asked Vilhelm. Yes, his girl had been there and washed up a little in one room. That sounded quite encouraging, indeed; then we met Gullik [Rønningen] going home for flour. We drove farther. But when I now saw there were neither windows nor plaster in the bedroom, it struck me as too much, and I was in low spirits all evening. After we had eaten and I had sat outside with Vilhelm, I was no longer depressed, it is true. But, God be praised, we are now here, have already been here more than fourteen days, and find more joy every day in being here. If only Vilhelm did not have to travel so much — he does not get much good out of his new home! But now it ought to be twice as cheerful for him to return home, and twice as pleasant for me to expect him.

To think that I have not written in my diary every day since we came here! Well, that brings its own punishment. Even if I should try now to recall each and every day (which I cannot), I could not describe them as I might have done. I shall try, however, to recall what I can.

Vilhelm went to Minnesota this morning, and when he is away I am usually better at writing, although now I have plenty to do before he returns eight days hence. Pastor Brandt will come with him. Sunday we shall have many guests; there will be various demands on my resourcefulness as a housekeeper, and there are many things I want done, provided the carpenter does not put a stop to everything, as it almost appears he will, for he has been here neither yesterday nor today. I hope Vilhelm stays well. He had a slight cold (for which he took Cherry Pectoral), which probably was what made him feel rather poorly before he left. I have now brushed and hung up the coat that I so much wanted him to take with him. I am forgetting that I must write a letter to "Mrs. Koshkonong" this evening so that Suckow can take it with him in the morning; therefore I dare not write more here. I believe Caroline [Linnevold] and Gudbrand are finally saying good night.[6]

Thursday, October 19. I am doing well by my diary, it seems to me! I just finished a letter to Mrs. Dietrichson and now I must add a few lines before I go out and cook dinner for the boy and myself. Since Caroline is home doing the washing, I must be the cook.

Let me see now what I can remember from the days we have lived here. There was the first Monday — then we had Suckow, Sven, the carpenter, and I do not know who all to set up the little hut for the stove; everything was supposed to go like lightning with so many workers, but they just stood about with their hands in their pockets. Yet, to be exact, let me not do Sven an injustice. First he got down on all fours and dug the ashes out of the stove and cleaned it; then he very energetically chopped dead branches from the old oak outside and would gladly have chopped up both what I wanted and did not want. That beautiful oak which the workers would disfigure in order to make it easier for themselves! No, they shall have my kind permission to go two steps around it instead. That was the day I treated them to salt spare ribs for dinner. I did better the next day and was praised by my husband; that was probably because he had cabbage with his meat. Sven was our guest for dinner; he came with Vilhelm from the confirmation class. He has been very kind and helpful; he brought us water, etc.

What a pity I cannot remember what we did those afternoons and evenings! I remember only it was very cozy and we were very happy in our new home. We walked about the fields, through the woods, which were still almost entirely fresh and green, and down to Tollef's farm, from which Vilhelm carried back a pail of water. Then Vilhelm was me-

[6] The pastor went to the Spring Grove area and possibly to Highland Prairie. Ayer's Cherry Pectoral was a patent medicine. "Mrs. Koshkonong" refers to Mrs. A. C. Preus. Gudbrand may have been Gudbrand Eriksen Egge, son of the Erik G. Egges who lived in Madison Township.

chanic and carpenter (I daily discover more perfections in him) and made contrivances with which to hold up the windows. Then he was to make an egg case for me, but there he stopped halfway and I got none. Then Caroline came.

For dinner Wednesday I had a special treat; roast fowl, a gift from one of the candidates for confirmation. Vilhelm went to Decorah and I ironed. Supper had been waiting for some time and I began to grow impatient when I heard: "May I put on the eggs now? The minister is coming." I answered, "Yes," and went to meet him, but had to hurry back and order more boiled eggs, for Jørgen Lomen was driving right behind him. Vilhelm came in with many things for the house; but when Jørgen unloaded, too, I thought they must have brought half the supplies in Decorah — knives, dishes, jugs, and I know not what, beside two stoves and the things from Lansing. So we had the house furnished all at once; and after Jørgen left, we were busy inspecting it all. It was good to get the Lansing things. So far, it is true, we have no other place for them than the case in which they came.

Vilhelm is really a very good buyer and thinks of many things I had forgotten. At times he brings quite original things, too, as for example that contrivance for turning pancakes. It may also be used for dishing up butter. The coal bucket, which he had intended for carrying out ashes, I have set aside to carry wood in, and it now serves in that capacity. I received many gifts during those days: carrots, potatoes, eggs, butter, prairie chickens, and, not to be forgotten, Mother Katterud's leg of dried mutton.

Thursday Vilhelm had his confirmation class. Meanwhile I was busy trying to get dinner ready by twelve o'clock and tidying up inside as much as possible, as there was to be a wedding at one o'clock. At twelve o'clock the chicken was on the table, the footstool, with a cover over it, ready for the bridal couple, and stools set out to sit on — we had only two chairs at that time. The bridal party came; the carpenter, the master mason, and their families were present, too. When that was over and we sat alone over our coffee, old Thrond [Lommen] came on horseback and paid us a visit. He left just in time for us to take a walk in the grove.

We talked of how in the future we would clear the brush there; then we went over to the little grove which I had not visited before, planned a bench under the pretty oak (it will be a pleasant spot to rest on our walks), and talked about an arbor on the knoll. Vilhelm has ideas as to how to make one so strong that it will not blow down, but I am wondering if an arbor of locust trees will not be more beautiful and also easier to enter. Thus we walked and made plans for the future. How much fun that is! And if they should not be fulfilled, at least we have had the pleasure of making them and of dreaming of the possibility of their coming true.

We did not walk far. I grew tired of rambling through the brush. Vilhelm had a real hog hunt when we came home. These impudent hogs and cattle — I wish I had Vige here; he would certainly keep them from licking the windowpanes! They did great damage in the summer kitchen one night; they drank up all the water and chewed the oven door and the teakettle cover to pieces. Gudbrand came Thursday evening, too; so now we have one more to carry water. He spends most of his time gathering chips for kindling; he has quite a pyramid already.

Friday Vilhelm went to Paint Creek and was away until Tuesday. Caroline and I had a busy time. We quilted five quilts and sewed straw mattresses. Then, in addition, I was interrupted on Saturday by the man whom we had applied to for pork, who hit upon the unhappy idea of slaughtering just at that time. It was not sensible on his part, hot as it still was, and it could hardly have been more inconvenient for me. There I was without salt, with nothing to put the pork into, and the cellar full of kindling. Well, Gudbrand and Sven had to leave the haystack they were making; the former had to go and borrow a barrel, the latter, salt. Meanwhile, while the meat was being weighed, I stood outside with a pencil and a large piece of wood to keep track of it. Luckily I was able to borrow what I needed and I got Sven to cut it up and help me salt. Then we managed to get the barrel into the cellar. That was the first time I put down salt pork.

Sunday: how well I remember that Sunday! I spent the greater part of the day writing home, made a visit to Skaarlia's, picked seeds and a bouquet of my mignonette, and got eggs from Guri. I think I have never seen such a beautiful evening here. The woods had a very faint autumnal aspect. It is just beginning to look like autumn here, and is still so beautiful. The first days when we were here I went from window to window all day long to watch the changing light and shade in the woods. It can be beautiful here at sundown. Think of sitting in the arbor on the knoll then!

Early Tuesday morning, just as we had taken down the quilt frame and Caroline was going to scrub the floor, Vilhelm returned. I was not at all pleased and told him he had better leave. But to make me relent, he brought out a sack of hickory nuts and a basket that had been given him. I had to yield. It was hardest on him, for he got a poor dinner. I thought I ought to serve some of the meat that had been given us, but it had become so salty we could hardly stand it and we had to be content with pork.

For a couple of days I had the well diggers, too, for dinner; and one day I expected all their helpers, but only half came. Sunday Vilhelm was to go to the western settlements. Before going he had the stove moved into the kitchen, to my great joy. A great deal was accomplished that day. Sven cleaned the cellar, Suckow plowed a firebreak, Vilhelm drove nails on which to hang all my kitchen utensils, and I prepared food for all these people. Dinner was ready early so that Vilhelm could get to McKay's, but his trip failed to materialize. On the contrary, we had visitors from afar all afternoon and did nothing but set the table and clear it.

All day Monday I sewed busily on Vilhelm's coat. As the

sun went down I walked over to Sørland's, arranged to get milk from Guri, and hurried straight home so that I would not lose my way in the woods, it was getting so dark. Just as I arrived, Vilhelm stepped from his wagon. That was nicely timed; I had not expected him so early.

On one of the days when Vilhelm was home we took down our bundle of letters, read here and there, and sorted them. It will be a pleasure, many a winter's evening, to re-read them and recall memories. Some real winter's night when Vilhelm has time and the fire is burning merrily in the stove and the room is cozy — that will be the right time. It is evening, everything is quiet in the house, and I am probably the only one awake. I do not even hear Pompadour. Kari Katterud was here this forenoon and gave me some melons and nuts. The well diggers were here blasting; I was warned several times that they were going to set off a charge, but heard it only once. They are having difficulties. It is late and I have let the fire go out, idiot that I am.

Friday, October 20, 1854. I am busy these days. I have to be, if I am to accomplish everything I want done before Vilhelm returns. Meanwhile, nevertheless, I find time to write and walk. This afternoon I went down to Skaarlia's. The sky was gray and it began to grow dark; I wished Vilhelm were with me. This evening it seemed very lonesome here alone. I wished I knew how Vilhelm was. Then I thought of my rambles last winter — how I would come home to the room (so frequently boiling hot) at Egge's, and to the smell of pork, how the light would then be lit and Helene's shears be brought out to trim it, and how I would take out my crochet work or my diary, and Erik would fill the room with tobacco smoke! No, now it is quite different to come home.

It was different, too, to come into our kitchen, which was fairly light from the fire in the stove, near which Caroline and Gudbrand were sitting on their wooden stools; and from there into the living room, where the fire also cast a friendly glow, thanks to Vilhelm, who started it before he left. Yes, it was with a warm and thankful feeling I sat down in the rocking chair, where I stayed until tea was ready. God be praised for this home! May it be a truly peaceful and loving home! May I do all I can to make it so!

In many respects this is really a new existence for me. I have more to look after, more duties. In a way it is as if I had just been married. This is more agreeable — better, too, perhaps. I hope I may be somewhat as I ought to be; not become cross or upset if something is not to my liking. I hope I can manage everything for Vilhelm as I desire.

Johanne was here this morning; she brought me some milk, and said Aadne had not been here because he was helping a man who had neither doors nor windows in his house, but would come in the morning.[7] I do not begrudge the man's getting windows in his house, but it is tiresome just the same that everything is at a standstill here. Per has not been here either — I shall probably not even get the door to the bedroom until they come.[8] I met Suckow on my walk. He had not found either onions or middlings, unfortunately. Then he said that soon we ought to burn for a firebreak; I thought he was to take care of that, but apparently not. I must try to get someone else. Now I am going to bed for this evening.

Saturday, October 21. It is really good to have the pipe up for the stove. Now I can sit here cozy and comfortable with the fire crackling in the stove while, outside, the rain is pouring down. What weather we had this afternoon! It beat into the kitchen and the loft so that Caroline had to move her bedclothes to the floor. I thought a new house would stand up better. The carpenter is here today; he gave me a fine spurtle yesterday. We had to try it out for dinner.

This morning I was out on household errands; first to Katterud's, to find out about flour and whether I might get straw for the mattresses, and to get my wool weighed; from

[7] Johanne was probably the wife of Aadne Aadneson, the carpenter. See footnote 5 to this chapter.
[8] Per was a plasterer or master mason who worked on the parsonage.

there to Kari's to have it carded and to ask Ola if he would
undertake to burn. Yes, he assured me he would be more
than glad to do so and thanked me for calling on him when
there was something he could do. I like Ola and Kari very
much, but I wish I did not have to hear about brother Nils
and his problems.

I hurried home to get started with the straw mattresses
while the straw was dry and newly threshed. I arrived a little
tired and very hungry, and so the smell of pancakes, which I
recognized from afar, was very welcome. But we were spared
filling the mattresses, the way the rain poured down. I have
sewed and sewed and at last have my black dress ready — a
tiresome job and I'm glad it's done. Now I must go to bed
and see if anything comes of my resolve to write Mrs. Treschow tomorrow.

Sunday, October 21 [22].Unfortunately, nothing came of
that good resolve. I do not know where the day has gone. Yet
I thought I had a good long day ahead of me. In the forenoon
I was interrupted by Per, who is ill; he has a pain in one
eye and came to me for advice. He stayed much longer than
was necessary. Then came the carpenter, and then another
man to get a book of sermons. This afternoon Helene was
here, from noon until sundown, and talked and chattered
and said "ma" over and over interminably.[9] Afterward I sat
so long in the twilight that Caroline no doubt thought it
was too long and came and asked if I did not want a light. It was
very pleasant here this afternoon. The stove threw out so
much light and everything looked so cozy that I could not
help wishing Vilhelm were home and were sitting just as
comfortably as I. Since we got the stove in, I believe he has
not been home one twilight hour, the best time of the day.

This evening I sat thinking of Mrs. Treschow and the
letter I wanted to write, and thus I was transported back to
the old scenes — old memories from home; farther and

[9] From Sunday, October 22, through Tuesday, October 31, each of Mrs.
Koren's date numbers is one day short. On Helene's use of the word "ma," see
chapter 10, footnote 4.

farther back in time, back to the twilight hours at home, to the time when Christiane used to play, and we danced, in the gloaming; farther back, to when she sat and played her melodies, while I sat in a rocking chair and listened and dreamed of I know not what, and then wakened. And I often used to wonder why people thought I did not care for music; probably because I was not at all musical and did not say much about it — a strange shyness that has always been with me. Whether it stems from the fact that I knew I did not have too deep an understanding of music and could only feel what appealed to me, or because music definitely was something that lay beyond my powers, I do not know. But while others might stand and enlarge upon the beauty of this and that, I could not say a word; I felt embarrassed, I think. (With a painting it would have been different.) Then I wondered whether it was necessary or taken for granted that, to enjoy and appreciate music, one should be able to recognize and name this or that selection. Yes, recognize them perhaps, but not so specifically name them, as some people seem to think.

But it is doubtless better to lay this aside; otherwise I am likely to lose myself again in old memories and then I should be sitting here all night. I wish I knew how Vilhelm is; he does not have so pleasant a room to sit in, I am sure of that.

Monday, October 22 [23]. Just a couple of words before going to bed. It is already late, but the day shall not be brought to a close until I have written a little here. God be praised for this day! It has passed peacefully and well. I have plenty to look after during the day; so time never hangs heavy, but rather passes quickly. How entirely different it is to be alone now! I do not long so much for Vilhelm, though indeed I wish every hour that he were here; he enjoys so seldom the comforts of our home — and how pleasant it can look, even with the confusion that still exists. I look forward to getting it a little more presentable before he returns. Today the doors were finished; now I can move things in whenever I please. Tomorrow I think the carpenter will be making a table in the kitchen; things are progressing. But the well digging is at a standstill; no workers have been here for several days.

From now on we shall escape being disturbed by Madame Pompadour, who has been provided a place of her own, with which she seems to be well content. I had a beautiful walk this afternoon toward sundown — I wish Vilhelm had been with me. He will not see how pretty the woods are now. They vary so much in color from day to day. I had better not write more; the lamp indicates it is time to say good night.

Tuesday, October 23 [24]. I am little in the mood for writing tonight, and it is sheer folly to attempt it. But it seems as if something is lacking when the day ends without my having written. I do not know what is the matter with me today. It is as if I can neither think nor undertake anything. I think, indeed, chiefly of a thousand things at once, without being able to bring order into them; at times I am stopped by some trifle or other without being able to get any farther, repeating the same sentence to myself over and over. It is not a pleasant state of mind; but I am not ill — just a little tired. I know well enough what I want; I want Vilhelm home. Then he would sit in the rocking chair, as is our custom in the evening — that would be delightful. I hope no one comes when Vilhelm returns this time. I am not likely to have the least bit of good from his visit — he must leave again Monday or Tuesday, probably. Oh, well, I shall enjoy his being here, just the same. Even if the house were full of strangers, there would no doubt come an hour for me, too. Just so he is home; that is good. And it is nice that Brandt is coming.

I had planned to write Mrs. Treschow this evening. I had the time, but what was the use when I was so entirely out of the mood for writing? It is too bad that so much time should elapse before she gets a letter. I wonder if there are not letters waiting at McKay's. Last Sunday it was a couple of days since Erik, my postman, had been there.[10] He will no doubt

---

[10] She is probably speaking of Erik Egge.

come on Saturday; then we shall see. I should like very much, before Vilhelm returns, to send Gudbrand to see if there is anything. But I cannot very well do without him; I must have help in various ways, and the house must be cleaned, and for that water is essential.

Today I got a kitchen table and a shelf for dishes. It is such fun to have everything in good order in the kitchen. Today Suckow brought me onions, although he had had a hard time getting them. He was my dinner guest. He said he would try to shoot some game before Vilhelm's return. I hope he will. I wish he had had his gun with him today, when he saw more than twenty prairie chickens! If I were a hunter, I would always take my gun with me; for, if one leaves it at home, he always sees something; and if one always had it with him, he would in all probability get something.

No, no more now this evening. I am very tired — my head is very tired — so it is best to rest.

Wednesday, October 24 [*25*]. What activity in the house, and how industrious everyone has been today! The carpenter made kitchen benches and shelves, worked upon a cutting board, and helped me move beds; Caroline scrubbed and cleaned; Gudbrand made a walk from leftover boards and, this evening, crushed spices with all his might, for tomorrow we shall bake — and I, I have gone back and forth from one thing to the other. The carpenter would come and summon me to decide on some important matter outside; then I would go to Gudbrand and show him how to do things, for otherwise I would never get them as I want them; then I would go to the cellar and look after the pork; then I pickled onions and put down beets, placed the kitchen utensils in order, sewed the down quilt, trimmed my hat, and did no end of things. I did not take a walk. I seem to see Vilhelm eyeing me because I have not taken my usual walk, but surely it is not needed when one is so active.

How pleasant it has been, all of it! I should not have had

so much pleasure, indeed, if I had come to a house with everything ready. Tonight I shall sleep in our new bedroom; it looks quite cozy, although for furniture we have only chests, and the bed cannot be placed where I had wanted it. It is bare and empty without the bed, but just wait until tomorrow — then it will be better.

Suckow gave me a chicken today; now I have a little to regale my pastors with. I wonder if Vilhelm is not a little curious about how things will look when he comes? Yes, no doubt he is; but perhaps he does not even think of it. Well, now there is only tomorrow; then Friday they come; and tomorrow I have a great deal to put in order — that will be enjoyable. Think, if there were no one to arrange the room and make it comfortable for, if it were only for myself. There would be little joy in that. No, God be praised, it is not so. Now I am tired and want to sleep.

Friday, October 26 [*27*]. I shall write a little, and then perhaps they will come. I am tired of waiting, for everything is ready. I half expected them for dinner and had food — —

Tuesday, October 30 [*31*]. I got so far Friday and Caroline put her head in the door and announced, "There comes the pastor, but he is alone." I answered, "You must be mistaken," and hurried out. But so it was. It was Vilhelm and, instead of Pastor Brandt, he had his buggy full of baskets and tinware — contributions toward the furnishing of the kitchen, which really was equipped well that day. In the forenoon I had received a large shipment of crockery — teapot, cups, plates, dessert plates, etc. Vilhelm is really remarkable, the way he remembers and looks for what we need. I hurried in with my tinware, took hammer and nails and hung it up as an additional decoration, and then went out again, impatient to get Vilhelm away from his horse and into the house, where, without more ado, he should have a look and say what he thought of it all. How much fun it was to show him everything and to hear that he, too, was well pleased and thought, as I do, that it is all very cozy.

We were really not much disappointed, either of us, that our guest failed us; it was better by far to be alone. How delightful to have Vilhelm home! I almost failed to give him anything to eat, although he had had nothing since morning, because I was so very happy to have him home again and so eager to talk about everything. We could not be happier if our home had been arranged and furnished with the greatest elegance than we are with it now in all its simplicity.

It is really fun to see how far a little can go; and, actually, is the room not attractive with the bookcases in one corner, the large table under one window, and the smaller table, with a white cover over it and two embroidered stools at its side, under the other? That is my place during the day; when I take my rest at noon I withdraw to my rocking chair with my book. And how pleasant it is to have a bedroom, and in the morning to go into a tidy room to a breakfast table all set, instead of first having to clear away the toilet articles before the table can be set, and then having to sweep the floor! We have really learned to prize all such little things, for such they are indeed, which at home it never occurred to us to think about. God be praised that we are now so well settled; may we indeed be duly thankful therefor!

Now Vilhelm has left again; he started this morning. God be praised for every hour that he was home! We are both at ease now when Vilhelm is away: he, because he knows I am comfortable here, and I, because I know I can make him more comfortable when he is home. I hope he will return next Tuesday. He has now no doubt completed his journey for today. Would he could look in to see how pleasant it is! The fire in the stove is burning merrily, the moon is shining in through the curtains, and I am sitting in the middle of the room, where I have moved my little table. It is snug and cozy. Too bad we did not need a fire while Vilhelm was home; it makes it so much more pleasant. But some day when he is home, the time will undoubtedly come. There is no hurry.

I had an amusing task today; Vilhelm would have laughed, had he seen me. Well, he can laugh when I show it to him on his return. I hope he was not too thinly clad when he left today; it has been blowing hard, and I did not even remember to send his Cherry Pectoral with him.

I took a brisk walk through the Sørland woods this afternoon. When I came home, I stirred up the fire. The moon shone in. I took an apple, sat down in the rocking chair, recalled the pleasant twilight hour we had yesterday, and was really so unreasonable — or whatever I should call it — that I thought it was very sad to sit here alone, and that it would be a terribly long time before Vilhelm would return, and more such fancies. But then I was ashamed of myself and chased such ideas out of doors; but just the same I could not help longing for Vilhelm, and I must be allowed to do that, no matter how pleasant things are. If Vilhelm were sitting here now, he would turn around from time to time from his work and look, first at the stove where the fire crackles, and then at me, as much as to ask, "Is it not really cozy, my dear?" This is a good place I have chosen; every evening I shall certainly move my table here.

On the Sunday when we expected Brandt, his family, too, were supposed to come for dinner. It would be just as well to expect them, Vilhelm said, although they knew nothing of it.[11] He added: "You can prepare for ten guests. If those to the west of us do not come, I shall ask others. But do not expect us before two." Nor did I expect them earlier. But by the sun I could see that four o'clock had come and gone; the table had been set and the food ready for I don't know how long. I took my ease and read for several hours before they came. And then there were only four — Brandt's two sisters, and Jørgen [Lomen] and [Johannes] Evenson. That was the whole party. It was so late that none of the others he had invited came, which really was rather fortunate; for my food

[11] No doubt they knew nothing of it because they had not yet been invited.

had so thickened and shrunk that I am afraid I should have been in a sorry pickle if ten guests had come with as keen appetites as the four who did. It was pleasant, however, to have them. They stayed some time after coffee, then left.[12]

Now came the pleasantest hour of all as we sat alone and read the letters Vilhelm had brought — from Christiane (everything is well at home, God be praised). But nothing from Johan and Marie. I wish so much I might get their letter before Vilhelm returns; I am a little afraid it is lying about somewhere, as did the last one. It was a pleasant evening. I read Christiane's letter to Vilhelm; then we talked of those at home until it was late and time to get some rest, which Vilhelm no doubt needed after the long, tiring service.

Monday morning, just as the breakfast things had been removed and I had put away the silver and was standing in the bedroom cutting out something, and while Vilhelm was talking to one of his parishioners in the other room, Gudbrand ran to the open window and cried, "Here comes Pastor Brandt driving!" And so it was. He had had such bad luck with the roads and means of transportation that he had been forced to walk more than forty miles carrying his bag. It was pleasant, however, that he came while Vilhelm was home and while Evenson happened to be here; B.'s two sisters had not yet gone home, so they came over. I had a busy time making hot chocolate and coffee and getting breakfast ready and was in quite a quandary over the chocolate. It goes twice as far as what I was accustomed to at home and consequently became so thick I had to thin it with all the milk I had in the house; even then it was so thick Vilhelm suggested plates and spoons to eat it with.

There were so many here that day. For breakfast I also had

---

[12] Brandt's two sisters were Anne, who was married to Ivar Ringestad, and Elisabeth Lomen. See chapter 10, footnote 7. Johannes Evenson took land in 1850 in the northeast quarter of Section 32, Madison Township; see chapter 12, footnote 14. In 1851 he was married to Catherine Helen Anderson. This marriage, performed by Pastor Nils O. Brandt, was the first recorded in Winneshiek County; Sparks, *History of Winneshiek County*, 16.

Magnus, Erik, John, and Per, the master mason, and had scarcely got them out before Brandt's sisters came. After much discussion it was decided that Brandt would go home with them in the afternoon. We would have dinner at three, we agreed, but I, poor creature, was not prepared for so many guests. The chickens from the day before would not go round. So I had to bring up a piece of pork from the barrel, salty as it was, and use it whether it was palatable or not. It turned out all right. Then I mashed turnips, made soup, and baked a souffle. All went well. We had dinner, drank coffee, spent a pleasant two hours together, and then they went home. Like everyone else, I think highly of Brandt; it would have been a pleasure if he had stayed longer. It will no doubt be a long time before I again have use for my silver and knives. Brandt, too, thought everything very cozy here.

I am now very tired of writing and cannot get my pen to behave. So I think I shall take my knitting and a book. I do so hope Vilhelm will not have a toothache this evening and that he is comfortable where he is staying. I cannot reconcile myself to the thought that he may not be as comfortable as I. As long as we were at Skaarlia's, it never occurred to me; but now I always keep thinking that perhaps Vilhelm is sitting in a little dismal room with a wick in a saucer of grease for a light, while I have everything so pleasant — but then it will seem good, too, to come home and be comfortable here.

As soon as he has driven away and I can see him no longer, I begin to look forward to the time of his return. I stood at the window when he left today — he simply would not look back — and wished that he were returning instead of leaving, or that I were with him. Only reluctantly, if at all, would I travel — but I should like to be with him. It is always so empty as soon as Vilhelm has left, and therefore I hurry to do something to keep from brooding. Today it struck me much more than before that it must be dreadful to sit and drive all day alone, as Vilhelm does constantly — often it is a hardship, too, I know. I hope it will not be too cold this winter!

333

19

This Is a Strange Time—This

All Saint's Day.[1] Alas, that Vilhelm should have to be away now, was my first thought both yesterday and today when, after a walk, I came home to a bright stove and moonlight and sat down in the rocking chair with an apple. My thanks to Vilhelm for the apples; they taste very good. Today it was even more pleasant and cozy than yesterday. Vilhelm has no chance to enjoy the moonlight at home this time. How it blew today! I hope the prairie fire has not caused any damage.

I have been at Sørland's. It is pleasant to have a grove like theirs to walk in when it blows so hard. While I was there, Embret returned from Lansing; so I had a chance to bargain for a little pork. It will not do to be without pork when there are so many of us. The girl from Minnesota has come.[2] This morning I read a sermon for the boy and girl; after that I wrote to Mrs. Treschow. It is well I finally got that done. Now I shall write to Christiane. But how time has flown! It

[1] A church festival observed November 1; Hallowmas.
[2] It has not been determined who the girl from Minnesota was.

334

seems only a short time ago I wrote home, and here it is already almost a month. I wonder how Vilhelm is; I do not even know where he is. That was stupid of me, not to ask him where he was going.

God be praised and thanked for the home we have! I am very happy over it, and everything is so comfortable. How different from last year at Egge's, or at Skaarlia's! It is so good to be here. Out in the kitchen I hear singing and talking; it is very pleasant indeed to have people about one. I hope I may be thankful enough for it all, for all the blessings I enjoy! At times I have been rather afraid I might take altogether too much pleasure in this house and its surroundings and think too much about food and such things. Yet I hope not. That was mostly when I had to arrange everything, when I expected Vilhelm and Brandt to come and all those from the western settlements. Since I am still an inexperienced young housewife, I shall have to comfort myself by believing that was the reason I gave so much more thought than necessary to such things. Now I must really write to Christiane, if that is to be done this evening.

Thursday, November 2. I wish Vilhelm were home this evening; a fire is burning frightfully all about us, and it is worst to the northwest. Now at last, after sitting in darkness a long time watching it, I have lit the lamp. I shall try to write a little, but I am very restless. I go to the window every few moments. I see the flames on every side. I became frightened when I first saw the fire. All afternoon, yes, all day I saw smoke. It had been blowing very hard, and I was sure there was fire abroad. Several times I sent Gudbrand up to the knoll, but he came back each time with the report that he could see nothing but some smoke far away. At sundown it smelled so strongly of smoke that I sent the girl over to the knoll to investigate; she came back with the same answer. I hoped then that perhaps it had been put out, and was really frightened when I looked out a moment later to discover virtually a sea of flames in three places.

I sent Gudbrand over to Ivar to find out what the situation was. He came back and said that Ivar and Nils Katterud had gone to Juul's, where the fire was then burning, and that a good many people were over there. He had also talked with Ola Tollefsjord; the latter was driving home, but coming back at once with his brother. Ola had also sent word not to start a backfire unless the fire came quite close to us. If we have to start a backfire, we shall need more help, I imagine. God grant that they succeed in mastering the fire before it does any damage! I think the wind has died down a little. Gudbrand has gone over to see how matters stand. I am not too uneasy, God be praised, but I wish very much Vilhelm were home. And he would wish it himself, too, if he knew how it looks here.

Caroline is at Thibaut's today; I wonder if she will bring letters from McKay.[3] This morning while I was in the kitchen there was a knocking at the door and in came Guri, bringing with her "a little drop of sweet milk and a dozen eggs," as she said. It was pleasant to see Guri; she was glad everything was so attractive, went about with me and inspected, but could not stay long. As usual, she was in a hurry. She was going to Rønningen's to buy wool and asked if I cared to go with her. I really should have finished sewing the pillow slips that were to be washed tomorrow, but I have wanted so long to visit Gullik's that I quickly decided to take my walk this morning instead of this afternoon. The wind was blowing so hard that at times we could scarcely make any headway; but it was a remarkably warm wind. What a wretched house they have! It is almost impossible to be neat and clean there; and if I had not seen with my own eyes how neatly the oldest daughter managed the coffee and biscuits that were served, it would have been difficult to persuade myself to take anything.

[3] Frank Teabout, founder of the village of Frankville in Frankville Township, Winneshiek County, settled there in 1851. He had a building that came to be known as "the emigrant store"; Sparks, *History of Winneshiek County*, 20, 115.

Gudbrand just returned and said that the fire from the north was headed toward Juul's, that he had been there, and that more and more men were coming; they hoped to put out the fire. Juul had saved his haystacks; the fire had almost reached them. God grant it does not cause too much damage!

Friday, November 3. How cold it was today! I suppose Vilhelm has enough clothes with him. I wish he had taken the little blue coat! If he is out driving now, he must certainly be freezing.

I went for a walk, first toward Kvale's, then north, then south, and so home again. Ah, how delightful it is to come home to a comfortable, warm room, seat myself in the rocking chair, let my thoughts roam where they will, eat an apple in the dusk, then light the lamp and write a little until tea is ready! How fortunate I am! The parsonage and its surroundings looked so pleasant and beautiful this evening. It will really be a pleasure to improve these grounds. If one could get hold of some beautiful roses, he would certainly have excellent soil for them. In this fertile soil they would not be much trouble. As one man said, "Aw, you just scratch the soil a little, throw in a little seed, and kick a little dirt over it; it will grow all right."

God be praised, nothing too serious came of that ugly fire last night; I have not heard that it caused any damage. Of course it is burning tonight, too, in several places, but today there is no wind. How glad I was to wake up this morning after a sound and undisturbed sleep! I went to bed last night thinking that in all likelihood I would be awakened during the night, the fire was burning so strongly in the north. I was not really uneasy, but I had a strange feeling. I wished Vilhelm were home, that is certain, and had half thought of having Gudbrand sleep in the kitchen in case anyone should come. The servants, meanwhile, went to bed very early; by that time the fire had died down somewhat. I, on the other hand, sat up very late and then lay awake for a long time.

Gudbrand ran errands all day and really provisioned the

house. First he went to Juul's to learn if he could haul stone. Juul's wife sent back eggs with a message that, if I wished to buy, she would gladly sell me all she had from now on. Since I have received the same message from everyone in the neighborhood who has eggs to sell, I ought surely to be provided for now. Then Gudbrand went to Sørland's for pork and turnips, and last to [Ola] Bergan's, where I got a room for the girl. Tomorrow I plan to send him to Freeport with a sack, to try, if possible, to get middlings. Well, Caroline brought me no letters; she was told that both the letters and newspapers had been sent Sunday. I should have known there would be no mail here from Sunday to Thursday. I pin my faith on Erik. Now I shall drink tea.

Sunday, November 5. How much different and how much better the Sundays are here than when I sat alone at Skaarlia's! Then, many a time, I became quite melancholy. Still, I would not want to be without all the pleasant hours I spent then, sitting on the bench behind the house or at my desk in that little cabin. But now it is better, indeed; here I do not become lonesome.

A little while ago I read a sermon for Caroline and Gudbrand. Then I went out and gave orders for dinner. And now I am sitting here finishing a letter to Mrs. Treschow. Outside it is really stormy — God grant that we be spared a prairie fire — but here it is comfortable, light, and pleasant. When Vilhelm *Mecanicus* comes home, however, I shall ask him to do something about the window that rattles so. How happy I am to have our cozy little kitchen! It is good to know that those who work there have pleasant surroundings, too; it is especially cozy at dusk, when there is a light from the stove. Yes, God be praised for everything in this little home, which we enjoy so much despite its shortcomings.

Yesterday, because of sheer laziness or industry, whatever one may call it, I wrote nothing. I was very much provoked at having to sit all morning over some yarn that Caroline was to have washed, but which she had managed to get so tangled that a most frightful zeal for doing things took possession of me for the rest of the day. And that was not so bad after all; I must keep busy now if I am to get anywhere.

But I did not neglect my apple at twilight in my rocking chair; I shall not easily give that up. It is definite, however, that Caroline will stay only for the time agreed upon; she must return to her Yankees. That is too bad. I would gladly have kept her — it will certainly not be easy to get a capable girl again.

I wonder where Vilhelm is today — perhaps at Brorby's. I look forward so eagerly to Tuesday. I hope he will return then — and he longs to, I know.

I have written to Christiane and Mrs. Treschow; I am very glad that is finally done. Now, if Vilhelm were only home, we should have a delightful twilight hour. The sun just went down like a red ball of fire. It reminded me, with the fleecy clouds overhead, of one of the beautiful sunsets at sea. To think that last year at this time we were still on the ocean — ugh, I certainly would not like to be there now. God be praised, I shall not be traveling this winter as I was last!

I have been interrupted by Juul, who came to talk about hauling stones. These people are really queer; they always sit down, and then either remain silent, or talk about how fine the weather is or how unusual the weather is, until at last I ask them if they wish to speak to the pastor.

I hope the well diggers, at least, will come tomorrow. When Vilhelm is away, everything stands still. I am writing almost in the dark now, so I had better stop. It is pleasant, all the same, to have the sunset just outside my window, for here it does not get dark as suddenly as it would elsewhere.

Saturday, November 11. Poor Vilhelm, who is jolting along in his wagon on the hard-frozen ground on that tedious road to Paint Creek! How cold it is today! I am glad he has the buffalo robe. I hope he gets rid of his toothache after this trip! And I sit here so snug inside. It strikes me as rather embarrassing, almost unfair, that I should be so comfortable, while Vilhelm is not. I am very happy over our new stove; we shall be satisfied with it, I am sure. It is nice to have it, at any rate. Well, we shall see how it acts this evening.

Vilhelm must be thinking of me and will write, too, provided he does not keep thinking how unreasonable I was this forenoon. Oh, no, he will not do that. The house is very empty, as it always is on the day Vilhelm leaves, and today even more so than usual, perhaps because it is so gray and melancholy outside, and thus it is even now, although the sun is beginning to peep out and things are dry and comfortable inside after the floor scrubbing; but it all serves only to make me wish even more that Vilhelm were home. I am a hard person to please, I know that well enough — but it is so pleasant when Vilhelm is home. How cozy it was yesterday — and now how lonely before I can hope to have him home three or four days hence!

Just see how beautifully the sun is shining! Vilhelm should be here now; then he would agree that it is pleasant to have real winter outside and be able to sit inside in a comfortable room. I fall to thinking so often of Egge's, now that I see snow on the ground — of all the times I sat at the window writing in my diary and froze each time they opened the door; and then, whenever Vilhelm surprised me, how happy I was. God be praised, how much better it is now!

As soon as Vilhelm had gone, I went out and made pork sausage and pickled onions. It was good to have something like that to do. Thus the forenoon passed. Meanwhile Caroline had finished polishing the stove and scrubbing the floor. Dinner was ready, but I thought it very melancholy to sit alone at the table and had no appetite. Nor did I desire to do anything. So I took my knitting and began to read *Svanehammen*, but nothing would really come right.[4] Vilhelm will want to scold me when he reads this; I am not supposed to be so fainthearted, or whatever I should call it. But now I feel

[4] The story referred to is "The Six Swans"; see *Grimms' Fairy Tales*, 232 (New York, 1944).

more cheerful and will go to work. Can I afford to be lazy? No. I will be cheerful and glad and remember that it is not really so desperately long until Wednesday.

I wonder if Vilhelm got any letters from McKay today? I almost wish he would not get them until his return, so that we can read them together. "When the sun sets in the west, thy Lalla then will work the best" will no doubt apply to me today. It is getting quite dark. I hope Vilhelm reached his destination safely by daylight.

It is a long time since I last wrote here — almost a week now, I believe. That is always a sign that Vilhelm has been home. He came Tuesday. We had eaten dinner some time before and I was sitting at the window, sewing and glancing out now and then, when whom should I see but Vilhelm driving by almost under the window. I certainly had not expected him from that direction, but had been keeping an eye out the other window all the time. It was wonderful to have him home again after eight long days, but he had had such a toothache, poor man. He had so many "honors" with him this time: fresh meat and pork, nuts, and a piece of cloth that will make a splendid shirt for Gudbrand. Yes, there were many "honors."[5]

Wednesday Vilhelm met with the candidates for confirmation. I kept the soup warm for him a long, long time and blamed the wedding because he did not come. At last Caroline came in and said that two wagons full of people were driving toward us. "Oh, they will certainly not come here," I thought and continued peacefully with my sewing. But that calm did not last long, for in no time both wagons actually stopped outside. I saw Vilhelm hasten toward me; then I knew what the situation was and hurried to clear the table and make the usual preparations before the large bridal party came in. There was a baptism, too, and Vilhelm talked so long with two of the group that I thought the soup would cook away entirely.

[5] "Honors" are gifts to the pastor.

But there was a little left, after all, when at last we got to the table; so we had a cozy time, drank coffee, and ate the cakes we had baked in the morning, for Vilhelm had thought of inviting some guests after the Bible reading on Thursday. But that plan was given up, wisely enough; it would have been too much, in the short time he could be at home. We had a long lovely twilight, with apples, the light from the stove, and all that goes with it.

Later in the evening Embret brought a hog, which he cut up and salted down for me. And the next day I treated the household to pork tenderloins. I was home alone and was the cook; the others were with Vilhelm. Kari Bergan, who came early in the forenoon, bringing butter and cheese, detained me so long that Vilhelm returned before the meal was ready — something that seldom happens. While we were drinking coffee, Mother [Anne] Aarthun brought us two roosters; so there is no end to my extravagance with fresh meat. When Mother Anne left, after having inspected everything carefully, Kari Katterud came. There were plenty of people here that day.

We went out for a little walk when the rain had let up, and investigated how far the prairie fire had gone the night before. It was a frightful fire. God be praised, Vilhelm was home, I say again. We had finished our evening meal and had moved the table to the middle of the room; I sat with my back to the window and had no inkling of trouble until Vilhelm sprang up with the cry, "Look, what a fire!" It was then quite light outside and flames came swiftly up the valley from Ivar's. Vilhelm went out — Gudbrand was already ahead of him — but came back at once for matches and something with which to beat out the flames; they were going to set backfires. Caroline ran out with the mop and some sacks and then went to rouse the Katteruds and Skaarlias, who were asleep and knew nothing of what was going on.

Meanwhile I went from window to window, watching how swiftly the flames traveled where Vilhelm and Gudbrand were setting backfires and how at Tollef's, too, men were setting backfires. More and more men came, and well they might, with such a fire and so strong a wind. At Ivar Kvale's, where all were fast asleep, the haystack almost caught fire. It was the worst fire I have seen, and, furthermore, was very near us. It was sad to see the flames lick through the woods and set fire to the trees. It centered in the wood on Tollef's land, but threatened to break through to ours at any moment. It was already halfway across the slope when Vilhelm went to stop it. He was successful and our pretty little grove was spared.

It was one o'clock before Vilhelm came back and we went to bed; the fire then had slackened considerably everywhere. Three large deer had been seen in the woods fleeing from the flames. Gudbrand so often sees deer. There must be quite a few here; they live in peace and freedom. Now I hope we may be reasonably free from fires for the rest of this year. God be praised, Vilhelm was home this time! Nothing was damaged except the sacks and the mopstick, which was so charred that Caroline almost despaired of making it usable again.

Yesterday morning we awoke to snow, the first this year, and a raw, cold wind, which was one reason that Vilhelm postponed his trip until today. Glad was I. It seldom happens, as it did yesterday, that he has a day to himself for his work at home, but how pleasant it is when he does! Then he sits at the large table with all his papers, and I at the window with my sewing. Hereafter, with God's help, it will not be so seldom.

There was this advantage, too, in not leaving until today: he got a buffalo robe which, I imagine, is proving its worth now. Gudbrand brought it and also the stove I am now enjoying, and which Vilhelm was good enough to set up before he left this morning. I have now had another cozy twilight hour. Yes, Vilhelm will really be pleased with his stove; it lights up very splendidly and heats very well, and it is fine to be able to put wood in it without worrying about the stove-pipe, thanks to Vilhelm, who put it up. I hope he is now as warm and comfortable as I am! But no doubt he is in a room where the door leads outside. Here I was supposed to busy myself with some real housework and not write until it became dark — then start in when I had a light. But this is the way it goes. I did knit very industriously at twilight; I shall comfort myself with that. Now I shall put this away and finish the heel of my stocking.

Sunday, November 12. It is already late, the sun will soon set, and here am I, who had thought to begin a letter home today. Yes, the evening is long, but I am not in the same mood as this morning. I should have written then; then Father would have had a cheerful letter. Now we shall see how it will go after the twilight hour is past. Indeed, my mood was better this morning when I read a sermon aloud, as I usually do, and then read a little to myself. I read some of Theremin, put on my things, and took a walk. I felt really virtuous about that; I had very little desire to go but felt it was my duty; and so I went and did not regret it, either.[6]

First I walked north, but it was so raw that way that I turned for refuge to the Sørland woods. It did me good to get out, and I found it pleasant indeed to come home to a warm room and steaming soup. Since then I have finished *Svanehammen* and read Oehlenschläger's poems without noticing the time.[7] Caroline is now home, as usual; Gudbrand fires his stove, and I mine. How seldom it is that Vilhelm is home on Sundays! It would be very pleasant if he were. I hope he is now in a warm house and does not have a toothache. I trust he is not at Sjur [*Sivert*] Vold's; I think of us there last winter, sitting as close to the stove as we could, and freezing. I have no desire now for a similar trip; I am being spoiled, I am so comfortable.

Monday, November 13. That was a job — making head-

[6] On Theremin, see chapter 13, note 15.
[7] Adam Gottlob Oehlenschläger (1779–1850) was a Danish poet who introduced romanticism in Danish literature.

cheese! It was the first time I had tried such a task, and it was really very difficult. Mother Winsnes insists that I sew the head around the edges, but it was no easy job to fasten the soft fragile pork rind. Now the head lies in press and I have a secret fear that it will break in two, and my almonds and other glorious things will be lost in the brine. That's the way it is when everything is to be so fine. Vilhelm will no doubt laugh if it falls to pieces. I did not take a walk today; I had enough exercise pickling pork. I have tripped about all day, and could not help thinking of Mrs. Linka and the bedbug.[8] The rocking chair and an apple suited me gloriously afterward. I just now lit the light. Tomorrow I intend to bake before Vilhelm returns, but just the same, he will not get what he wants. Gudbrand will be my assistant. Caroline is going home to do a washing. I wonder if Vilhelm will come Wednesday or Thursday. I should like to know; most likely not before Thursday.

They have begun to haul logs for the stable, I see to my great surprise. Magnus and Erik [Skaarlia] have been here. I wonder if Vilhelm knows of it. Naturally, however, neither the carpenter nor the well digger has been heard from. Vilhelm is away and so everything is at a standstill save what pertains to the affairs of the household. The household affairs, yes, they all go just splendidly; we wash, we iron, we bake and scrub and put things in order.

Yesterday, just as it was getting light, I was awakened by Madame Pompadour, who was very restless and barked violently. She can make herself heard, small as she is, and she kept on so long and so continuously that I hardly knew what to think until I heard another larger dog begin, too. It was probably someone driving by.

Nothing came of my writing home yesterday, unfortunately. When will it now be done? And I ought to write to Horten, too — well, not to the lazy bridal couple, but to Vil-

[8] This may be the incident mentioned in *Linka's Diary*, 187. When the Herman Preuses arrived in Wisconsin, they spent a night in a hotel in Milwaukee sitting up in chairs because the bed was infested.

helm's mother.[9] Instead of writing yesterday, I buried myself in *Hrolf Krake*. It is strange I had not read it before, but it perhaps did not appeal to me when I read Oehlenschläger earlier.[10] Now I must get busy; it is too bad I do not get any sewing done. With whom is Vilhelm sitting and chatting this evening, I wonder?

Tuesday, November 14. I become quite alarmed when I realize that we are already writing the 14th. I wish I could detain time a little; it goes all too quickly for me. I do not accomplish half of what I ought; I am not industrious enough, I suppose. Certainly I have not been so today. I lay in bed and read and rested for a long time after I had eaten dinner. Perhaps it was the baking and the task of being cook that affected me so much. The whole morning was wasted, too, for I was interrupted by Ingeborg [Hauge], who came to talk about her sister, whom I may get as a girl; then she took some wool with her to spin for me. When I saw it was already one o'clock, I thought, "Well, we do nothing but cook." This is the month for slaughtering, and I suppose they are now busy with it at home, too. Erik Skaarlia was here with logs this morning; he is always out early. Tollefsjord Ola, too.

How beautiful the sunset is this evening! And I have not been outside in this lovely mild weather! I was so tired, I really did not have the courage for it earlier; now it is too late to go walking alone. Well, if Vilhelm were home — but he perhaps is admiring the sunset on the banks of the Mississippi this evening. Possibly I can expect him tomorrow; I hope he comes. It is charming to have the sunset just outside the window — the heavens are so beautiful and in here it is so pleasant. Last night I sat up rather late. I had been very busy finishing my sewing, but was chased to bed earlier than I expected. While I was sitting there, I was frightened by a crash that no doubt sounded twice as loud as it was, since

[9] The lazy bridal couple were Johan and Marie Louise Koren.

[10] Adam G. Oehlenschläger, *Hrolf Krake, et heltedigt* (Hrolf Krake, an Epic Poem, in *Samlede verker*, vol. 3 — Copenhagen, 1845).

everything was so hushed and quiet. At first I thought it was the stovepipe or the chimney that fell, but it was Per's plastering behind the stove that collapsed. Now it is falling piece by piece. It is very unpleasant to be disturbed like that when one is the only person awake in the house. Then I always hurry to bed as fast as I can. When I get my head under the quilt I am safe.

Sunday, November 26. It is seldom that even a few lines are written here now; but that is a good sign, for it means Vilhelm is home much of the time. It is Sunday and consequently I am alone. Vilhelm is in the western settlements. He left this morning after a very substantial breakfast — fried chicken, headcheese, soft-boiled eggs, and coffee, too. Yes, I am thankful we have our own ménage. Gudbrand is with him, too, resplendent in new clothes from top to toe; he was pleased with them. Vilhelm will probably return tomorrow; I dare not expect him tonight. It is true that the weather has changed from this morning's sleet and cloudiness to clear sunshine, but he is not likely to come tonight. It would really be extremely pleasant, however, if he should surprise me, as he did the other evening; I had already lit the light when he came so unexpectedly from John Axdal's.[11]

I am really glad I took my walk in the forenoon. I feel I should walk, but I seldom have a desire to when Vilhelm cannot be with me. The wind blew me from place to place. First I tried the Sørland road; no, that was hopeless. Then over to Tollef's farm; there it was bearable, and I came home with a good appetite for a bowl of steaming cooked rice. I have been smart today and have copied everything for Vilhelm, but it is at the expense of my diary. I am tired and must stop. There goes the sun, too.

Everything is wonderful now, with Vilhelm home so regularly. Yesterday was a lovely day, the twilight hour the best of all. Outside it was raw and cold; here it was warm and comfortable. God give us many such days! When Vilhelm re-

---

[11] On John Axdal, see chapter 8, note 16.

turned from Paint Creek last Wednesday, he brought letters from home. That was delightful. And I had one lying here for him from Nilsine Breda — an old one from last May, but it was good to get it just the same.[12] Since then he has been in the western settlements a couple of days, and on the east prairie one day, but home most of the time.

The days are not all quiet here, however. For dinner each day I have two carpenters, who keep on pounding until my head aches, and the well diggers, too, though they are very irregular. One noon I had three men who were putting the roof on the stable and who won my special approval; one was an old man from Valdres, a friend of the dean, to whom he asked me to send many greetings. We are continuing to mold candles, which Vilhelm made so much fun of at first but now thinks quite splendid, since he sees that I get more than the five which he predicted; moreover, he was unable to buy oil the last time he tried. It goes slowly — only five at a time.[13]

Tomorrow Embret is coming with an enormous pig; then I shall have plenty to do. The worst of it is that I have no barrel to salt it down in, so I am afraid it will lie in a corner of the cellar and we shall have to cut what we want, slice by slice, from the whole hog. Wednesday I shall have all the helpers for dinner; I shall no doubt have to prepare the little pig that Anne Aarthun sent over the other day, if I can only get it roasted properly. I have so much fresh meat now; there is always a chicken hanging in the loft. Anne Rønningen gave me the last one; she was here one morning. It is just as well that I can no longer see, for otherwise I should very likely keep on writing, and that does me no good.

Sunday, December 3, 1854. Sunday, November 26 — Sunday, December 3 — the entries are not very regular in my

[12] Nilsine Breda was a friend in Norway.

[13] "The wicks were fastened to sticks and dipped in hot tallow, and then hung, stick after stick as long as there was room, between the ropes of one of the old-fashioned beds which had a knitted rope support for the mattress; when the tallow had stiffened, the wicks were dipped again, and the process was repeated until the candles were thick enough"; Naeseth, in *Folkekalenderen 1933*, 11.

diary any more. I have so many more important matters that must come first. It seems too bad that December has already started. Vilhelm is at Turkey River, but I am no longer alone. Anne is here, she and her little son; that brings life into the house.[14] Vilhelm undoubtedly wonders at times how things will go, whether we shall get through safely, and whether I am a contented child or a silly one, as when he was home. Oh, no — I am now sensible and well satisfied to have Anne here. She is so kind and agreeable, too, that I could never hope for a better person; but I am afraid it will be less pleasant for Vilhelm.

We talk very sensibly; I receive good advice and instruction. At the moment I hear her in the kitchen, where she spends a part of the day with her boy. What a fool I am, to dread so many things I need not have dreaded! When Vilhelm returned Tuesday and told me Anne was coming on Thursday, I felt quite unhappy at the idea, and at the thought of trying to wash without water — of disorder in the house, too. Contributing also to my mood, no doubt, was the fact that Vilhelm came home after I had gone to bed. That seemed so annoying to me, too. Oh, well, there is no accounting for me these days; it is not worth thinking about.

The evening had seemed very long to me last Sunday. The indoors, I found, held so little charm that I went to bed very early and had just put out the light when Vilhelm knocked on the windowpane. I had never expected him at that hour. It was really silly of me to go to bed. Think how cozy it could have been, instead of his having to wander about in cold rooms. And then I think he found no food except two rooster legs which he brought in, gnawing away at them, and a bowl of hickory nuts, of which I ate my fair share.

Wednesday the church trustees met here. For dinner a large beef roast, a gift from [Johannes] Evenson, which caused me no little trouble to roast because of its size; and besides I

[14] This is believed to have been Anne Rønningen (1807-93), wife of Gullik Rønningen. See chapter 6, footnote 19.

had to bake a rice pudding. I had six trustees and four workers at the table, and they seldom lack good appetites. I stayed in the bedroom that day and had the pleasure of seeing Gudbrand drive up with a large barrel for the hog, which, sure enough, had been put away in a corner of the cellar Monday. He brought no letters. Letters in the autumn — they always come by a marvelous route. On the other hand, we got two numbers of the *Semi-weekly Times*, thanks to the consul. It is interesting to get them; there is always something worth reading.[15]

Thursday the candidates for confirmation were here and tracked up my newly scrubbed floor so much that I was in a bad humor for a time; Vilhelm insisted that it was because he had teased me about a cake, or else because the roast was so salty. We had received a large piece of venison as a gift, with which I was to regale the household; but it had been salted, and so thoroughly, that I had to go out and warm up some of the preceding day's roast. Whatever it was, it is certain I was not in too agreeable a humor. But fortunately my mood changed in the afternoon so that, after the bed had been moved in, preparatory to Anne's coming, and we had taken a turn outside in the lovely moonlight, we had a delightful twilight hour.

When it was so late that we had almost given up, Anne finally came with her husband and child. The next morning Vilhelm left. Now I hope Wednesday will see him at home. Anne said today that he is to preach on Christmas Eve at Erik Egge's.[16] I cannot believe that; that would be too bad. Should he not be home on Christmas Eve? He no doubt hopes to return the same day, provided wind and weather do not interfere.

The room is now very crowded. There are two tremendous beds (it is amazing how much room they take; nor can they remain where they are; but Vilhelm will have to decide that)

[15] *The Semi-weekly Times* (New York, 1855?–95).
[16] On Erik G. Egge, see chapter 13, footnote 24.

and in addition the colporteur's chests, and a washstand that pleases me very much.[17] When I get a chest of drawers, all will be splendid; and it is kind of Vilhelm to have it made now.

Tomorrow the hog must be salted; I do not dare let it lie longer, although the vinegar smell is not yet quite gone from the barrel. Anne will have charge of the salting. I have now eaten some hickory nuts; that was to have been a diversion for the twilight hour, but Gudbrand was not here then to crack them. I took a walk this afternoon with Anne. We went as far as Sørland's. Afterward I was the cook, for Caroline was visiting her sister. I wonder if anyone gave Vilhelm such well-prepared roast and rice pudding as I gave my people today? When I started writing, I thought I would write either home or to Marie Horten, but I dare not — it irritates me. This is a strange time — this.

What an uproar there is in the kitchen! I suspect they are putting on a dance with music — all of them — for little Gudbrand.[18].

[17] A colporteur in this connotation is a hawker or distributor of religious books or tracts. It is believed that a colporteur's chest was a small, compact trunk that could be pressed into service as a piece of furniture; these chests must have come from Norway.

[18] The diary ends here; Henriette Koren was born December 12, 1854.

20

My Own Little World

LITTLE IOWA PARSONAGE
January 28, 1855

MY OWN DEAR FATHER:

Bright and refreshed, I am just back from a walk in most beautiful winter weather, and since my little bird is sleeping just as sweetly as when I went out, I hasten to make use of the opportunity. It is not many days since I wrote home, and nothing special has happened since then. The baby, God be praised, is well and active, and I, too.

My husband is in Paint Creek, where he is having services today. Toward the end of the week I think he will come for a little visit to see how we all are before he sets out for Turkey River. As you see, his old life of travel has begun again and no doubt will continue a long time almost without interruption, since he has now spent so much time in this settlement. I hope, however, that eventually there may be a change and that he will not go to Paint Creek so often but rather will remain longer each time; thereby he will be able to spend longer periods at home, and that will be no slight gain. If he could only get his study — how I long for that! It is r ally a shame it is not yet ready. But now it looks a little more as if it might soon be finished, for some lumber has arrived. Lack of materials is causing the delay; it is hard to get the least bit of lumber.

On this trip Vilhelm used a sleigh for the first time this winter. It is a good thing, for a great deal of snow has fallen lately. I am well pleased when he can use a sleigh. It is so much warmer than a wagon, even if it pulls rather heavily now and then, for he must be his own snowplow most of the time; at any rate, on the road to Paint Creek there is a long tedious stretch through one of those "barrens" where almost no one but Vilhelm drives. This sleigh of his, by the way, is a curiosity, quite in a class by itself. I do not know if it is Vilhelm's own invention; if it is, I must do him the honor of saying it is very comfortable, for there is even a support for one's back, as in a chair.[1]

I seem now to have regained my strength; I take a walk every day if the northwest wind is not too bad. When I was out today, I saw two large deer. They stood motionless and gazed at me awhile before they took off at full speed into the little wood near our house. There, the baby is crying; I must go.

It is now late in the day and the baby is sleeping again. I am afraid she is sleeping for tonight as well as today. One of my greatest delights is to stand and watch her when she wakes. She yawns and stretches and makes the most comical faces you can imagine, until at last there is a little cry, and then she is fully awake. Vilhelm always tries so many experiments when he holds her; first he taps her hand, then he snaps his fingers to see what she will do. She knows how to smile now; I can get her to look at me and smile whenever I wish. When I last wrote, Vilhelm said, "You will write only about the baby now, I suppose." So perhaps I did — and now

[1] On the sleigh, see chapter 8, footnote 15.

I am beginning the same way again. Are you tired of it, dear Father? I cannot help it; it comes of itself. If I could talk to you, I would tell you all such little details. For lack of that — well, writing shall make up for it; so with good conscience I shall keep writing every detail, about both the baby and myself. I know you will like it.

I have now neither politics, literature, social life, nor any such thing to write about — just my own little world; and that comprises only Vilhelm, the baby, my home, and its immediate surroundings, including such appurtenances as the horse, dog, hens, and other animals that we have — and of this little world you shall receive detailed information.

When I start the garden in the spring I shall tell you of everything I plant and sow. I wish I had a few flowers from home; there are not likely to be many here, I imagine. I have no great expectations for the garden this year. I shall be content if it is plowed, a fence placed about it, and the underbrush cleared away so I can put it in, for the soil is of the best; if only the gophers do not play me too many tricks. Just think — we are already at the end of January. Spring will be here before I realize it. Time indeed hurries on. I hope I can manage to look after the garden properly. Perhaps the baby will monopolize my time; I get nothing done except looking after her. But by that time she will be larger, of course, so perhaps it will be better.

Well, it is "a tremendous lot of work," as Embret Sørland said when Vilhelm asked if it had not been livelier in their home since their little boy arrived. "Well, sir, it's a tremendous lot of work; but it's work that's a tremendous lot of fun, too." How tired I can become at times when she is awake too long! And she is a heavy little thing, too, you may be sure. Yes, it is a different matter to be left home now; even if Vilhelm is away, I am no longer alone, for I have the baby to occupy me. And in addition I have so many other things to do, when I can, that the days pass very swiftly.

Here we are in February already. It is Saturday evening —

ah, if you could just look in on us, dear Father! Then you would be glad to see how comfortable we are. Outside it is biting cold, but here it is comfortable and warm. I am sitting in the middle of the floor with the cradle at my side. Yes, it is different to be home alone now. You ought to see how sweetly the baby is sleeping with her small hands up to her face. I have tucked her in for the night and now, before I go to bed, will devote the rest of the evening to this dear occupation. You must have Vilhelm's letter by this time — I hope so. Every day I think of it and try to picture to myself how you must have looked when you read it. I hope that all was well at home, so that you could really rejoice over it. I am eager for a reply, but must allow time for an answer to come.

Vilhelm came home, as I anticipated, for a brief visit — and a day earlier than I expected him. Yesterday morning he left again in fine, mild weather, which changed quickly, however, to such a cold and biting wind that for a time I felt quite sure he would turn back. I wish I knew whether he got through safely. Fortunately, he is not going very far. This time he will be gone twelve days. When he returns there will be services here, and I hope then the baby will be baptized.

I had an unexpected visit when last Vilhelm was away. One morning Pastor Clausen drove in. He was on his way home from Iowa City — came this far by stage and got off at Aarthun's in order to go on from there. But he had scarcely got inside before he became so violently ill that a doctor had to be sent for. He looked very sick, but could not be persuaded to stay. He was hurrying home because of his wife; all I could do was give him a little of Ayer's Cherry Pectoral, which is good for a cold; Vilhelm usually takes a small bottle of it with him on his travels. He invited us warmly to visit him — he wanted us to be sure to come this summer. Who knows, if all goes well, but it might happen that some fine day we will travel even farther in the "Far West" — especially if the Preuses should visit us and keep us company? That would be interesting.

I have so much to do while Vilhelm is away this time and have only the evenings, usually after supper, to myself. Even though the baby is exceptionally good, I have to be with her all day long, for she seldom sleeps save at night. That sweet little child! You cannot imagine how happy she makes me. She is sweeter and sweeter every day. And now good night. At home at this time the maid comes in and banks the stove for the night.

Well, when am I going to get this letter off? It is already the twenty-second today. I do not do much writing now, but I must get this on its way, even if I do not get any more written. I do not like to have you wait for letters, but it seems too bad to send only half of what I wanted to write.

Sunday — Shrove Sunday — the baby was baptized.[2] Her name is Henriette. What a pity that none of our family could be present at her baptism, she who could have had both grandfather and grandmother for sponsors! Guri Skaarlia carried her and thereby probably offended half the settlement, for ordinarily she refuses to be a sponsor. The other sponsors were old Thrond Lommen and Thore Skotland. You should have seen how sweet the baby was that day, dear Father. Here one cannot come for the baptism only and leave right afterward; everything is too crowded and there are too many people. I had to be there with her from beginning to end. She did not sleep a wink, but was sweet and quiet. You should have seen how she looked about her and listened when the hymn singing began.

She has made great progress since I began this letter. She has grown and, God be praised, has not been sick a moment. She begins to recognize me. Of course, I think she is beautiful, too; but you know the fable of the snipe.[3] She really has pretty blue eyes and a fair, clear complexion. She is beginning

---

[2] Shrove Sunday is the Sunday before Lent.

[3] The fable of the snipe is to be found in Peter Christen Asbjørnsen and Jørgen Moe, *Norsk-folkeeventyr*, 48 (Norwegian Fairy Tales — Christiania, 1874). For an English version see G. W. Dasent, *Tales from the Norse*, 139 (London, n. d). The point of the fable is that each one thinks his own children the handsomest of all, though others may consider them very ugly.

to babble, too, and has laughed four times — really laughed aloud, you understand; and the way she works her arms and legs is a sight to behold. How I wish you could see her when she lies in my lap, and is so contented, and seems to try to talk! She has also learned the art of sucking her fingers — just as many as she can get into her mouth. She always does that when she is hungry. Once in a while when she is reaching for me at night, she lies and sucks her fingers so she can be heard far off. Yes, she is a treasure, our little baby.

The sponsors and their wives were here for dinner (you may be sure the women crowded around me after services to see the baby); moreover, we had invited the families with whom we had lived, of whom, however, only the Erik Egges came. I served roast chicken, salt pork (you should taste it!) with creamed potatoes (the only vegetable I can furnish), and rice pudding — there has to be solid food — and everything went well.

Many greetings from Vilhelm. Tomorrow he goes to Paint Creek, returns next Thursday, preaches here Friday, and leaves again Saturday. I hope it will be milder than today. I really wish he had a wolfskin coat. If anything would keep him warm, that would. Do you know what I should like very much, dear Father? It would be — if it were possible — to get one or two sleigh bells from home. I know they would please Vilhelm, and therefore, if they are to be had, I wish you would send one or two of those large single bells we had at home. It would be so much like home to hear their jingling. I have still another request, dear Father. If ever a daguerreotyper comes to Larvik, I should like daguerreotypes of Marie, Tom, and Lina.[4] I so often wish I had them. Then I would have you all. I should be happy if this could be done. You will not be offended at my asking, dear Father? No, I am sure you will not! The baby and I often look at your daguerreotype,

---

[4] Marie, Tom, and Lina were Elisabeth's sisters and brother. See chapter 8, footnote 22 and chapter 14, footnote 9. Thomas Fasting Hysing (1838–1922), Elisabeth's youngest brother, became a minister; Johnson, *Slekten Koren*, 1:189.

you may be sure, and then I tell her of her grandfather. Think of when she can understand me!

Now it will not be long before sweet snowdrops will be peeping forth — ah, your dear garden at home! Have you had many flowers this winter? I wish I were near enough to get slips from you. I should so much like to have flowers in the windows. Now I must indeed say good-by, my dear, good Father. God grant I may soon have good news from home again.

Your own
LEIS

LITTLE IOWA PARSONAGE
May 4, 1855

MY DEAR, GOOD FATHER:

We have now received the letters we so much longed for. It was good to hear how happy you all are over our little treasure. A thousand thanks for what you have written, dear Father!

It had been a busy day at the parsonage on Saturday, when we got the letter. We were busy with spring work; we had four horses, six oxen, and five men here. The men had just eaten and left when Vilhelm brought your letter. Of course I knew Vilhelm's letter would bring you joy at the manor house, but it is different, nevertheless, to read of it ourselves, and it brought us a happy evening hour. Thank you for that, dear Father. It was just as if something were lacking until I knew that you shared our joy.

It is Rogation Day and evening is here. I am sitting with a light at Vilhelm's worktable. He left yesterday for Paint Creek and will return Thursday. I am much pleased with the new arrangement of his trips to Paint Creek; he is there now a week at a time, and thus can be home for longer periods.

It is beautiful here now. The aspen has had its pretty, fresh foliage for some time. The oaks are still far from fully leaved out, yet have come far enough to make the woods beautiful. How slow the oaks are! Nor do they have a fresh green color but are rather yellowish-green. The plum and cherry trees are in full bloom; I am noting well where they stand so that I can find them again in the autumn. Yes, it is now becoming attractive and beautiful at the parsonage. It will be nice to have a little shade outside this summer. How many times I wished for a tree near the house when we were staying at Skaarlia's!

The wheat is coming up everywhere and the first spring work is over. Were our neighbors not kind to do all our work for us?

I have just come back from a walk with the baby. We went as far as the field and looked at a flock of sheep. Then our walk took us to the barn to look at a large, black hen, which is sitting on eighteen eggs. I now have one on fourteen and one on eighteen, and soon the largest hen will have twenty for her pleasure. We are likely to have a whole poultry farm, aren't we?

It is Sunday again. Vilhelm came home Wednesday; the next day there was a baptism here — people who were about to move far away. And people came and went all day. After Pentecost Vilhelm will make a long trip to Minnesota; people there keep besieging him to come.[5] It will be good when once they get a pastor. Munch, I suppose, is not thinking of going to Minnesota, now that he has received another call?

So many of those who emigrated last year are going through here, practically all of them to Minnesota. I wonder what state will be next, or whether there will finally be an end to this continual bird-of-passage life. It is unpleasant — this constant restlessness among people here. If they would sell out and go home, that would be very understandable, as our nearest neighbors, two young men, apparently are think-

[5] Pentecost: the seventh Sunday after Easter, or Whitsunday.

ing of doing if they can get enough for their valuable property.[6]

Is the beech wood in leaf for the Seventeenth of May this year? We, too, have a beech wood, the largest of our groves; we call it the beech wood, but it really consists of only oak and poplar — not that that matters much, however. We have names for all the places hereabouts: "Østerdal"; "Gudbrandsdal," where Gudbrand goes for water; "Valdres," where a family from Valdres is living; "Haugen," in which Vilhelm has named a "Mont Blanc" and I a "Cannon Mountain"; and "Jordfalden," the little grove on the slope behind the house. Then, of course, the "Plain" is in front of the house. The most amusing place is one which Vilhelm calls "Lofoten," though there is not a drop of water in the gullies there.[7]

Have I told you about the bowls, or whatever they are called, which Vilhelm brought from one of his trips? They are no doubt a kind of gourd; in any event, they grow like them and usually are shaped like scoops or round bottles with long necks. They have very hard shells and are useful containers. I have seed for them and shall sow some. If they turn out well, I should like to send some home. Mother would surely find use for them in the kitchen and dining room.

Ascension Day.[8] It is afternoon; Vilhelm is on a visit to the sick. While he is away and the baby is sleeping, I will use the time to finish my letter. Services were held in the schoolhouse today; I was present, too, though it has rarely been possible for me to attend this winter. Would you believe that the services in the small houses here make a stronger and

[6] Usually immigrants from Norway spent a year, or at least a winter, in older settlements such as Illinois or Wisconsin before going on to take land in the new areas opened for settlement. The two young men were probably Ola and Halvor Tollefsjord.

[7] Østerdal is the easternmost of the extended valleys in Norway. It lies east and north of Oslo (Christiania) and is about 150 miles long. Gudbrandsdal is a valley in central Norway, and Valdres is a valley northwest of Oslo. *Haugen* is the Norwegian word for "hill," and *jordfalden* indicates a sinking of the ground; see chapter 15, footnote 6. The Lofoten Islands are off the northern coast of Norway. Cannon Mountain has not been located.

[8] Ascension Day, or Holy Thursday, is the Thursday forty days after Easter, on which is commemorated Christ's ascension after his resurrection.

more satisfying impression on me than those at home? I do not know why it should be. I think it is the ardent singing of the hymns and the crowded room, whereby the pastor and the congregation come into a much closer and more intimate relation to each other.

Yesterday Vilhelm and I went to Decorah, a beautiful drive. Decorah has a good deal of traffic, and large stores for so small a town.

Vilhelm has been troubled lately by a cold and hoarseness because of the extreme changes of weather. This is a rigorous climate. He is well again.

We are living high these days on venison, which was given us by Suckow, who shot a deer. The deer are thin at this season but it is a rare thing now to get fresh meat. Today we had venison and cottage cheese. I give Vilhelm the latter dish regularly, for he is very fond of it. The other day Eli Sørland brought us some fresh fish. It was just one year since I had tasted fish.

I am very happy over the refreshing rain we are having today. It has been so hot and dry that I was quite worried about my garden. For afternoon coffee we now sit outside regularly and enjoy the cool shade and beautiful woods — and at times make believe that the blue prairie is the distant sea. Ah, how beautiful it is at home now! The beautiful water! Hearty greetings to all from

VILHELM AND YOUR LEIS

LITTLE IOWA PARSONAGE
Sunday, June 10, 1855

MY DEAR FATHER:

Thank you very much for your last letter, and God be praised that all is well at home. Letters from home are coming through very well now, but none has come so quickly as this last one — only twenty-three days from Larvik.

Each day I wonder why my garden grows so slowly; yet we have had rain and warm weather. Perhaps things grow slowly here to begin with; but they must grow very fast later to reach the luxuriance found here.

On one of the first nights in June there was such a hard frost that the potatoes and corn froze in many places and also the tops of oaks and small sumacs.

Vilhelm held services in the schoolhouse today and now holds communion service at one of the neighboring farms, for there is not enough room in the schoolhouse. Since then I have packed Vilhelm's things and seen him leave; he will no doubt be gone at least fourteen days.

The 17th, Sunday evening. At home it is light now all night, but here it is dark by eight o'clock. The sun goes down at half past seven and twilight is soon over. Ugh, how oppressively hot it has been these last days! The stove has been moved out of the kitchen; all the windows are open and covered with mosquito netting. Oh, if we only had the same climate as at home! If it is just as hot where Vilhelm is, I do not understand how he can keep on preaching day after day, as I know he does — or how he could, even if there were churches! When July and August finally come with their heat, he must certainly keep within the limits of Little Iowa at least; otherwise he will lose his strength completely.[9]

In this settlement there has been little progress in building a church. At the last meeting, which was to decide definitely upon a building site, Vilhelm met only disappointment, and came home soaked through by one of those sudden and violent rainstorms which occur so often. This time it began with hail, hail as big as a small walnut, and that in the month of June![10]

[9] Pastor Koren's letter of call came from three congregations: Little Iowa, Paint Creek, and Turkey River. In addition, he served and helped organize other congregations in Allamakee, Winneshiek, Howard, Chickasaw, Fayette, and Clayton counties in northeastern Iowa, and Houston and Fillmore counties in southern Minnesota.

[10] The first church was built on the parsonage land in 1855. It was erected of logs, mostly elm with some oak, "whittled down fine." The whole neighborhood came for the "raising" when the frame was ready. On the interior the boards were planed; on the outside the siding was painted white. This church served until the present stone structure was dedicated and put into full use, December 19, 1873.

Today I am having strawberries for the second time this year. It is not easy to get anyone to pick them, for no one buys them here. I hope Vilhelm returns before they are gone. We are thinking of transplanting some to the garden this fall, and I also want to plant grapes on the south wall between the windows. They will look nice. I found a wild flower and transplanted it in the garden; it is an unusual flower. I will send you seed when I get some. I keep transplanting flowers when I find any I want; otherwise the cattle destroy them.

Vilhelm helped me plant cabbage; the occasion for this was my birthday. On the whole Vilhelm takes about the same interest in the garden as Christiane did when she and I had a garden together; she was willing to have her share in the cherry tree, but left the flowers to me. Vilhelm, too, enjoys seeing things thrive and bloom if he escapes the work.

The 28th. Vilhelm is now home, in good health, God be praised, after his trip, the most strenuous since our arrival here. He was gone fourteen days. He made the longer drives during the first part of the trip, held seven services during the last eight days, traveled every day, and furthermore had so many communicants and baptisms that, although he began at half past ten, he often was not through until half past four. Friday he will set out again. There will be constant traveling next month. I hope he gets a little rest in August. You must not be alarmed if you read of Indian troubles. The Indians in question live in the very westernmost part of Iowa and we in the easternmost; here it is peaceful enough.

[LEIS]

LITTLE IOWA PARSONAGE
September 9, 1855

DEAR FATHER:

We are now home, safe and sound, from our outing to Cedar River.[11] We arrived last Friday evening, just in time

---

[11] The Cedar River flows past St. Ansgar, Iowa. C. L. Clausen was pastor there.

363

to get under shelter before a severe thunderstorm broke loose. As the food at the tavern where we stopped at noon was almost unfit to eat, we returned with splendid appetites; but of course we did not have a bite of bread in the house and it was too late to go down to Sørland's to borrow. Fortunately Gudbrand, who had come back the day before, had brought the cows home; so we had milk and were able to cook mush. The next morning we had a delicious breakfast consisting of hot biscuits, corn on the cob, and excellent *knaost*, a gift from Mrs. Clausen.[12]

We had been away eight days. It was high time we returned, too, for Vilhelm had asked the trustees to meet here Saturday. Sunday he was to preach, and Monday, to have a meeting of the congregation. Saturday, then, I was busy getting dinner ready. But first I had to go out and look around, and found, to my comfort, that the hens had not been taken by the hawks, nor the melons by the pigs, nor the shocks of wheat and oats torn down by the cattle. I had been somewhat uneasy, for there was not a soul on the place — only a neighbor boy who came up once a day and fed the chickens. For dinner the trustees had roast pork, of course, corn on the cob, pancakes, pickles, cucumbers, and sour milk soup.

At the congregational meeting it was decided that our house should have siding and be painted white, on the outside of course; we were greatly pleased, you may be sure, for otherwise, to keep the rain out at all, it would be necessary to caulk between the logs every year. The work is to be done this autumn, at least as far as they can go with the materials available.

At the same time I think they will build an additional room opening off the living room on the north side, where the entry is now. That will be the study. This year, however,

---

[12] *Knaost* is a kind of soft cheese made from skimmed milk that has soured. Bergretha Pedersen Brekke Hjort, the widow of H. E. Hjort, became Pastor Clausen's second wife in 1847. See Svein Strand, "Pastor C. L. Clausen," in *Symra*, 213 (1913); and Malmin, Norlie, and Tingelstad, *Who's Who among Pastors*, 102.

no more will be done than the frame and sheathing. If, as I hope, the well diggers come soon, the carpenters, and Ivar, that Hardanger boy who is to stay with us this winter, I shall have plenty of people here, indeed. That is fine. There is still a long way to go before I reach the bottom of my pork barrel.

Tuesday after we got home Vilhelm came in and said, "Tomorrow the threshing machine will be here." Well, I went out and told Oline to set bread, and the next day we had twelve men for meals.[13] Fortunately they did not all stay overnight, for some of them were our nearest neighbors, who came to help us of their own good will. Our neighbors have surely been very friendly and helpful on every occasion. And now we have more wheat than we need to supply ourselves, and about 240 bushels of oats. Then there is the corn to cut and husk, as they call that operation here.

At the last meeting the congregation also expressed a wish that the parish be divided, and stated that it was willing to double the present salary. The same action will no doubt be taken in the other settlements, where Vilhelm is now. What will be most difficult, in all likelihood, is to get a pastor from Norway. How glad I should be if this division could be brought about! It has also been decided that in Little Iowa alone five separate churches are to be built. At first only three were considered. But people had fixed ideas and would not make concessions and preferred to build their own churches. So the result is that those who live on the east prairie, about one Norwegian mile from here by a bad road, will build their own church instead of uniting with those here; and likewise it follows that there probably will be only two real churches and three large meetinghouses.[14] The church here is to be located on the parsonage land, not far from our house. I doubt, however, that we shall be able to see it because of the slight elevation west of us. There is talk of building it of wood with a tower; it is difficult to get stone.

[13] Oline was the Koren's hired girl at that time.
[14] One Norwegian mile equals seven English miles.

Vilhelm is going to the Synod meeting soon. In fourteen days we expect Pastor Clausen; then the two will set out overland Monday morning. Vilhelm asks if I want to go, but I do not; it is too late in the year to go traveling with the baby. No, we two will stay home and look after the house and chickens. Vilhelm will have seven delegates with him at the meeting.

Vilhelm is in Paint Creek and will be away one more Sunday. He is making the circuit now before he goes to Wisconsin, where he expects to spend three weeks, including the trip down and back. It will be wonderful when the railroad comes to Prairie du Chien, as it no doubt will within two years; it is already built part way. Then, instead of the present four or five days, we shall need scarcely two to get to Preus's.

Your loving daughter,

LEIS

LITTLE IOWA PARSONAGE
October 28, 1855

DEAR FATHER:

Vilhelm has been in Wisconsin, and you may be sure he surprised me when he returned long before the appointed time. I had a good many things to do while he was away. I was lucky enough to find a seamstress and so I got a new morning dress (the first new dress since I left home), a new sash for Vilhelm's dressing gown, and dresses for the baby. Then I lay on the floor a couple of days stitching quilts. I do not have a table large enough, and for the heavy ones that I am tying I do not need a frame. So we chose the floor. There, then, I had lain all day long and was very tired, and very happy to be finished. The seamstress had left, the baby was settled for the night, and so I sat, putting the last touch on one of the small dresses, and thinking it would be best to bake the next day, so as to be all ready.

I did not expect him for four or five days, and was debating about sending word to the butcher, when the door to the kitchen opened and Vilhelm walked in as softly and calmly as if he had never been away. They — Clausen and his delegate were with him — came much too soon, according to my calculations. But I was glad to have Vilhelm home well and strong; when he left, he had such a bad cold and felt poorly.

They had to make the best of what I could give them: soft-boiled eggs are my stand-by. Pastor Clausen was in a hurry to get home. We had a busy time preparing a chicken fricassee for early next morning. Then he left.

Vilhelm had bought a large buffalo robe for himself, and I am very happy over that, for it has been my constant worry that he has been too poorly equipped for the trips he has to take. I began to bombard him with questions about the Synod meeting, Spring Prairie, etc.; but first I had to give an account of everything at home, and then I was told that next time the Synod is to meet with us. The housing problem will be acute, indeed, especially if there should be, as they expect, fourteen pastors instead of nine. I hope by that time that there may be some young pastor's wife in the neighborhood who can come and help me.

Vilhelm was well satisfied with the meeting and all that took place. He came close to being elected to go to St. Louis, Columbus, and several other places, which two pastors are to visit, to investigate I do not know exactly what at the German universities there. However, he gave advance warning that it was useless to vote for him; he would not be able to undertake it because of his congregation — he would have to be away too long. So Brandt and Ottesen were chosen, and perhaps no one else has more time and opportunity than they have. I am glad it turned out thus. Vilhelm is away enough as it is, without also making a three-to-four-months' trip. The pastors who are members of the church council will hereafter be charged with the duty of visiting all congregations, both those which have and those which do not have pastors. Pastor Clausen is

our dean; when he comes we shall slaughter our fattest calf
— but I am afraid that it will have to be our fattest rooster.[15]

Vilhelm compares his various trips here with living in
Christiania and having Drammen, Ullensaker, and Drøbak
as annexes, and sometimes Eidsvold — and I do not remember
what corresponds to the settlements farther up in Minnesota;
and then occasionally having a trip about as far as from
Larvik to Sandefjord. Tomorrow is All Saints' Day, which,
with Epiphany, has been included among the festival days
of the church here; Vilhelm is then to make a trip as if to
Sandefjord; then the day after tomorrow he leaves early for
Paint Creek, which is Drammen; from there to Turkey River,
to Norway and the Clermont settlement, which is Drøbak;
and then, after twelve to fourteen days, comes home. And
after that, indeed, the same going back and forth to Minnesota again; he must go up in November; that is Eidsvold.

From November 14 until New Year's Eve (forty-eight days)
Vilhelm has functions away from home on thirty-two days,
all preaching days, with two or three exceptions. Moreover,
in the same period he must travel at least four or five hundred
English miles. The district to be served is seventy English
miles from north to south, and forty from east to west.

They are beginning in a small way to build the church
here. We shall be able to see the spire and a portion of the
building from our living room.

When this letter reaches you, it will perhaps be very near
Christmas. God grant that all is well at home and that you
may have a joyous and blessed Christmas.

My loving greetings to all.

LEIS

[15] Brandt and Ottesen, as a result of their visits, recommended at the next
Synod meeting in 1857 that a Norwegian professorship be set up at Concordia
Seminary in St. Louis, the theological school of the Missouri Synod. The
Norwegian Synod adopted this recommendation and decided at the same time
to raise funds for a school of its own. As a result, Professor Laur. Larsen
joined the staff of Concordia Seminary in 1859 and Luther College opened
in Decorah in 1861. See *Kirkelig maanedstidende* (Monthly Church Times):
1857, p. 476; 1858, p. 7; 1859, p. 80. This paper was published at Inmansville
(Luther Valley), Wisconsin.

Mrs. Koren's Conclusion
to the Norwegian Edition

Little did I dream that what I recorded in my diary as a very young and inexperienced wife during our first years in this country, and what I wrote in letters, so that my dear ones in Norway might have as detailed news of us as possible, would ever be printed and given to the world.

I was able to reconcile myself to the idea that the diary and letters should be copied; the close fine handwriting had become almost illegible; we had little paper at the time. To do that, I thought, was proper for the sake of the children. But when the children also wished to have them printed, I found myself very much opposed to it, and still cannot believe that these simple, unadorned notes are worth it.

Many memories press on me as I think back over these sixty-one years — that first Christmas evening at Egge's, when I went up to the loft and found the last little piece of chocolate in our trunk. To me that was almost like a last reminder of civilization.

Then the summer at Skaarlia's, where as a rule I was alone

on Sundays — without seeing a living soul. It was humble enough there, but kind Guri Skaarlia was very good to me.

I used to take long walks and look for flowers and bushes, gather seeds, and make mental notes of what I should like to plant in the garden I eagerly looked forward to in the future.

I remember also the reading services we used to have. There were so many congregations that of necessity there had to be several weeks between services. During the intervals we gathered in the various houses, the schoolteacher read the sermon and examined the children, and it was very edifying to see the devotion and reverence for the Word of God which was shown.

It is strange now to sit in my large cheerful room and think back to the winter of '56, which was so bitterly cold. Despite the cold, people stood outside the windows at the schoolhouse and listened to the sermon on Christmas Day.

At New Year's Koren became very ill. There was no doctor to be had. It was so cold that we could not keep our little house warm (it consisted of a living room, a little sleeping room, and a kitchen) and had to go about inside fully clad as for a journey.

We saw hardly a person except those in the house; it was too cold. But God helped us then as always. Koren eventually regained his health, and then all was well.

With gratitude I look back on my long life here in this land, and think of the many now dead who received us with so much friendliness and surrounded us with love all our lives.

Possibly some of their descendants may be interested in reading these notes.

ELISABETH KOREN

WASHINGTON PRAIRIE PARSONAGE, NOVEMBER, 1914.

Index

For the convenience of readers the character ø, which occurs frequently in Norwegian names, is alphabeted as o.

371

Consider Becoming a Vesterheim Member

All members receive discounts at the Vesterheim Sales Shop and on tuition for the museum's craft classes; free admission to the museum; and the quarterly illustrated newsletter *Vesterheim News*. Choose from five levels of membership:

Associate Member ($15 per year)
Contributing Member ($25 per year)
Supporting Member($50 per year
Life Member ($200 contribution)
Fellow ($1000 contribution)

Members also may take advantage of the following
Special Interest Services :

Vesterheim Rosemaling Letter ($8 per year)
A quarterly publication with patterns, articles on painting, and information on contests, exhibitions and seminars.

Vesterheim Genealogical Center ($8 per year)
Genealogical Center subscribers receive the quarterly newsletter *Norwegian Tracks* and a discount for genealogical research.

Vesterheim Woodworking Newsletter ($8 per year)
A quarterly newsletter sharing information about and promoting woodworking in the Norwegian-American tradition.

Postage outside the U.S.: For *each* membership AND *each* special interest, add $2 for Canada and Mexico, $4 for all other countries.

(1994 prices, subject to change)

For more information, write to:
Vesterheim Norwegian-American Museum
502 W. Water Street, Decorah, IA 52101